The Soviet Union since Stalin

THE
SOVIET UNION
SINCE
STALIN

EDITED BY

Stephen F. Cohen
Alexander Rabinowitch
Robert Sharlet

INDIANA UNIVERSITY PRESS
Bloomington

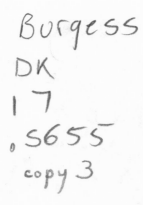
Library of Congress Cataloging in Publication Data
Main entry under title:

The Soviet Union since Stalin.

Based on papers presented at a conference organized
by the Indiana University Russian and East European
Institute in 1978.
Includes index.
1. Russia—Congresses. I. Cohen, Stephen F.
II. Rabinowitch, Alexander. III. Sharlet, Robert S.
DK17.S655   947.084'2   79-3092
ISBN 0-253-32272-3   3   4   5   84   83   82   81
ISBN 0-253-20236-1 pbk.

CONTENTS

EDITORS' PREFACE   vii

Introduction   *Alexander Rabinowitch*   1

Part One / POLITICS

The Friends and Foes of Change: Reformism and
    Conservatism in the Soviet Union   *Stephen F. Cohen*   11

The Stalin Question   *Roy A. Medvedev*   32

Khrushchev Reconsidered   *George W. Breslauer*   50

Changing Soviet Perspectives on Leadership
    and Administration   *Erik P. Hoffmann*   71

De-Stalinization and Soviet Constitutionalism
    Robert Sharlet   93

Part Two / THE ECONOMY

Soviet Economic Planning and Performance
    Arthur W. Wright   113

Post-Stalin Agriculture and Its Future   *James R. Millar*   135

Soviet Regional Development   *Robert N. Taaffe*   155

Part Three / SOCIETY AND CULTURE

The "New Soviet Man" Turns Pessimist *John Bushnell*   179

Georgia and Soviet Nationality Policy *Ronald Grigor Suny*   200

The Soviet Family in Post-Stalin Perspective
  Peter H. Juviler   227

New Aspects of Soviet Russian Literature *George Gibian*   252

Part Four / FOREIGN POLICY

The Stalinist Legacy in Soviet Foreign Policy *Charles Gati*   279

RESPONSES

The Soviet Union and the West *William Zimmerman*   305

The Soviet Union and Eastern Europe
  Roger E. Kanet and *John D. Robertson*   312

The Soviet Union and the Third World
  Alvin Z. Rubinstein   324

THE CONTRIBUTORS   333

INDEX   337

EDITORS' PREFACE

This book grew out of a multidisciplinary conference on "Continuity and Change in the Soviet Union since Stalin," organized by the Indiana University Russian and East European Institute in 1978. The conference marked both the twenty-fifth anniversary of Stalin's death and the twentieth anniversary of the Institute.

In planning the conference and then this book, the editors attempted to draw upon the knowledge of leading scholars, most of them with firsthand experience in the Soviet Union or Eastern Europe. We asked of our authors that their contributions reflect the most recent scholarship in their respective fields, that they address the central question of continuity and change, and that they be accessible to nonspecialists as well as to other scholars. Otherwise, no effort was made to impose a single approach to the subject or a single interpretation of the twenty-five years since Stalin died. As a result, the essays gathered here reflect the great complexity of the post-Stalin era as well as differences of opinion among Western scholars about these developments. This is, we believe, as it should be. And while space limitations have constrained us in some respects, we have tried to insure that major trends and developments in the broad areas of politics, economics, society, culture, and foreign policy received appropriate attention.

The editors wish to thank the institutions and individuals whose support made this project possible. The original conference at Indiana University was partially funded by grants from the Research and Development Committee of the American Association for the Advancement of Slavic Studies and from the United States Office of Education to the Indiana University Slavic Language and Area Center. We want to express keenest appreciation to the other scholars who participated in the conference and contributed to its success; they include Edward J. Brown, Abraham Brumberg, Elizabeth Clayton, Vera Dunham, Maurice Friedberg, Loren Graham, Darrell P. Hammer, Dodona Kiziria, Linda Lubrano, Peter B. Maggs, Phillip Raup, and Joel Shapiro. Our thanks, too, to Rodney B. Sangster and the staff of the Russian and East European Institute, who handled conference arrangements.

Our greatest debt is, of course, to our authors, who responded to our editorial interventions and met our deadlines. We also acknowledge our gratitude to Oxford University Press (London) for permitting us to include the essay by Roy A. Medvedev. Finally, we thank Janet Rabinowitch of Indiana University Press for editorial advice and steadfast support from the outset.

S. F. C.
A. R.
R. S.

The Soviet Union since Stalin

Introduction

Alexander Rabinowitch

"The heart of Josef Vissarionovich Stalin, Lenin's comrade-in-arms and inspired continuator of his work, wise leader and educator of the Communist Party and the Soviet people, has stopped beating." This terse TASS bulletin of March 6, 1953, anticipated since the initial announcement two days earlier that the aging Soviet dictator had suffered a massive brain hemorrhage, conveyed news of momentous import. Stalin's sudden demise brought to an end an extraordinary quarter century in Russian history—an era shaped most of all by Stalin himself.

Beginning in the late 1920s, Stalin, who had emerged victorious over all his political rivals, reversed earlier, more moderate policies and embarked on an unprecedented program of national economic transformation. This drastic course was ultimately to change the Soviet Union from a relatively underdeveloped, still largely agrarian society into the world's second greatest industrial power. The brutal social and economic revolution that Stalin directed began with the collectivization of some 125 million peasants, often by force. During the course of this "revolution from above" in the early 1930s, the tolerance and diversity that had characterized the economy, culture, and, compared to what followed, even politics in the years of the New Economic Policy gave way to extreme centralization and regimentation. Supported by a powerful, extralegal secret police and a swollen, privileged bureaucracy, Stalin subsequently carried out the Great Purges, which decimated the country's elites, and which destroyed the Communist Party as the ruling political institution. In part by means of mass terror, Stalin imposed the most ruthless and powerful dictatorship in modern history. This system, commonly known as Stalinism, became nearly inseparable from the personality of the man who created it. Two of the system's most characteristic features were an almost permanent reign of terror, which left millions dead and millions more in labor camps, and a fanatic public cult of Stalin, which daily, for more than twenty years, proclaimed Stalin as the greatest and wisest man alive.

Despite these demographic and other losses of the 1930s, the Stalin government led the Soviet people to a great triumph over German fascism during World War II. In terms of human costs and physical devastation, the price of victory was colossal. The fruits, however, were also considerable. The Soviet Union became a superpower with global interests; its only real rival for some time after the war was the United States. At the same time, Stalin reimposed a draconian political regime and launched an ambitious and exhausting program of postwar economic recovery. Taking advantage of the changed circumstances abroad, he established subservient communist dictatorships in the nations of occupied Eastern Europe. In 1948, after Tito balked at bending to his absolute authority, Stalin branded him a traitor and excommunicated Yugoslavia from the communist camp. Stalin hoped to take further advantage of Western weakness and postwar social unrest to acquire greater influence and power in Asia, the Middle East, and parts of Western Europe. However, except for the victory of the Chinese Communists in 1949, which for Stalin was at best a mixed blessing, the primary result of Soviet probing in these far-flung areas was to increase world tension and intensify the Cold War.

Signs of Western resolve to face up to the Soviets, such as the Berlin air lift and the formation of NATO, impelled Stalin, in the last two years of his life, toward a tactically less militant stance in relations with the outside world. Domestic repression and regimentation, however, incessantly justified by the alleged danger of an all-out military conflict with capitalist powers bent on destroying the Soviet Union, reached their apogee. The Soviet people were again forced to make incredible sacrifices for the security of the Soviet state and to worship the invincible Stalin.

Stalin's twenty-five-year domination of the Soviet system did not necessarily mean that his death would lead to an end of his coercive policies or even to a relaxation of the Stalinist police state. There was not even any certainty that his demise would bring an easing of international tensions. In the initial days and weeks after Stalin's death, the general consensus among Western political observers was, to the contrary, that the impending struggle for Stalin's mantle would be accompanied by continued harshness at home and by adventurism and instability in foreign policy. Averell Harriman, U.S. Ambassador in Moscow from 1943 to 1946, expressed this troubled reaction to the latest news from Moscow in a statement to the *Washington Post* the day after Stalin's grave illness became known. Harriman warned, "With the end of Stalin's control will come a period of extreme tension and terror throughout Russia. . . . These tensions will continue not just until his successor emerges, but until that man proves his ability, if he can, to dominate the Communist party, the secret police, the army, in fact the whole Soviet apparatus." Harriman added, "Grave danger could come from reckless action on the part of the new Kremlin leadership, undertaken to divert attention from internal problems."

Events were to prove these gloomy predictions inaccurate. In retrospect it is clear that Stalin's death triggered nearly a decade of reform which ultimately affected, to a greater or lesser degree, virtually every area of Soviet politics and society, as well as foreign policy. Signs of this new direction came quickly. During the initial infighting among Stalin's potential successors, Georgi Malenkov, prime minister from 1953 until 1955, promised to let up on the development of heavy industry in favor of a higher level of consumer-goods production and housing construction. Nikita Khrushchev, appointed first secretary of the Communist Party Central Committee in September 1953 and prime minister in 1958, sought to stimulate agricultural production with concessions to peasants such as lower taxes and higher prices for collective-farm products. The so-called Doctors Plot—sensational criminal charges against several Kremlin doctors trumped up at Stalin's direction in January 1953, apparently as a pretext for another large scale purge—was revealed by Lavrenti Beria, head of the secret police, to have been fabricated. Spring 1953 also saw the first "thaw" in Soviet literature, as censorship and ideological controls became less pervasive and oppressive.

Following Beria's own ouster and execution in 1953, the secret police was stripped of considerable authority and for the first time since before the purges of the mid-thirties was put firmly under party control. At first hundreds and thousands and subsequently nearly all of the millions of Stalin's political prisoners still languishing in labor camps were amnestied. Many of these prisoners, although by no means all of them, and countless other political victims who did not survive the Stalin years, were in time legally and politically rehabilitated.

In foreign policy, concrete moves toward more normal relations with the noncommunist world, foreshadowed in Stalin's last years, also came very quickly. A more flexible and less aggressive spirit in foreign affairs was reflected in policy statements emanating from Moscow within weeks of Stalin's death and in such later events as the Korean armistice of July 1953; the partial rapprochement between the Soviet Union and Yugoslavia, the relinquishing of Soviet military bases in Finland, and the arrangement of a peace settlement with Austria, all in 1955; and Khrushchev's energetic pursuit of "peaceful coexistence" with the West, capped by his memorable visit to the United States in 1959. Moreover, in the late 1950s scientific, cultural, and personal contacts between the Soviet Union and the West finally began to be developed. These events early in the post-Stalin period were indications of the waning of the Cold War and the beginning of detente.

Within a short time after Stalin's death, official adulation of the late dictator began to subside. Stalin was mentioned less and less frequently in the press and on the radio, and the phrase "cult of personality" came into official use as a code word for criticism of Stalin's terroristic and despotic rule. A number of important social welfare measures were adopted. Reform of the legal system greatly clarified and strengthened legal procedures, making the application of law significantly less arbitrary.

Most fundamentally, government by means of terror was ended, and, especially under Khrushchev, the emphasis became less on control through intimidation and coercion than on efforts to win popular support for the post-Stalin regime. Some of Khrushchev's reforms have reasonably been criticized as ill-conceived, or, more bluntly, as "hare-brained." Such was the case with his abortive bifurcation of the regional party apparatus which, at least in the eyes of entrenched officials, threatened to cause administrative chaos. Nonetheless, it was also under Khrushchev that lower-level authorities were given considerably greater latitude in policy implementation. Direct control from Moscow over political, economic, and cultural affairs in the national republics was reduced. Further, while the government remained a one-party authoritarian dictatorship, the political process became significantly more open, and local party activists, scientific and technical specialists, and competing institutionalized interest groups of all kinds were encouraged to participate in public affairs in ways which contrasted strikingly with the situation under Stalin.

A parallel process of internal liberalization and decentralization took place in Eastern Europe. The Soviet Union gradually curtailed economic exploitation of the East European countries, and the latter took advantage of looser control from Moscow to gain a significant measure of independence and freedom of action.

Major events in what was referred to increasingly often in the West as "de-Stalinization" included Khrushchev's sensational repudiation of

Stalin both at the Twentieth Party Congress in 1956 and at the Twenty-second Party Congress in 1961. Following the Twenty-second Party Congress, Stalin's personal disgrace was symbolized by the removal of his embalmed body from its resting place alongside Lenin in the mausoleum on Red Square. Throughout the Soviet Union places and institutions that had been named for Stalin were hastily renamed; most dramatically, Stalingrad became Volgograd. A renewed thaw in culture stimulated by Khrushchev's 1961 exposé of Stalin's crimes, which unlike his anti-Stalin speech of 1956 was immediately made public, was reflected in the publication, in November 1962, of Alexander Solzhenitsyn's frank description of conditions in Stalin's forced labor camps, *One Day in the Life of Ivan Denisovich.*

The main highlights in the de-Stalinization process are easily listed; however, the impact and broader systemic significance of these changes have been difficult to evaluate. Part of the difficulty Western scholars have had in assessing post-Stalin reformism stems, of course, from continuing problems with access to key sources of information. Western analysis of change in the Soviet Union since Stalin has also been complicated by the fact that almost from the start, reformism was subject to sharp zigzags. Some of these political shifts reflected give and take among advocates and opponents of liberalization in the party leadership. Other shifts were reflexive reactions to major world developments. The first cultural "thaw" that began in 1953, for example, was halted and in fact temporarily reversed in October 1956, following the eruption of popular ferment in Poland and the uprising in Hungary. Khrushchev was the individual most closely identified with reform; yet even during his administration, reformism tended to be erratic. Thus in December 1962, just weeks after publication of *One Day in the Life of Ivan Denisovich,* Khrushchev, evidently under strong pressure from conservative leaders, caused a scandal by publicly berating avant-garde artists at an exhibition of modern art at the Moscow Manege. The "excesses" allegedly exposed at the exhibition were subsequently used as a pretext for retightening ideological and cultural controls.

Then too, some important reforms adopted in good faith simply did not take hold. This was the case both during Khrushchev's rule and after his ouster in October 1964. Thus the new leadership headed by Leonid Brezhnev, general secretary of the Central Committee and since 1977 also president of the Soviet Union, and Alexei Kosygin, prime minister, introduced major economic reforms with great fanfare in 1965. Aimed at considerable decentralization of economic planning and control, these reforms encountered many obstacles, including strong resistance throughout the system, and were substantially modified by

1967. Soon afterward, an extended period of conservative reaction to reformist policies began and it has continued to the present.

In considering developments in the Soviet Union during this most recent period, it is necessary to emphasize that today's modern, consumer-goods-hungry Soviet society, not to speak of the international context in which the present leadership must operate, is vastly more diverse and complex than was the case in Stalin's time. This means, for one thing, that contemporary policy makers, irrespective of their personal inclinations, must contend with the views of the many competing institutional interest groups that first became meaningfully involved in public affairs under Khrushchev, as well as with international public opinion. There is also no denying that many of the significant changes adopted in the reform period have been retained and legitimated by present leaders. To cite some examples, the Brezhnev regime has remained steadfastly committed to the ultimate political primacy of the party; to rationalizing decision making; and to improving the responsiveness and efficiency of the vast administrative bureaucracy while avoiding Stalinist bureaucratic excesses.

Although the availability of consumer goods in recent years has fallen well short of popular expectations, Brezhnev has also given high priority to upgrading the material quality of Soviet life, often at the expense of increased investment in science and technology and the more rapid development of heavy industry. Moreover, although vigorously championing Soviet interests and exploiting Western weakness worldwide, Kosygin and Brezhnev, like Khrushchev, have generally adhered to a policy of coexistence or detente (that is, the abjuration of all-out nuclear war, the pursuit of peaceful political competition, and the practice of strictly controlled interaction and accommodation with the capitalist West), as the international course best suited to the country's present needs. This orientation has impelled the present regime to accept concessions to Western public opinion such as Jewish emigration and tolerance of a level of political dissent and cultural diversity which, however modest by Western standards, would have been unthinkable under Stalin.

At the same time, it is equally undeniable that between 1964 and 1968, the reformist impulse in the Soviet Union declined sharply. After August 1968, when the Soviet leadership felt compelled to use Soviet Army tanks and troops in Czechoslovakia to crush liberalization carried out by the reformist Dubcek government, de-Stalinization ceased. With a conservative mood plainly ascendant, not only among top party leaders but within society generally, political and cultural controls were considerably tightened. The freer, more open political climate of the

Khrushchev years was rapidly dissipated. The government, concerned most of all with maintaining stability and making the economy function more smoothly, increased economic and moral incentives to conform, routinely violated civil rights of nonconformists, and in a number of extreme cases, confined individuals deemed guilty of political deviation to mental hospitals or prison camps. All the while, as the distinguished Soviet dissident historian Roy Medvedev shows in his chapter in this volume, influential neo-Stalinists have pressed, as yet with only mixed success, for Stalin's rehabilitation and, presumably, for further repressive measures reminiscent of Stalinism.

The scope and longevity of the conservative reaction under Kosygin and Brezhnev, especially the present regime's stance on civil rights, its harsh treatment of political dissent, and the apparent resurgence of neo-Stalinism, inevitably raise profound questions. How many of the changes of the post-Stalin reform period have survived a decade and a half of reaction? How does the Soviet Union today differ from that of Stalin's Russia and, no less important, what are the prospects for the future of Soviet politics and society? It is hoped that the chapters which follow will help shed light on the answers to these fundamental questions.

Part One / POLITICS

The Friends and Foes of Change: Reformism and Conservatism in the Soviet Union

Stephen F. Cohen

> The combination of conservative institutions with revolutionary ideas meant that the Republic was the first successful attempt to reconcile the conservative and revolutionary traditions in France. But it also meant that in the twentieth century the forces of change were resisted and obstructed to the point of frustration.
>
> DAVID THOMSON,
> *Democracy in France*

> The theme of the meeting, "Tradition and Innovation," offers an occasion to talk about serious things.
>
> MIKHAIL ROMM (1962)

Change in the Stalinist system, and stubborn resistance to change, have been the central features of Soviet political life since Stalin's death in 1953. The rival forces of "innovation and tradition," to use the language of the official press, have become "two poles" in Soviet politics and society, which are expressed through "sharp clashes between people standing on both sides of the psychological barrier."[1]

© 1980 by Stephen F. Cohen.

This essay grows out of a larger project supported at different times by the John Simon Guggenheim Memorial Foundation and the Center of International Studies at Princeton University. I wish to express my gratitude to these institutions. I wish to point out also that though I speak here of "the Soviet Union," my discussion really applies to the Russian nation within that multinational union.

Western students of Soviet affairs were slow to perceive this deep-rooted conflict. Accustomed to seeing only one political tradition and thus only continuity in Soviet history, and to imagining the Soviet Union as a frozen "totalitarian" system, most scholars began to think seriously about change and the large controversies it has engendered only in the mid-1960s.[2] Although a valuable scholarship on the subject now exists,[3] it remains inadequate in important respects. Conflict over change is often treated narrowly—either in terms of high Soviet politics and thus apart from society itself, or, at another extreme, in terms of avowed dissidents and thus outside the official political system. No less important, many treatments of the subject lack historical dimensions; and quite a few are couched in a jargon-ridden or value-laden language that obscures more than it reveals.

I propose to argue that the fundamental division between these "two poles" in Soviet life is best understood as a social and political confrontation between reformism and conservatism in the sense that these terms convey in other countries. In generalizing about different aspects of this great conflict during the quarter of a century since 1953, I shall raise some questions that I cannot answer. My overview of the post-Stalin era should therefore be read also as a proposed agenda for further discussion.

Reformism and Conservatism

The terms "reformist" and "conservative" do not embrace the full diversity of political outlook, ranging from far left to far right, that has emerged so dramatically in the Soviet Union since the 1950s. As in other societies, these terms designate only mainstream, not extremist, attitudes toward the status quo and toward change. Even a spectrum of political outlook inside the Soviet Communist Party, for example, would require at least four categories: authentic democrats, reformers, conservatives, and neo-Stalinist reactionaries.[4] But while full-fledged democrats and neo-Stalinists may respectively share many reformist and conservative attitudes, the policies of either would mean radicalism in the Soviet context today, not reform or conservatism. In times of profound crisis, reformism and conservatism everywhere usually give rise to extremist trends and may even grow into their most extreme manifestations—revolution and counterrevolution.[5] But apart from extraordinary historical moments, reformers and conservatives represent the majority of mainstream antagonists—the friends and foes of change—in the Soviet Union as well as in other countries.

Though most scholars use other words to characterize these antagonists in the Soviet Union,[6] the terms reformer and conservative are preferable in important ways. Unlike "functional technocratic modernizer" and similar contrivances, they are not jargonistic or exotic. Unlike "liberal and dogmatist" or "revisionist and orthodox," they do not prejudge or simplify the nature of Soviet reformism and conservatism, which are complex amalgams of opinion and attitudes requiring further analysis rather than restrictive labels. (It is a serious analytical mistake, for example, to insist that real change or reform in the Soviet Union must mean "liberalization" or "democratization" in our sense of these words.) The terms anti-Stalinist and neo-Stalinist are very important, but they identify components within the larger conflict. Above all, archetypical reformers and conservatives are, as even the reticent Soviet press makes clear, "two popular types" in Soviet life, and the universal meaning of reformism and conservatism corresponds fully to the "partisans of the two directions" in the conflicts of the past twenty-five years. Or as the conservative Molotov put it, "There are . . . reforming Communists, and then there are the real Communists."[7]

Reformism and conservatism, therefore, are concepts that require no special definition in the Soviet context. Both tendencies take on certain national characteristics in different countries because they are expressed in the different idioms of those political cultures. (Soviet conservatives today often speak, for example, in a neo-Stalinist or nineteenth-century Slavophile idiom.) Moreover, the full nature of reformism and conservatism everywhere is always historical, changing from one period to another. (Liberalism and conservatism in England, France, and the United States are not the same today as they were earlier in the twentieth century.) But despite these cultural and historical variations, the basic antagonism between reformers and conservatives is similar in different countries, including the Soviet Union.

Reformism is that outlook, and those policies, which seek through measured change to improve the existing order without fundamentally transforming existing social, political, and economic foundations or going beyond prevailing ideological values. Reformism finds both its discontent and its program, and seeks its political legitimacy and success, within the parameters of the existing order. This distinguishes it from radicalism. The essential reformist argument is that the potential of the existing system and the promise of the established ideology—for example, Marxist socialism in the Soviet Union or liberal democracy in the United States—have not been realized, and that they can and must be fulfilled. The reformist premise is that change is progress. Unlike the conservative, the reformer everywhere therefore tends to be agnostic about history and cults of the past. He is opposed to "prejudices inherited from the yesterday of our life," to the "tendency to accept as generally valid many propositions that were appropriate for only one period of our history."[8]

The pivot of conservatism is, on the other hand, a deep reverence for the past, a sentimental defense of existing institutions, routines, and orthodoxies which live on from the past, and an abiding fear of change as the harbinger of disorder and of a future that will be worse than the present as well as a sacrilege of the past. Conservatism is often little more than the sum total of inertia, habit, and vested interests. But it can also be a cogent philosophical justification of the status quo as the culmination of everything good in the historical past and thus the only sturdy bridge to the future.[9] Many conservatives can distinguish between stability and immobilism, and they do not flatly reject all change. But the conservative insistence that any change be slow and tightly controlled by established authority, based on law and order, and conform to prevailing orthodoxies is usually prohibitive. In the end, conservatives usually prefer cults of the past and those authorities (notably, the armed forces and the political police) which guard order against change, native tradition against "alien" corruption, the present against the future.[10]

Authentic reformism and conservatism are always social and political. Both trends are expressed below, in society, in popular sentiments and attitudes, and above, in the middle and higher reaches of the political system, in groups, factions, and parties. And still higher, so to speak, they take the more exalted form of ideological and philosophical propositions.

Both reformism and conservatism have been apparent as antagonists on all three of these levels in the Soviet Union since the 1950s. Although we lack the kind of polling and other survey information available for other countries, we know, for example, from firsthand accounts, that profoundly conservative attitudes are widespread among ordinary citizens and officials alike.[11] Detailed scholarly studies point out the sustained struggles between reformist and conservative groups inside the high political establishment, including the party itself.[12] And, as we shall see, the ideological and even philosophical dimensions of this quarrel have become particularly evident in recent years.

What we do not know, and indeed barely perceive, is the relationship between these trends in society below and in the political apparatus above. Though this is partly a problem of inadequate information, it derives also from the untenable but persistent notion that Soviet party-state officialdom is somehow insulated from society itself. This conception makes no empirical sense in a country where the state employs almost every citizen and the party has 18 million members. All of the trends in society, even those expressed by dissidents, also exist, however subterraneanly, inside political officialdom. There is at best, as one Western scholar argues, a "soft boundary" between the two.[13] Once we abandon the commonplace image of a gulf separating political officialdom and society, and see them instead, in the imagery of a Soviet dissident, as "upstairs" and "downstairs,"[14] the fuller social dimensions of the political conflict between Soviet reformism and conservatism will at least come into view.

At the level of politics and policy, the conflict between reformism and conservatism derives its scope and intensity from the fact that it is simultaneously a quarrel about the past, the present, and the future. The historical agnosticism of the reformer and the historicism of the conservative are therefore especially antagonistic in a country such as the Soviet Union, where what its citizens call "living history" has been unusually traumatic. Not only the immediate Stalinist past but also the remote tsarist past are subjects of fierce controversy. Conservatives bitterly protest the reformist "deheroization" of the past and the view in which "the past, present, and future . . . turn out to be isolated, shut off from each other." The conservative extols the "continuity of generations"; the reformer replies, "If the children do not criticize the fathers, mankind does not move ahead." For conservatives, reformist perspectives "distort the past"; for reformers, conservatives "idealize the past" and try "to save the past from the present."[15]

These historical controversies have been an essential part of almost all policy disputes throughout the post-Stalin era. They reflect the political struggle between the forces of reform and conservatism inside Soviet officialdom from 1953 to the present—from an official reformation to a far-reaching conservative reaction.

From Reformism to Conservatism

Because of the unusually despotic nature of his long rule, Stalin's death unleashed a decade-long triumph of Soviet reformism which was disproportionate to its actual strength in society or officialdom. Virtually every area of Soviet life was affected (and improved). Though bitterly opposed, often contradictory, and ultimately limited, the changes of the 1950s and early 1960s constituted a reformation—within the limits of the authoritarian system—in Soviet politics and society, as indicated by a brief recitation of the most important reforms.

The kind of personal dictatorship exercised by Stalin for more than twenty years ended and the Communist Party was restored as the ruling political institution. Twenty-five years of mass terror came to an end and the political police, the main agency of Stalin's dictatorship, was brought under control. Millions of prison camp survivors were freed and many who had perished in the terror were legally exonerated, thereby enabling survivors and relatives to regain full citizenship. Many administrative abuses and bureaucratic privileges were curtailed. Educated society began to participate more fully in political and intellectual life. A wide array of economic and welfare reforms were carried out. Major revisions were made in Soviet censorship practices, in the official ideology of Marxism-Leninism, and in foreign policy.

Insofar as this was official reformism, or reform from above, Nikita Khrushchev was its leader, and his overthrow in 1964 marked the beginning of its political defeat.[16] Khrushchev himself was a contradictory figure. His background and career made him the representative of the old as well as the new; and some of his policies, as in certain areas of science, favored conservative forces. But in terms of his overall administration, Khrushchev was, as Russians say, a great reformer (velikii reformator).

Nonetheless, Khrushchev and his faction at the top were only part of a much broader reformist movement inside Soviet officialdom. During the decade after 1953, the struggle between the friends and foes of change spread to all areas of policy making—to the areas of administration and planning, industry and agriculture, science, history, culture, law, family matters, welfare, ideology, and foreign affairs.[17] In each of these areas, reform found notable spokesmen and important allies.[18] Like conservatism, whose adherents ranged from old-line Stalinists to Tory-style moderates, Soviet reformism must be understood as an amalgam of diverse types and motives. It included technocrats in search only of limited change in their special areas as well as authentic democrats; it derived from self-interest as well as idealism. But in relation to the overarching question of change, something akin to two distinct parties—reformist and conservative—emerged inside Soviet officialdom, and within the Communist Party itself, counterposing rival interests, policies, and ideas over a wide range of issues in all political quarters.[19]

Conservatism, as a defense of the inherited Stalinist order, was more fully formed as an ideological and policy movement in the years immediately following Stalin's death. By the early 1960s, however, reformers had developed a characteristic cluster of reformist policies, historical perspectives, and ideological propositions. Most of these were developed, both as critique and program, in opposition to conservative ones, which still drew heavily upon the Stalinist past. There were many of these reformist ideas by the early 1960s, and they cannot easily be summarized. A few examples must suffice.

While conservatives eulogized the tsarist and Stalinist pasts, and particularly the 1930s when many existing Soviet institutions took shape, reformers rehabilitated the radical intelligentsia of the nineteenth century, the Soviet 1920s, and a generation of old Bolsheviks purged by Stalin. While conservatives accented the authoritarian stands in Marxism-Leninism, the Stalin cult, and the dangers of revisionism, reformers stressed socialist democracy, Lenin himself, the criminality of Stalin, and the dangers of dogmatism. Against the conservative themes of Russian nationalism, Soviet hegemony in the communist world, and xenophobia, reformers emphasized internationalism, different roads to socialism, and an opening to the West. In contrast to the conservative preference for heavy-handed censorship, reformers promoted varying degrees of cultural and intellectual liberalism. As opposed to the overly centralized Stalinist system of economic planning and administration, with its decades of heavy industrialism, agricultural retardation, waste, and austerity, reformers advocated the market, decentralized initiative, efficiency, consumer goods, and innovations in order to encourage private initiative in the collective system. Against the Stalinist tradition of terror, reformers called for rule of law and due process.[20]

Soviet reformers won many victories during the Khrushchev years. But reform from above everywhere is always limited in substance and duration, and it is usually followed by a conservative backlash. This circumstance is partly a result of the nature of reformism, which struggles against the natural inertia of people and institutions on behalf of limited goals. Many adherents of reform are quickly satisfied, many allies are easily unnerved, and many who only tolerated reform are soon driven to oppose further change. All become part of a neoconservative consensus, defenders of the new, reformed status quo, and critics of reformist "excesses." Indeed, this reformist-conservative rhythm is thought to be axiomatic in American and British politics, where Republicans and Tories are expected to follow Democrats and Labourites.

The overthrow of Khrushchev in October 1964 reflected this swing of the pendulum in Soviet officialdom, and possibly in society as well. His fall ushered in, after an interlude of uncertain direction in 1964–65, a far-reaching conservative reaction, which brought an end to major reform, and even some counterreform in most areas of Soviet society, from economics and law, to historiography, culture, and ideology. Since 1966, and especially since the Soviet overthrow of the reform communist government in Czechoslovakia in 1968, the Brezhnev administration has been a regime of conservatism. It has revived many of the conservative practices noted above as well as the preeminent symbol of the past, Stalin himself. Its antireformist spirit and policies have been expressed in a galaxy of refurbished conservative catch phrases and campaigns—"stability in cadres," "law and order," "the strengthening of organization, discipline, and responsibility in all spheres," "military-heroic patriotism," "developed socialism," "vigilance against bourgeois influences," and more.[21] It has, in short, reasserted conservative views on the past, the present, and the future.

The conservative reaction since 1964, though far-reaching, has not meant a restoration of, or return to, Stalinist policies. With society and politics themselves, conservative attitudes and policies change. Stalinism no longer defines Soviet realities, and therefore mainstream Soviet con-servatism, as it did in the early 1950s. The Brezhnev government re-versed some reforms of the Khrushchev years; but, for the most part, it has tempered and administered already accomplished reforms as part of the new status quo, while deploring earlier "excesses" and setting itself against further change. (Republicans and Tories did the same upon returning to office in the United States and England in the 1950s.)

Some ideas and policies once associated with Soviet reformers—con-sumerism, higher investment in agriculture, welfarism, scientific man-agement, legal proceduralism, detente, repudiation of Stalin's "excesses" —have even been incorporated into the new conservatism. This does not demonstrate, as some Western observers have thought, the reform-ist spirit of the Brezhnev government, because these once reformist ideas have been infused with deeply conservative meaning. "Economic reform," for example, has been an official idea intermittently since 1964; but the original reforms have been stripped of their essentials—the role of the market and decentralization—so that, in the words of one re-former, they have become "purely superficial, partial changes which do not affect the essence of the prereform system."[22] The official re-pudiation of reform since the mid-1960s is clearly understood by people inside the Soviet Union: "We are ruled not by a Communist or a fascist party and not by a Stalinist party, but by a status quo party."[23]

By the late 1960s, the increasingly censorious conservatism of the Brezhnev government had muted reformist voices, and thus explicit conflict, in many policy areas. At the same time, however, and possibly for this reason, the conflict between reformers and conservatives broke out dramatically in a different way in the official press: in an often abstract controversy about the nature of Russia as a historical society. Focusing on philosophical, cultural, and even religious themes, the two rival outlooks have now been openly at odds for more than a decade.[24] This controversy echoes the split between Westerners and Slavophiles in nineteenth-century Russia, but its real importance is contemporary and intensely political. It is a confrontation, couched in a philosophical and older Russian idiom, between present-day Soviet reformism and conservatism. The traditional idiom of the conservatives, with their advocacy of Russia's "eternal values," has become particularly forthright, leading reformers to protest that their ideas are "borrowed, transcribed, taken on hire from the storehouse of conservative literature of the past century."[25]

This neoconservative philosophy, which is in many respects congruent with the policy spirit and Russian nationalism of the Brezhnev government, has spread throughout the Soviet press (and *samizdat*) and demonstrated remarkable appeal to many segments of the population. Its popularity tends to confirm firsthand evidence that official conservatism is not a regime-made artifice but a reflection of broad and deep currents in Soviet officialdom and society.[26] It has become clear that the great reforms of the Khrushchev years derived more from unusual historical circumstances than from the actual political and social strength of reformism in the Soviet Union. For a fuller perspective on the post-Stalin era and on the future, we need, then, at least a brief look at the historical origins of contemporary reformism and conservatism in the Stalinist past.

The Stalinist Roots of Reformism and Conservatism

The first great reform in Soviet history was the introduction of the New Economic Policy (NEP) in 1921. Intended to replace the extremist practices of the civil war years, NEP quickly grew into a whole series of policies and ideas which Lenin, the father of NEP, called "a reformist approach."[27] For four years after Lenin's death in 1924, NEP remained official Soviet policy, with Nikolai Bukharin as its interpreter and great defender. Thus, when Stalin forcibly abolished NEP in 1929, he inadvertently created a historical model for future generations of communist reformers. Since that time, and especially after 1953, NEP— with its dual economy, concepts of market and plan, cultural diversity, more liberal politics, and Leninist legitimacy—has exercised a powerful appeal to anti-Stalinist party reformers everywhere, from Moscow to Eastern and Western Europe. Soviet reformers have revived many NEP economic ideas; reformist historians have studied NEP admiringly; cultural liberals have cited its tolerant censorship; and reform politicians have sought legitimacy in it.[28]

With the defeat of the Bukharinist opposition (or "right deviation"), the end of NEP, and the onset of Stalin's revolution from above in 1929, party reformism became the special enemy and victim of Stalinism. There were at least two serious attempts by high officials to initiate reform from above during the Stalin years. The first involved the so-called Kirov group in the Politburo in 1933–34, which proposed to ameliorate the terrible hardships of forcible collectivization and heavy industrialization. The second was in 1947–48; it apparently involved similar proposals, by the Politburo member Nikolai Voznesensky and others, for change in economic policy. Both attempts to reform Stalinism ended horribly—in the great terror of 1936–39 and in the Leningrad purge of 1949 and Voznesensky's execution.[29]

Nonetheless, this melancholy history of failed reform shows that even during the worst Stalin years, there was a reformist impulse among high party and state officials. These early strivings toward a "Moscow Spring" (as an insider termed them in 1936) were the official antecedents of Khrushchev's reformism, as he tacitly acknowledged by associating his de-Stalinization campaign with the Kirov affair and by rehabilitating Voznesensky. But it also shows that reform from above stood no chance in the conditions of Stalin's terroristic autocracy and in the face of his personal hostility, which remained adamant to the end.[30]

And yet while Stalin martyred reform at every turn, his system and policies were creating the future political and social base of reformism. The historical Stalinism of 1929–53 was an extraordinary composite of dualities. Stalinism began as a radical act of revolution from above and ended as a rigidly conservative social and political system. It combined revolutionary traditions with tsarist ones; humanitarian ideas of social justice with terror; radical ideology with traditional social policies; the myths of socialist democracy and party rule with the reality of personal dictatorship; modernization with archaic practices; a routinized bureaucracy with administrative caprice.

Reformism and conservatism grew out of these dualities after Stalin in two general ways. First, the values and ideas of both post-Stalin reformers and conservatives had been perpetuated in Stalinism. Russian nationalism, terror, and privilege came to dominate, for example, but their opposites remained part of the official ideology. They were maintained in an uneasy state of latent conflict, as a kind of dual Soviet political culture, by the Stalin cult and the terror.[31] After Stalin's death, these currents went separate political ways into the conflicts of 1953–79, especially into the conflict between anti-Stalinism and neo-Stalinism, which in the 1950s and early 1960s played a special role in the confrontation between reformers and conservatives.

The second way in which the Stalinist system prepared its own reformation was, as Marxists say, dialectical. Stalinism created within itself an alternative model of political rule.[32] The agent of this potential change was not, as Marxist critics of Stalinism had hoped for so long, an activist working class, but Stalin's own political-administrative bureaucracy. Having grown large and powerful under his rule since the 1930s, the leading strata (*nachal'stvo*) of the party-state bureaucracy gained almost everything—income, privilege, status, power over those below. But what they lacked was no less important: security of position and, even more, of life. Stalin's terror inflicted one demographic trauma after another. And no one was more vulnerable after 1934 than the party-state *nachal'stvo*.

The history and ethos of Stalinism made this bureaucracy profoundly conservative in most political and social ways.[33] It yearned, however, for one great reform that would free it from the capricious, terroristic regime at the top, and allow it to become a real bureaucracy—that is, a conservative force based on stability, personal security, and predictability. While Stalin lived, even the highest officials felt themselves to be "temporary people" and sought protection against the abnormality of the terror in various legalisms.[34] But normality in this sense could come only with the end of the autocrat.

Both reformism and conservatism were thus already in place when Stalin's death finally came in March 1953. The first words of his heirs, imploring the population to avoid "panic and disarray," revealed them as fearful conservatives (who always imagine disorder below) in important respects. But fear of retribution from below and another terror from above led them quickly to major reforms, from which others followed: the dismantling and curtailment of Stalin's primary institutions (his secretariat, the terror system, and the cult) and the restoration of party dictatorship and collective leadership.[35] Restoring the party to political primacy was in itself a major change that had far-reaching ramifications. It proved to be remarkably easy, reformist rather than revolutionary, partly because it promised at last protection from terror to high officials throughout the system. Indeed, this was the essential reformist meaning of Khrushchev's "secret" speech against Stalin in 1956. For most high officials, this may have been not only popular but also sufficient.

These circumstances help to explain the success of Khrushchev's initial reforms, even though reformism probably was, and remains, a minority outlook in Soviet officialdom. His successes and rise to power in 1953–58 were based on a kind of reformism, or de-Stalinization, which had broader appeal in these special historical circumstances. The majority of Soviet officials and elites wanted, it seems clear, an end to terror, a diminishing of the police system, some historical revisionism, relaxation of international tensions, and certain welfare reforms (in pensions, for example) which benefited them as well. They wanted, and got, a thaw—but not a spring.

After 1958, Khrushchev's reformism and renewed de-Stalinization campaign began to mean something different. They came to include quasi-populist policies, or ideas, that impinged directly upon the nature of the central party-state bureaucracy and its relations with society, rather than with the regime above.[36] The quiescent conservative majority emerged and began to resist. Khrushchev became an embattled leader. That he managed to achieve as much as he did after 1958, despite the opposition, his many ill-conceived policies, and his personal inadequacies as a reform leader,[37] is probably explained partly by the momentum and political appeal of anti-Stalinism. When this cause was spent in the early 1960s, so, too, were Khrushchev's great reforms.

Soviet Conservatism and the Future of Reform

The real obstacle to future reform in the Soviet Union is not this or that institution, group, faction, or leader, but the profound conservatism that seems to dominate them all, from the ordinary family to the Politburo, from local authorities to the state *nachal'stvo*. It can be argued that the Soviet Union has become, both downstairs and upstairs, one of the most conservative countries in the world.[38] Real discussion of the prospects for further change therefore must await fuller scholarly study of this political and social conservatism, which manifests itself daily, in all areas of life, as a preference for tradition and order and a fear of innovation and disorder.

It may be argued that a system born in revolution and still professing revolutionary ideas cannot be called conservative, but history has witnessed other such transformations, as well as the inner deradicalization of revolutionary ideologies.[39] Indeed, the conservative aftermath of a great social revolution may be a kind of historical law.[40] If so, we might expect this to have been doubly the case in Russia, where revolution from below in 1917 was followed by Stalin's revolution from above in 1929–33. Early Bolsheviks worried that even their own party might end in this way. One warned: "History is full of examples of the transformation of parties of revolution into parties of order. Sometimes the only mementos of a revolutionary party are the watchwords which it has inscribed on public buildings."[41]

There are, in addition, many specific, and mutually reinforcing, sources of Soviet conservatism. Although specialists disagree as to the most important factors in Soviet political life, almost all of these factors have contributed to its conservatism. There is the legacy of tsarist Russia, with its own bureaucratic and conservative traditions. There is the subsequent bureaucratization of Soviet life in the 1930s, which proliferated conservative norms and created a *nomenklatura* class of zealous defenders of position and privilege.[42] There is, in this connection, the persistent scarcity of goods and services, which redoubles the resistance of vested interests. There is the increasing age of Soviet ruling elites. And there is even the official ideology, whose domestic thrust turned many years ago from creating a new order to extolling the existing one.

Underlying all of these factors is the Soviet historical experience with its particular combination of monumental achievements and mountainous disasters. In sixty years, man-made catastrophes have repeatedly victimized millions of ordinary citizens and officials alike—the first European war, revolution, civil war, two great famines, forcible collectivization, Stalin's great terror, World War II, and more. Out of this experience, which is still autobiographical for many people, have come the joint pillars of today's Soviet conservatism: a towering pride in the nation's modernizing and Great-Power achievements, together with an abiding anxiety that the next disaster forever looms and that change is "some sinister Beethovean knock of fate at the door."[43] This is a conservatism at once prideful and fearful, and thus powerful. It appears to influence most segments of the population, even many dissidents, to be a real bond between upstairs and downstairs and therefore the main obstacle to change.

Much would seem to favor, then, only conservatism in Soviet politics. And yet, as we have seen, this has not been the entire story of the post-Stalin years; nor is it now. Advocates of change, however weak their position and however diverse their reformist aspirations, continue to exist in most policy areas and even to hold responsible positions in lower and middle levels of the party-state officialdom.[44] Indeed, one enduring reform of the post-Stalin years has been a broadening of the political system sufficient to tolerate such people even during a conservative regime. Therefore, some of the general factors favoring a resurgence of official reformism must also be taken into account. Leaving aside the possibility of serious domestic crises, and assuming that Soviet reformers stand a chance only in an international environment of diminishing tensions, three weaknesses of Soviet conservatism should be emphasized because they point to permanent sources of reformism in the Soviet system.

Like conservatives everywhere, Soviet opponents of change need a usable past in order to justify and defend the status quo. The relevant past includes, however, the criminal history of Stalinism. Soviet conservatives have coped with this problem in two ways since the fall of Khrushchev. They have selectively rehabilitated the Stalinist past, largely in terms of the great Soviet victory over Germany in World War II, and without fully rehabilitating Stalin himself.[45] And they have groped toward a surrogate past in tsarist history. Neither seems to be a durable solution. Historical de-Stalinization, which is a powerful source of political reformism, retains its appeal not only because tens of millions died, but because millions of wartime casualties can be blamed directly on the Stalinist government. As for the tsarist past, though partially rehabilitated under Stalin and of considerable appeal today, its traditions are nonetheless contrary to the ideas of the Russian revolution, which official conservatives still embrace as the main source of their legitimacy. These two traditions cannot be durably reconciled. Ultimately, they inspire rival currents, conflict not harmony in political life, as was the case in post-revolutionary France.[46]

The second conservative weakness, and source of reformism, is the plain discrepancy between the official ideology and everyday Soviet realities. Except for a small segment of the population, this is not foremost a discrepancy between democratic ideas and dictatorial practices, but something more fundamental. As an official ideology, Soviet communism has come increasingly to mean, in addition to Russian nationalism, consumer goods plus the welfare state. These commitments are exceedingly important to ordinary citizens, to middle-class officials, and to the government. They have been the main domestic pledges of the conservative Brezhnev government since the mid-1960s, as well as its most glaring failures.[47] Though elementary welfare provisions were achieved much earlier, low standards of living, chronic shortages of basic foodstuffs and housing, and the scarcity of other consumer goods remain widespread and intractable problems of everyday Soviet life.

As repeatedly expressed ideological commitments, to officialdom as well as to society-at-large, these consumer-welfare promises cannot be easily withdrawn or forever deferred. They are a relentless threat to Soviet conservatives because they attract constant attention to the inadequacies of the centralized economic system and thus keep meaningful economic reform permanently on the agenda. And, as both reformers and conservatives understand, this kind of economic reform, involving decentralization and the market, must have reformist implications in political life as well.[48]

The third factor favoring reform also involves official ideology. The role of Marxism-Leninism, or communism, may have declined in recent years, but it remains the essential framework for discourse and conflict throughout official Soviet politics. No reformist or conservative movement anywhere can be successful if it is estranged from established political norms and culture. Soviet conservatives and reformers must have a Soviet face; they must find inspiration and legitimacy somewhere within historical Marxism-Leninism. Conservatives are trying, as reformers complain, to fill "Marxist formulas" with their own meanings.[49] But Marxism-Leninism is an unreliable conservative vehicle because it is an ideology, even in its dogmatized version, based upon the very idea, desirability, and inexorability of change. Soviet reformers miss no opportunity to make this point: "Any apologetics for things as they are is alien to the materialistic dialectic. . . . This applies to any particular form society may have assumed at any stage in its development. To search constantly for new and imaginative ways to transform reality—that is the motto of the dialectic."[50]

In this respect, Soviet reformers have an important advantage over their nineteenth-century counterparts in tsarist officialdom, whose experience may be highly relevant.[51] Struggling against a conservative majority of Russian officials in the decades leading up to the major reforms from above in the 1860s, tsarist reformers were seriously hampered by an official ideology thoroughly hostile to the idea of real change. They had to seek ideological inspiration and legitimacy elsewhere, in suspect "foreign" cultures. Official Soviet reformers do not have this problem, or at least not as acutely. Moreover, they can, and regularly do, point to existing models of communist reform in Eastern Europe as examples which are Marxist-Leninist, and thus fraternal rather than "foreign."[52]

The experience of official reformers under tsarism suggests another important perspective. The growth of reformist sentiments and "enlightened" officials was a slow, cumulative process. It extended over decades and included many setbacks. During the long winters of reform, such ideas could openly circulate only outside the bureaucracy, in circles of nineteenth-century nonconformists, before percolating into the bureaucracy to influence policy. The role of today's Soviet dissidents and their *samizdat* discussions is pertinent to this process. Incapable of effecting reform themselves, since it can come only from above, their real function must be to contribute to the growth of reformist ideas and thus to the "enlightenment" of future officials.[53] Viewed in this way, it could be argued that the sudden, escalating reforms of the Khrushchev years were premature, that the "enlightenment" process was just beginning in officialdom, and that the still ongoing conservative reaction is not the end but only a stage in the history of post-Stalin reform.

This perspective raises a final question. Successful reform is always a result of political coalitions, a fact of special importance to Soviet reformers, who apparently represent a distinct minority of officials. Unable to draw strength directly from protest movements below, as reformers in other societies have done, and advocating economic policies that threaten many petty administrators and even workers,[54] Soviet reformers can find allies only among the conservative majority of officials, who have seemed more attracted by neo-Stalinism in recent years. Is this a real possibility?

"The boundary between progressive and conservative runs through each of us," remarked a Czech official during the Prague Spring.[55] Soviet reformers must appeal to this "progressive" element in moderate conservatives. Historians tell us that conservatives are uncomfortable reformers but that many become reformers to save what they believe is most important in the existing order of things.[56] There is some evidence that in the 1960s a consensus for change was forming between moderate reformers and moderate conservatives, at least among the party intelligentsia. It seemed to center on commonly perceived problems such as the degradation of country life, declining labor productivity, drunkenness, the Stalinist past, and the heavy-handed censorship that frustrated conservatives as well as reformers.[57] The emergence of such a consensus may not yet be in the making, but it is the best, and probably only, hope for reform.

Notes

1. A. M. Rumiantsev, "Vstupaiushchemu v mir nauki," *Pravda*, June 8, 1967; "Kogda otstaiut ot vremeni," *Pravda* (editorial), January 27, 1967; and O. Latsis, "Novoe nado otstaivat'," *Novyi mir*, no. 10, 1965, p. 255. The theme of innovation versus tradition has been the subject of endless polemics since 1953. It also runs persistently through Soviet fiction, from Vladimir Dudintsev's *Ne khlebom edinym*, published in 1956, to Aleksandr Zinov'ev's *Svetloe budushchee* (Lausanne, 1978).

2. For critical discussion of these habits in Soviet studies, see Stephen F. Cohen, "Bolshevism and Stalinism," in Robert C. Tucker, ed., *Stalinism: Essays in Historical Interpretation* (New York, 1977), pp. 3–29; Carl A. Linden, *Khrushchev and the Soviet Leadership* (Baltimore, 1966), pp. 1–9; and William Taubman, "The Change to Change in Communist Systems," in Henry W. Morton and Rudolf L. Tökés, eds., *Soviet Politics and Society in the 1970's* (New York, 1974), pp. 369–94.

3. Among the most interesting studies are Zbigniew Brzezinski, "The Soviet Political System: Transformation or Degeneration?," in Zbigniew Brzezinski, ed., *Dilemmas of Change in Soviet Politics* (New York, 1969), pp.

1–34; Jerry F. Hough, *The Soviet Union and Social Science Theory* (Cambridge, Mass., 1977), chap. 1; George W. Breslauer, "Khrushchev Reconsidered," *Problems of Communism*, September-October, 1976, pp. 18–33; and George W. Breslauer, *Five Images of the Soviet Future: A Critical Review and Synthesis* (Berkeley, 1978).

4. My categories derive from, though they do not fully correspond to, the following firsthand accounts: Roy A. Medvedev, *On Socialist Democracy* (New York, 1975), chap. 3 and *passim*; Alexander Yanov, *Detente After Brezhnev: The Domestic Roots of Soviet Foreign Policy* (Berkeley, 1977); and Igor Glagolev, "Sovetskoe rukovodstvo: Segodnia i zavtra," *Russkaia mysl'*, August 31, 1978. Considerable information on trends in the party is available in *Politicheskii dnevnik* (2 vols; Amsterdam, 1972 and 1975).

5. Arno J. Mayer, *Dynamics of Counterrevolution in Europe, 1870–1956: An Analytic Framework* (New York, 1971), chap. 2.

6. There are important exceptions. See Sidney I. Ploss, *Conflict and Decision-Making in Soviet Russia: A Case Study of Agricultural Policy, 1953–63* (Princeton, 1965); Linden, *Khrushchev and the Soviet Leadership*, which includes an excellent discussion of this spectrum (pp. 18–21); and Moshe Lewin, *Political Undercurrents in Soviet Economic Debates: From Bukharin to the Modern Reformers* (Princeton, 1974).

7. Alexander Yanov, *Essays on Soviet Society* (*International Journal of Sociology*, vol. 6, no. 2–3; Summer-Fall, 1976), esp. pp. 75–175; G. Kozlov and M. Rumer, "Tol'ko nachalo (Zametki o khoziaistvennoi reforme)," *Novyi mir*, no. 11, 1966, p. 182; F. Chapchakhov, "Pod vidom gipotezy," *Literaturnaia gazeta*, August 16, 1972, which is an attack on, and an inadvertent confirmation of, Yanov's two "types"; and Molotov, quoted in Giuseppe Boffa, *Inside the Khrushchev Era* (New York, 1959), p. 108. The word conservative (*konservator*) is commonly used in the Soviet Union. Various words or expressions are used to express "reformer," though the English word (*reformist*) is coming into use. See Valentin Turchin, *Inertsiia strakha* (New York, 1977), p. 5. Soviet writers often use these concepts, with obvious implications for the reader, in analyzing other political societies. See, for example, M. P. Mchedlov, *Evoliutsiia sovremennogo katolitsizma* (Moscow, 1966).

8. V. Lakshin, "Ivan Denisovich, ego druz'ia i nedrugi," *Novyi mir*, no. 1, 1964, p. 230; Medvedev, *On Socialist Democracy*, p. 41.

9. For the range of factors (fear, self-interest, philosophy) that animate conservative opposition to economic reform in the Soviet Union, for example, see the series of articles by A. Birman in *Novyi mir* between 1965 and 1968, and especially his "Sut' reformy," in no. 12, 1968, pp. 185–204.

10. For a summary of the extensive literature on modern conservatism, see Clinton Rossiter, "Conservatism," *International Encyclopedia of the Social Sciences*, vol. 3 (New York, 1968), pp. 290–95.

11. See, for example, Turchin, *Inertsiia strakha*; Medvedev, *On Socialist Democracy*; Yanov, *Essays on Soviet Society*; Andrei Amalrik, *Will the Soviet Union Survive Until 1984?* (New York, 1970); and note 9 above.

12. In addition to the titles cited in note 6, see Michel Tatu, *Power in the Kremlin: From Khrushchev to Kosygin* (New York, 1969); and H. Gordon Skilling and Franklyn Griffiths, eds., *Interest Groups in Soviet Politics* (Princeton, 1971).

13. See Lewin, *Political Undercurrents in Soviet Economic Debates*, pp. 262, 298.

14. Alexander Yanov, *The Russian New Right: Right-Wing Ideologies in the Contemporary USSR* (Berkeley, 1978), p. 15.

15. *Politicheskii dnevnik*, I, p. 123; F. Chapchakhov, "Pod vidom gipotezy," *Literaturnaia gazeta*, August 16, 1972; *Politicheskii dnevnik*, no. 66 (samizdat; Moscow, March 1970), p. 36; A. Iakovlev, "Protiv antiistorizma," *Literaturnaia gazeta*, November 15, 1975.

16. See Linden, *Khrushchev and the Soviet Leadership*; and Breslauer, "Khrushchev Reconsidered."

17. In addition to the titles cited in notes 6 and 12 above, see the sections on the 1950s and 1960s in the following works: Nancy Whittier Heer, *Politics and History in the Soviet Union* (Cambridge, Mass., 1971); Peter H. Juviler and Henry W. Morton, eds., *Soviet Policy-Making: Studies of Communism in Transition* (New York, 1967); Peter H. Juviler, *Revolutionary Law and Order: Politics and Social Change in the USSR* (New York, 1976); Gail Warshofsky Lapidus, *Women in Soviet Society: Equality, Development and Social Change* (Berkeley, 1978); Aron Katsenelinboigen, *Studies in Soviet Economic Planning* (White Plains, N.Y., 1978); Timothy McClure, "The Politics of Soviet Culture, 1964–1967," *Problems of Communism*, March-April, 1967, pp. 26–43.

18. Individuals such as Aleksandr Tvardovskii in literature; A. Birman, V. G. Venzher, and G. S. Lisichkin in economics; A. M. Rumiantsev and F. M. Burlatskii in the social sciences; M. D. Shargorodskii in law; V. P. Danilov and M. Ia. Gefter in history; and so on. One *samizdat* writer has suggested that "it would be truer to call the epoch of Khrushchev, the epoch of Tvardovskii," because of his editorship of the reformist journal *Novyi mir*.

19. *Pravda* (January 27, 1967) discussed the reformist journal *Novyi mir* and the conservative journal *Oktiabr'* in terms of the "two poles" in Soviet politics. Soviet intellectuals sometimes spoke of them privately in the 1960s as the "organs of our two parties."

20. To give a few more cryptic examples of code words in the conflict, reformers and conservatives emphasized, respectively, the following: bureaucratism as the main danger—anarchy as the main danger; the Lenin of 1921–23—the Lenin of 1918–20; the importance of the intelligentsia—the importance of the worker and the soldier; the 20th and 22nd Party Congresses—the 23rd, 24th, and 25th Congresses; modernism in art—traditionalism in art; internal problems—external threats; women's rights—the stability of the family; innovation—discipline; renewal of cadres—stability of cadres; social interests—the organic unity of society.

21. See, for example, *Razvitoe sotsialisticheskoe obshchestvo: Sushchnost', kriterii zrelosti, kritika revizionistskikh kontseptsii* (Moscow, 1973); P. M. Rogachev and M. A. Sverklin, *Patriotizm i obshchestvennyi progress* (Moscow, 1974); and the editorials in *Pravda*, February 5 and 24, and October 17, 1978. For discussion of important aspects of these conservative policies, see T. H. Rigby, "The Soviet Leadership: Towards a Self-Stabilizing Oligarchy?," *Soviet Studies*, October, 1970, pp. 167–91; his "The Soviet Regional Leadership: The Brezhnev Generation," *Slavic Review*, vol. 37, no. 1 (March 1978), pp. 1–24; and Breslauer, "Khrushchev Reconsidered."

22. Quoted in Iu. Subotskii, "Upravlenie, khozraschet, samostoiatel'nost'," *Novyi mir*, no. 7, 1969, p. 265.

23. Lev Kopelev, quoted in *The New York Times*, December 3, 1978, p. 14.

24. The controversy began with the rival journals *Novyi mir* and *Molodaia gvardiia*, but it has since spread to many publications. For an excellent survey and analysis, see Frederick C. Barghoorn, "The Political Significance of Great Russian Nationalism in Brezhnev's USSR With Particular Reference to the 'Pseudo-Slavophiles'" (unpublished paper delivered at the AAASS Conference, Washington, October 1977).

25. Yanov, *Essays on Soviet Society*, p. 124. For similar protests, see A. Dement'ev, "O traditsiiakh i narodnosti," *Novyi mir*, no. 4, 1969, pp. 215–35; Iakovlev, "Protiv antiistorizma," *Literaturnaia gazeta*, November 15, 1975; and the running objections in the *samizdat* journal *Politicheskii dnevnik*. Though the idiom is plainly Russian, it is sometimes universally conservative, even Burkean. See, for example, the eulogy of "social authority" and the "continuity of generations" in S. Semanov, *Serdtse rodina* (Moscow, 1977), pp. 92–3.

26. See note 11 above.

27. See Stephen F. Cohen, *Bukharin and the Bolshevik Revolution: A Political Biography, 1888–1938* (New York, 1973), pp. 132–38. Soviet reformers have been eager to identify NEP as "the first reform." See, for example, A. Birman, "Mysli posle plenuma," *Novyi mir*, no. 12, 1965, p. 194.

28. See, for example, Lewin, *Political Undercurrents in Soviet Economic Debates*, chap. 12 and *passim*; G. S. Lisichkin, *Plan i rynok* (Moscow, 1966); M. P. Kim, ed., *Novaia ekonomicheskaia politika: Voprosy teorii i istorii* (Moscow, 1974); and A. Rumiantsev, "Partiia i intelligentsia," *Pravda*, February 21, 1965.

29. Cohen, *Bukharin and the Bolshevik Revolution*, pp. 341–47; Ploss, *Conflict and Decision-Making in Soviet Russia*, pp. 28–58.

30. This was also the case in foreign policy. See Robert C. Tucker, *The Soviet Political Mind* (rev. ed.; New York, 1971), chap. 4.

31. For a cultural approach to Stalinism, see Robert C. Tucker, "Stalinism as Revolution From Above," in Tucker, ed., *Stalinism*, pp. 77–108. For the conservative aspects of Stalinism, see note 33 below.

32. As Moshe Lewin has argued in "The Social Background of Stalinism," in Tucker, ed., *Stalinism*, pp. 133–35.

33. See Vera S. Dunham, *In Stalin's Time: Middleclass Values in Soviet Fiction* (Cambridge, England, 1976); Leon Trotsky, *The Revolution Betrayed* (New York, 1945); Nicholas S. Timasheff, *The Great Retreat* (New York, 1946); and Frederick C. Barghoorn, *Soviet Russian Nationalism* (New York, 1956).

34. Lewin, "The Social Background of Stalinism," pp. 133–35; and Robert H. McNeal, "The Decisions of the CPSU and the Great Purge," *Soviet Studies*, vol. 23, no. 2, October 1971, pp. 177–85. The quote is from *Khrushchev Remembers* (Boston, 1970), p. 307.

35. For the fearful atmosphere surrounding these decisions, see *Khrushchev Remembers*, pp. 315–53.

36. See Breslauer, "Khrushchev Reconsidered."

37. For a critical discussion of Khrushchev's inadequacies by two dissident reformers, see Roy A. Medvedev and Zhores A. Medvedev, *Khrushchev: The Years in Power* (New York, 1978).

38. This does not mean that there are not special bastions of Soviet conservatism such as the elites of the KGB, the Komsomol, the Trade Unions, and the Political Sector of the Army. It does mean, however, that we should not assume that the division between reformers and conservatives is a function of generations. Older people played a major, even leading, role, for example, in the struggles for economic and cultural reform in the 1950s and 1960s. More generally, there is evidence that Soviet youth is no less conservative than its elders. For a discussion of this question, see Walter D. Connor, "Generations and Politics in the USSR," *Problems of Communism*, September-October 1975, pp. 20–31.

39. See Robert C. Tucker, *The Marxian Revolutionary Idea* (New York, 1969), chap. 6.

40. This does not mean that the revolution must be repudiated. Often it is simply reinterpreted in a conservative fashion, as has happened in the Soviet Union and the United States. See Michael Kammen, *A Season of Youth: The American Revolution and the Historical Imagination* (New York, 1978).

41. Cohen, *Bukharin and the Bolshevik Revolution*, p. 186.

42. See Bohdan Harasymiw, "*Nomenklatura*: The Communist Party's Leadership Recruitment System," *Canadian Journal of Political Science*, vol. 2, no. 4 (December 1969), p. 512; and Mervyn Matthews, *Privilege in the Soviet Union: A Study of Elite Life-Styles Under Communism* (London, 1978).

43. The phrase is Yanov's, used in another context. *Essays on Soviet Society*, p. 85. The Soviet press sometimes asks, "Where do the conservatives come from?" (R. Bakhtamov and P. Volin, "Otkuda berutsia konservatory?," *Literaturnaia gazeta*, September 6, 1967.) Although this historical explanation may not be sufficient, it is essential.

44. The sources cited in note 4 relate to the post-Khrushchev period. See also Abraham Brumberg, "A Conversation With Andrei Amalrik," *Encounter*, June 1977, p. 30. Reform proposals, though of a lesser sort, continue to be expressed by responsible officials in the Soviet press.

45. See, for example, G. A. Deborin and B. S. Tel'pukhovskii, *Itogi i uroki velikoi otechestvennoi voiny* (2nd ed.; Moscow, 1975).

46. David Thomson, *Democracy in France* (London, 1960).

47. For the importance of this "contract," see George W. Breslauer, "On the Adaptability of Welfare-State Authoritarianism in the USSR," in Karl Ryavec, ed., *Soviet Society and The Communist Party* (Amherst, Mass., 1979), pp. 3–25. Interviews with Soviet emigres over a thirty-year period suggest the great importance citizens place on the welfare provisions of the Soviet state. See Alex Inkeles and Raymond A. Bauer, *The Soviet Citizen* (Cambridge, Mass., 1959), esp. chap. 10; and Zvi Gitelman, "Soviet Political Culture: Insights From Jewish Emigres," *Soviet Studies*, vol. 29, no. 4, October 1977, p. 562.

48. Lewin, *Political Undercurrents in Soviet Economic Debates*, chaps. 6–9.

49. Iakovlev, "Protiv antiistorizma," *Literaturnaia gazeta*, November 15, 1975.

50. P. Kopnin quoted in Yanov, *Essays on Soviet Society*, p. 76. Similarly, see A. M. Rumiantsev, "Vstupaiushchemu v mir nauki," *Pravda*, June 8, 1967; and A. Bovin, "Istina protiv dogmy," *Novyi mir*, no. 10, 1963, pp. 180–87.

51. My comments here are based on a reading of S. Frederick Starr, *Decentralization and Self-Government in Russia, 1830–1870* (Princeton, 1972); Richard S. Wortman, *The Development of a Russian Legal Consciousness* (Chicago, 1976); and W. Bruce Lincoln, "The Genesis of an 'Enlightened' Bureaucracy in Russia, 1825–1856," *Jahrbucher für Geschichte Osteuropas*, vol. 2, no. 3, June 1972, pp. 321–30.

52. The connection between East European and Soviet reformers has been very important since 1953. Since the Soviet overthrow of the reform communist government in Czechslovakia in 1968, Soviet conservative literature on the dangers of "right-wing revisionism" has grown into a virtual industry aimed implicitly at domestic reformers as well. Nonetheless, reformers continue to make the point. See, for example, P. Volin, "Liudi i ekonomika," *Novyi mir*, no. 3, 1969, pp. 154–68. For the reform movement in Eastern Europe, see Vladimir V. Kusin, "An Overview of East European Reformism," *Soviet Studies*, July 1976, pp. 338–61.

53. This perspective has been adopted by some dissidents. See, for example, Medvedev, *On Socialist Democracy*; and, for a more systematic statement, L. Okunev, "Slovo—tozhe delo," *Politicheskii dnevnik*, no. 68 (Moscow: Samizdat, May 1970). But many dissidents have lost all hope of reform in recent years and now address their activities and thoughts not to Soviet officialdom but to Western governments.

54. See Karl W. Ryavec, *Implementation of Soviet Economic Reforms* (New York, 1975), pp. 299–300.

55. Quoted in H. Gordon Skilling, *Czechoslovakia's Interrupted Revolution* (Princeton, 1976), p. 495.

56. Rossiter, "Conservatism," pp. 292, 294.

57. For example, journals with different outlooks began to emphasize the same social problems. *Novyi mir* is of particular interest in this connection. Well-known as a kind of reformist community, the journal published, or favorably reviewed, conservative writers such as Efim Dorosh and Vladimir Soloukhin. It also published many newer fiction writers who identified with conservative rural values, but whose writings depicted a post-collectivization countryside in need of reform. The new *samizdat* publications *Pamiat'* and *Poiski*, which include authors of different political outlooks, may be a sign of a similar development in dissident circles.

The Stalin Question

Roy A. Medvedev

Three years after Stalin's death, the Twentieth Congress of the CPSU was held in Moscow. It began on February 14, 1956, and immediately after the opening ceremonies, delegates and guests stood in silence to pay homage to the memory of the man who so recently had been their "father and teacher."

In the course of eleven days of concentrated sessions, delegates were able to pick up a considerable amount of information both from official speeches and reports and in the lobbies of the hall. The new leadership of the party most certainly had achievements to its credit. In agriculture there were clear signs of a change for the better in 1954–55, after the crisis situation of the last years of the Stalin era. The exorbitant taxes strangling the countryside were sharply reduced, and there was an appreciable rise in the purchase price for collective farm products. Plans for industrial production were revised so as to promote the manufacture of consumer goods and the construction of housing; at the same time the development of the service sector was accelerated.

There were also a number of achievements in foreign policy. The new leadership brought about a marked change in relations with Yugoslavia as well as with other countries such as India and Egypt, and relations with China showed some improvement too. It was in 1955–56 that the term "detente" first made its appearance in our political vocabulary.

Adapted from *On Stalin and Stalinism* by Roy A. Medvedev, translated by Ellen de Kadt, © Oxford University Press 1979. Reprinted by permission of Oxford University Press. Footnotes denoted by asterisks have been added by the editors of this volume.

In his report to the Twentieth Congress, the first secretary of the Central Committee, Nikita Khrushchev, declared that it was possible and necessary to prevent a new war between the great powers and that the arms race should give way to "peaceful coexistence," economic competition, and even cooperation between countries having different social systems.

After the events of 1953,* the security organs were brought under effective party control, and their staff and functions were substantially curtailed. It is true that millions of prisoners continued to languish in the dense network of prisons and camps spread throughout the country, since the only case to be reviewed immediately was the "Leningrad affair" of 1949–50.** But within a year, other cases were being reexamined and rehabilitations were begun. By the time the Twentieth Congress was convened, approximately 12,000 persons had been released from imprisonment, for the most part Komsomol and party workers arrested in the 1930s; some of them were even invited to attend the congress. In the report of the Central Committee, Khrushchev mentioned only the defeat of the "Beria gang" and nothing was said about Stalin. When Mikoyan spoke, however, he touched on the theme of the "cult of personality," commenting in very guarded language on the serious consequences of this cult, and referring to the rehabilitation of Kosior and Antonov-Ovseenko.***

Judging from the stenographic record, the congress ended on February 25, but in fact it formally came to a close on the evening of February 24. Of the 125 members of the Central Committee elected at the Nineteenth Party Congress, only 79 became members of the new Central Committee; 54 additional members were chosen so as to consolidate Khrushchev's personal position. And while the first organizational plenum of the Central Committee was being held in the Kremlin, delegates were discussing the results of the congress among themselves and making their preparations to return home. Suddenly, shortly before midnight, all the delegates were summoned back to the Kremlin. On this occasion no guests or delegations from other communist parties were present in the Great Hall. Participants were told that there was to be a special closed session of the congress. Then Khrushchev rose to the podium and in the name of the recently elected Central Committee

---

*When Lavrenti Beria, head of the secret police, and several other high police officials were arrested and executed.
**A purge of high Leningrad party officials.
***Two of the thousands of old Bolshevik leaders who fell victim during Stalin's great purge of 1936–39.

read his celebrated four-hour speech, "On the cult of personality and its consequences."*

The astonished delegates listened to the speech in silence, interrupting him only occasionally with expressions of amazement or indignation. Khrushchev spoke of the illegal mass repressions approved by Stalin, of the savage torture inflicted on many prisoners, including members of the Politburo, and of their letters written on the brink of death. He mentioned the dubious circumstances surrounding the death of Kirov and the possible implication of Stalin in this incident.** Delegates were told of Stalin's breakdown at the beginning of the war, of his virtual desertion of his post during those first vital days, and of his direct responsibility for the massive defeats of the Red Army in 1941–42. According to Khrushchev it was Stalin who initiated the mass repressions of the postwar period, Stalin who was to blame for the critical state of agriculture and for the miscalculations of Soviet foreign policy. Stalin himself had encouraged the cult of personality and falsified the history of the party.

Khrushchev's speech was not followed by any debate or general discussion. In its official resolution, which was not published until several months later, the congress approved the speech of N. S. Khrushchev and instructed the Central Committee "consistently to carry out measures with the object of fully overcoming the cult of personality, which is alien to the principles of Marxism-Leninism, and eliminating its consequences in every aspect of party, state, and ideological activity."[1]

There was of course no way of concealing Khrushchev's speech from the outside world. Within a day the foreign press was reporting that a secret session of the congress had taken place, and several weeks later the United States Department of State distributed a complete text of the speech in English.

Khrushchev's speech made an enormous impact on world public opinion and on the communist movement, but I shall not go into that question here.[2] I want to suggest merely that the widespread criticism leveled at Khrushchev for his omissions and for the superficiality of his speech do not take into account the complexity of his position at the time.

*Published in English in several editions, including Nikita S. Khrushchev, *The Crimes of the Stalin Era* (New York: New Leader Pamphlet, n.d.).

**Sergei Kirov, head of the Leningrad party organization and a member of the Politburo, was assassinated in Leningrad on December 1, 1934. Stalin, whom many scholars believe organized the crime, used the murder as a pretext to begin his great purge of the 1930s.

In early 1956, conditions within the Central Committee made it impossible for Khrushchev to have access to any kind of systematic investigation of the issue. He had to proceed with extreme caution, in view of the fact that he was obviously acting against the interests of many members of the Central Committee as well as members of the Presidium such as Molotov, Kaganovich, Voroshilov, Malenkov, and others. After the execution of Beria, his closest associates were put on trial in various cities, but Stalin's name was never mentioned in these trials and the entire responsibility for lawlessness was attributed to the NKVD-MGB.* As he prepared his address to the Twentieth Congress, Khrushchev was taking an enormous personal risk. It was crucial for him to act independently, decisively, and quickly, relying on his most trusted aides. The fact that neither Khrushchev nor his immediate circle were free of guilt made them immensely vulnerable. If they too bore their share of responsibility for the crimes of the Stalin era, surely the exposure of Stalin could turn against them as well. Sowing the wind, would they then have to reap the whirlwind? No one could anticipate the outcome. Yet as it turned out, the gamble paid off. In the long-term perspective the positive effect of Khrushchev's dramatic revelations by far outweighed any temporary problems.

To this day, foreign communists and Western sovietologists continue to discuss the question of Khrushchev's *motives*. His decision was undoubtedly the result of a number of considerations. According to one version, Khrushchev devised his partial denunciation of Stalin's crimes in order to rationalize the system of bureaucratic rule. Therefore he placed greatest emphasis on the illegal arrest of officials in the party-state apparatus, as if to assure the higher echelons of the bureaucracy that repression of this kind was a thing of the past; in this way he would improve the functioning of the totalitarian system and strengthen the privileges of the *nomenklatura.***

We know now, of course, that although no one could be immune from the terror in the years of Stalin's rule, the upper strata of the apparatus were in fact particularly vulnerable. And just as Napoleon's generals eventually grew tired of continuous warfare, so the men in Stalin's entourage, even those entirely obliged to him for their elevated rank, were weary of his morbid suspiciousness and the ever-present fear of sudden arrest. Undoubtedly these sentiments were shared by Khrushchev and influenced his decision to expose the Stalin cult; clearly

---

*As the internal security forces were then called.
**A system of appointment lists, controlled directly or indirectly by high party authorities, covering virtually all responsible posts in the country.

he was assured of the initial support of a basic part of the party cadres. But this is just one aspect of the story and certainly not the most important one. The Stalinist bureaucracy could hardly be interested in an account of Stalin's crimes so blunt that their own authority might be undermined as well. These people were afraid of being held responsible for their own complicity in Stalin's actions and for them Khrushchev's speech, even with its many evasions and reservations, must have seemed too dangerous a step.

Even more frequently it has been suggested that Khrushchev's speech was the decisive episode of the power struggle. Seizing the initiative as he did, Khrushchev struck a blow against Stalin's closest comrades-in-arms such as Molotov, Malenkov, Voroshilov, Kaganovich, and Mikoyan, who were convinced of their own stronger claim to "inherit" the power of the departed despot. Although Khrushchev never referred to any of these men by name, they were all obviously intimately involved in those monstrous crimes which had been the subject of his remarks at the closed session of the Twentieth Congress. With this well-timed stroke, Khrushchev knocked the ground from under the feet of these "leaders" who were left with a simple choice: they could either submit to his authority or lose power altogether. There is undoubtedly a great deal of truth in this version also.

It is apparent from the speech at the Twentieth Congress as well as from later speeches that the young Khrushchev's passionate devotion to Stalin had long since given way to carefully concealed emotions of hostility and fear. Stalin repeatedly mocked the simple-minded "Nikita," frequently in a humiliating and insulting manner. "Nikita, dance for us!" demanded Stalin during one of his usual soirees when the news came that Kiev had been taken. Khrushchev described how Stalin would sometimes summon him to the southern dacha near Sukhumi, or to some other place, make him wait in the reception room for several hours, and then casually walking past him would ask in a surly tone: "What are you doing here? Go back." Evidently this long-suppressed hatred of Stalin erupted at the first opportunity, when Khrushchev found himself at the summit of power.

Much of Khrushchev's behavior in 1955–56 was bound up with his commendable personal qualities, for he managed, to a greater extent than any of the others in Stalin's entourage, to retain a capacity for doing good and for repentance. Among all the members of Stalin's Politburo, Khrushchev seems to have been the only one to keep up direct contacts with the workers, and even more important, with the countryside. He was very troubled by the tragic plight of Russian and Ukrainian peasants living in appalling conditions, and it was with a heavy heart that he carried out instructions from Stalin or Malenkov calling for massive requisitions of agricultural produce while the countryside still suffered from the ravages of war.

I am inclined to take the view, however, that many of Khrushchev's actions as first secretary were at least to some extent determined by his formative experience as a regular party worker; for the rest of his life Khrushchev was to retain certain qualities that were typical of local party leaders in the 1920s. This new generation of men who rose from the ranks during the devastating years of revolution, civil war, and NEP* were more united, although less well educated, than the highest leadership of the country. Working in extremely difficult conditions, trusting each other, and sharing the same interests, these people were bound by that special friendship of party functionaries which can be compared only to the attachment between officers hardened together in battle. The middle strata of party leaders were more impressed by Stalin's external simplicity, and even his rudeness, than by the educated refinement of the arrogant Trotsky or the erudite dogmatism of Zinoviev and Kamenev with their typical intelligentsia indecisiveness. This factor may well have played a greater role in bringing about Stalin's victory over the Left Opposition than any theoretical disagreements. The second generation of party leaders were largely men of action rather than theoreticians, although of course this does not imply that all their actions can stand up to scrutiny. Almost all of them were wiped out during the years of terror in the second half of the 1930s. Khrushchev was spared, having accepted the norms of behavior dictated by Stalin. But he never became an out-and-out Stalinist: in his heart of hearts there were always doubts about the arrest of his oldest friends and about the guilt of party figures of the older generation such as Vlas Chubar or Stanislav Kosior who had guided the beginning of his career in the party. When Khrushchev was finally at the head of the Central Committee Secretariat, having eliminated the Beria group with the help of Malenkov, Zhukov, and Bulganin, in addition to all his economic preoccupations he was determined to restore the reputations of his former friends, whose families he immediately brought back from exile. When the widows and children of his friends from the Ukrainian and the Moscow party organizations returned to the capital, much of what they had to tell was a revelation for Khrushchev—personal bitterness and indignation were certainly a part of the motivation for his speech at the Twentieth Congress.

*The New Economic Policy of 1921–29.

Although the speech was never published in the Soviet Union, it was not kept secret from the Soviet people. By the second half of March, the speech was read out in full by representatives of district and city party committees at mass meetings attended by nonparty people as well as by party members. One must assume that this also took place on the initiative of Khrushchev.

Needless to say, the acknowledgements of the appalling crimes of the Stalin era was a painful ordeal for the entire communist movement. In Western countries, many Communists left the party. Until very recently communist parties everywhere had been rejecting rumors and reports of illegal repressive measures in the USSR as slanderous inventions of the bourgeois press. Now suddenly the news came from Moscow, from the Congress of the CPSU, that much of what had been written in bourgeois papers was absolutely true, and that even worse things had happened that they could not know about. For all admirers of the USSR and supporters of socialism, this was very hard to bear, but it was a fitting and inevitable payment for past sins, and in any case the past could not have remained hidden for long. To conceal Stalin's crimes might have led to even more drastic consequences in the future.

Of course there was only one way to overcome the enormous shock of these unexpected revelations, and that was to inaugurate bold changes in the style and methods of party leadership in line with policies laid down by the Twentieth Congress. Unfortunately, however, subsequent political developments pursued some sort of zigzag path. In the months following the Twentieth Congress, attempts by individual Communists to continue discussion of the problem of the "cult of personality" were cut off. Some of them were given party penalties, and the editorial board of *Voprosy istorii* (Questions of History) was broken up after the journal published an extremely cautious article criticizing Stalin's errors in March, 1917. An article appeared in *Pravda*, translated from the Chinese paper *Jen Min Jihn Pao*, in which it was argued with the aid of a certain amount of sophistry, that Stalin's "mistakes" could even "enrich" the historical experience of the dictatorship of the proletariat. After several months Khrushchev himself was compelled to declare that Stalin was a "great Marxist-Leninist" and a "great revolutionary," that the party would not allow "Stalin's name to be delivered up to the enemies of communists," and that the concept "Stalinism" was an invention of anti-Soviet propaganda.

Yet other events were taking place in the USSR at the same time: the mass liberation of almost all political prisoners, the rapid review of dossiers, and the rehabilitation of most of those who died in camps and prisons in the period 1935–55. On Khrushchev's personal instructions, approximately 100 special commissions were set up, each one containing a representative of the Procuracy and of the Central Committee, and a party member who had been released from imprisonment and rehabilitated in 1954–55. These commissions, endowed with the widest powers, set out from Moscow to all "islands" of the *Gulag*. Prisoners' cases were scrutinized and quickly dealt with. Members of the commission looked at the indictments and had a brief conversation with the prisoners of the camp, after which they pronounced judgment—usually it was a decision for release, and it was final. They also set free those considered to have been guilty but whose sentence had long since been completed. Also freed and rehabilitated were all former prisoners of war and "displaced" Soviet citizens who had never in fact collaborated with the enemy. Thus toward the autumn of 1956, several million prisoners had been released.

In terms of its effect on domestic affairs in the USSR, this return to their families of millions of prisoners as well as the posthumous rehabilitation of millions of victims of the terror was no less important a result of the Twentieth Congress than the public denunciation of Stalin.

There were, of course, elements of indecision and compromise in the work of the commissions on rehabilitation, both in Moscow and at the camps. For example, there was no party rehabilitation for leading members of the party oppositions of the 1920s. No formal reconsideration was given to the sham political trials of 1928–31 or 1936–38. After the Twentieth Congress, the widow of Nikolai Krestinsky spent seven years trying to obtain the rehabilitation of her husband, who was convicted together with Bukharin in 1938. When she was finally informed by the Central Committee that her husband had been rehabilitated and reinstated as a party member, she had a heart attack and died, falling on the floor right by the telephone. Bukharin's widow was allowed to return to Moscow after seventeen years of prison and exile; she was rehabilitated, but her husband has not been formally rehabilitated to this day. Even the trial of Tukhachevsky, Yakir, and other Red Army commanders was not reviewed until the end of 1957. The illustrious leader of the October insurrection in Petrograd, Fedor Raskolnikov, was rehabilitated only in 1963.

Soon after the Twentieth Congress a special Central Committee commission was set up and given the task of investigating the circumstances of Kirov's murder, the organization of the "show trials" in 1936–38, the background of Ordzhonikidze's suicide,* and other of

---

*Sergo Ordzhonikidze, a Politburo member and reportedly an opponent of Stalin's encroaching terror, died mysteriously in early 1936. It appears that he was forced to commit suicide.

Stalin's crimes including the murder of the prominent Transcaucasians
Khandzhian and Lakoba. The work of this commission proceeded very
slowly, however, and came up against quite a number of obstacles.
Moreover, the 1956 events in Hungary and Poland had the effect of
sharpening a struggle for power within the Central Committee, with
Khrushchev and a group of his closest supporters on one side, and on
the other, the obvious Stalinists such as Molotov, Kaganovich, Malenkov, and Voroshilov, who were soon joined by Bulganin, Pervukhin,
Saburov, Shepilov, and certain others. On the surface this struggle appeared to be about economic questions, but in fact the real issue was
the continuation and development of the line of the Twentieth Congress. And although after a number of dramatic incidents Khrushchev
finally prevailed, preserving his personal power and then substantially
increasing it—he took on the chairmanship of the Council of Ministers
as well—he was for some time reluctant to come forward with any
new disclosures about Stalin. The sarcophagus containing Stalin's body
continued to lie in the mausoleum on Red Square. Many cities, thousands of streets, squares, plants, factories, collective farms, and institutes continued to bear Stalin's name. In the years 1956–60, the Soviet
press would still never mention any anniversary associated with the
lives of the most prominent party and government figures who had
fallen victim to the Stalin terror, although almost all of them were
fully rehabilitated posthumously. However the entire press devoted
much space to the eightieth anniversary of Stalin's birth on December
21, 1959. The periodical *Kommunist* wrote at the time:

> December 21 marks the eightieth anniversary of the birth of J. V.
> Stalin, one of the most eminent and energetic figures of our Com-
> munist Party and the international communist movement. J. V. Stalin
> was a distinguished Marxist theoretician, organizer, and staunch
> fighter for communism, true to Marxism-Leninism and dedicated to
> the interests of the working people. He carried out the most impor-
> tant party commissions and for more than three decades occupied the
> post of general secretary of the Central Committee. He has performed
> great services for the party, for the Soviet Motherland and people, and
> for the international communist and workers' movements.[3]

The period between the June plenum of the Central Committee
(1957) and the Twenty-second Congress (1961) witnessed a profu-
sion of institutional changes and reform programs, including several
reorganizations of the management of industry and agriculture, the
alteration of the educational system, the abolition of machine tractor

stations, an urgent drive to increase the production of meat and milk, etc.—the list could be extended considerably. Toward the beginning of the 1960s the intricacies of the international situation also became rather complex. Periods of detente in East-West relations alternated with bitter flareups of Cold War confrontation. Once again there were strained relations with Yugoslavia, while steadily deteriorating relations with China had reached a state of chilly hostility. Khrushchev's personal authority continued to grow in these years, yet at the same time he was losing popularity among broad sections of the population. With this problematic state of affairs as a background, preparations were under way for the Twenty-second Congress of the CPSU, due to take place in the autumn of 1961.

The congress was ostensibly convened in order to debate and adopt the new party program. According to this program, the Soviet Union would catch up with and overtake the United States economically (in the production of goods and services per capita) within the next decade, i.e., towards 1970, and within twenty years the USSR would "in the main" be a communist society. The publication of the draft of the program did not, however, arouse great enthusiasm among the population. Agriculture had been stagnant in 1959–61, with a noticeable decline in the supply of meat and milk to the cities and a reduction of income for collective farmers. The popular mood quite naturally was determined by the increasing difficulties of the present rather than the still very distant prospect of complete affluence in the future. The fall of his prestige in almost all main sections of the party-state apparatus was particularly serious for Khrushchev. It was due largely to impatience with his interminable reorganizations. All this provided favorable conditions for what could be called a "neo-Stalinist" reaction. Both Khrushchev and his personal "cabinet" undoubtedly were aware of the growing disaffection within the ruling apparatus, and it was partly this which prompted Khrushchev openly to raise the question of Stalin once again at the Twenty-second Party Congress.

It is known for certain that when the Presidium discussed the agenda of the forthcoming party congress, the decision was taken not to broach the subject of Stalin or to mention the "antiparty group of Malenkov, Molotov, Kaganovich, and its adherent Shepilov." However, on October 17, 1961, to the surprise of many members of the Presidium, Khrushchev, rising to the podium, raised the question of the Stalin cult in a relentless, harshly worded speech. What is more, he went much further in the scale of his revelations, referring openly not only to Stalin, but also to his closest aides and accomplices. "At first," declared Khrushchev,

Molotov, Malenkov, Kaganovich, and Voroshilov put up determined resistance to the line of the party; they opposed the condemnation of the cult of personality, the development of inner-party democracy, the denunciation of all abuses of power and their correction, and the exposure of specific perpetrators of repression. It is no accident that they took this stand, since they bear personal responsibility for mass repressions directed at party, economic, military and Komsomol cadres as well as for other similar events which took place during the period of the cult of personality.[4]

This last-minute alteration of Khrushchev's address provoked animated discussion in the lobbies of the hall, but it also meant that the delegates themselves could no longer avoid referring to the crimes of the Stalin era in what were, it must be remembered, *open* sessions of the congress. All participants hurriedly rewrote their prepared texts. One of the first to speak, K. T. Mazurov, described in detail how Malenkov annihilated the party cadres of Belorussia. The crimes of Molotov and Kaganovich were dealt with by Furtseva and Polyansky. Speaking on October 24, Mikhail Sholokhov demanded that members of this faction be expelled from the party, a suggestion greeted with applause by the delegates. Particularly detailed information about the crimes of Stalin, Molotov, Voroshilov, and others was given in the speeches of Ilichev, Shvernik, Shelepin, and Serdyuk, who cited what were then sensational aspects of the evil deeds of 1936–39. Summing up the discussion, Khrushchev returned in his concluding remarks to the question of the crimes committed by Stalin and his entourage, devoting even more attention to this theme than in his opening report.

Before the Congress came to a close, representatives from the Leningrad, Moscow, Georgian, and Ukrainian delegations demanded that the sarcophagus containing Stalin's body be removed from the mausoleum, for as Demichev said, "to leave it there any longer would be blasphemy." The congress thereupon approved a special resolution in which it was stated:

To keep Stalin's sarcophagus in the mausoleum any longer is recognized to be unsuitable in view of the serious violations by Stalin of Lenin's legacy, the abuse of power, and the mass repressions against honest Soviet citizens; these and many other acts committed during the period of the cult of personality make it impossible for his coffin to remain in Lenin's mausoleum.[5]

Approval of the resolution took place the morning of October 30. It was put into effect the evening of October 31. In his poem "The Heirs

of Stalin," which caused something of a sensation, the well-known poet
Yevgeny Yevtushenko wrote:

> Mute was the marble. Mutely glimmered the glass.
> Mute stood the sentries, bronzed by the breeze.
> Thin wisps of smoke curled over the coffin. And breath seeped
>   through the chinks
> as they bore him out the mausoleum doors,
> Slowly the coffin floated, grazing the fixed bayonets.
> He also was mute—he also!—mute and dread.
> Grimly clenching his embalmed fists,
> just pretending to be dead, he watched from inside . . .
> He was scheming. Had merely dozed off.
> And I, appealing to our government, petition them
> to double, and treble, the sentries guarding this slab,
> and stop Stalin from ever rising again and, with Stalin, the past.[6]

But no sentry was placed near the slab under which the remains of
Stalin lay. A deep pit was dug in the ground not far from the mausoleum, into which they lowered the coffin. And instead of filling the
grave with earth, they brought several dump trucks with liquid concrete and poured it on top of the coffin lying at the bottom of the pit.
A granite slab was placed on top, later to be engraved with the simple
inscription: "J. V. Stalin." By the time Khrushchev brought the
Twenty-second Congress to a close on October 31, 1961, Stalin's body
was no longer in the mausoleum.

The Twenty-second Congress had gone much further in discrediting
and condemning Stalinism than had the Twentieth Congress. It was not
only a question of a new information or the fact that many of Stalin's
accomplices were exposed at the congress. The crucial difference was
that these questions were discussed in open rather than closed sessions
and that the texts of all speeches were published in the press. Each
day for almost two weeks, people eagerly read the papers, fascinated
by every new disclosure. The question of the new party program inevitably receded into the background. Only after the Twenty-second
Congress did it become possible to eliminate many of the symbols of
the Stalin cult. Cities, squares, and streets were renamed, as were plants
and factories, collective farms and state farms. Monuments to Stalin
had been pulled down in a number of cities in 1956. For example, the
huge monument on the Volga-Don Canal, for which Stalin personally
had ordered the bronze, was cut up and sent to be melted down. In
many cities, however, the statues had been left standing, but after the
Twenty-second Congress they all disappeared from sight. Only in

Georgia could one still come across "Stalin Street" or "Stalin Embankment" or even small museum exhibitions devoted to his memory.

The Twenty-second Congress opened the way for scholarly research and publication on many themes which until then had been forbidden territory. Scores of books and hundreds of articles were published in 1962–64 providing facts about the atrocities perpetrated by Stalin and his henchmen. All central and local newspapers began to carry obituaries devoted to the memory of Stalin's victims: political figures, economists, military leaders, writers, and artists. After the Twentieth Congress, certain individuals, in absolute secrecy, decided to write memoirs of their tragic experience. Now scores, even hundreds, of people began to write such memoirs, not surprisingly with varying degrees of talent and objectivity. The "camp theme" also found its reflection in literature. A particularly significant event was the publication of Solzhenitsyn's *One Day in the Life of Ivan Denisovich* in Alexander Tvardovsky's journal, *Novyi mir* (New World). But there were also other works written on the same subject—some were published in the USSR (e.g., the memoirs of General Gorbatov*) while others were circulated there in typescript (Evgeniia Ginzburg's *Into the Whirlwind*, Varlam Shalamov's *Tales from Kolyma*), all leaving an indelible impression on their readers.** It was essentially after the Twenty-Second Congress that the Soviet Union experienced something like those complex and difficult processes of catharsis and reappraisal that occurred in Western communist parties after the Twentieth Congress. For this reason we conventionally refer to the "line of the Twentieth and Twenty-second Party Congresses."

Among the many accusations lodged against Khrushchev during his overthrow at the October plenum of the Central Committee in 1964, nothing was said about the line of the Twentieth and Twenty-second Party Congresses. On the contrary, one of the most serious charges against him was that while condemning the cult of Stalin, he had begun to propagate a cult of his own, abusing the power of his office, and violating the principles of collective leadership and Leninist norms of party life. Thus, the decisions of his celebrated party congresses were on this occasion used against Khrushchev himself.

*The memoirs of General A. V. Gorbatov, who was arrested in 1938 and released on the eve of World War II in 1941, appeared in the March through May 1964 issues of *Novyi mir*. They are translated into English as *Years Off My Life* (New York, 1965).

**After circulating in *samizdat*, both were published abroad: Evgenia S. Ginzburg, *Into the Whirlwind* (London, 1967); Varlam Shalamov, *Kolymskie rasskazy* (London, 1978).

Many of the institutional changes carried out during the "great decade" were reversed in the months immediately following the October plenum. In some cases, more time was needed before various reforms could be altered or dismantled. Many of Khrushchev's innovations were retained, however, when it appeared that it was either inexpedient or too late to do anything about them. Even in Khrushchev's time, the publication of "camp" literature was virtually discontinued—the flood of these documents apparently proved alarming for Khrushchev himself or his closest advisers. But a number of books and articles containing criticisms of Stalin did still appear after the October plenum. For example, only after Khrushchev's departure was it possible to expose the activities of Lysenko and his group, and a considerable amount of material was published about the pernicious effect of the Stalin cult on biology and medicine.* The names of scores of the most prominent scientists, defamed and annihilated in the 1930s, were restored to the history of Soviet science. In 1965–66, books by Alexander Nekrich, Yuri Trifonov, Boris D'iakov, Ivan Maisky, Ts. Agayan, P. Oshchepkov, and others took up the theme of Stalin's cult of personality.**

In the first months of 1965, however, a group of influential ideologists, leading military figures, and some writers was actively beginning to press for a reconsideration of the decisions of the Twentieth and Twenty-second Congresses as well as for a virtual rehabilitation of Stalin. The group included Sergei Trapeznikov, the head of the Central Committee Department of Science, General Yepishev, the head of the Political Department of the army, and Petr Pospelov, the director of the Institute of Marxism-Leninism. This revival of the neo-Stalinists, who were on intimate terms with the new leadership of the Central Committee, aroused anxiety in the wider circles of the creative intelligentsia. It was precisely in these months that a whole variety of manuscripts and materials began to circulate among the intelligentsia, protesting in one form or another against the rehabilitation of Stalin. This was the beginning of the phenomenon soon to be called *samizdat*. At the same time, Andrei Sinyavsky and Yuli Daniel were arrested and charged with writing and publishing abroad "slanderous inventions, defamatory to the Soviet political and social system."

From the beginning of 1966, materials related to the forthcoming Twenty-third Party Congress came up for discussion, and some influ-

*For this episode in the history of Soviet science under Stalin and Khrushchev, see Zhores A. Medvedev, *The Rise and Fall of T. D. Lysenko* (New York, 1969).
**The first four items refer to A. M. Nekrich, *1941 22 iiunia* (Moscow, 1965); Iurii Trifonov, *Otblesk kostra* (Moscow, 1966); Boris D'iakov, *Povest' o perezhitom* (Moscow, 1966); and the fragmentary memoirs of the Soviet diplomat Maisky.

ential groups tried to take advantage of preparations for the congress to encourage a partial or indirect rehabilitation of Stalin. In was rumored that a demand of this kind was made in a letter signed by a large number of marshals and generals and sent to the Central Committee. The trial of Sinyavsky and Daniel in February 1966 was essentially intended to serve the same purpose, and despite the many protests in the Soviet Union and abroad, they were sentenced to seven and five years, respectively, in a strict-regime corrective-labor camp.

These developments intensified the concern of the intelligentsia: a great many letters were received by the Central Committee and the Presidium of the congress, objecting to the possible rehabilitation of Stalin. One letter in particular made a major impression—it was signed by twenty-five leading members of the Soviet intelligentsia. One can only suppose that this letter had some influence on those in power.* In any case, Stalin's name was never mentioned at the Twenty-third Congress, although the "line" of the Twentieth and Twenty-second Congresses was given a notably vague reformulation so as to preserve freedom of action for both camps: those who pressed for further criticism of Stalin as well as those demanding his political rehabilitation. It is not surprising that the acute, if largely discreet, struggle around the question of Stalin continued after the congress came to an end. This is not the place for a detailed examination of even the most telling incidents in this controversy—suffice it to say that towards the end of 1968, the odds were predominantly on the side of the neo-Stalinists.

The year 1969 began with a conspicuous ideological offensive launched by the Stalinists. The question of the ninetieth anniversary of Stalin's birth was already under discussion in the Central Committee. Although it would not occur until December, preparations were under way long in advance. The tear-off calendar for 1969, published in an edition of ten million copies, noted the ninetieth birthday and included a short article about Stalin on the reverse side of the page for December 21, mainly devoted to his "services" in the struggle for socialism and only obliquely referring to the "cult of personality, alien to Marxism-Leninism."

In the spring of 1969, apparently at the level of the Central Committee Secretariat, it was decided to take certain measures to commemorate Stalin's ninetieth birthday. Although these plans were not made public, they were communicated to senior personnel concerned with ideological questions. It was intended, for example, to erect a

*The letter, which appeared originally in the *samizdat* journal *Politicheskii dnevnik* (No. 18, March 1966), is translated in *Political Diary*, edited by Stephen F. Cohen (New York: W. W. Norton, 1980).

statue on Stalin's grave near the Kremlin and to hold a meeting of workers and war veterans at its unveiling ceremony. A special scientific session would be arranged at the Institute of Marxism-Leninism, devoted to the memory of Stalin. A long editorial article about Stalin would appear in *Pravda*. One Moscow printing house received an order to produce a large batch of Stalin portraits, and several studios began making arrangements to manufacture busts of Stalin. Both the portraits and the busts were to go on sale in the second half of December. A volume of his collected works was prepared for publication. There was some discussion about turning one of Stalin's dachas on the outskirts of Moscow into a memorial museum. It was also planned to make certain "organizational" changes, particularly the removal of Alexander Tvardovsky as editor of *Novyi mir* and the breakup of the editorial board of what was the most distinguished Soviet journal.*

In the first months of 1969 there were cautious but quite definite signs of the projected rehabilitation of Stalin. Thus, for example, a long article appeared in *Kommunist* (no. 3) entitled "For Leninist *Partiinost'* in the Interpretation of the History of the CPSU," the collective effort of five authors. Since it was the most outspoken attempt to vindicate Stalin since the Twenty-second Congress, it naturally evoked numerous protests. In September 1969, *Oktiabr'* began to publish an extremely scandalous novel by its editor Kochetov, entitled *What Do You Want Now?*, which not merely appealed for the rehabilitation of Stalin but blatantly called for the restoration of the entire system that prevailed in the party and in the country at large during the Stalin years. Kochetov openly attacked all the innovations of the post-Stalin period.** The serial film *Liberation*, made with the assistance of the writer Yuri Bondarev, also served in a different form to resurrect Stalin's political and military "reputation."

Toward the middle of December 1969 it appeared that the question of the Stalin jubilee had already been decided. A long *Pravda* article under the headline "Ninety Years since the Day of Stalin's Birth" was ready and approved for publication. The article with an accompanying photograph, set in type and kept in the safe of the editor-in-chief of *Pravda*, was also distributed to the editorial offices of papers in all the capital cities of the union republics as well as to the major party papers

*Under Tvardovsky, *Novyi mir* was the leading anti-Stalinist journal published officially in the Soviet Union in the 1950s and 1960s. Tvardovsky and his editorial board were finally ousted in 1970.

**Under its editor Kochetov, *Oktiabr'* was a leading neo-Stalinist journal and the arch-rival of Tvardovsky's *Novyi mir*.

of the socialist countries. The intention was to publish it in *Pravda* on December 21 and in the other papers on the following day. However, the Stalin question was also being discussed in the leading bodies of other communist parties, and the Central Committee of the Polish and Hungarian parties came out decisively against publishing the article. There is evidence to suggest that Janos Kadar and Wladyslaw Gomulka came to Moscow on an urgent unofficial visit to try to persuade the Central Committee not to allow the publication of materials rehabilitating Stalin. They warned that their own parties would be compelled to dissociate themselves from such a disastrous step. There could be no doubt that the communist parties of a number of Western countries and of Yugoslavia would react in a similar way, and this was too serious a threat to be ignored.

Two or three days before the anniversary, the question of Stalin was once again discussed by the Politburo, and according to one well-informed source, it was decided by a small majority of votes to cancel a large part of the arrangements for celebrating the Stalin "jubilee." The bust which had already been placed on Stalin's grave was unveiled without any kind of formal gathering. The grand sessions that were planned for the Institute of Marxism-Leninism and in Georgia were called off. It was decided not to publish the long *Pravda* article but to print instead a short note, fundamentally different in content. The capitals of the union republics and of other socialist countries were of course immediately informed of this decision, but the Central Committee official responsible for liaison apparently failed to ring Ulan-Bator (where the time was seven or eight hours ahead of Moscow), with the result that on December 22 the long sympathetic article and portrait appeared in the Mongolian language paper, *Unen*. A notice informed the reader that the article had been reprinted from *Pravda* of December 21, although in fact *Pravda* had published something very different on that day—a brief article entitled "On the 90th Anniversary of J. V. Stalin's Birth" that emphasized the "mistakes and perversions associated with the cult of personality" rather than his "services" to the cause of socialism. In a specially made frame, this clipping, like a cherished photograph, stood on Alexander Tvardovsky's desk until his very last day in the editorial offices of *Novyi mir*.

The events of December 1969 were a defeat for all those who so persistently sought the rehabilitation of Stalin. Essentially, the question of Stalin and his rehabilitation was removed from the agenda in the USSR, and it did not come up at the Twenty-fourth or Twenty-fifth Party Congresses. Still, many elements of the pseudo-socialist system created by Stalin remained more or less intact, and they are still with us in the 1970s. The struggle against Stalinism and neo-Stalinism in all its manifestations, whether open or veiled, continues to be one of the most important problems facing the world communist movement.

Notes

1. *XX s"ezd KPSS: Stenograficheskii otchet* (Moscow, 1956), p. 498.

2. When the closed session of the congress was over, delegations from certain other communist parties were given the chance to become acquainted with the contents of Khrushchev's speech. They were only allowed to have the text for several hours and were asked to keep its substance an absolute secret. Even Khrushchev himself, shortly after the congress, publicly denied rumors of some kind of secret report. The leaders of many Western communist parties did not read the speech until it was published by the U.S. State Department in June 1956.

3. *Kommunist*, 1959, no. 18, p. 47.

4. *XXII s"ezd KPSS: Stenograficheskii otchet* (Moscow, 1962), vol. 1, p. 105.

5. Ibid., vol. 3, p. 362.

6. *The Poetry of Yevgeny Yevtushenko* (New York, 1965), p. 161. Translated by George Reavey.

Khrushchev Reconsidered

George W. Breslauer

Nikita Khrushchev's approach to political participation was a key aspect that distinguished his leadership from Stalin's. Most Western scholars who have written about the 1950s and 1960s would agree that Khrushchev's emphasis on mass political participation was a Soviet form of populism. Khrushchev attempted to draw the broad masses into the "building of communism" and to create a tacit alliance between himself and the masses against the bureaucrats, in order to foster administrative control and responsibility. Most scholars would also agree that the Brezhnev regime rejected Khrushchev's populism and favored a more bureaucratic approach. At the same time, the sources of Khrushchev's populism, and the varied components of mass political participation in the Soviet Union that shaped it, have not been clearly defined. As a result, there has been considerable implicit disagreement among Western scholars about the meaningfulness of the measures taken, the motives behind Khrushchev's efforts, the character of changes since Khrushchev, and the prospects for a populist revival in the future.[1] This chapter will explore the character and sources of the Khrushchevian approach to political participation after Stalin and will propose a conceptual framework for thinking about the nature of post-Stalin change in that area.

Since Stalin, several forms of mass political participation have received sustained attention in the Soviet Union, as Stalin's successors

An earlier version of this chapter appeared in *Problems of Communism*, September-October 1976.

sought to expand authentic mass initiative, critical feedback, and the boundaries of the political arena. Specifically, four forms of mass political participation came to be reevaluated and redefined: (1) expanded involvement or "drawing in" (*privlechenie*) of the citizenry into the administration of public affairs; (2) expanded input on the part of workers, peasants, and members of the intelligentsia before decision making; (3) expansion of the rights of citizens vis-a-vis their hierarchical superiors; and (4) transfer of functions from performance by full-time officials to performance by social activists.

Changing economic, administrative, and political realities after Stalin necessitated the expansion and redefinition of these varied forms of mass political participation. However, such changes in the terms of political participation invariably conflicted with the tendency among Soviet party and state officials to protect their political and bureaucratic autonomy[2] against unregulated criticism or initiative in the non-official sector. In the light of these conflicts, and in the absence of either a Stalinist restoration or a breakthrough into socialist or liberal democracy, two likely variants of these forms of mass political participation are apt to prevail: a managerial approach and a populist approach.

A managerial approach, such as was advocated by Malenkov and has been practiced by Brezhnev, would seek to vary the relative political status of groups in the official and nonofficial sectors in order to heighten official responsiveness to societal inputs. But it would not advance these changes to the point of either status equalization or an adversarial relationship between officials and masses. Nor would it seek to redefine the language, areas, or scope of political conflict in ways that challenged the political and bureaucratic autonomy of Soviet officials.

In contrast, a populist approach would attempt to define the language, areas, and scope of political conflict in ways that challenged prevailing conceptions of political and bureaucratic autonomy. It would challenge the higher political and ideological status of state and party officials vis-a-vis the masses; and it would attempt to reduce the immunity of officials to criticism of their political prerogatives and decision-making styles.

The latter approach was chosen by Khrushchev. Despite the fact that he propagated a personality cult of his own and sought to keep initiative and criticism within bounds determined by the dominant coalition in the Politburo, he led an attack on elitism among Soviet officials. Khrushchev's adoption of a populist approach to authority relationships was not merely an instrumental feature of his power struggle or his efforts to foster administrative control. It was also a product of his belief that economic policy effectiveness required an expansion of authentic initiative and criticism, which he saw as incompatible with prevailing definitions of political status after Stalin. Moreover, Khrushchev's vision of political community called for the creation of an active, self-regulating society of like-minded individuals; this vision, he came to believe, was also incompatible with prevailing conceptions of political and bureaucratic autonomy. By 1961, therefore, when Khrushchev's economic, social, and political programs had faltered, his personal political difficulties fed into his populist approach to political participation, leading him to sponsor a far-reaching redefinition of authority relationships between officials and masses.

Khrushchev and Stalin's Legacy

While during the Stalin era ultimate political authority resided in the hands of Stalin himself, Soviet officials, within their domains, exercised almost unlimited discretionary power over the masses in the execution of his will. It was taken for granted among Soviet officials that decompression of police controls would lead to "anarchy" and that most groups in the nonofficial sector of society could not be trusted to advance regime goals in the absence of coercion. Distrust and fear of the masses were accompanied by a profound distrust of the critical instincts of the scientific intelligentsia. Dogmatic controls were imposed on most areas of inquiry, and there was an almost paranoid concern for political reliability in recruitment. The institutional expression of these orientations was a secret-police hierarchy that sought to atomize society and a highly prescriptive bureaucratic system that aspired to reduce an individual's discretion to a minimum. Though the regime professed to want Soviet citizens to exercise "initiative" and to criticize official malfeasance, the paranoid atmosphere of the time, coupled with the inordinate emphasis on political control, militated against such initiative.

Khrushchev, however, was more interested in stimulating the growth of the Soviet economy than in reinforcing the political controls of late Stalinism. He operated on the basis of a core belief that problems of economic growth could not be solved without eliciting authentic mass initiative—and he searched constantly for new methods of mobilization and leadership that might elicit such initiative. In the process, Khrushchev was forced to confront the exclusivist, dogmatic, and heavy-handed orientations of Stalinist officialdom. This eventually led him to the opinion that only a radical redefinition of authority relationships could create the conditions for genuine mass initiative. Let us look in greater detail at the evolution of his outlook.

Khrushchev's much-noted economic "pragmatism" forced him to address some very controversial questions of political life in the USSR: What should be the status of the peasantry in a socialist society? Could technical specialists be freed from the shackles of dogma and included in decision-making processes without threatening the integrity of the ideology and the political prerogatives of officials? How much discretion and local initiative could be delegated to the citizenry without stimulating "spontaneity"? The issue, then, was one of *trust*: Could the new socialist society be trusted? Had it been decisively reconstructed?

Khrushchev's repudiation, at the Twentieth Party Congress in 1956, of the Stalinist dictum that the "class struggle intensifies as the building of socialism advances,"[3] was perhaps his most dramatic attack, during the initial years of his tenure, on the notion that society still could not be trusted. Yet, if one examines his speeches during 1953–59, one notices that, in varied forms, the calls for "trust in society" were a constant refrain in his exhortations to central and local officials.

In the case of the peasantry, Khrushchev argued that the regime could no longer afford to base its relationship with the peasant on forced exploitation, confiscation, and neglect.[4] Yet, establishing a national commitment to rural development required more than just an instrumental recognition of the impact of agricultural depression on urban consumption. According to Khrushchev, it also called for a dilution of the Stalinist distrust of the peasant and peasant initiative. This crucial sociopolitical definition of the problem occurred frequently in Khrushchev's speeches. For example, in attempting to prevent local officials from confiscating the seed reserves of collective farmers, Khrushchev pointed out, "We have long since been without a kulak class in the countryside."[5] Thus, in attempting to modernize Soviet agriculture, Khrushchev was led to confront the question of political community. The peasant, he contended, could be trusted; he no longer embodied the threat of restoration. Hence, he ought no longer be mobilized by Stalinist methods.

If Khrushchev must be credited with convincing the Soviet elite that the status of the peasant had to be reevaluated, he must also be credited with integrating the scientific and technical intelligentsia into the political community. Throughout his tenure in office, Khrushchev could be found arguing, *not only* for an end to dogma in many fields, but for a new approach to the political status of specialists as well. His secret speech denouncing Stalin had many motives, but surely one of them was to expand the boundaries of decision-making arenas ("collective leadership") so as to incorporate multiple competences. Moreover, his speeches are replete with calls for party officials to treat specialists with "consideration," to create good working conditions for them, and to respect their knowledge.[6]

Khrushchev's campaigns to draw nonfunctionaries into the decision-making process, regardless of their political status, naturally brought him into conflict with the exclusionary propensities of Stalinist officialdom. As early as 1954 we can find examples of the Khrushchevian approach to the problem: "Both party and nonparty comrades are present at this meeting. Both are involved in the same general business. Therefore we criticize both party workers and nonparty. . . ."[7]

Even at the highest levels, Khrushchev would invite nonparty specialists to Central Committee meetings to offer their expertise. When frustrated in his efforts to move talented and energetic young people into positions of authority within the party apparatus, Khrushchev defined the problem in familiar terms: "The young must be trusted."[8] In sum, Khrushchev's ideal conception of decision-making processes envisaged cooperative problem solving among talented actors. The first secretary had little patience with institutional boundaries or conceptions of political exclusiveness that inhibited such interaction.

The issue of official exclusiveness arose in other contexts as well. In 1956 Khrushchev argued that all Soviet citizens should be subject to the performance principle in evaluations of their work. A party official should be no more exempt from meeting economic performance goals than any other citizen, and his pay should reflect this philosophy. Apparently there were objections to these proposals by those who felt that party leaders did not need material bonuses as incentives in light of their higher level of political consciousness. Khrushchev did not accept this argument, declaring, "party workers are not the only principled [*ideinye*] people among us. Each Soviet person—worker, collective farmer, and member of the intelligentsia—is principled."[9]

All of these citations are from Khrushchev's speeches of the 1950s— before the radical changes introduced at the Twenty-second Party Congress in 1961. Thus, in the early years of his rule, Khrushchev was already confronting the problem of equal accountability in a reconstructed socialist society. A persistent theme in his statements during the 1950s was that the boundaries of the political community had to be expanded to include the previously repressed, neglected, or distrusted groups within Soviet society.[10] Beyond this, Khrushchev believed that party cadres and nonparty people alike required material incentives to induce them to contribute to national performance goals. Thus, judging performance by the performance principle rather than simply by political reliability was a leveling process, in that it no longer accepted the contention that party cadres were privileged.

Toward the Active Society

Khrushchev perceived a redefinition of authority relationships to be necessary to the advancement of still another goal: eliciting mass initiative through new patterns of leadership. He envisaged a society in which the masses would contribute actively, enthusiastically, and voluntarily to the pursuit of centrally prescribed goals. The key (in his mind) to synthesizing this centralist mode of integrating society and the vision of an enthusiastic, involved citizenry was the debureaucratization of leadership. Khrushchev wanted to make Soviet centralism more effective by purging it of its bureaucratic-statist component. In this way, the citizenry would develop a greater sense of identification with the policies and personnel of the regime and would have greater incentive to become personally involved in the administration of public affairs.

Throughout the de-Stalinization campaign, Khrushchev called upon Soviet officials to abandon "leadership from the desk," "rule by fiat," and "commandism," and demanded that they acquire the inspirational skills necessary to mobilize the masses without recourse to terror.

If party leaders alienated the masses with their behavior, Khrushchev felt, it would not be possible to develop local initiative. All forms of noncoercive incentives, after all, require a measure of trust on the part of those being led, for there is some degree of deferred gratification in any endeavor that does not promise a guaranteed payoff. It was critical, therefore, that local leaders impart to the masses a sense of confidence that a job well done would be rewarded as promised. Or, as Khrushchev put it with characteristic bluntness: "It is necessary to speak the truth to collective farmers, to persuade them, so that they will continue to believe you, so that they will believe your every word, because their pay will arrive in the spring, whereas the harvest must be collected in the winter."[11] Thus, "trust in the masses" was a prerequisite for establishing greater "trust in government."

Khrushchev aimed at changing the basis for maintaining compliance from command to inspiration. This, he believed, required the establishment of direct ties between the leaders and the led and the eradication of the indirect, bureaucratized style of leadership that had been dominant under Stalin. Indeed, as first secretary of the Communist

Party in the Ukraine as well as of the CPSU, Khrushchev was a model of the mobilizational leader; his forays among the people and his concern for firsthand contact with local conditions were characteristic of his approach.

In addition to these efforts to change the leadership style of Soviet officials, Khrushchev sponsored a three-pronged effort to expand the quantity and quality of mass participation and to elicit initiative from all those who had been driven into passivity by the orientations of the "dictatorship of the proletariat." First, there began in 1957 a vast expansion in the size of the party, in the number of party and nonparty activists, and in the role of social organizations in the discussion and implementation of policy. Under Khrushchev, this form of *privlechenie* had a distinctly anti-elitist tinge. For example, the party's adult political education program, a means of recruiting activists, was expanded and transformed; the program now began to emphasize training of nonparty, nonofficial citizens.[12]

The anti-official character of measures to expand mass participation also found expression in a movement toward expanding the rights (*rasshirenie prav*) of such mass organizations as the soviets and the trade unions. This movement was in line with Khrushchev's call for such organizations to "wrangle really hard"[13] with state officials and to protect their constituents from arbitrary behavior by their hierarchical superiors. In addition, there emerged at this time a movement for the transfer (*peredacha*) of some administrative functions of the state to public corporations or social organizations.

Khrushchev was clearly in favor of such a transfer, since it was entirely consistent with his belief in the need for debureaucratization of leadership. Not surprisingly, this brought him into conflict with the political orientations of party and state officials whose distrust of unregulated political initiative and whose broad definition of "political" reinforced a bureaucratized style of leadership. It was in response to these orientations that Khrushchev publicly developed his ideas about popular *self*-regulation.[14] As far as he was concerned, the bureaucratization of all tasks and the pervasive state regulation of social behavior had been based upon a belief in the untrustworthiness of the population and a conviction that its behavior needed to be circumscribed in all spheres. Perhaps for this reason at the Twenty-first Party Congress in 1959 Khrushchev called for a diminished role for formal state agencies and the transfer of many social functions to public organizations that would work "alongside and parallel to . . . state agencies."[15] Popular initiative would be stimulated by the depoliticization of many social initiatives, thereby legitimizing their removal from formal sub-ordination to state officials.

Such depoliticization implied greater trust in society, for it assumed that a decompression of political controls would not foster political deviance. Indeed, the interpretation of the concept of *obshchestven-nost'* (public-spiritedness) under Khrushchev differed strikingly from that employed under Stalin. Under Stalin, the *obshchestvenniki* were, in practice, the party and soviet officials themselves.[16] By the late 1950s, however, the term *obshchestvenniki* referred to a stratum of mobilizers drawn from all groups in society and not just from among the full-time paid officials of the party and state bureaucracies. Efforts were made to enlist these activists from among the more technically com-petent "opinion leaders" in society.[17] It was hoped that the didactic relationship involved in mobilization would be based upon interaction among social peers and would thus be less susceptible to considerations of ego, status, or formal position in the hierarchy.

Naturally, there was considerable resistance to this trend, as Soviet officials tried, wherever possible, to regulate the behavior of the non-official activists, to give them menial tasks rather than real influence, and to blunt their ability to penetrate the inner workings of the deci-sion-making process.[18] What was at stake was the political autonomy of Soviet officialdom: its prerogative to define the nature of problems; to establish criteria for evaluating success; and to judge whether a spon-taneous initiative constituted political deviance. For those who feared that genuine self-regulation would lead ultimately to anarchy, the right to channel all political initiative was jealously guarded. To Khrushchev's way of thinking, on the other hand, social and political cohesion were not threatened by decompression, precisely because he believed in the basic trustworthiness of the population and in the ability of rank-and-file activists to maintain control and to exercise leadership without the regime's having to resort to "administrative methods" and police power.

Frustration and Reaction

As is well known, Khrushchev's ambitious plans for social transfor-mation and economic growth were frustrated as early as the first years of the seven-year plan (1959–65). During this period serious questions were raised about the wisdom of his policy of using pressure to try to elicit extraordinary economic performance. His campaigns for greater social homogeneity were also strongly resisted by both officials and nonofficials. And behind the scenes, efforts were made to dilute the ideological innovations articulated at the Twenty-first Party Congress. By 1961 serious doubt had been cast upon the efficacy of Khrushchev's social, economic, and political programs. The party program of 1961, in fact, is noteworthy for its repudiation of "revolutions from above," for its advocacy of a policy of channeling mass initiatives through state agencies (thereby diminishing the status of self-regulation), and for its view of sociopolitical transformation as a measured outgrowth of long-term economic growth.[19]

Moreover, as many have observed, Khrushchev's counterattack against these trends was highly unpopular with many Soviet officials. They disapproved of his efforts to purge the party and state administrations through the establishment of a "rotation system" among officials; his large-scale recruitment of specialists into generalist positions within the party apparatus, bypassing political training in party schools; his bifurcation of the party and state hierarchies into industrial and agricultural branches; and his broad mobilization of the masses to check up on the behavior of officials in discharging their administrative responsibilities. The Western interpretation of these moves is usually cast in instrumental terms, viewed solely from the perspective of Khrushchev's concern for the solution of economic and administrative problems or for the protection of his personal power. However, there was an additional dimension to Khrushchev's undertakings that is ignored by any single-factor explanation of his policies: namely, the sociopolitical dimension that has been highlighted in this chapter. For what we find during the 1961–64 period are continuing attempts by Khrushchev to solve economic problems through the further expansion of the boundaries of decision-making arenas and the further diminution of the political status of Soviet officials.

Indeed, a careful reading of Khrushchev's speeches at the Twenty-second Party Congress reveals an intensification of his efforts along these lines. Ideologically, the first secretary sought to undermine still further the notion that officials have a higher level of political consciousness than the masses and therefore that they are entitled to regulate mass initiative and make decisions *in camera*. In announcing that the USSR had emerged as a "state of all the people," for example, Khrushchev indicated that this was a new form of state whose institutions were becoming nonpolitical organizations of the working people. Similarly, in depicting the CPSU as a "party of all the people," Khrushchev sought to upgrade the ideological status of the activists at the expense of the party bureaucrats.[20]

Such calls for depoliticization and debureaucratization could be legitimized only by a consensual image of society. Khrushchev supplied this as well, noting that the "overwhelming majority" of Soviet citizens "reason like Communists."[21] For similar reasons, Khrushchev needed to downgrade the notion that existing class differences warranted the continuation of an elitist pattern of decision making at the local levels: "The distinction between the working class and the peasantry have been eliminated in their major, decisive aspects; the final eradication of class differences will now proceed at an ever faster pace."[22]

Of course, Khrushchev remained thoroughly committed to the notion that the New Man was still to be created, but he felt that the locus of resocialization had to shift. Accordingly, he tried to downgrade still further the formal, educational function of party and state officials in a statement that would be repudiated by Brezhnev ten years later:

> The molding of the new man is influenced not only by the educational work of the party, the Soviet state, the trade unions and the Young Communist League, but by the entire pattern of society's life. . . . All economic, social, political, and legal levers must be used to develop people's Communist consciousness.[23]

The anti-official emphasis in Khrushchev's remarks should not, however, be taken as a sign of liberalization within the system at large. After all, it was precisely during this period that Khrushchev, in response to widespread signs of corruption, sponsored the extension of the death penalty to economic crimes and a witchhunt against "parasites." Nevertheless, Khrushchev was trying to maintain a highly organized and centrally coordinated system without simultaneously reinforcing the administrative methods and exclusionary policies that had pertained under Stalin.

Thus, while pressure was used increasingly during the early 1960s, a series of measures to reduce the scope of discretion of Soviet officials vis-a-vis their subordinates was simultaneously introduced. Elected production committees were established in the factories as a means of broadening worker participation in decision making. A campaign was launched by the trade union newspaper *Trud* during 1961–63 to encourage factory union committees to protect workers against illegal overtime, dismissals, and underpayment for work done.[24] Within the party, Khrushchev pushed, unsuccessfully, to reduce the size of the secretariats, so as to force party officials to rely more on the bureaus and the activists in decision making.[25] Moreover, during 1961–62 the number of nonstaff party instructors was greatly increased. An independent Party-State Control Commission was to see to it that "those who spoke critically of party leaders in report meetings received equal time with other speakers."[26]

An additional clue to Khrushchev's dual motives during this period appeared in the semiannual slogans of the Central Committee. In October 1961, for the first time in the entire postwar period, all references to "labor discipline," "technological and production discipline," and "state discipline" disappeared from the slogans, not to reappear until October 1965.[27] Under Soviet conditions, the reinforcement of social discipline is often effected by increasing the discretionary powers of officials vis-a-vis their constituents. Since this was precisely what Khrushchev was trying to move away from, it is understandable that he sought to decouple the traditionally paired concepts of "organization" and "discipline" in order to further his calls for cohesion based upon new patterns of social leadership.

Given the anti-official character of all these innovations, it should not surprise us that Khrushchev would later be accused of: (1) having "counterposed" the state of all the people to the dictatorship of the proletariat;[28] (2) having turned the legislative organs of the state administration against the executive organs;[29] and (3) having overemphasized the degree of homogeneity and consensus in society in order to denigrate political criteria in party recruitment.[30] Nor, for that matter, is it unusual that "certain authors" would later be accused of having claimed that the state had already lost its "class essence."[31] For the innovations sponsored by Khrushchev unleashed social forces throughout the system which, for reasons of their own, were hostile to the political prerogatives of Soviet officials.

The Lessons of Khrushchev

Khrushchev's successors have not dealt kindly with his historical image, presenting him as little more than a harebrained schemer and arbitrary interventionist. A more balanced appreciation of Khrushchev's contribution to Soviet history, however, would at least give him credit for addressing the most crucial sociopolitical dilemma of de-Stalinization: the relationship between initiative and criticism, on the one hand, and political authority and status, on the other. On this score, Khrushchev opened something of a Pandora's box. He sought to integrate previously repressed social groups into the political community by changing their political and ideological status, and he attempted to elicit their initiative by urging them to criticize obsolete policies and recalcitrant officials. However, his Stalinist legacy came through in his continued commitment to central definition of the direction and rate of change and his heavy emphasis on citizen obligation. He envisaged a society in which all would "participate in the construction of com-

munism as a single monolithic labor collective."[32] Thus, he never idealized the distinctiveness of the peasantry, the intelligentsia, or other
groups. He would fight for their recognition as citizens who could be
trusted, but he himself always treated them as equally liable to mobilization by a political leadership that made no binding commitments to
specific interests in society. Accordingly, he would encourage the critical intelligentsia to criticize but would then feel impelled to urge them
not to "overgeneralize" their criticism, lest this challenge the centralist
bases of the system.[33]

The commitment to centralism left Khrushchev with relatively few
options in trying to stimulate initiative and criticism. He found common cause with certain liberal dissenters who urged the development
of legal norms to protect the citizen against arbitrary behavior by state
and party officials, but he could not countenance the constraints on his
own actions that would have been imposed by an independent legal
order. Similarly, he flirted with the notion that the primary contradiction in society lay between "the state" and "society." This flirtation
strengthened the hand of those liberal academic philosophers who accepted the Yugoslav critique of bureaucratic centralism and argued
against their more traditional colleagues that "bureaucracy," not "anarchy," was the main danger in Soviet society.[34] However, the first
secretary could not explicitly endorse such a theoretical position because he was not interested in a genuine pluralism and dispersal of
power. These would only have tied his hands and slowed his campaigns for social transformation. In the event, one of the few options
that remained was for him to propagate a personality cult as a means
of bolstering his own authority and to "ally" with the social activists
against the full-time officials. Politically, this was a rather weak position, given the dominance of Soviet officials in the political system.

Yet the circumstances that pertained in the early 1960s make it hard
to assess exactly how weak this position was, for Khrushchev combined his commitment to centralism with a commitment to urgency,
pressure, and optimism. Thus, he called upon the activists to inspire
people to deny their own self-interest at the same time that he applied
pressure to induce workers and peasants to work very hard for a rather
low reward. His use of pressure often frustrated efforts to upgrade the
role of legislative branches of party and state and thereby to draw
nonofficial activists into local decision making; pressure simply reinforced the tendency of party secretaries to make decisions rapidly and
in camera.[35] Resort to high pressure was also detrimental to attempts
to elicit a new leadership orientation, since insisting on rapid conformity to extreme demands was hardly conducive to a posture based upon

persuasion and trust. (The campaign to communalize private peasant livestock was a case in point, and it cast serious doubt on the Khrushchevian belief that high pressure was consistent with voluntary compliance.) Finally, Khrushchev's commitment to pressure alienated many of the specialists and technocrats whom he was championing, for they recognized the need for a more contemplative, "scientific" approach to the solution of economic and administrative problems, even as they were resentful of the dogmatic and exclusionary practices of Stalinist officials.[36]

It is possible, then, that some form of alliance with the nonofficial activists against Soviet officials is a viable political strategy in a Soviet-type system (though the Maoist experience suggests that this would require police power). The Khrushchev experience is inconclusive on this score, clouded as it is by the disruptive impact of the first secretary's simultaneous commitment to high pressure, rapid transformation, and personal rulership. Yet, within the context of a dictatorial system, Khrushchev's primary insight may have been that genuine initiative could not be elicited on a broad scale without offering the citizen opportunities for regular public criticism of his hierarchical superiors. Moreover, Khrushchev was also aware that such criticism could not be elicited without either upper-level or extra-bureaucratic protection from retribution, and his efforts toward redefining the political and ideological status of Soviet officials were directed toward creating these conditions.

From this standpoint, Khrushchev was far more than a transitional leader, for one of the central thrusts of the Brezhnev-Kosygin regime has been to restore the political status and prerogatives of official organs.

The Brezhnev-Kosygin Approach

Khrushchev's successors probably raised their stock with the Soviet masses by further extending certain trends that had begun after Stalin's death: more rational economic and administrative policies, reduced reliance on pressure (despite Khrushchev's commitment to the use of pressure, his employment of it did not in any way match Stalin's in intensity), and assurances to the masses (lived up to in practice) that political conformity ensures physical security and that hard work means the opportunity for advancement and a higher standard of living. However, the price of these changes, and the accompanying end of "revolutions from above" as mechanisms for social transformation, has been the abandonment of populist efforts to redefine the status of political authority. On this score, the Brezhnev-Kosygin regime represents very much of a "conservative reaction."[37]

In contrast to the Khrushchevian emphasis on trust in society, one now finds continual reference in elite articulations to the need for "trust in cadres." Most of the "diploma specialists" recruited directly into the party apparatus during 1962–64 were purged shortly after Khrushchev's overthrow, and the importance of training in a party school before advancement into, and within, the party apparatus has been restored.[38] The dismantling of the Party-State Control Commission eliminated an out-of-channels source of protection for those inclined to criticize party officials. The practice of expanded plenary sessions of the Central Committee, attended by nonparty specialists, has been dropped, as has the publication of transcripts of Central Committee proceedings. In addition, the role of the nonparty population in the adult political education program was rapidly reversed.

None of these trends is necessarily incompatible with greater openness on the part of Soviet officials to the advice of experts. Nor do they preclude a more rational division of decision making among the various institutional centers of power in the system. These trends do, however, point to the determination of Soviet officials after Khrushchev's fall to regulate both the quantity and quality of popular involvement in public affairs and to arrogate to themselves the right to decide which decisions are routine (and therefore can be safely delegated) and which are fundamental or "political."[39]

Thus, despite the fact that more and more citizens have been "drawn into" public affairs, the entire ethos of elite articulations about the terms of this participation has changed radically since Khrushchev's overthrow. Calls for "discipline" have filled the press, and the term returned to the Central Committee slogans in October 1965.[40] During the 1970s, special efforts have been made to activate party members and to increase the number of "social assignments" performed by them; however, this campaign has been linked with continual calls for "iron discipline" among party members, rather than with efforts to upgrade the relative ideological status of the activists vis-à-vis the party apparatus.

The current Soviet leadership has also redefined the problem of "self-regulation" in order to reassert both the higher political consciousness of Soviet officials and the right of these officials to channel political initiatives into a bureaucratic, rather than a public, arena.[41] And the current regime rejects the Khrushchevian contention that societal activity is the principal area in which popular consciousness is to be raised. Instead, it reasserts the educational function of formal organs, thereby also diminishing the relative political status of the activists. Thus, in contrast to Khrushchev's doctrinal innovation of 1961 (see above, footnote 23), Brezhnev, at the Twenty-fourth Party Congress in 1971, defined doctrinal orthodoxy as follows: "The moral and political qualities of Soviet people are molded by the entire socialist tenor of our life, by the entire course of affairs in society, but *above all* by the purposeful, persistent ideological-upbringing work of the party and all its organizations."[42]

There has likewise been a marked constriction of the terms of discussion in the ideological literature concerning political organization, in contrast to the more heterogeneous discussion of certain socioeconomic and administrative issues. The "state of all the people" and "party of all the people" have been redefined (but not dropped, for reasons discussed below) in order to purge them of all components that contributed to "anarchy, disorder, and lack of discipline."[43] It is now routine for Soviet leaders to refer to the CPSU as the "political leader [*vozhd'*] of the working class, of all working people, of all the people," and to stress:

> Under conditions of developed socialism, when the Communist Party has become a party of all the people, it by no means loses its class character. By its nature, the CPSU has been and remains a party of the working class.[44]

Similarly, there is no more flirtation in the ideological literature with defining the "state of all the people" as an entity evolving rapidly toward a nonpolitical form of self-regulation. Rather, the emphasis is on the political organization of society, achieved through the strengthening of the state. Also, incessant calls for "discipline" and "order" are now the mode in the ideological literature, and those who see bureaucracy as the main evil do not receive much press. Predominant attention in the literature on political participation is given to "drawing in" and expanded input; expanded rights and transfer of functions are less salient as current imperatives and are now discussed in ways that do not suggest an adversarial definition of the relationship between state and society.[45]

With the end of the anti-Stalin campaign (which had implications far beyond mere historiography), and with the changes in policy and ethos noted above, Soviet citizens know quite well that criticism of the political prerogatives of Soviet officials is not likely to receive support at the top or in a Party-State Control Commission. The scope of individual criticism on social and economic issues—instrumental feedback

—has probably expanded. But when leaders and newspapers suddenly speak continually of "trust in cadres," "strengthening the state," and the need for "iron discipline," one wonders how many citizens are likely to exercise their right to engage in criticism directed toward political innovation. And under these circumstances, one also wonders how many Soviet citizens will exercise their right to criticize their hierarchical superiors for anything but the most flagrant abuses of authority.

It is noteworthy, however, that the regime has continued to affirm that the Soviet Union is directed by a party and state of "all the people," instead of reverting to Stalinist formulations. This is not merely a manipulation of symbols, for although the anti-official component of Khrushchev's innovations has been rejected, the other component—the post-Stalin recognition that socialism has been fully victorious and that the regime need not face the masses in a posture of ideological confrontation—has remained. In a sense, this is testimony to the success of Khrushchev's efforts to expand the boundaries of the political community and to recognize the needs of "all the people." Soviet theorists now distinguish their own conception of the relationship between officials and masses from those of both Titoists and Maoists.[46] Titoists are accused of counterposing the interests of the state to those of groups in society and thereby fostering "anarchy"; Maoists are accused of going too far in the opposite direction in maintaining a militant-transformist approach to society. In contrast to each of these, the Soviet affirmation of the "class essence" of the state and party of "all the people" upholds the higher political status and autonomy of executive organs but treats the state as no longer relating to society in an arbitrary and revolutionary posture.

The current Soviet regime, then, is hardly a return to Stalinism. Contemporary calls for "discipline" lack the paranoid insistence on compulsive displays of political conformity that characterized the Stalin era. Today, "discipline" usually means that the masses are expected to be politically conformist and to remain sober, arrive at work on time, labor hard and conscientiously, upgrade their skills, and participate in such occasional rituals as the *subbotniki* (donations of off-work time to state projects) and political lectures. Moreover, while the political prerogatives of official organs have been restored, there has been no return to the commandist and heavy-handed leadership of earlier years. Indeed, the leadership style of most Soviet officials has probably become less harsh and disciplinarian (at least toward the politically conformist) since Khrushchev's overthrow because of the reduced pressure for attaining unrealistic goals. This reduction in pressure has also expanded the opportunities for official consultation with specialists before decisions are made. A relatively low pressure, bureaucratic regime has replaced a relatively high pressure, populist regime.

The assumption of the Brezhnev-Kosygin regime, however, is that mass initiative can be stimulated without status equalization between the officials and the activists and that even-handed treatment in social and economic policy is more important to various groups in the population than is equalization of political status. Soviet leaders assume that most Soviet citizens prefer a bureaucratic political system that is responsive to their basic socioeconomic needs, rather than a pattern of public politics in which officials of local party organizations are subject to unregulated mass criticism.

Conclusion

The Brezhnev administration's managerial approach to political participation encourages expanded popular involvement in public affairs, as well as expanded public input into decision-making processes. It even accommodates a concern for the transfer of functions to public organizations and, as the recent Soviet constitution demonstrates, further expansion of the rights of Soviet citizens.[47] This arrangement may well be more stable than that under Khrushchev because it accords material and physical security to the populace. However, at the conceptual level the managerial approach must be clearly differentiated from a populist approach for several reasons: (1) it resists challenging the political and bureaucratic autonomy of party and state officials by ensuring that *they* decide which functions are transferable and which organizational leaders can be trusted to keep the initiative of mass organizations within bounds; (2) it resists the establishment of extra-bureaucratic institutions, independent of the local party organization, which might provide a powerful channel of appeal against official retribution for criticism; (3) it does not permit expansion of the rights of citizens to be defined in terms of an adversarial relationship between local party officials and the masses; (4) it places greater ideological, political, and practical emphasis on the unity of interests between central and local political organizations than on the unity of the central organization and the masses against the local political organization; and (5) it does not encourage doctrinal status equalization between party bureaucrats and activists.

Although this state of affairs has survived the test of fifteen years, a managerial approach to political participation contains inherent tensions that provide incentives and opportunities for future change in the terms of participation. First, various groups—blue-collar, white-collar, specialist, party and nonparty activists—may push for still further enhancement of their ideological status vis-a-vis officialdom. Second, maintenance of a managerial approach may frustrate the efforts of a leadership coalition seeking to reorganize public administration or to make Soviet officials more responsive in practice to the advice of experts. Such a coalition will be tempted to ally with groups in the nonofficial sectors in order to broaden the scope of political conflict against recalcitrant officials.[48] Third, a leadership coalition seeking an ideological revival for its own sake might be drawn to a populist revival in hopes of thus generating authentic mass initiative and expanding the legitimacy of the regime.

The probability of a populist revival—for instrumental reasons or as an end in itself—is difficult to estimate. More important than prediction, however, is an appreciation of the tensions within any mode of political organization, and of the interests which could, for reasons of their own, exploit those tensions to transform the terms of political participation. Khrushchev's populist approach and Brezhnev's managerial approach define variants set within parameters that exclude either a Stalinist restoration or some form of institutionalized (or constitutionalized) democracy. The future, of course, is open. But if it proves to be the case that neither Stalinism nor democracy is on the agenda for the foreseeable future, and if the tensions within Brezhnev's managerial approach push toward a limited redefinition of the terms of political participation, we may witness a selective reinclusion of components of Khrushchevian populism. "De-Brezhnevization" would be as different from "de-Stalinization" as Brezhnev is from Stalin. In addition, the personality and predispositions of Brezhnev's successor are likely to be quite different from Khrushchev's. Hence, the character and degree of populism included in such an effort would be different from that experienced under Khrushchev. Still, the populist impulse appears to have systemic roots that provide continuing temptations.

Notes

1. See George W. Breslauer, "Khrushchev Reconsidered," *Problems of Communism* (September-October 1976), pp. 18–20, for fuller discussion and citation of this literature.

2. "Bureaucratic and political autonomy" refers to the right of party and state officials to define the language, arenas, and scope of legitimate political action.

3. Leo Gruliow, ed., *Current Soviet Policies II: The Documentary Record*

of the 20th Party Congress and Its Aftermath (New York: Frederick A. Praeger, 1957), p. 177.

4. Nikita Khrushchev, *Stroitel'stvo kommunizma v SSSR i razvitie sel'-skogo khoziaistva*, 8 vols. (Moscow: Politizdat, 1962–1964), vol. 1, p. 77 (hereafter, *Stroitel'stvo kommunizma*).

5. *Stroitel'stvo kommunizma*, vol. 1, p. 319. For analogous exhortations during the early years after Stalin's death, see Khrushchev, in *Pravda*, September 15, 1953, and in *Stroitel'stvo kommunizma*, vol. 1, p. 180; also, *Stroitel'stvo kommunizma*, vol. 2, pp. 36, 91, 106. In his memoirs, Khrushchev makes special note of Stalin's implicit sociopolitical definition of the problem: "For Stalin, peasants were scum." See *Khrushchev Remembers: The Last Testament* (Boston: Little, Brown, 1974), p. 112.

6. For examples from the early years after Stalin's death, see *Pravda*, September 15, 1953; *Stroitel'stvo kommunizma*, vol. 1, pp. 108–111, 178, 402 and vol. 2, pp. 94–95, 376–377, 416, 425.

7. *Stroitel'stvo kommunizma*, vol. 1, p. 192, for analogous articulations during these early years, see *Pravda*, September 15, 1953, and March 21, 1954; also *Stroitel'stvo kommunizma*, vol. 1, pp. 183, 357, and vol. 2, pp. 31, 62, 65, 69, 94, 96–97, 114, 124, 125.

8. *Pravda*, October 17, 1959.

9. *Stroitel'stvo kommunizma*, vol. 2, p. 384.

10. At a higher level of generalization, one scholar interprets post-Stalin reform in Soviet-type regimes as a process of "inclusion" of previously excluded groups; see Kenneth Jowitt, "Inclusion and Mobilization in European Leninist Regimes," *World Politics*, 28 (October 1975), pp. 69–96.

11. *Stroitel'stvo kommunizma*, vol. 1, p. 126.

12. Ellen Mickiewicz, *Soviet Political Schools* (New Haven: Yale University Press, 1967), pp. 10, 13.

13. Gruliow, *Current Soviet Policies II*, p. 59.

14. See Khrushchev's speech at the congress of the Young Communist League in April 1958, as reprinted in *Stroitel'stvo kommunizma*, vol. 3, especially pp. 170–173.

15. Leo Gruliow, ed., *Current Soviet Policies III: The Documentary Record of the Extraordinary 21st Congress of the Communist Party of the Soviet Union* (New York: Columbia University Press, 1960), p. 67.

16. Moreover, Paul Cocks notes that these officials harbored a profound distrust of nonofficial party activists, whose numbers were, in any case, very small. See his "Controlling Communist Bureaucracy: Ethics, Rationality, and Terror," unpublished manuscript.

17. See William Conyngham, *Industrial Management in the Soviet Union* (Stanford: Hoover Institution Press, 1973), p. 84.

18. This resistance is well documented in Cocks, "Controlling Communist Bureaucracy," and Conyngham, *Industrial Management*.

19. See Richard Lowenthal, "Development vs. Utopia in Communist Policy," in Chalmers A. Johnson, ed., *Change in Communist Systems* (Stanford: Stanford University Press, 1970), pp. 33–116; and George A. Brinkley, "Khrushchev Remembered: On the Theory of Soviet Statehood," *Soviet Studies* (January 1973), p. 396.

20. Charlotte Saikowski and Leo Gruliow, eds., *Current Soviet Policies IV: The Documentary Record of the 22nd Party Congress of the Communist*

Party of the Soviet Union (New York: Columbia University Press, 1962), pp. 102, 71–72.

21. Ibid., p. 114. Stalin, in his election speech of February 1946, also denigrated the party-nonparty distinction, but this must be interpreted in terms of Stalin's larger effort at the time to reassert the ideological primacy of his own authority. Obviously, it was not accompanied by the pervasive Khrushchevian concern for transforming the authority relationship between officials and masses.

22. Ibid., p. 66.

23. Ibid., p. 104.

24. Mary McAuley, *Labor Disputes in Soviet Russia, 1957–1965* (Oxford: Clarendon Press, 1969), p. 123.

25. Conyngham, *Industrial Management*, p. 148.

26. Cocks, "Controlling Communist Bureaucracy," p. 491.

27. These slogans appear regularly in *Pravda* and *Izvestiia* in April and October of each year. The word "discipline" was entirely expunged from the slogans during the period from October 1962 through April 1965. In October 1961 and April 1962 it appeared only with reference to "military discipline."

28. D. Chesnokov, in *Pravda*, February 27, 1967.

29. A. Luk'ianov and B. Lazarev, "Sovety: razvitie i ukreplenie demokraticheskikh osnov," *Kommunist*, no. 13, 1961, p. 57.

30. Speech by I. V. Kapitonov, "The CPSU After the 23rd Party Congress," *World Marxist Review*, no. 9, 1966, p. 6.

31. Ts. A. Stepanian and V. S. Semenov, eds., *Klassy, sotsial'nye sloi i gruppy v SSSR* (Moscow, 1968), p. 27.

32. *Pravda*, March 8, 1963.

33. For an excellent example of Khrushchev's effort to balance these conflicting requirements, see his speech to the Writers' Congress, *Pravda*, May 24, 1959.

34. See F. Burlatskii, *Gosudarstvo i kommunizm* (Moscow, 1963), pp. 172–173, 207ff.

35. Conyngham, *Industrial Management*, p. 203.

36. These included the academics, many of them liberalizers, whose hopes soared so high after Khrushchev's overthrow—paradoxical as it may seem. On the one hand, they supported Khrushchev's de-Stalinization campaign and its implied attack on the political prerogatives of Soviet officials. On the other hand, they hoped that his overthrow would reduce the pressure for social transformation and thereby allow the extension of political changes begun under Khrushchev. See, for example, A. I. Lepeshkin, in *Sovetskoe gosudarstvo i pravo*, February 1965, pp. 5–15; F. Burlatskii, in *Pravda*, January 10, 1965; and A. Rumiantsev, in *Pravda*, February 21 and September 9, 1965.

37. In the original version of this essay I referred to this as a conservative restoration. However, Stephen F. Cohen's chapter in the present volume has persuaded me of the utility of distinguishing between a conservative reaction and a conservative restoration.

38. Conyngham, *Industrial Management*, p. 260.

39. It is also important to bear in mind that greater secrecy of deliberations is not necessarily associated with greater dogmatism in the resolution

of social and economic issues, though this may be the case, depending upon the realm of policy in question. For contrasting conclusions on this score, see Peter H. Solomon, Jr., "Specialists in Policy-Making: Criminal Policy 1938–1970," in Karl Ryavec, ed., *Soviet Society and the Communist Party* (Amherst, Mass.: University of Massachusetts Press, 1978), pp. 156–176; and George W. Breslauer, "On the Adaptability of Soviet Welfare-State Authoritarianism," ibid., pp. 3–25. Thus, evaluators of change in the USSR must distinguish four dimensions of political change: richness and freedom of debate; access to officials; responsiveness by officials to certain types of messages; and secrecy of deliberations (regardless of who takes part in them).

40. This means that the period between October 1961 and April 1965 is the only time in the entire postwar period (1946–78) that the concept of discipline (other than "military discipline") does not appear in the slogans.

41. The commitment to channeling politics into a bureaucratic arena and hostility to the creation of an autonomous public arena are features that markedly distinguish the Soviet regime from liberal-democratic ones. On this point, see Kenneth T. Jowitt, "National, State, and Civic Development in Marxist-Leninist Regimes," paper presented to the September 1975 meeting of the American Political Science Association in San Francisco. In this paper, Jowitt has also pioneered new ways of conceptualizing the role and status of party activists in "Leninist" regimes.

42. *Pravda*, March 31, 1971.

43. *Prvada*, December 6, 1964.

44. *Pravda*, February 25, 1976.

45. The literature is extensive but rather homogeneous. For a sampling, see A. Butenko, "O razvitom sotsialisticheskom obshchestve," *Kommunist*, no. 6, 1972, pp. 48–58; G. N. Naumov, "Sovetskoe gosudarstvo—glavnoe orudie postroeniia sotsializma i kommunizma," *Sovetskoe gosudarstvo i pravo*, no. 5, 1971, pp. 10–19; N. P. Farberov, "Ukreplenie sovetskogo gosudarstva i razvitie sotsialisticheskoi demokratii," ibid., no. 8, 1971, pp. 3–11; and A. P. Kositsyn, *Sotsialisticheskoe gosudarstvo* (Moscow: Iuridicheskaia literatura, 1970). For a dissent from the contemporary orthodoxy by one who strongly supported de-Stalinization, see F. Burlatskii, *Lenin, gosudarstvo, politika* (Moscow: Nauka, 1970), especially pp. 388, 393, 404.

46. For a typical example, see I. Kuzminov, *Pravda*, April 16, 1969.

47. For the text of the new Soviet constitution as amended and ratified, see *Pravda*, October 8, 1977. See also the comprehensive analysis of this document in Robert Sharlet, *The New Soviet Constitution of 1977: Analysis and Text* (Brunswick, Ohio: King's Court, 1978).

48. For an analysis of Brezhnev's leadership strategy, which documents Brezhnev's awareness of this temptation, see George W. Breslauer, "Dilemmas of Leadership in the Soviet Union since Stalin, 1953–1976" (unpublished manuscript), chs. 9–13.

Changing Soviet Perspectives on Leadership and Administration

Erik P. Hoffmann

Stalin's view of the ideal political organization of society has been characterized as "monolithic" in the Soviet Union and as "totalitarian" in the West.[1] Westerners stress that its essential features were the assumption of an extraordinary range of responsibilities by the national government and the extension of state power into virtually all areas of human life. Soviet writers emphasize that Stalin's basic aim was to unify the civic values, attitudes, and beliefs of the entire population, and to mobilize all material resources and human energies for the task of rapidly creating a "socialist" society and eventually transforming it into a "communist" one. The impressive build-up of heavy industry, the brutal but thorough collectivization of agriculture, and the waves of mass terror against the Soviet people are the best-known of Stalin's policies in the 1930s. Also important were his efforts to enhance the national defense capabilities of the USSR throughout the decade, and to consolidate the mature Stalinist system of the late 1930s by strengthening Soviet law and the Soviet family, by promoting scientific-technical and vocational education, and by recentralizing the political indoctrination machinery (Agitprop) and expanding its programs.

The political order that Stalin created to accomplish these goals was itself a vital product of "the third revolution" following NEP. By 1937 Stalin had replaced the previous oligarchic dictatorship of the Communist Party with a personal dictatorship or one-man rule. The CPSU was in no sense a ruling or sovereign party. Its highest organs met with increasing infrequency in the years 1934 to 1953, and over a million of its members (almost half of them) were arrested or perished in the mid and late 1930s.[2] The party was reduced to more or less equal status with the other major bureaucracies—the secret police, army, and state apparatus (councils of ministers and soviets). Stalin, through loyal agencies, dominated all of these institutions, using them as instruments of his policy and personnel preferences and inner needs for power and adulation. Stalin deliberately pitted officials of these institutions against one another and established overlapping and imprecise spheres of bureaucratic jurisdiction. He did so to ensure that major (and many minor) political decisions and disputes would be resolved by him personally, and to increase the likelihood of obtaining accurate information from various organizational sources and speedy compliance with his commands. To ensure further that his dictates would be followed —and that lower-level officials would pursue national goals in the absence of precise and consistent directives and adequate resources— Stalin created an elaborate system of rewards and sanctions, which included extraordinary opportunities for career advancement as well as life-and-death power over all officials (and citizens).

Stalin's most important goals were few and clear-cut, and the polity he molded emphasized heavily the unquestioned support of the leader and the effective fulfillment of policies and targets, not the efficient use of resources or cooperation among organizations and groups. For instance, planning was focused on ends, not on means, and generous bonuses were given only for complete fulfillment (or overfulfillment) of assigned tasks, and for immediate, rather than long-term, benefits. Hence, the political-administrative system was designed to allow institutions and individual officials considerable flexibility in choosing the methods of achieving centrally prescribed aims and in competing with one another for political power and material and human resources to do so. As Merle Fainsod pointed out, "The bureaucratic hierarchies . . . operated as centers of influence in their own right. . . . Behind the monolithic facade of Stalinist totalitarianism, the plural pressures of professional bureaucratic interests found expression."[3] But group participation in the formulation and frequent reformulation of public policies was not a part of the theory or practice of Stalinism. The power to determine and choose among policy alternatives was highly concentrated in Stalin's personal secretariat (not in the party Politburo) and, above all, in the hands of Stalin himself.

During World War II Stalin was compelled to enter into a political, economic, and military alliance with the major Western democracies, and to allow greater institutional and ideological diversity within the USSR. Collaboration with the United States, "different roads to socialism" in the world communist movement, and relaxation of controls at home—all were paths that former Soviet leaders had unsuccessfully advocated in the 1920s but which had to be explored in time of crisis.

Yet after World War II Stalin reestablished the Soviet political system of the late 1930s. In time of peace and of "cold war," Stalin reaffirmed his commitment to the prewar resource allocation priorities and institutional relationships. Despite the leader's caution or indecision as reflected in the Varga affair, despite the intensified jockeying for power among the major bureaucracies, and despite considerable public yearning for a less coercive polity, Stalinism was reimposed and the industrial production of the USSR was revived with remarkable rapidity in the time-tested ways (e.g., autarkic economic development, political indoctrination, forced labor). Stalin's chief effort abroad, the forging of a totalitarian interstate system which included Eastern Europe and eventually China, was primarily intended to meet internal economic and national security needs; it was surprisingly successful (at least in the short run).

The shortcomings of Stalin's policies and policy-making procedures became increasingly evident to Soviet officials and foreign observers in the new domestic and international conditions after the war. As Alfred Meyer observed, "This crude, primitive, but effective Stalinist system . . . became obsolete because of its success. Having built an industrial society, it was poorly equipped by its own structure and operating methods [e.g., terror, command, centralized control] to maintain, manage, and improve this [more complex, heterogeneous, and interdependent] society."[4] That is, Stalin had achieved absolute power to issue commands; he did not have to persuade or reason with anyone to gain compliance with his specific directives. But the political system he created did not have the capacity to provide its leader with the information needed to make large numbers of feasible, timely, and integrated policies and commands in the increasingly complex sociopolitical, economic, and scientific-technical environments of the postwar era. Nor did Stalin have the capability, or in some cases the will, to utilize the policy-relevant information he received. The Stalinist political order repressed creativity and initiative in most fields, and it lacked the flexibility to adjust plans and decisions to rapidly changing domestic and international conditions and to unanticipated opportunities and problems. Robert C. Tucker has succinctly stated that when Stalin died, the question was not, "Who shall replace him?" but "What shall take the place of Stalin*ism* as a mode of rule and pattern of policy and ideas?"[5]

Khrushchev's Views on Leadership

The response of Stalin's successors, as is well known, was to revitalize the Communist Party and to reassert its predominant role in Soviet society. The CPSU's power vis-a-vis the other major bureaucracies increased, its involvement in industrial management and operations in the countryside expanded, and its membership grew. Less recognized is that Nikita Khrushchev, like Stalin, conceived of the party as primarily an administrative organ for implementing policies formulated by the top leader. By the late 1950s Khrushchev had gradually put together a "grand design": a coordinated set of new domestic and international goals and policies that included peaceful coexistence with the West; allocation of more resources to agriculture and consumer goods; systematic application of scientific discoveries and technical innovations to production problems; and social and economic egalitarianism. He then tried to develop various reform programs to implement these central ideas. Such programs included decentralization of economic decision making; major changes in Soviet law; and curtailed defense expenditures.

Khrushchev was not very successful in attaining his objectives. His lack of accomplishment was in part the result of poor planning, formidable bureaucratic resistance and inertia, unfavorable external developments, and the intractability of human nature. The first secretary's inability to mobilize institutional support for his policies was especially frustrating, and it prompted his increasingly persistent, even frenetic, search for public acclaim and new administrative measures to accomplish his cherished (and often unchanging) aims. Khrushchev, by almost any yardstick, was less effective and efficient in achieving his chief goals than Stalin was in achieving his. Carl Linden has noted that "Khrushchev's power and prestige were, to a far greater extent than Stalin's, dependent on the success of his policies."[6] Whereas Stalin could govern either *through* or *over* the party,[7] Khrushchev found it more and more difficult to do either.

The difficulties of being Stalin's successor may well have been enhanced by residual elements of Stalinism in Khrushchev's conceptions of authority. Khrushchev apparently believed that all party and state officials should actively help to administer national policies which they had little or no part in shaping, and that they could be made to carry out their responsibilities by means of job insecurity and a peculiar mix of performance and moral incentives. The new CPSU leader most assuredly did not conceive of himself as an arbiter of competing "interests" or claims from the major institutions and social strata, or from scientists, technical specialists, or economic executives, to whom power to shape national policy was devolving or should devolve.

Khrushchev did seek, as George Breslauer has observed, "to expand the boundaries of decision-making arenas," and his "ideal conception of decision-making processes envisaged cooperative problem-solving among talented actors."[8] But increased elite and popular participation in administration do not necessarily lead to greater democratization of the policy-making process, and Khrushchev almost surely did not intend them to do so. The first secretary had a highly instrumental view of scientific, technical, economic, and managerial expertise. He vigorously strove to use the contributions of the specialized elites and the masses to implement *his* vision of the national interest and to refine *operational*, not strategic, decisions. Khrushchev sought competence and initiative wherever he could find them, in order to help translate his general goals into reformist policies and to carry out workable programs expeditiously within the spirit, if not always the letter, of the party statutes and the law.

The grand design advocated by Khrushchev consisted primarily of substantive goals; he was less clear about the means by which these goals were to be achieved. Khrushchev does not seem to have given careful thought to the interrelationships between ends and means, or he lacked the political-administrative skills to link them. To be sure, Khrushchev made an enormous contribution to Soviet politics by foreswearing terror as a means of resolving political disputes. But this decision eliminated any possibility of his ruling *over* the major bureaucracies and having them compete with one another to realize his objectives. Also, Khrushchev probably assumed (incorrectly) that the elimination of physical coercion against party and state officials would increase bureaucratic support for his policy preferences. Khrushchev apparently failed to recognize that new decision-making procedures and institutional reorganizations are not likely to be very effective if important groups of bureaucrats perceive them to be illegitimate or threatening. For example, the first secretary insisted on disbanding the economic ministries in 1957 and on bifurcating the regional party apparatus in 1962—administrative changes that were quite unpopular with state and party officials, respectively.

For Khrushchev, appropriate political processes were, by definition, those which augmented the prestige and supported the policies of the top leader, and not the goals of other officials, organizations, and social groups. Political power and the policy-making system were not perceived as ends in themselves, but as means to promote centrally prescribed objectives. Khrushchev frequently refused to accede to his

Presidium colleagues when his policies and programs faltered. When he was increasingly forced to do so, Khrushchev responded by trying to break away from the bonds of oligarchic party rule—for example, by appealing for the support of public opinion and of "his" regional CPSU officials and scientific-technical experts. In the process, Khrushchev alienated, one by one, the leaders and many of the lesser officials of all the major Soviet bureaucracies, including the party.

Khrushchev's ouster in 1964 stemmed mainly from his quite authoritarian ideas about the preponderant power of the party leader over even the highest party bodies;[9] his cavalier treatment of party and state bureaucrats; his penchant for grandiose but insufficiently planned projects; and his demanding, unpredictable, disruptive, and impatient political style. Important but probably secondary factors were his often far-sighted and idealistic policies and priorities. Khrushchev's colleagues objected less to the content of his grand design than to his methods of advocating and implementing it.

Brezhnev's Views on Leadership

Khrushchev's policy-making procedures had a major impact on his successors' conceptions of power and authority. The Brezhnev administration, especially between 1964 and 1969, devoted considerable effort to establishing stable and agreed-upon decision-making methods to promote cooperative problem solving and institutional checks and balances to ensure the "mutual control" of top officials.[10] At the same time the new "collective leadership" gradually formulated the comprehensive domestic and foreign policies elaborated at the Twenty-fourth Party Congress in 1971. The content of Brezhnev's grand design was quite similar to Khrushchev's: it included detente with the United States; the use of advanced Western technology to spur Soviet economic development; and the improvement of wages for the lowest paid workers. However, Khrushchev's grand design consisted largely of substantive policies, whereas Brezhnev's incorporated significant policy-making practices in addition to domestic and international goals. Brezhnev's program, adopted at the Twenty-fourth Congress, was not imposed from above; rather, it was the product of extensive consultation, controlled debate, and bargaining among the top leaders; the major bureaucracies; the scientific, technical, managerial, and educational elites; and, to a much lesser extent, rank-and-file Communists.

Key elements of the emerging new policies on how to make policy were the following: broader and deeper participation by specialists at different stages and levels of decision making; group decision making in party committees and departments; major compromises *before* innovative programs were launched; prior consolidation of bureaucratic support for policy implementation; "trust in cadres"; clearer and more stable spheres of responsibility; a strong preference for incremental change; and expanded opportunities for party and state executives to assess the consequences of decisions before *and* after they were made, especially at official CPSU meetings. Also, sociopolitical, economic, and scientific-technical information were to be actively solicited throughout the party hierarchy and at various stages and levels of decision making and administration. Particularly encouraged were the evaluation of data on the effects of prior decisions, and practical suggestions for formulating more feasible social, economic, and research and development programs, and for improving the planning and organizational work needed to implement general party goals.

Today's Soviet leaders and management theorists view goal setting and decision making as a complex and ongoing process, requiring large amounts of diverse information, technical and administrative skills, coordination and control, institutional stability, and bureaucratic perquisites. "Problem situations" can be managed but rarely eliminated. Policy outcomes must be continuously monitored, and decisions and decision-making procedures must be periodically adjusted to take into account unanticipated consequences, changing conditions, and new management techniques and organizational technology. CPSU and government officials view the political-administrative system as increasingly permeable to internal and external influences, and many consider these growing interdependencies necessary to promote economic and social progress, and not a source of weakness or vulnerability.

Leading Soviet officials and theorists consider it a prime challenge to enhance the directive, responsive, and "learning" capacities of the central political organs. Particularly important is the adaptation of traditional principles, such as integrated economic and social planning and "democratic centralism," to dramatically changing scientific-technical and socioeconomic conditions.[11] Other perceived challenges are to avert the possibility of an increasingly unfavorable competitive position vis-a-vis the industrialized nations of the West, and to utilize advanced Western techniques and technology without promoting the "technocratization" of the Soviet intelligentsia or the "embourgeoisement" of Soviet society.[12]

Brezhnev and Kosygin, much more pragmatic than their predecessor but different from one another, recognized clearly the significance of establishing uncontested and regularized methods of governing to meet these challenges. Specifically, they saw numerous benefits in creating more permanent institutional relationships and more consensual, responsive, and routinized policy-making and administrative procedures. For example, the collective leadership's reunification of the regional party committees, which had been recently divided by Khrushchev into industrial and agricultural units, and the reconstituting of strong, centralized ministries were organizational changes of major importance. Above all, the highest Soviet leaders hoped that these and other adjustments in the policy-making process would generate greater support and contributions from the officials and specialists whose cooperation and skills were essential in formulating, as well as carrying out, comprehensive and successful national programs.

From Khrushchev's experience, Brezhnev and his colleagues seem to have developed a keener understanding of the close connections between the effectiveness and legitimacy of policies and the ways in which they are made. Khrushchev was unable to accomplish his central aims in the face of bureaucratic obstructionism at home and a frequently unresponsive, even hostile, political environment abroad. Khrushchev's problems made his successors aware of the inseparability of ends and means, of politics and administration, of domestic and foreign policy and policy-making practices, and of the substantive and procedural aspects of successful leadership.

Significantly, the current CPSU leaders apparently believe that the processes by which policies are made, as well as the content and effectiveness of these policies, determine their legitimacy. Khrushchev had a distinctive vision of the national interest and found it very difficult to compromise with his domestic political opponents, except in response to overwhelming opposition or the obvious failure of his policies. Somehow, he never lost the power to propose or initiate programs, such as the development of chemical fertilizers for agriculture and rapprochement with the West in 1959 and 1963. But when accomplishments fell short of his clearly stated aims, responsibility rested squarely with the first secretary. Indeed, some Soviet leaders may have formally supported Khrushchev's decisions in the expectation that they would fail and thereby reduce his influence. In contrast, Brezhnev's authority is much less dependent on the success of his policies. The power to determine purposes and to define success is exercised by a collective leadership comprised of representatives of all the chief party and state institutions. Hence, responsibility is widely diffused among many individuals and organizations.

Initially, the Brezhnev Politburo and Secretariat apparently assumed, or hoped, that more legitimate policy-making procedures would produce more effective policies. The leadership efforts to increase bureaucratic acceptance of the policy process have been quite successful. Indeed, the present Soviet political system probably enjoys a high degree of legitimacy among virtually all of the bureaucratic elites. Many administrators seem to like the current decision-making and recruitment practices because they chiefly assign responsibility for specific segments or phases of a task, because they do not impose inordinate pressures to learn new skills, and because they provide very considerable professional and personal security to competent and/or loyal bureaucrats, especially at the highest levels. Even when an administrative unit or grouping does not get much or most of what it seeks, it has very likely had an opportunity to make its view heard, and it will feel—and top party officials will communicate expectations and incentives to make it feel—an obligation to carry out the probably incremental policy changes agreed upon at the center. It is not surprising, then, that the predominant majority of party bureaucrats and state administrators seems willing to abide by the present decision-making rules.

Stalin and Khrushchev had a much greater distrust of professional bureaucrats than Brezhnev has. Stalin developed powerful rewards and sanctions to motivate officials, whereas Khrushchev, by choice and circumstance, placed considerably more reliance on public supervision over their activities. Stalin, in hopes of improving administrative performance, fostered in cadres the fear of losing life and job; Khrushchev proscribed terror but tried to manipulate the official's fear of losing his job; Brezhnev, until 1969–70, did neither. Brezhnev's approach to administrative productivity and motivation has been reminiscent of the executive who assures his subordinates of career security and ample material and psychological rewards, and then tells them "Now get to work!" In contrast to Khrushchev's personnel policies, Brezhnev's have been characterized by a low turnover of executives and reduced shifting of officials from one assignment to another. Brezhnev assumed that greater administrative stability and clearer delineation of rights and responsibilities would markedly improve the quality of work in many fields. Only since the early 1970s has Brezhnev begun to lose patience with the concept of "trust in cadres" and increasingly linked job performance with job security in his public pronouncements.[13]

Brezhnev no longer seems to believe that legitimate political processes are necessary *and* sufficient to produce effective policies. The Soviet elites' widespread acceptance of the present policy-making system has not been accompanied by a significant rise in bureaucratic accountability or responsiveness to national goals and initiatives. More and more technical and administrative contributions have been forthcoming to implement the top leadership's general conception of the national interest. But organizational and departmental interests are still quite powerful. If anything, they are becoming increasingly formidable because of their greater direct representation in the Politburo and Central Committee, the diverse policy preferences of key leaders (especially after the difficulties encountered by the Twenty-fourth Party Congress program), and the growing international ties between Soviet and foreign political and economic institutions.

Almost a decade ago two Western specialists observed that "the [Soviet] leadership has recognized that its own authority can best be maintained if various groups are given more leeway to pursue independently the general interest of society."[14] But the top party leaders have more and more sought to enhance the center's capacity to plan, budget, and "manage by objectives," to elicit organizational contributions in support of *national* goals, and to control the chief bureaucracies.[15] This trend does not necessarily represent a return to a more authoritarian form of government. Rather, it may be a kind of holding action to prevent what Jerry Hough has called "the devolution of power to the major institutional centers" and the transformation of the leadership's role to that of "a broker mediating the competing claims of powerful interests."[16]

Special interests are well entrenched in the myriad party and state organizations in Moscow, as well as in the localities. Politburo officials themselves have different views and continuously debate the merits of current objectives, programs, and priorities. However, a unified national perspective, and if at all possible a widely supported set of comprehensive and feasible domestic and foreign policies, is the officially stated and quite possibly the operative goal of most Politburo members. The Politburo is the only organ in the Soviet polity committed to formulating a long- and short-term conception of the common good and to making it prevail over group and individual interests and immediate pressures. After all, the capacity to plan and manage the economy and society in the interests of all the people, not just the wealthy or powerful, is allegedly one of the fundamental advantages of a Soviet-type socialist system. In order to develop and utilize this capability, the CPSU leadership must pay close attention to the party's relations with other major institutions in the USSR.

The Role of the Party in "Developed Socialism"

Soviet leaders and theorists stress the growing significance of the Communist Party in "developed socialist society," the official name for

the socioeconomic order achieved by 1967. The traditional functions of
the party—to provide political, organizational, and ideological leadership—are to remain the same. But these activities will become more
important as their content and interrelationships change. The reasons
given include the following: the greatly increased scale and complexity
of the present-day tasks of "communist construction"; the need to mobilize the specialized elites and masses to help fulfill these tasks; the
need for integrated social and economic forecasting; the need to nur-
ture "socialist democracy" through more effective political education
work; and the need to direct the USSR's international relations in
the era of the worldwide "scientific and technological revolution"
(STR).[17] In a word, the Soviet polity and the CPSU are both viewed
as "dynamic" organisms, whose purposes, activities, and structure are
constantly evolving. To quote an official Soviet interpretation, "Developed socialism is at the same time developing socialism, the mechanism
of its functioning being inseparable from the mechanism of its improvement."[18]

   The enhancement of "the leading role of the party" is nonetheless an
ambiguous idea, which is in need of considerable theoretical elaboration and is no doubt the subject of continued dispute among CPSU
and state leaders. For example, does the "growing" importance of the
party refer to its accumulation of power relative to that of other institutions in Soviet society? Prominent officials and theorists deny this,
suggesting instead that there is a trend toward a more equal distribution of power among Soviet institutions. This trend, coupled with the
greater scope and complexity of the problems to be managed, increases
the significance of the party's "coordinating" and "unifying" activities.
V. S. Shevtsov comments, "The growth in the party's role does not,
and cannot, imply any increase in its rights vis-a-vis other organizations of the working people. What it really means is a growth in the
party's obligations, in the significance of its ideological and political
guidance, and in the scale of its activities."[19]

   Theorists of developed socialism and of "the scientific management
of society" still stress the traditional Leninist idea that a "conscious"
party leadership must impose its view of the national interest on the
"spontaneity" of the masses. But the present emphasis is on improving
the CPSU's capacity to elicit contributions from all strata of society
and from all state and public organizations, in order to help formulate
and implement decisions in a collaborative manner for the benefit of
all. The party's role is to be the "decisive coordinator," "integrator,"
"regulator," "synthesizer," "adjuster," "mobilizer," and "energizer" of
the activities of an increasingly well-educated and politically sophis-

ticated general population. As a Soviet text states, "The Communist
Party joins together all of the links of the socialist political system,
directing their activities [and subordinating them] toward a single goal
[communism]." The CPSU, comprising the "nucleus" of the polity
and of all state and public institutions, "ensures organization, unity, and
singleness of purpose of the entire system."[20]

The policy-making procedures of the Brezhnev administration are
proving to be less successful than anticipated. That is, the power of the
present Politburo and Central Committee to *make* decisions is greater
than their power to *implement* these decisions, and this gap appears to
be widening. The problem is not as serious as it was under Khrushchev,
but top party leaders are clearly concerned about it. A senior political
analyst asserts: "It must be especially emphasized that real collective
leadership is not only freedom of discussion and debate, but also the
active struggle for putting into practice the collectively reached decisions."[21] Brezhnev himself noted at the Twenty-fifth Party Congress in
1975 that the Politburo and Secretariat had "devoted far more attention
than in the past to control over and verification of the fulfillment of
adopted decisions." He felt constrained to deny that "any alarming
situation has developed in the party" with respect to "decisions [that]
are not fulfilled or are fulfilled imprecisely or incompletely,"[22] and he
implied that the leadership's perception of and impatience with the
problem had increased, not the problem itself.

Although Brezhnev did not offer reasons why party decisions are
sometimes inadequately carried out, the beginnings of a most interesting
official explanation can be pieced together from various sources. The
key idea is that "the Communist Party, as a higher form of social organization, is not connected with any professional, departmental interests."[23] The state organs, in contrast, *are* reportedly developing stronger
occupational and organizational interests. And the source of the accompanying "technocratic and bureaucratic manifestations" is the scientific and technological revolution, or STR.[24]

Why is this "nonantagonistic contradiction" occurring? Because the
growing use of scientific and technical advances in management and
production calls for greater specialized training and professionalization,
which simultaneously pose opportunities and problems to Soviet political authorities. Although the development of "negative tendencies"
(in the ministries, scientific-technical research institutes, and economic
production units) is not "fatally inevitable," their "neutralization" is
not an "easy or automatic matter." "The more the STR adversely affects the sphere of management, the stronger and more effective must
be party and social control, ensuring the timely removal of possible
elements of a technocratic and bureaucratic approach to leadership by

social life."[25] The party, despite its extraordinary size and differentiation,[26] is allegedly "monolithic" or free of such divisive and harmful tendencies.

P. N. Fedoseev, a prominent Soviet theorist, links this general interpretation to larger questions concerning the nature and development of socialist democracy.

> In the Soviet Union the professionalization of the executive bodies of management is combined with enhancing the role of the representative bodies—the soviets at all levels and the social and political mass organizations: party, trade union, and youth organizations, production conferences, and so on. In the socialist countries systematic work is conducted to develop the activity and effectiveness of all democratic bodies in every possible way, to ensure their control over the activity of the executive organs of government and to draw the masses, on an increasingly larger scale, into the administration of state affairs. This is facilitated by raising the general and the political education of the population, their cultural and professional level, by their growing social consciousness and maturity.[27]

Note the sharp distinction made between party and state. The CPSU is viewed as united, selfless, and unaffected by the onerous consequences of the worldwide STR. The state is fragmented, parochial, and vulnerable to the STR's harmful side effects. Only through the persistent combined efforts of "the democratic bodies," especially the party, can the technocratic tendencies within "the executive organs of government" (the state ministries and committees) be curbed, and can "the unity of scientific, technological, social, and moral progress" be ensured.[28]

What is implied, but never stated, in contemporary Soviet writings is that the CPSU is the sole centripetal force in a society consisting of increasingly powerful centrifugal forces. Among the centrifugal factors are portentous socioeconomic developments such as manpower shortages and strong ethnic loyalties, and amorphous forms of "spontaneity," such as alcoholism, juvenile delinquency, and "indifference to politics." Also, the centrifugal elements now include a very large number of administrative and production units. Only the party's "great authority . . . enables it to accommodate the interests of different organizations and departments, to coordinate their work, and unify and direct it. In so doing, the party gives the whole political organization of Soviet society a purposefulness that multiplies its strength many times."[29]

However, the CPSU has not been able to perform these functions to the satisfaction of the leading party officials of the Khrushchev and Brezhnev administrations. Members of the collective leadership bemoan the declining influence of the party in industrial management, for example.[30] Despite (or because of) Brezhnev's emphasis on the political education of scientific and technical specialists, the manageability of the major Soviet bureaucracies is an article of faith, not an accomplished fact. Growing problems are being caused by the multitude of administrative units, the unintentional overlapping of responsibilities, and the lack of sufficient interorganizational coordination in the planning and management of the economy—a phenomenon aptly described as "bureaucratic pluralism."[31] Hence, the chief constraint on centralized socioeconomic planning and societal guidance, and on the effective use of information in decision making and administration, is *not* technological. Rather, it lies in the highly differentiated and bureaucratized nature of the myriad party and state political-administrative bodies and alliances, whose members are reluctant to relinquish their group or organizational power to anything but a strongly unified Politburo interpretation of the national interest.[32] The Manichean pronouncements regarding the positive influences of the STR on the Party and the STR's negative effects on the state (discussed above) clearly signal high-level concern about the difficulties of providing effective leadership in a complex bureaucratized society. Such assertions possibly foreshadow a Party crackdown on state agencies at all or some levels. Much more likely, these statements are part of an effort by the national CPSU leadership to delegate still greater responsibility to the major bureaucracies, while at the same time guarding against the possible dissipation of national initiative and control over the policy process.

The present-day Politburo and Secretariat are well aware that the broadening and deepening of specialized elite participation in decision-making in some ways enhances, but in other ways reduces, the central party bodies' capacity to lead. This "nonantagonistic contradiction," which has been and will continue to be exacerbated by the contemporary STR, produces ongoing tensions in party-state relations. At issue are the CPSU's role in economic decision making and its recruitment and deployment of party and state officials, for example. Such choices necessitate continuous reassessment of risks and costs by all of the Soviet bureaucratic elites. For example, shifts of power are likely to occur within administrative units when new organization technology and management techniques are introduced. Soviet writers on developed socialism have just begun to grapple with the fact that "much aggregation of interests takes place within and between the ministerial apparatuses," and that the highest party officials must continuously strive to ensure that "the final aggregation process occurs in the Politburo." In other words, major decisions must be at least approved by, if not actually made by, the central Party bodies. Some top Soviet leaders might privately agree with David Lane, one of the few Western observers who refuses to view the present-day CPSU as a "ruling" party, and who stresses instead "the real powers of social forces and institutions outside it."[33]

Soviet theorists are beginning to catch up with practicing administrators in their understanding of the capacity of politicians, politician/experts, and experts to influence one another, and of the political implications of their increasingly close cooperation. Soviet analysts contend that "the socialist intelligentsia" must put its expertise at the disposal of the party committees and the soviets, thereby broadening elite and popular participation in decision making and administration. "And the more the intelligentsia succeeds in fulfilling this task, the greater becomes its moral and political authority in socialist society, its influence on the political decision making."[34] Hence, Soviet scientists, engineers, and managers are exhorted to contribute their skills and knowledge to the solution of centrally prescribed economic and sociopolitical tasks. In return, scientific and technical specialists, many of whom hold responsible positions in the party and in other major bureaucracies, are promised increased, but carefully circumscribed, power to help determine the basic purposes and nature of those tasks.

In short, Soviet writers imply that the inherently competitive nature of the relationship between political leaders and experts, and the obvious potential benefits of their close collaboration in formulating and implementing feasible national policies, enhance the responsibilities of the party in the era of the STR. This "contradiction" and its uncertain political and administrative implications may help to explain why key aspects of Soviet leadership theory, such as democratic centralism and party-state relations, lie so heavily in the normative realm, and why there are still many ambiguities regarding the evolving "leading" role of the CPSU in developed socialist society.

Conclusion

The Brezhnev administration has made sustained efforts to improve the central party organs' capacity to lead and manage society in the era of the scientific and technological revolution. To do so, the collective leadership has experimented with various ways to rationalize policy making and implementation. The current Soviet interpretation of rationality includes many elements. As David Holloway has observed, "It stresses the hierarchical nature of administrative structures; it points to the possibility of optimal decision making; it emphasizes the role of information flows in administration . . . and the uses of the new data processing technology; and it assumes that the self-regulation of Soviet society is to be achieved through the interaction of two subsystems: the controlling and the controlled."[35] The emerging Soviet views on societal guidance are founded on a modified cybernetic or "steering" model of government and place heavy emphasis on improving the efficiency or "technocratic rationality" of administrative processes.[36]

Whether these current Soviet perspectives are elements of continuity or change since Stalin is a highly subjective question. Did Khrushchev and Brezhnev alter the essence of Stalinism, or merely adapt fundamental characteristics of the Stalinist system to new conditions? One's answer depends heavily on one's view of the basic features of Stalinism and of the importance of certain undeniable post-Stalin changes in policy making and administration.[37]

On the one hand, it is difficult to conceive of Stalin agreeing with the contemporary Soviet analysts who acknowledge "the impossibility of decision making from the center on many, let alone all, questions,"[38] or who assert: "One of the basic criteria of the democratic nature of any political organization is its capacity for critical analysis of its own activity in order to bring to light its own mistakes and take effective measures to prevent them recurring in the future."[39] On the other hand, one must give serious consideration to the elements of secrecy, orthodoxy, arbitrariness, inertia, evasiveness, inefficiency, and mendacity—in short, the Stalinist legacy—in present-day Soviet politics. To be sure, Brezhnev and his colleagues have encouraged the bureaucratic, scientific-technical, and educational elites to contribute their expertise on policy-relevant questions, and they have actively supported the introduction of modern managerial techniques and information technology. Yet the present leaders continue to suppress criticism of Stalinism and its consequences, which greatly reduces the effectiveness of their renewed emphasis on political and administrative rationality and on the "democratic" side of democratic centralism in party and state activities. Traditional, but not necessarily Stalinist, bureaucratic patterns, such as strong personal loyalties and resistance to innovation, and communication pathologies, such as reluctance to transmit accurate information about shortcomings to one's superiors, also persist.[40]

Generally speaking, the top Soviet leaders' *perspectives* on policy making have undergone greater changes since Stalin than the actual *styles* of leadership and administration. As we have seen, the Politburo functioned in very different ways under Stalin, Khrushchev, and Brezhnev. But Khrushchev and Brezhnev, using quite different methods, were both frustrated by their inability to alter Stalinist attitudes and behavior in the major bureaucracies and economic production units. For example, Soviet factory managers strongly opposed the Kosygin economic reforms in 1965.[41] What this reveals is a persistent and perhaps increasing tension between national and local or departmental perspectives in the post-Stalin polity and society. It also suggests that there are growing pressures on the current Politburo to consider seriously major changes in institutional relationships and bureaucratic incentives, and to maintain highly unified positions on public policies.

The Stalin, Khrushchev, and Brezhnev "cults of personality" must be seen in this light. The glorification of the top leader is clearly an element of continuity in the style of Soviet politics after Lenin. But the content and functions of the Stalin, Khrushchev, and Brezhnev cults differ in important respects. Stalin sought to create the impression that he was an omniscient and omnipotent leader who possessed a deep understanding of the "laws" of historical development and of the contemporary relevance of the authoritarian politico-religious relationship between the tsars and the masses. Khrushchev portrayed himself as a man of the people who was eager to support practical initiatives and to meet individual citizens' material and cultural needs, rather than to promote conservative bureaucratic interests. Brezhnev has cultivated the image of an effective, responsible, businesslike executive who knows how to manage large organizations and complex forces, domestic and foreign.

Correspondingly, Stalin's cult served as a means of strengthening personal dictatorship and of mobilizing institutional and public support for the radical transformation of society "from above." Khrushchev's efforts to enhance his popularity among the masses were an attempt to circumvent collective leadership in the Presidium and to pressure party and state bureaucrats who opposed his reformist policies and his unsettling policy-making and administrative practices. The growing official adulation of Brezhnev is perhaps a collectively agreed-upon method of increasing the power of the Politburo vis-a-vis the major bureaucracies, of improving the effectiveness of group decision making by establishing the general secretary as "first among equals," and of producing a prestigious chief-of-state to further Soviet interests in contemporary international relations. The Brezhnev cult may be simply a partisan effort to strengthen the hand of one faction within the collective leadership. But the chief function of the public praise of Brezhnev is apparently to promote gradual or controlled change and to help manage or cope with powerful socioeconomic and scientific-technical forces "from below" and from abroad. Thus, Stalin, Khrushchev, and Brezhnev all developed distinctive cults and used them to pursue rather different goals, each deliberately enhancing the cult of Lenin and seeking to identify current aims and methods with Lenin's.

The sine qua non of developed socialism is the "scientific management" of Soviet society, of which the key element is "scientific leadership." Today there are at least three competing Soviet perspectives on scientific guidance—one that seeks to rationalize centralized party leadership through the use of new techniques, technology, and incentives; another which advocates reducing CPSU supervision over the major nonparty bureaucracies; and a third which calls for greater regional planning and decision making by party and state organs. The first is currently the dominant perspective. Yet there appears to be growing support among the Soviet bureaucratic elites for the second and third alternatives, or for some new kind of synthesis. For example, future national party officials may well feel compelled to experiment with further institutional decentralization—greater autonomy to the production associations and more effective regional planning, at the very least—in order to formulate and administer more feasible *centrally prescribed* goals and policies.

In summary, the Brezhnev collective leadership clearly recognizes that the "revolutionary" socioeconomic and scientific-technical changes since World War II are increasing the volume and interconnections of political decisions of one-party systems at a rate faster than Stalinist or Khrushchevian methods could handle. Current top CPSU officials acknowledge that the extraordinary complexity of modern production has increased the interdependence of Soviet institutions and society with one another and with those of other nations, and has made the Soviet polity more sensitive or permeable to powerful domestic and international economic forces. Furthermore, party leaders have recognized the need to be responsive to, but not to be dominated by, the rapid advances of modern science and technology, whose sociopolitical and ecological consequences are often difficult to anticipate and control. Soviet analysts stress that the STR has created opportunities, problems, and uncertainties which make necessary the closer "correlation" of domestic and foreign policy, "dynamic" and "comprehensive approaches" to planning and decision making, and more "creativity," "flexibility," and "integration" of specialist and public contributions to society. Thus, Brezhnev and his colleagues have cautiously encouraged social theorists and politician-administrators to do some fresh thinking about the theory and practice of leadership, and about the many questions concerning the present era "which have only been touched upon and await profound analysis."[42]

Because of the imminent transfer of power to a new generation of Soviet leaders, competing perspectives on policy making and administration are likely to play an especially important role in the politics of the USSR in the near future. Brezhnev has worked hard to establish stable and effective decision-making procedures, but an even more important part of his legacy may be his legitimation of serious theoretical and politicized discourse on the guidance and management of an industrialized society in a domestic and international environment characterized by complex interdependence. Like the policy processes of Stalin and Khrushchev, Brezhnev's collective leadership may have a considerable impact on his successors' views of power and authority. These evolving perspectives, intertwined with the struggle for position and influence after Brezhnev's departure and with some real policy alternatives and a serious need for organizational rationalization posed by the STR, could produce notable changes of *various* kinds in the structure and functioning of the Soviet polity.

Notes

1. E.g., Carl Friedrich and Zbigniew Brzezinski, *Totalitarian Dictatorship and Autocracy* (Cambridge, Mass.: Harvard University Press, 1956), especially pp. 9–10. Cf. Gregory Grossman, "The Solidary Society," in Gregory Grossman, ed., *Essays in Socialism and Planning in Honor of Carl Landauer* (Englewood Cliffs, N.J.: Prentice-Hall, 1970), pp. 184–211; T. H. Rigby, "Stalinism and the Mono-Organizational Society," in Robert C. Tucker, ed., *Stalinism: Essays in Historical Interpretation* (New York: W. W. Norton, 1977), pp. 53–76.

2. Andrei Sakharov, *Progress, Coexistence, and Intellectual Freedom* (New York: W. W. Norton, 1968), p. 55.

3. Merle Fainsod, *How Russia is Ruled* (2nd ed.; Cambridge, Mass.: Harvard University Press, 1963), p. 579. See also Jerry Hough and Merle Fainsod, *How the Soviet Union Is Governed* (Cambridge, Mass.: Harvard University Press, 1979), pp. 184–191.

4. Alfred Meyer, "The Soviet Political System," in Samuel Hendel and Randolph Braham, eds., *The USSR after 50 years: Promise and Reality* (New York: Alfred A. Knopf, 1967), p. 51. See also Alfred Meyer, "Authority in Communist Political Systems," in Lewis Edinger, ed., *Political Leadership in Industrialized Societies* (Huntington, N.Y.: Krieger Publishing Co., 1976), pp. 84–107.

5. Robert C. Tucker, *The Soviet Political Mind: Stalinism and Post-Stalin Change* (New York: W. W. Norton, 1971), p. 173 (emphasis in original).

6. Carl Linden, *Khrushchev and the Soviet Leadership, 1957–1964* (Baltimore: Johns Hopkins Press, 1966), p. 15.

7. See Leonard Schapiro, *The Communist Party of the Soviet Union* (2nd ed.; New York: Vintage, 1971), pp. 556 and passim.

8. George Breslauer, "Khrushchev Reconsidered," *Problems of Communism*, 25, 5 (September-October 1976), pp. 21–22. This essay contains a thoughtful discussion of Khrushchev's "populist" or non-Stalinist views on authority.

9. Richard Lowenthal, "The Revolution Withers Away," *Problems of Communism*, 14, 1 (January-February 1965), p. 11.

10. See, e.g., T. H. Rigby, "The Soviet Leadership: Towards a Self-Stabilizing Oligarchy?" *Soviet Studies*, 22, 2 (October 1970), pp. 167–191. Relatively few substantive policy choices were made in the first four to five years of Brezhnev's leadership, prompting some Western analysts to observe "degeneration" and "immobilism" in the Soviet political system. The most portentous and difficult decision—the intervention in Czechoslovakia—was a response to powerful external influences. The Kosygin economic reforms and the heightened repression of dissidents were also major decisions.

11. See, e.g., A. S. Akhiezer, *Nauchno-tekhnicheskaia revoliutsiia i nekotorye problemy proizvodstva i upravleniia* (Moscow: Nauka, 1974).

12. See, e.g., D. M. Gvishiani, *Organizatsiia i upravlenie* (2nd ed., Moscow: Nauka, 1972).

13. This last point is developed in George Breslauer, "On the Adaptability of Soviet Welfare-State Authoritarianism," in Karl Ryavec, ed., *Soviet Society and the Communist Party* (Amherst, Mass.: University of Massachusetts Press, 1978), pp. 7–8, 16–17.

14. Donald Barry and Harold Berman, "The Jurists," in H. Gordon Skilling and Franklyn Griffiths, eds., *Interest Groups in Soviet Politics* (Princeton: Princeton University Press, 1971), p. 293.

15. Paul Cocks, "The Policy Process and Bureaucratic Politics," in Paul Cocks, Robert Daniels, Nancy Heer, eds., *The Dynamics of Soviet Politics* (Cambridge, Mass.: Harvard University Press, 1977), pp. 156–178; Paul Cocks, "Retooling the Directed Society: Administrative Modernization and Developed Socialism," in Jan Triska and Paul Cocks, eds., *Political Development in Eastern Europe* (New York: Praeger, 1977), pp. 53–92.

16. Jerry Hough, "The Soviet System: Petrification or Pluralism?" *Problems of Communism*, 21, 2 (March-April 1972), pp. 32, 33, 37ff. See also Jerry Hough, *The Soviet Union and Social Science Theory* (Cambridge, Mass.: Harvard University Press, 1977); and Hough and Fainsod, *How the Soviet Union Is Governed*, especially pp. 518–555.

17. E.g., G. Kh. Shakhnazarov, *Sotsialisticheskaia demokratiia: nekotorye voprosy teorii* (2nd ed.; Moscow: Politizdat, 1974), pp. 112ff.; *Razvitoe sotsialisticheskoe obshchestvo: sushchnost', kriterii zrelosti, kritika revizionistskikh kontseptsii* (2nd ed.; Moscow: Mysl', 1975), pp. 272ff.; V. I. Kas'ianenko, *Razvitoi sotsializm: istoriografiia i metodologiia problemy* (Moscow: Mysl', 1976), pp. 173ff. On the STR, see Erik P. Hoffmann, "Soviet Views of the 'The Scientific-Technological Revolution,'" *World Politics*, 30, 4 (July 1978), pp. 615–644; Erik P. Hoffmann, "The 'Scientific Management' of Soviet Society," *Problems of Communism*, 26, 3 (May-June 1977), pp. 59–67; T. H. Rigby and R. F. Miller, *Political and Administrative Aspects of the Scientific and Technical Revolution* (Canberra: Australian National University, Occasional Paper No. 11, 1976).

18. *Sotsialisticheskoe obshchestvo* (Moscow: Politizdat, 1975), p. 6.

19. V. S. Shevtsov, *The CPSU and the Soviet State in Developed Socialist Society* (Moscow: Progress, 1978), p. 65.

20. *Razvitoe sotsialisticheskoe obshchestvo*, pp. 163–164.

21. P. A. Rodionov, "Leninskii stil'—vazhnoe uslovie uspekha partiinogo rukovodstva," in *Partiia v period razvitogo sotsialisticheskogo obshchestva* (Moscow: Politizdat, 1977), p. 74.

22. Leonid Brezhnev, "Central Committee Report," in *Current Soviet Policies VII* (Columbus, Ohio: American Association for the Advancement of Slavic Studies, 1976), pp. 24–25. Brezhnev added: "At times, after some decision or other is not fulfilled, a second, occasionally even a third, decision is adopted on the same question. In terms of content, they may seem rather good. But the point is that something should have already been done. The question automatically arises: Isn't a new decision on an old subject something like a concession, isn't it a manifestation of liberalism? Isn't the result a lowering of exactingness? We must put an end to this practice!"

23. *Razvitoe sotsialisticheskoe obshchestvo*, p. 164.

24. Iurii Volkov, "Vlianie nauchno-tekhnicheskaia revoliutsiia na sistemu vlasti i demokraticheskie uchrezhdeniia," in *Sotsiologiia i sovremmenost'* (Moscow: Nauka, 1977), vol. 1, p. 89.

25. Ibid.

26. The party consists of a central apparatus of more than 20 departments, regional and local secretariats, a national and 14 union republic central committees, 154 territory and province party committees, 10 regional party committees, 4,243 city and district party committees, and 390,000 primary party organizations.

27. P. N. Fedoseev, "Social Significance of the Scientific and Technological Revolution," in Ralf Dahrendorf et al., *Scientific-Technological Revolution: Social Aspects* (Beverly Hills, Calif.: Sage Publications, 1977), p. 103.

28. Ibid., pp. 103–105.

29. Shevtsov, pp. 63–64. CPSU leaders may have been attracted to Western "systems analysis" in the 1960s precisely because of its *lack* of emphasis on purposes and motivations other than those prescribed by the central political authorities. Systems analysis is now especially attractive to many Politburo and probably all Secretariat members, because it explains and justifies the need to increase party supervision over state organs and to reduce subsystem autonomy (or parochialism) in the major bureaucracies and society. That is, comprehensive approaches to policy making and administration necessitate the subordination of departmental and local interests to national party policy, within the framework of greater elite and mass participation in the formulation and implementation of many decisions. Also, some top Soviet officials may consider systems approaches to be a useful means of increasing the consistency and clarity of central directives, and of promoting unified national support for *their* policy preferences.

30. See Darrell Hammer, "Brezhnev and the Communist Party," *Soviet Union*, 2, 1 (1975), especially pp. 8–12.

31. Alec Nove, *The Soviet Economic System* (London: Allen and Unwin, 1977), pp. 60–84ff.

32. For detailed information on the character and difficulties of altering the highly bureaucratized Soviet political system, see Roy Medvedev, *On Socialist Democracy* (New York: W. W. Norton, 1975).

33. David Lane, *Politics and Society in the USSR* (New York: New York University Press, 1978), pp. 230.

34. E. M. Babosev, "Scientific and Technological Revolution: The Growing Role of Scientific and Technological Intelligentsia," a paper presented at the 8th World Congress of Sociology, Toronto, August 17–24, 1974, pp. 15–16.

35. David Holloway, "The Political Use of Scientific Models: The Cybernetic Model of Government in Soviet Social Science," in Lyndhurst Collins, ed., *The Use of Models in the Social Sciences* (London: Tavistock, 1976), pp. 116, 121.

36. Ibid., pp. 116–117ff. See also, e.g., Donald Schwartz, "Recent Soviet Adaptations of Systems Theory to Administrative Theory," *Journal of Comparative Administration*, 5, 2 (August 1973), pp. 233–264.

37. On the most essential or fundamental elements of the Soviet system, see especially John Hazard, *The Soviet System of Government* (4th ed., Chicago: University of Chicago Press, 1968), pp. 201–214ff.

38. V. G. Afanas'ev, *Pravda*, May 2, 1976, p. 2.

39. Shakhnazarov, pp. 72–73.

40. See Erik P. Hoffmann, "Technology, Values, and Political Power in the Soviet Union: Do Computers Matter?" in Frederic Fleron, ed., *Technology and Communist Culture: The Socio-Cultural Impact of Technology Under Socialism* (New York: Praeger, 1977), pp. 397–436; Erik P. Hoffmann, "Information Processing in the Communist Party of the Soviet Union: Recent Theory and Experience," in Ryavec, pp. 63–87; Erik P. Hoffmann, "Soviet Metapolicy: Information Processing in the Communist Party of the Soviet Union," *Journal of Comparative Administration*, 5, 2 (August 1973), pp. 200–232. Cf., e.g., Viktor Afanas'ev, *Sotsial'naia informatsiia i upravlenie obshchestvom* (Moscow: Politizdat, 1975).

41. See Karl Ryavec, *Implementation of Soviet Economic Reforms: Political, Organizational, and Social Processes* (New York: Praeger, 1975).

42. *Razvitoe sotsialisticheskoe obshchestvo*, p. 275.

De-Stalinization and Soviet Constitutionalism

Robert Sharlet

De-Stalinization, understood as the politics and process of post-Stalin reform, has been underway in the Soviet Union at varying tempos for the
past quarter of a century since the death of Stalin.[1] In 1977 de-Stalinization interacted with the older tradition of Soviet "constitutionalism"
(the tendency of Soviet leaders during the past sixty years periodically
to define and redefine the structure and functions of the Soviet system)
to produce the fourth Soviet constitution. The latest Soviet constitution continues the progressive Romanization of Soviet legal culture,
which was revived by Stalin in the mid-1930s, and the traditional Bolshevik ambivalence toward formal legalism.[2] Since de-Stalinization and
constitutionalism both originated from and are controlled by the party
leadership, their interaction in generating the new Soviet constitution
of 1977 was hardly coincidental.

The 1977 constitution, superseding the "Stalin constitution" of 1936,
provides an unusual opportunity to explore in broad outline the question of change and continuity in the Soviet system since Stalin. As the
most ambitious constitutional description of the shape and appearance
of the Soviet system to date, the new document represents a careful
distillation of six decades of Soviet rule and particularly of the developments of the post-Stalin period.[3] Consistent with Soviet political tradition, the new constitution is more important for its comprehensive
spirit than for its function as a fundamental legal document; it represents a broad, historical policy statement or, more precisely, a "metapolicy": a policy on policy making and implementation. However,
departing from past practice, the constitution of 1977 is intended as

a prescriptive and normative declaration, signaling the party's public commitments with regard to nearly all aspects of the Soviet system. In the absence of the Stalinist reliance on terror, and given the post-Stalin leadership's much greater dependence on public consensus requiring the maintenance of the elite's credibility, these constitutional commitments have not been made lightly.[4]

The 1977 constitution is clearly a metapolicy to be taken seriously. I will argue that the Brezhnev regime has attempted to use the document as a means for codifying both the scope and the limits of de-Stalinization.[5] De-Stalinization as post-Stalin reform has generally been taken to mean decentralization and the "diffusion of administrative authority"[6] as well as the "debureaucratization of leadership" and the "depoliticization of social initiative."[7] Among other things, this broad reform has resulted, in practical terms, in "increased operational independence" for middle-level political, administrative, and economic elites; solicitation and accommodation of expert advice in policy making; invigoration of secondary organizations and the stimulation of "mass participation in the implementation of official policy"; and a less coercive social policy toward the individual.[8] Within the context of contemporary Soviet constitutionalism, I will examine the consequences of de-Stalinization as it has affected policy making, policy implementation, and the relationship of the state and the individual in Soviet society.

De-Stalinization and Policy Making

The drafting, discussion, revision, and ratification of the 1977 constitution reflected the scope and limits of de-Stalinization as it affected the policy-making process. Comparing the "making" of the constitutions of 1936 and 1977, it is apparent that the high concentration of political resources and the severely restricted access to policy-making arenas that were characteristic of Stalinism have given way to a greater dispersal of political resources and far more access to these arenas in the post-Stalin period.[9] An obvious comparative measure is that the 1936 constitution was little more than a year and a half in the making, including the public discussion, while preparation of the 1977 constitution required nearly two decades of intermittent activity.

Certain similarities are evident in the constitution-making processes of 1936 and 1977. Stalin had formally chaired the constitutional commission, and his successors Khrushchev and Brezhnev later followed suit, underscoring that a new Soviet constitution was considered not merely a technical instrument of government but a policy statement of some magnitude. Secondly, the political symbolism of the two documents is similar; both followed periods of intensive internal change—Stalin's dramatic transformation of Soviet society and his successors' longer, slower, reformist reconstruction of the post-Stalin USSR. Finally, the ultimate products, the constitutions of 1936 and 1977, were intended to consolidate, institutionalize, and legitimate Stalinism and post-Stalin reform respectively.

As a result of the decentralization that marked the post-Stalin period, the current Soviet constitution passed through a relatively more open, factionalized policy-making process. The accommodation of diverse and conflicting interests was involved in the composition of this comprehensive and overarching policy document. Members of the Constitutional Commission were expected to represent their regional and/or institutional interests in the drafting and revision process.[10] Numerous institutional interest groups were consulted and the advice of a variety of academic specialists was solicited in the long drafting process. Over the years the main themes of the several drafts put forward were discussed repeatedly in the Politburo and by the Secretariat of the Central Committee, so that the final draft published for discussion in June 1977 was the product of national and regional elite, institutional, and even selective individual policy-making inputs.

The most decisive inputs, as one might expect, came from the national elite and from the legal profession, which was recruited to fill a staff role in the constitution-making process. As a former participant reported, specialized groups of legal scholars drafted the different sections of the prospective constitution under the guidance of a senior official of the USSR Ministry of Justice in the preliminary stage of the final drafting process. These draft sections, in turn, were forwarded to the Administrative Organs Department of the Secretariat of the party's Central Committee; at that point the department head exercised political supervision over the drafting process. Everything that eventually appeared in the published draft was subject to preliminary approval at this stage of the process.

Conversely, certain draft proposals were terminated at this level by political veto. For example, a group of reformist jurists drafted an article providing for the establishment of administrative tribunals in which citizens could bring suits against governmental actions as a kind of judicial oversight of administrative decisions. Another group of more conservative jurists opposed the limiting implications of this proposal and joined the issue as both groups lobbied the Ministry of Justice. Although there was significant ministerial opposition, Justice Minister V. I. Terebilov decided in favor of the reformist proposal, seeing in it the opportunity of augmenting the authority of his office. The draft article calling for an administrative tribunal was then sent to the Central Committee; here delegations representing the divided jurists presented arguments for and against the proposal to the head of the Secretariat's Administrative Organs Department, which is responsible for party supervision of the legal system. Ultimately, the department head rejected the reformist proposal on the grounds, among others, that administrative tribunals might afford dissidents additional leverage in their struggle against the Soviet regime.

Proposals that were approved by the Administrative Organs Department, presumably along with inputs from other departments of the Secretariat, were then passed on to Brezhnev's personal staff; at this point final decisions were taken and communicated to the Constitutional Commission for incorporation into the draft text.[11]

Typical groups active within the higher elite structure of the drafting process represented women, youth, and the union republics. Women as a group sought, but failed to obtain, inclusion of the right of part-time work in the "equal rights" clause of the draft constitution, but did manage to gain some concessions in the revised text.* The youth "lobby" succeeded in getting the age for electoral candidacy to all soviets lowered from twenty-three to eighteen in the draft, but had to compromise at twenty-one for election as a deputy to the USSR Supreme Soviet in the final, ratified document. In internal discussion of an earlier working version of the draft, union-republic elites collectively managed to beat back attempts to abolish the federal structure in favor of a unitary state, and eventually succeeded in influencing a greater constitutional diffusion of administrative authority to their advantage.[12]

The nationwide discussion of the draft constitution that took place in the media and within the system during the summer of 1977 provided additional opportunities for group participation in the constitution-making process. Although predictably the draft was not substantially revised during the fall ratification process, approximately 150 amendments and clarifications were made in 110 articles. The great majority of these changes occurred in response to organized group activity and mass participation during the discussion period.[13]

Some groups merely wished to join the roster of organizations and occupations given constitutional notice in the draft, such as the armed

*See the translation of the 1977 constitution in *Current Digest of the Soviet Press* (Vol. XXIX, No. 41, Nov. 9, 1977, pp. 1–13), reprinted in Robert Sharlet, *The New Soviet Constitution of 1977: Analysis and Text* (Brunswick, Ohio: King's Court, 1978), pp. 73–131.

forces, the people's controllers, and the state arbitrators. In fact, writers, television producers, and sports officials, among others, did manage to acquire the prestige of constitutional mention in the final text, but other groups such as peer justice personnel lobbied to no avail and had to settle for the lesser recognition of being referred to in a generally inclusive phrase in the revised preamble of the constitution.[14]

In addition to institutional group activity, a number of anomic groups surfaced in the public part of the discussion, usually in quest of more constitutional emphasis on their particular concerns. "Grass roots" law-and-order advocates used the discussion in the media to seek a tightening up of constitutionally imposed discipline on the individual generally. A small but prominent group of civil libertarians, for the most part ignored in the revision process, made numerous proposals for strengthening specific clauses intended to buffer the citizen from the state. Establishment scientists and a hybrid environmental coalition deluged the press with letters advocating more constitutional attention to their respective interests.[15]

By far the largest anomic group of individuals was barred from any significant visibility in the media discussion of the draft because of the political sensitivity of their demands. This was the vast "better-housing" lobby, which took advantage of the party-sponsored decision to swamp the Secretariat of the Constitutional Commission, where all communications eventually arrived, with the greatest volume of letters on a single issue—the housing clause. Most of the letter writers were ordinary Soviet citizens complaining of their housing conditions and seeking a larger or better apartment as their constitutional due. Brezhnev took no notice of this group in his report on the proposed revisions to the draft constitution.[16]

In spite of the partial opening up of the policy-making arenas in the post-Stalin USSR, the limits of de-Stalinization with regard to the policy-making process are evident in the opening chapter of the 1977 constitution. While the party is mentioned twice in rather narrow terms toward the end of the Stalin constitution,[17] Article 6 of the post-Stalin document proclaims *de jure* the party's *de facto* hegemony over domestic and foreign policy making. Moreover, nowhere in the new constitution (except perhaps in the right of the mass organizations to make formal legislative proposals) did the Brezhnev regime accord any constitutional legitimacy to the *de facto* process of interest-group articulation that has become almost a regular, though *sub rosa*, aspect of Soviet policy making, and which contributed substantially to the making of the 1977 constitution itself.

De-Stalinization and Policy Implementation

The scope and limits of de-Stalinization are also evident in the constitutionally mandated policy-implementation process, the means by which policy and legislation are executed in the Soviet system. Basic social processes that were highly flexible and manipulable under Stalin have now become more stable and institutionalized under his successors. Similarly, roles and structures that were loosely defined in the Stalinist system have progressively become more specialized and differentiated in the post-Stalin period. Basically, these developments reflect the steadily increasing tendency under both of Stalin's successors to define the system in the language of formal legality.[18]

Ironically, the roots of this phenomenon can be found in the 1936 constitution, which was designed to consolidate and codify the changes in the society and the system resulting from Stalin's "revolution from above." In particular, the Stalin constitution marked the reversal of then prevailing anti-juridical trends and mandated legal reforms and codification intended to replace the NEP codes still in force. Some progress was made in the late 1930s, especially in preparing new draft criminal and civil codes, but the reform program was abruptly abandoned on the eve of the war, leaving intact a Soviet "dual state" still heavily skewed in favor of the "prerogative" sphere, with its reliance on force and arbitrariness.[19]

The 1936 constitution was frequently amended over the years, but this was a patchwork process merely intended to keep the constitution, as a reflective instrument, generally consistent with changes in the structure of the administrative system. As a result, Stalin's heirs inherited a relatively shapeless system below the top, a system ideally suited to revolutionary breakthroughs, but less amenable to the more exacting tasks of managing and maintaining the growth of the large, complex Soviet industrial economy of the post-Stalin period. One consequence of the poorly defined lines of administrative authority and overlapping jurisdictions is the contemporary chaos of Soviet economic legislation, a labyrinth of thousands of often conflicting economic decisions and administrative decrees. Only in recent years have the codifiers begun to classify and compile them into an orderly body of law.[20]

Against this background, de-Stalinization of policy implementation has above all taken the form of greater rationalization of the administrative system through increasingly precise clarification of lines of authority, jurisdictional boundaries, and institutional relationships. Most of these changes have been accomplished through resumption of the aborted legal reforms of the late 1930s. In fact, it is necessary to say that de-Stalinization in general, and the de-Stalinization of policy implementation in particular, has relied very considerably on the post-Stalin legal reform process for its concretization and investiture into the rhythm of official life in the USSR. Like the de-Stalinization process itself, the legal reforms have unfolded slowly and with a good deal of deliberation and compromise between reformist and conservative jurists and politicians. The long list of completed reforms now stretches from the 1955 reform of the Procuracy to the contemporary reforms of technical legislation.[21]

New criminal and civil basic legislative principles (*osnovy*) and codes were completed by the early 1960s under Khrushchev. His successors continued the process by systematically reforming the legal framework for administrative behavior through codification or recodification of the legislation concerning the enterprise (1965); the collective farm (1969); land (1968); labor law (1970); public health (1969); education (1973); and, most recently, minerals (1975) and forestry (1977).[22] Only the administrative law reforms, which are in preparation, remain to complete the major parts of the post-Stalin legal reform program carried out under Khrushchev and Brezhnev.

As Brezhnev emphasized in his May 1977 report on the draft, the post-Stalin reform legislation was one of the major sources of the new constitution.[23] In fact, there is little in the 1977 constitution that is actually new. Many of the novel clauses for Soviet constitutional law merely express in compact form reforms already in existence. For instance, the core of the Kosygin-Liberman economic reforms can be found in Article 16, the basic enterprise clause; the participatory feature of the labor law reform has been given a prominent constitutional place in the clause on workers' collectives; and more routine aspects of the labor reforms have been included in the expanded right to work and right to rest clauses.[24]

In contrast, however, the constitutional chapters that concern the administrative system, in addition to reflecting existing practice, foreshadow the final codification of the reform of this central component of the implementation process. The relevant clauses bring greater constitutional order and clarity to the shape and dynamics of the administrative process of the Soviet system.

Comparing the 1936 constitution (amended through 1976) with the new constitution, it becomes apparent that the constitutional powers of the Council of Ministers have been considerably enlarged and are now defined in far greater detail. In general language, the 1936 document simply empowered the Council of Ministers to "coordinate and give direction" to the work of subordinate bodies and "take measures to carry out the national-economic plan."[25] In sharp contrast, the 1977 constitution spells out the increased responsibilities at some length in Article 131–1.

Similarly, the 1936 chapter on the local soviet was primarily devoted to a short description of its formal structure and a brief recitation of its functions, which included supervision over subordinate agencies, the protection of law and order and citizens' rights, local economic and cultural development, and the creation of the local budget.[26] As a reflection of the local soviet's enhanced status in the implementation chain, Articles 146 and 147 of the new constitution reflect the increased operational independence now granted to local administrative officials.

The de-Stalinization of policy implementation as reflected in the constitution of 1977 suggests that post-Stalin leaders, especially Brezhnev, have been steadily transforming the Stalinist system from a blunt instrument for rapid mobilization and directed development into a more sophisticated and better articulated party-led constitutional bureaucracy. However, the result falls far short of a *Rechtsstaat* in the full meaning of the term. While the party clause, Article 6, appears to bind subordinate party organizations to the norms of constitutional behavior, it stops well short of making the party a juridical entity. Still describing itself very much in the language of the Stalin constitution, the contemporary party of Lenin continues to retain its ultimate metajuridical or extra-constitutional status, thus reserving to itself an immense, unchecked residual power that potentially limits de-Stalinization of policy implementation in the USSR.

De-Stalinization and Citizen-State Relations

The key for assessing the accomplishments and limitations of de-Stalinization in the new constitution is the relationship it expresses between the state and the individual in post-Stalin Soviet society. The delineation between the political and social systems, or between the public and private spheres, which was indistinct during the Stalin period, leaving the citizen generally exposed and constantly vulnerable to state arbitrariness has since the early 1950s been more clearly indicated and significantly strengthened to the individual's advantage. As a consequence, the citizen of the post-Stalin USSR enjoys a greater degree of personal security than before and is now more reliably buffered against state action in general. This is the result of the post-Stalin leadership's shift from relatively greater dependence on rule by force to the more benign reliance on rule through law. In the spirit of the

Soviet dual state, this has meant a substantial expansion of the "normative" sphere of social regulation and the concomitant contraction of the prerogative sphere.[27]

However, de-Stalinization of citizen-state relations as reflected in the 1977 constitution presents a complex picture. Many of the contemporary citizen's rights and duties have been carried over from the 1936 constitution, a fact that can be attributed to Brezhnev's emphasis on the theme of constitutional continuity.[28] Nevertheless, there is both a qualitative and a quantitative difference between the two constitutions on the subject of rights and duties. The basic contract theory of rights for duties remains unaltered, but the scope of the rights granted and honored, and the number and diversity of duties required of the citizen, has changed dramatically from the 1936 to the 1977 document. The 1936 constitution contained the implied social contract between the state and the citizen. The state undertook certain obligations towards the citizen, who thereby received the corresponding rights; conversely, the receipt of these rights obligated the citizen to the state and to the performance of several enumerated constitutional duties such as safeguarding socialist property and defending the fatherland.

A similar compact has been built into the post-Stalin constitution, except that the present-day Soviet state has undertaken far more obligations vis-a-vis the citizen. These obligations are now honored more consistently in practice. In the same spirit, the citizen's general civic obligation has been particularized in a number of different constitutional clauses, with the added factor that many specific rights are qualified through direct linkage to the corresponding duty.

Thus, while the constitutional image of the citizen in Stalin's time was of a rhetorical defender of the newly established status quo of the 1930s, the citizen of the post-Stalin period is expected to play the multiple roles of the activist conservator of the "developed socialist society." In the process, however, the coercive approach to social policy of the Stalinist past has yielded to a more benevolent welfare state, in which the quality of life has noticeably improved. Nevertheless, just as the rights and duties section has been moved from the back of the 1936 constitution to the front of the 1977 constitution, the regime's expectations of the citizen have grown proportionately to the individual's notably enhanced status vis-a-vis the state.

In its sections on citizen-state relations, the constitution of 1977 essentially codifies and constitutionally legitimates the major post-Stalin legislative reforms in the socioeconomic, civil, and political position of the citizen, while creating a few new constitutional rights and several new duties. The spirit of post-Stalin citizen-state relations is conveyed in the opening clauses of the new constitution, which pledge the state to observe "socialist legality," a commitment reiterated in Article 57, and to promote the development of "socialist democracy." The individual, in turn, is accorded a wide array of corresponding rights and liberties, the enjoyment of which are explicitly linked with the general performance of his duties in keeping with the image of the citizen-conservator in this constitution. Thus, the individual's relationship to the state is framed within the two new "linkage" clauses (Articles 39 and 59), which form a tight nexus between the performance of one's civic duties and the realization of one's socioeconomic, civil, and participatory rights and liberties. In the following pages, I shall evaluate the scope and limits of de-Stalinization as defined by these rights and liberties in the new Soviet constitution of 1977.

Socioeconomic rights. The Soviet citizen is now constitutionally assured of more and stronger socioeconomic rights consistent with the more highly developed and affluent post-Stalin society; simultaneously, these new and improved benefits are accompanied by additional constitutional duties, obligations, and qualifications. The rights of "choice of occupation" and "type of employment" have been added to the 1936 right to work clause, but they are subject to the general requirement of prevailing public priorities in Article 40. A new right of housing has been introduced in Article 44, but it is conditional upon citizens "taking good care of housing allocated to them." "Freedom of scientific, technical, and artistic creation" is now guaranteed the Soviet citizen in Article 47, but only "in accordance with the goals of communist construction."

Collective farmers have now been included in the previous right-to-rest clause, although the length of their work time and leisure has been constitutionally delegated to the "collective farms," creating a potential constitutional inequity. Reflecting the post-Stalin health law reforms, the right to health care has been raised to full constitutional status in Article 42. However, the constitutional draftsmen apparently deferred full implementation by promising in other clauses future delivery of improved health services in both city and countryside. Similarly, the familiar right of education clause, Article 45, has been upgraded by the guarantee to the Soviet public of universal secondary education, while elsewhere in Article 25 this commitment seems to hinge on "improving the existing educational system." This qualification casts some doubt on the regime's ability to fulfill its educational promises in the near future.

Possibly the most important socioeconomic development in terms of improving the day-to-day quality of life for the Soviet population has been the constitutional reconfirmation and modest amplification of the former Stalinist clauses on the personal garden plot and private economic activity. However, the post-Stalin leadership has hedged in these traditional economic rights as well, through new injunctions to the citizen in Articles 13 and 17, respectively, to use his plot in a "rational" way and his entrepreneurial skills "in the interests of society."

Civil liberties. Probably no other part of the 1936 constitution was subject to more serious abuse under Stalin than the civil liberties clauses. As a result, the reduction of terror and a less coercive social policy became an immediate priority for his successors. During the decade after 1953 they successfully carried out the systematic reform of those branches of the legal system that most directly affected the implementation of existing civil liberties. In the process, they significantly strengthened and even broadened these individual rights, especially in connection with the criminal justice system.[29] The record of these reforms, as reflected in the 1977 constitution, while generally good, is a combination of constitutional advance and shortfall. Although the current constitution does not create any new civil liberties, the mere enumeration of the rights institutionalized in post-Stalin legislation and judicial practice serves to constitutionally legitimate this profoundly important aspect of de-Stalinization in citizen-state relations.

Except for slippage in one area, the constitution of 1977 registers the substantial improvements in personal security and procedural rights realized by the Soviet citizen in the post-Stalin period. The one regression occurs in the nearly verbatim transfer of the Stalin constitution's "bill of rights" clause into Article 50 of the new constitution.[30] This in itself is not surprising, but Stalin's successors have gone the next step in abridging the citizen's basic political liberties by now requiring the additional "test" that constitutionally approved exercise of free speech, press, and assembly must contribute to the *development* as well as to the strengthening of the Soviet system. However, the further curtailment of these rights has been partially offset by Article 58, the citizen's new constitutional right of complaint against official abuse and arbitrariness, including the right to resort to the courts for rectification of a wrong and even for financial compensation under certain circumstances.[31]

The contemporary constitutional record is generally better in the sections on procedural rights, which functionally constitutionalize the regime's prior legislative commitment to a qualified "due process." The opening clause in the section on the legal system implicitly but clearly signals the post-Stalin reconstruction and ascendancy of the normative over the prerogative sphere of regulation in Soviet society. In the language of Article 151, "justice is administered *solely* by the courts" (my emphasis), we find constitutional acknowledgement of the previous elimination in both fact and principle of the notorious "special boards," the principal Stalinist vehicle for the extra-judicial administration of justice.

Equally notable, a new "presumption of innocence" clause has been added to the citizen's list of constitutionally sanctioned procedural rights. A product of compromise from the debates on criminal procedural reforms in the late 1950s, Article 160 reads: "No one can be adjudged guilty of committing a crime and subjected to criminal punishment other than by the verdict of a court and in accordance with law." Though it falls far short of the explicit declaration advocated most recently in the discussion of the draft constitution by civil libertarians, the new clause nonetheless enshrines in constitutional form recognition that the Stalinist principle of the presumption of guilt has been abolished.[32]

Finally, the criminal defendant now enjoys a constitutionally enhanced right of defense housed in a separate clause, although it too is well short of the earlier admission of counsel sought by liberal jurists in the recent constitutional discussion and previously in the procedural reform debates.[33] Still, the improved post-Stalin right of defense is, in addition, constitutionally buttressed by the elevation to constitutional status of the defense bar and the institution of supplementary lay counsel.

Aside from constitutional strictures implying possible connections between such duties as assisting in the maintenance of law and order and the enjoyment of procedural rights among others, the most serious deficiency and limit on the de-Stalinization of civil liberties is that most of these rights are effectively denied to dissidents. Dissidents become "political cases," which are adjudicated, with full party complicity, in the spirit of a jurisprudence of political expediency.

The traditional Soviet ambivalence toward formal legality becomes fully apparent in the regime's treatment of its dissidents. The Marxian elasticity retained in the course of the post-1936 Romanization of Soviet legal culture comes to the fore in the form of *ad hoc* legality. In political cases, Soviet-style "due process" is arbitrarily violated, substantive legal rules are expediently interpreted, and relevant constitutional safeguards are essentially ignored. These practices reflect the spirit of the "reserve clause" of the Soviet "bill of rights," which implicitly denies civil rights to those citizens whose exercise of such rights are deemed by the authorities not to be in the national interest. Even more pernicious, and frequently below the level of public notice, is that many dissidents are repressed by means of administrative justice, for which no secure legal remedies are available in either Soviet legislation or the constitution, even to the non-dissident.[34]

Participatory rights. The final aspect of citizen-state relations is the relatively new constitutional domain of participatory rights. During the Stalin years, the reins of power and even the levers controlling implementation of policy were held tightly from above. Mass participation did occur within the policy-implementation process, but it was primarily a pro forma phenomenon, designed mainly to socialize and mobilize the population toward attainment of long-term party goals. In contrast, during the post-Stalin years both governmental and nongovernmental institutions below the all-union level have been invigorated. Subnational institutions are more actively involved in policy implementation, with commensurate growth of the authority of middle and local elites in the process.

Simultaneously, the opportunities for mass participation in facilitating policy execution through these revived organizational channels have been measurably increased. Although participation remains largely within the policy-implementation process, it now involves interpretation by subnational elites and application of national policy and legislation at various levels of the system through greater involvement of the mass public rather than by the rote behavior and pro forma involvement of the past. In brief, there is now more participatory opportunity within the Soviet system, and it is mapped out in the 1977 constitution through a network of clauses running thoughout the document.

The general public has been granted the constitutional right of discussion and referendum; mass social organizations have been revitalized in constitutional form; workers' collectives have been constitutionally activated; and citizens now enjoy the general right of participation, as well as the specific constitutional right to criticize governmental officials with impunity for shortcomings in their work.[35] Similarly, all levels of government below the all-union level have been delegated increased discretionary authority in the implementation process within their respective jurisdictions.

Finally, to ensure that the participatory channels remain open, the new constitution has made authority structures more accountable to their constituencies, at least in terms of apprising them about what their governmental representatives are doing on their behalf. People's deputies are now bound to report to their constituents on their public activity; local soviets must regularly inform the population of their decisions; and executive committees are expected to report periodically to their soviets as well as to the public at large. Greater responsiveness

and accountability is even required of local judges, individual administrators, and the national bureaucracy in general.[36]

In short, the post-Stalin constitutional commitment to more participation seems to be heading toward a party-controlled, elaborate system
of "checks and balances" within the administrative apparatus of the
Soviet system. As for the limits of de-Stalinization in this undertaking,
they are inherent in the recent constitutionalization of participation,
with its characteristic Brezhnevist preference for formal structures,
stable access routes, and professional inputs, over the former Khrushchevian participatory reliance on informal organizations, flexible
patterns of involvement, and greater popular spontaneity.[37]

Conclusion

Although the Soviet constitution of 1977 bears the discernible im-
prints of Lenin, Stalin, and Khrushchev, Brezhnev's "signature" is evident throughout the document as well, especially in what appears to be
his attempt finally to lay to rest Stalin's ghost as a divisive issue in Soviet
leadership politics.[38] Characteristically, his approach to this problem
has been to seek a pragmatic compromise. By constitutionalizing both
the accomplishments and the limits of de-Stalinization, Brezhnev has
presided over the creation of a centrist post-Stalin constitution that is
neither anti-Stalin nor neo-Stalinist.

However, it cannot be denied that the constitution of 1977 is a triumph for conservatism in Soviet politics. Although it may be a centrist
document in the letter, a tilt toward the conservative camp is evident
in its spirit. Since the constitution was drafted under the aegis of a
conservative leadership, it embodies the extremely cautious and tightly
controlled conception of change characteristic of the conservative reaction led by Brezhnev against Khrushchev's reformism since 1964.[39]
Fundamentally, the 1977 constitution is a document of the post-Stalin
and post-Khrushchev status quo. Stability is based on a "juridicized"
society[40] peopled by citizen-conservators constitutionally charged with
a host of duties. These duties range from "socially useful" employment
and the protection of public property to the preservation of culture
and the conservation of nature.[41]

Presumably one of Brezhnev's major purposes was to bring an authoritative and definitive end to de-Stalinization and what it came to
mean politically—the politics of reformism—by codifying its scope and
limits in the new constitution, the first since Stalin. It is characteristic
of Brezhnev and his conservative colleagues that they chose a legal
instrument to carry out this political purpose. Traditionally, law in

Soviet society has been considered a stabilizing force and has been philosophically and functionally juxtaposed to the dynamism of politics. In this sense, Soviet history can be viewed as a cycle of political change followed by consolidation through law. Hence, it is not surprising that the reform-to-reaction cycle of post-Stalin politics in the USSR has been defined in the basically conservative form of law. Whether or not this juridical framework will succeed in the long-term containment of the reformist impulse in Soviet society remains, of course, to be seen.

Beyond arresting reformist change, Brezhnev seems to want to leave behind the constitution of 1977 as a monument to his "administration," fixing in place the modernized, institutionalized, and now presumably stabilized Soviet system, if his eventual legacy remains intact.[42]

Notes

1. See Robert C. Tucker, "The Politics of Soviet De-Stalinization," in his *The Soviet Political Mind* (rev. ed., New York, 1971), pp. 173–202.
2. Constitutionalism with quotes is intended to deflect any implication of the Western conception of "limited" government. The previous constitutions were adopted in 1918, 1924, and 1936. See Robert Sharlet, "Stalinism and Soviet Legal Culture," in *Stalinism: Essays in Historical Interpretation*, ed. Robert C. Tucker (New York, 1977), pp. 155–79.
3. As with the previous constitutions, the new document is primarily reflective of the Soviet system. However, by design, the 1977 constitution also has programmatic content to a far greater extent than its predecessors. See Robert Sharlet, "The New Soviet Constitution," *Problems of Communism*, September-October 1977, pp. 5–8.
4. See Robert Sharlet, "Soviet Legal Policy-Making," in *Social System and Legal Process*, ed. Harry M. Johnson (San Francisco, 1978), pp. 209–29, esp. 212–14.
5. Following Tucker's analysis of Khrushchev's secret speech, I begin from the premise that de-Stalinization was a limited undertaking at the outset, essentially leaving unquestioned the transformational aspects of Stalin's "revolution from above" up to Kirov's assassination in 1934. See Tucker, "The Politics of De-Stalinization."
6. Ibid., p. 196.
7. See George W. Breslauer, "Khrushchev Reconsidered," in the present volume.
8. See Jeremy R. Azrael, "Varieties of De-Stalinization," in *Change in Communist Systems*, ed. Chalmers Johnson (Stanford, 1970), esp. p. 143.
9. This is an elaboration of my earlier writing on the defining characteristics of the Soviet political system. See, e.g. Robert Sharlet, "Law in the Political Development of a Communist System," in *The Behavioral Revolution and Communist Studies*, ed. Roger E. Kanet (New York, 1971), pp. 259–75.

10. See Robert Sharlet, *The New Soviet Constitution of 1977: Analysis and Text* (Brunswick, Ohio, 1978), p. 27.

11. Ibid., p. 58, note 10. The preceding account is based on comments made by Dr. Konstantin Simis, a former participant in this process, during a panel discussion, "The New Soviet Constitution and the Legal System," at the Tenth Annual Convention of the AAASS, Columbus, Ohio, October 14, 1978. An amplification of Dr. Simis's commentary will appear as a note in a special issue on law of *Soviet Union*, vol. 6, no. 2, 1979.

12. Information in the paragraph is based on interviews with Soviet jurists.

13. For an analysis of the amendments, see Sharlet, *The New Soviet Constitution of 1977*, pp. 45–55.

14. The phrase added to the preamble in the revision process is "communist social self-government," a familiar Khrushchevian phrase intended to include comrades' courts, people's voluntary patrols, and other institutions.

15. Sharlet, *The New Soviet Constitution of 1977*, pp. 24–45.

16. Interview with a Soviet jurist. For Brezhnev's report see *Current Digest of the Soviet Press*, October 26, 1977, pp. 1–7 and 13.

17. Constitution of 1936, Arts. 126 and 141.

18. See Sharlet, "Law in the Political Development of a Communist System." In Russian in the Soviet legal press, the tendency toward formal legality is expressed by the verb *uzakonit'*. The literal translation of this term is "to juridicize," in the context of defining party-directed relationships in formal legal terms. See Robert Sharlet, "Constitutional Implementation and the Juridicization of the Soviet System," in *Soviet Politics in the Brezhnev Era*, ed. Donald R. Kelley (New York, 1980).

19. See Ernst Fraenkel, *The Dual State: A Contribution to the Theory of Dictatorship*, tr. E. A. Shils (New York, 1941), esp. pp. 1–75, and my modification and application of his thesis and concept to the Soviet system in Sharlet, "Stalinism and Soviet Legal Culture," esp. pp. 155–58. To the best of my knowledge, Fraenkel's concept was first introduced into Soviet studies by Darrell P. Hammer, "Bureaucracy and the 'Rule of Law' in Soviet Society," in *The Soviet World in Flux*, ed. Mark W. Hopkins (Atlanta, 1967), pp. 87–110.

20. See Peter B. Maggs, "Improving the Legal Mechanisms for Economic Change," in *Soviet Law After Stalin: Part II—Social Engineering Through Law*, eds. Donald D. Barry, George Ginsburgs, and Peter B. Maggs (Alphen aan den Rijn, Netherlands, 1978), pp. 117–38. This is part of the larger task of compiling the *Svod zakonov SSSR* (Collection of USSR Laws), which is scheduled for completion in 1985.

21. On the Soviet legal reforms under Khrushchev and Brezhnev, see the three volumes under the series title *Soviet Law After Stalin*, ed. Donald D. Barry, George Ginsburgs, and Peter B. Maggs. The three volumes are: Part I, *The Citizen and the State in Contemporary Soviet Law* (Leiden, 1977); Part II, *Social Engineering Through Law*; and Part III, *Soviet Institutions and the Administration of Law* (Alphen aan den Rijn, Netherlands, 1979).

22. The basic legislative principles of Soviet land, labor, public health, and education law are translated in *Fundamentals of Legislation of the USSR and the Union Republics* (Moscow, 1974).

23. See Brezhnev's May report in *Current Digest of the Soviet Press*, July 6, 1977, pp. 6–10.

24. For the legislative antecedent of Art. 8, see *Fundamentals of Legislation of the USSR*, p. 125, Art. 97.
25. See the 1936 constitution, Art. 68.
26. Ibid., Art. 97.
27. See Robert Sharlet, "Legal Policy Under Khrushchev and Brezhnev: Continuity and Change," in Barry et al., *Soviet Law After Stalin*: Part II, *Social Engineering Through Law*, pp. 319–30.
28. Brezhnev's May 1977 report.
29. See Harold J. Berman's "Introduction" to Harold J. Berman and James W. Spindler, eds., *Soviet Criminal Law and Procedure: The RSFSR Codes* (2nd ed., Cambridge, Mass., 1972), pp. 3–124; and Christopher Osakwe, "Due Process of Law Under Contemporary Soviet Criminal Procedure," *Tulane Law Review*, 50 (January 1976), pp. 266–317.
30. See the 1936 constitution, Art. 125.
31. This is not new in post-Stalin reform legislation. See Donald D. Barry, "The Soviet Union," in *Governmental Tort Liability in the Soviet Union, Bulgaria . . . Yugoslavia*, ed. Donald D. Barry (Leiden, 1970), pp. 54–70. For current proposals to expand the right of complaint, see Sharlet, "Constitutional Implementation and the Juridicization of the Soviet System."
32. Sharlet, *The New Soviet Constitution of 1977*, pp. 38–44.
33. Ibid. See also John Gorgone, "Soviet Jurists in the Legislative Arena: The Reform of Criminal Procedure, 1956–1958," *Soviet Union* (1976), vol. 3, no. 1, pp. 1–35. See the 1977 constitution, Art. 158.
34. See Robert Sharlet, "Dissent and Repression in the Soviet Union," *Current History* (October 1977), pp. 112–117 and 130; and Robert Sharlet, "Dissent and Repression in the Soviet Union and Eastern Europe: Changing Patterns Since Khrushchev," *International Journal* (1978), 32, 4, pp. 763–795. Although *ad hoc* legality continues, a major difference in the post-Stalin period is that the dissident-defendant actually appears in court, usually pleads innocent to the political charges, customarily defends himself vigorously, and is sometimes ably represented by a skilled lawyer as well. The paradox of post-Stalin political justice is that the victim routinely uses Soviet law in his defense. As the regime proceeds from political motives to prosecute him, the dissident responds with a legalistic defense. In instances of administrative abuse (e.g., arbitrary eviction or dismissal), legalism is less effective, so dissidents tend to rely on publicity abroad as a "defense." In contrast, the nondissident subjected to administrative arbitrariness has traditionally been able to resort to the potential political remedy of turning to the local party organization for possible corrective action. Since 1977 the average citizen's narrowly defined right to seek judicial review of administrative actions has been enhanced and augmented in Article 58 of the constitution. Soviet jurists are currently discussing the implementation of this clause, and their proposals for judicial review include a wide range of administrative actions affecting the individual's civil and economic rights. See above, page 103 and note 31.
35. See 1977 constitution, Arts. 5, 7, 8, 48, and 49, respectively.
36. See ibid., Arts. 107, 94, 149, 152, 49, and 125, respectively.
37. Art. 102, the "voters' mandate" clause, was the one new article added to the draft in the revision process. It is exemplary of Brezhnev's approach to participation. For a comparison of Khrushchev and Brezhnev, on this

subject, see Breslauer, "Khrushchev Reconsidered," esp. p. 19ff.; and Breslauer's "On the Adaptability of Welfare-State Authoritarianism in the USSR," in *The Communist Party and Soviet Society*, ed. Karl W. Ryavec (Amherst, Mass., 1978), pp. 3–25.

38. No doubt this was related to the Stalin centenary in 1979.

39. See Stephen F. Cohen, "The Friends and Foes of Change: Reformism and Conservatism in the Soviet Union," in the present volume.

40. In commenting on an earlier version of this chapter, Professor Peter B. Maggs observed that the new constitution affords greater juridical recognition and protection to the personal property (e.g., savings accounts, dachas, and cooperative apartments) of the propertied stratum of the population in contrast to Khrushchev's previous hostility toward these property relationships. See Arts. 13 and 17, and generally on the juridicized society see Sharlet, "Constitutional Implementation and the Juridicization of the Soviet System."

41. See the 1977 constitution, Arts. 14, 60, 61, 12, 67, and 68, respectively.

42. John N. Hazard, "A Constitution for 'Developed Socialism,'" in *Soviet Law After Stalin*: Part II, *Social Engineering Through Law*, eds. Barry et al., pp. 1–33, esp. pp. 28–29.

Part Two / THE ECONOMY

Soviet Economic Planning and Performance

Arthur W. Wright

I. Introduction

The late 1970s are not likely to fix any milestones or leave any high-water marks on the economic history of the USSR. Still, they are a convenient and appropriate time for a retrospective view of Soviet economic achievements and problems since Stalin. The quarter century of the post-Stalin era is now equal in length to the Stalin era itself. Moreover, the Soviets themselves are not celebrating any significant anniversaries; thus our chances of achieving a balanced perspective on the period since Stalin are enhanced. How do the economic policies of Stalin's successors compare with those of the earlier, turbulent, formative period? And how do their accomplishments stack up against those of the man who left his mark on so many aspects of Soviet society?

Implicit in the theme of this book is the hypothesis that the death of Stalin caused fundamental changes in the USSR. Such an hypothesis is not new in the economics literature. J. M. Montias, for instance, has pointed out that elaborate models of economic growth, which otherwise capture much of Soviet economic history since 1928 (and East European economic history since 1945), cannot explain the impact of Stalin's death on communist economic policies and institutions.[1] Similarly, the hypothesis underlies Alexander Gerschenkron's remark that a "good deal of Soviet economic history could be written in terms of answers to the question, 'Why did Stalin change his mind?' "[2] With Stalin no longer around to make up his mind, let alone change it, things were bound to be different. And Stanley H. Cohn has contrasted the stark, "quixotic" Stalin era with the "bountiful post-Stalin years."[3]

An alternative hypothesis holds that underlying economic conditions dominate personalities in determining economic strategies and policies, at least over the observed or even the likely range of Soviet political institutions. One should not, of course, play down Stalin's unique dictatorial powers, but they should be seen, in this view, as having largely short-term significance in the long-term sweep of Soviet economic history. Thus, Stalin's death might be likened to the resignation of President Nixon in 1974: it brought welcome relief from a disturbing time of troubles but nonetheless left the basic system intact.

In this chapter we explore the issues raised by these rival hypotheses, with emphasis on two particular aspects of the post-Stalin Soviet economy. The first aspect is the so-called reforms of planning and management—their origins, their intended goals, and their results to date. The second is the performance of the Soviet economy in the past quarter century. We conclude with an assessment of the two rival hypotheses about Stalin's economic role and a look at the Soviet economy's prospects for the future.

II. The Stalin Era in Brief Perspective

The outstanding feature of the Soviet economy during the Stalin era is the industrialization drive and the institutions and policies that accompanied it. The year 1928 saw the first steps in a massive effort to transform the Soviet economy—then a large peasant agricultural sector with a modest industrial base appended—into a world-scale industrial power, within the space of a few short years. The strategy for effecting the transformation involved heavy investment and reinvestment in the means of production. To implement the strategy, Stalin adopted a "combination of ancient measures of oppression with modern technology and organization."[4] The oppression that harked back to Petrine and other tsarist practices included the collectivization of agriculture; stringent forced-saving measures; and a variety of forms of forced labor. The modern technology was channeled (along with capital and labor resources) into a few favored branches of heavy industry—steel making and its suppliers, machine building, electric power capacity, construction—while other sectors of the economy made do with what they could get, when they could get it. The modern organization consisted of what we now call "command planning," which centralized resource allocation in a government bureaucracy on a scale and with a scope that were unprecedented, even in wartime.

The Soviet economy was,[5] of course, centralized in the sense of ownership; the state claimed the rights to the means of production and appropriated the returns associated with those rights. Through Stalinist command planning, however, the Soviet economy was also centralized in the sense of operating authority. Both in plan formulation (to which the term "planning" usually refers in the context of a market economy) and in plan implementation, the Soviet government sought to control the detailed operating decisions that governed the uses of the means of production. The instrument of control was a bureaucracy of planners, accountants, statisticians, and auditors that translated central economic decisions into rules and instructions ("commands") to individual firms and farms. Centralization and bureaucracy combined to allocate resources through an aggregate economic plan that was, *ex ante* as well as *ex post*, identically equal to the sum of its parts.[6] Realizing ("fulfilling") the plan presented an intricate administrative task in which there was at best only a small tolerance for error in any component of the plan. The urgency of Stalinist economic goals considerably complicated that task.

Formulating the annual plan (it, not the celebrated five-year plan, was the basic operating unit of Stalinist command planning) involved exchanges of information between the central planners and the operating enterprises, via the bureaucracy. In the process known as "plan/counterplan," the center transmitted its production goals for key commodities down the chain of command, and the enterprises transmitted their estimated input requirements for meeting the goals back up the chain. Overall plan consistency was worked out iteratively, with the center having the final say—ending the process by transmitting the final plan to the enterprises.

Implementing the annual plan, once it had been formulated, was a matter of getting the enterprises to do what the center wanted—that is, to fulfill the plan. That meant spelling out the plan in intricate detail, first prescribing flows of vast numbers of inputs and outputs, by origin and destination, and then providing the authorizations ("documentation") for those flows to occur. A carrot-and-stick approach was used to encourage enterprises to fulfill their plans. Money rewards of managers and workers were tied to an array of "success indicators" that, on the surface, were bewilderingly complex. In principle, all the indicators were supposed to be met; in practice, however, only a small subset of them could be met, forcing the assignment of tacit priorities. The resulting ordering of priorities can be described as lexicographic, with the target for gross output assigned the letter "A" position; thus, gross output took precedence over any of its rival plan targets. If the carrot of the success indicators was not persuasive enough, there was also the stick of direct controls—bureaucratic, statistical, and financial —on enterprise behavior.

Command planning gave the Soviet leadership the extensive control over resource allocation required for their ambitious industrialization drive. It was not, however, without its costs. For one, the interlocking character of the plans made their success highly sensitive to errors either in formulating or in executing the plans. For another, the planning mechanism was relatively expensive just to operate, and it tended to become more so as industrial development proceeded—that is, as the planning targets themselves were achieved. The reason, as Robert W. Campbell has pointed out,[7] is the dysfunctions that emerge when hierarchical directives interact with nonhierarchical flows of real inputs and outputs. As modern industrialization occurs, those flows grow increasingly complex. In consequence, it becomes necessary to devote more and more resources to the planning process if the planners are not to lose the control that is the raison d'être of the process in the first place. We shall return to this point in the next section, which deals with the "reforms" of Stalinist command planning introduced in the mid-1960s.

How well did Stalin succeed with his strategy of economic development and its supporting institutions and policies? If we focus on the roughly fifteen years when the USSR was not preparing for, waging, or recovering from World War II, the strides made in the growth of heavy industrial output were impressive indeed. In Gerschenkron's phrase,[8] those strides were "unprecedented in the history of modern industrialization in Russia." They were also comparable to the most impressive bursts of modern economic growth in any country. Total industrial output (including consumer goods) grew at better than 10 percent a year (on the average) during the first two five-year plans (1928–32 and 1933–37) and again in the first half of the 1950s. For individual heavy industrial goods, the average annual growth rates were much higher than 10 percent during most of the 1930s and attained at least that level or better in the early 1950s.[9]

The obverse aspect of the impressive Soviet industrial growth record under Stalin was its heavy cost. The toll of human misery exacted during collectivization, the purges, and the repression of the early 1950s needs no detailed rehearsal. (Nor shall the issue of whether that toll, or indeed Stalin himself, was "necessary" tempt us away from the business at hand.) More mundane but no less telling is the course of real wages and per capita income between 1928 and 1953. According to the received estimates of Janet Chapman, real wages declined by almost half during the 1930s.[10] Naum Jasny estimated that the real per capita income of wage-earners declined by some 25 percent over the entire Stalin era; for the rural population the decline was about 40 percent.[11]

While it is exceedingly difficult to test it directly against quantitative evidence, the proposition that the Stalinist model was wasteful, or economically inefficient, would meet with broad agreement among economists who study the Soviet economy. Thus from 1928 to 1953 the Soviet economy operated well off the cost curve: more industrial growth could have been achieved at the same cost, or the same growth could have been attained at lower cost. A related question is whether Russia would have or could have achieved rapid modern economic growth without the October Revolution or under a different Soviet growth strategy. Again, received doctrine is that after World War I Russia under practically any regime would have been able to continue at least the broad pattern of growth that began in the 1890s.[12] In a recent study, Mischa Gisser and Paul Jonas have used econometric and simulation techniques to compare a "Bukharinesque" growth strategy, stressing agriculture and decentralized resource allocation, with the Stalinist strategy; they conclude that the Bukharinesque model would have outperformed the Stalinist model by achieving either greater total industrial growth with the actual costs or lower costs with the growth actually realized.[13]

III. The "Economic Reforms"

"De-Stalinization" was not extended to the Soviet economic system until 1965: the Stalinist central planning mechanism remained intact in all essential respects not only during the Malenkov-Bulganin-Khrushchev transition (1953–57) but also throughout the Khrushchev era (1957–64). The reorganization of production ministries along regional lines that accompanied Khrushchev's ascendancy in 1957 altered none of the "basic institutions and operating principles of the Soviet economic system," nor did it involve "decentralization" in any useful allocative sense.[14] Thus a dozen years elapsed between the death of Stalin and the first serious attempt to modify the planning mechanism developed during his reign. That does not mean, however, that there is no link between the event of his death and the reforms of Soviet planning and management of the late 1960s. In fact, there are two such links, both (as might be expected) having to do with politics as well as economics.

First, none of Stalin's successors became the despot he had been. Despite loose references in the Western press to the "cult of personality" and despite the repression of civil liberties, both Khrushchev and Brezhnev have been products of a relatively open (if still one-party) political process, with the attendant constraints on policies and programs. In particular, like politicians elsewhere, the post-Stalin leaders have had to deliver results, including the articulation and resolution of economic problems, in order to build and maintain governing constituencies within the Communist Party.[15] According to one common view, the consequent politicking caused party leaders to tackle such problems as agriculture and consumer goods production while simultaneously continuing to pursue "Stalinist" goals for heavy industry.[16] The frustrations that emerged from those attempts in the late 1950s and early 1960s are thought to have sparked interest in changing the system of planning and management.

Second, the death of Stalin brought with it the eventual relaxation of curbs on public discussion of economic policy issues. The USSR had experienced economic problems before 1953. Now, especially after Khrushchev gained a firm political foothold in 1957, it became possible to mention such problems openly and, more important, to criticize the system as one source of the problems and to propose alternatives— within rather well-defined bounds, of course. An ancillary development was the "rediscovery" of (in fact, the resumption of nonclandestine work on) economic analysis that focused on optimal choice and not on the application of Marxian categories under socialism. Thus a vigorous discussion of the defects of Stalinist command planning, and of possible remedies for them, began in the early 1960s.

The familiar list of the defects of Stalinist planning is a long one.[17] The inherent incompatibility between "vertical" ministries and commands, on the one hand, and "horizontal" input or output flows, on the other, led to longer and longer lines of communication as the economy grew in size and complexity. Interministerial coordinating committees were set up to shorten those lines, but they made planning more cumbersome. At the enterprise level, the distortions of effective incentives (relative to the planners' intentions) were legion. Enterprise managers sought lower, not higher, plan targets and deliberately avoided exceeding them by very much, for fear of being saddled with more challenging targets in the future. Managers also resisted innovation, either in the products they produced or in the techniques they used in production: anything new was uncertain and hence increased the chances of underfulfilling the gross-output plan. The lexicographic priority assigned to increasing output weakened the incentive to hold down costs; wasteful use of inputs could easily be concealed in the mass of detail that the central authorities had to monitor. The aggregation required to reduce detail in measuring performance distorted output mixes and interfered with the meshing of supplies and demands, because the weights used did not reflect the relative scarcities implicit in the aggregate plan.

An additional deficiency of Soviet planning in the early 1960s was Khrushchevian, not Stalinist in origin—namely, the regional "councils of the national economy" (*sovnarkhozy*, in the Russian abbreviation) introduced in mid-1957.[18] Originally billed as a "reform" of Stalinist planning but motivated in no small part by political considerations as well, the sovnarkhoz system began to creak badly soon after it was set up. Aptly characterized as "ramshackle,"[19] this experiment in reorganization had created a "near-chaotic situation" by the end of its tenure[20] and, overall, represented a distinct failure.[21]

The debate on planning and management in the first half of the 1960s was lively and wide ranging. At the risk of oversimplifying a discussion that at many points spilled over into broader issues,[22] it is possible to identify a "liberal" camp and a "conservative" camp in the debate, with a middle-of-the-road position in between. The liberals advocated restructuring the planning system to reduce the degree of detail at the center, to increase the autonomy of operating enterprises, and to simplify the entire vertical structure of plan formulation and implementation. At the fringe of the liberal position, arguments were advanced that, when fully spelled out, implied the dismantling of most of the command-planning apparatus—including the primacy of "planners' preferences." The conservatives grudgingly conceded the need for some change in the Stalinist planning mechanism, but only of minor degree; in effect, theirs was the traditional view, in which "self-criticism" was necessary to improve the status quo.

The middle-of-the-road view was that any changes in planning and management should focus on the question of enterprise success indicators. This view, the most celebrated adherent of which was Evsei G. Liberman, appeared to have the tacit endorsement of the Soviet leadership. The essence of Liberman's proposal, first articulated in an article in *Pravda* in 1962[23] and developed more fully in a subsequent monograph,[24] was the replacement of gross output by a rate of profit on total assets as the main enterprise success indicator. Liberman also proposed a number of supporting changes, but the important point was that the basic framework of Soviet central planning would remain intact under his proposal: only selected parts of the inner workings would have to be changed materially.

A different split between the parties to the debate distinguished "decentralizers" and "recentralizers" or "computerizers."[25] The former group included the liberals cited earlier and most of those in the middle of the road—those, that is, who espoused the modification of central controls to one degree or another. The latter group, unlike those we called the conservatives, also favored changes in Soviet planning and management but in the opposite direction. The source of the problems with planning and management, in the computerizers' view, was not too much centralization but too little—in particular, the inability of the center to carry it off properly. Under the Stalinist system, it was necessary to resort to some decentralization—whether explicit (e.g., in labor markets or the collective-farm markets) or implicit (e.g., the toleration of expediters who could secure chronically short inputs through extra-legal channels)—just to enable the economy to function. Such decentralization, however, meant the loss of central control and hence the misallocation of resources relative to the center's wishes. The solution advanced by the computerizers was to exploit modern mathematical progamming and computational techniques to permit the central planners to run the Soviet economy more tightly. It should be noted, in passing, that not all Soviet mathematical modelers endorsed the computerizers' position; many of them in fact wanted to use modeling techniques to enhance the decentralization of planning and management.

The transition from debate to the actual implementation of reforms began in the autumn of 1965, when Premier Alexei Kosygin outlined a proposed reform program to a plenary session of the Central Committee of the Soviet Communist Party.[26] The Kosygin program first of all abolished the sovnarkhozy and established a ministerial economic structure that resembled in essential respects the one in effect through 1957. (By this time, Nikita Khrushchev was no longer around to defend the product of his first major initiative after his Central Committee victory of June 1957.) Other than this structural change (which was not all that drastic), the Kosygin program focused on changes in planning and control at the enterprise level.

The 1965 reforms gave enterprises more latitude in deciding how to employ their resources. At the same time, the incentives and constraints they faced were revamped to try to induce the managers to use their new latitude to greater advantage—defined, of course, in terms of plan goals and targets. There were to be fewer success indicators than before,[27] and the all-important output indicator was to be measured in terms of realized deliveries or "sales," not the gross value of output at the plant gate as before. Enterprises were granted more say in determining input use, although the true significance of this change was effectively reduced by the impact of centrally determined norms and prices.[28] Incentives were redefined in terms of three special enterprise funds, based in part on the rate of profit on assets (*à la* Liberman) and on increases in total profits or sales over the year before. One of the funds could be used by enterprises for investments of their own choosing; here again, however, central controls constrained the degree of effective enterprise choice.[29] A minor breakthrough in cost accountability was the levying of a percentage charge (6 percent, with some exceptions) on the undepreciated value of assets. Finally, an effort was made to provide incentives to seek more ambitious plans, reversing the earlier pattern, by having enterprise bonuses vary in proportion to the *target* profit rate.[30]

Two other aspects of the Kosygin reform program should be mentioned. First, the use of sales and profits in constructing enterprise success indicators, coupled with the desire to do away with budget subsidies to enterprises (in the interests of greater autonomy), placed a heavier allocative burden than previously on the prices used in interindustry transactions. As a result, the reforms had to include a revision of the industrial wholesale price structure; an ambitious, economy-wide price reform was introduced in mid-1967. Second, the 1965 program envisioned that the amalgamation of enterprises into large associations, begun in the early 1960s, would continue and even accelerate.[31] The benefits of amalgamation were thought to extend to research-and-development as well as to line production enterprises, and the eventual goal was to place whole industrial ministeries on a *khozraschet* (financial accountability) basis. The inclusion of the amalgamation measures in a reform program that purportedly gave enterprises more autonomy from central control and interference seems more than paradoxical.[32]

The introduction of the reforms was accompanied by considerable political fanfare and exhortation.[33] Expectations were high, in spite of the past Soviet record of unfulfilled hopes for tinkering with economic institutions and policies.[34] Yet assessments by Western observers are virtually unanimous that the impact of the "reforms" has been quite modest—enough so to warrant enclosing the word in quotes.[35] Why should this have happened? We can answer this question both descriptively and analytically.

To recast an old aphorism, the road to reform of Soviet planning and management turned out to be paved with good intentions. In Eugene Zaleski's words, "the principal texts on the reforms of October 1965 contain numerous declarations of intentions to promote liberalization."[36] Yet while the supporting rhetoric may have been borrowed from the liberal camp in the debate of the early 1960s, the Kosygin program itself was adapted from the middle-of-the-road positions of

Liberman and others. What is more, neither the design of the reforms nor their implementation was bold or imaginative enough to accomplish the stated purposes, even stripped of public-relations excess.

Writing in 1967, two years after Kosygin's speech to the Central Committee, Campbell argued that "the reform measures so far introduced constitute neither a coherent system, nor a sufficient departure from the norms and behavior of the command economy to really solve the ills that prompted the reforms."[37] Some four years later, Alec Nove could corroborate Campbell's conjecture, citing dysfunctions under the reforms and reversions to all too familiar practices from an earlier era. In a paper bearing the subtitle, "The Reform That Never Was," Nove concluded that the "deficiencies or contradictions must be seen as the *consequences of non-reform*" (his emphasis).[38] The 1967 revisions (not "reforms") of prices had not been extensive enough to provide the scarcity signals, or the cash flow to enterprises, required to achieve the intended autonomy of industrial enterprises. As a result, the old, comfortable practice of centrally allocating goods in chronic excess demand had been maintained and even strengthened. The modifications of contract law and especially enforcement required to permit enterprises to deal directly with one another had not emerged;[39] hence the old system of centrally stipulating deliveries from given producers to designated customers still survived.[40]

As a description of the course of the reforms since 1965, the following epigram by Deborah Milenkovitch is apt: "The reforms were less liberal than the discussion [of the early sixties]; the implementation was cautious; and the key elements of the reforms were ultimately jettisoned."[41]

What can we say about why the good intentions of Soviet reformers came to so little? Possible reasons include timorousness, stupidity, and cupidity on the part of Soviet leaders. The first reason is difficult to believe, even at two or three political generations' remove from Stalin. The second reason is difficult to measure and thus, as a null hypothesis, unsportsmanlike. The third is difficult to deny (in any society) but does not satisfy as a causal factor *at the margin*: vested interests exist in any halfway stable society, and social change must always overcome (or compensate) them.[42]

A more satisfactory explanation, especially for an economist, can be found in certain propositions, now more or less received doctrine, about command-planning institutions and the way they interact with other kinds of allocative devices. At the core of these propositions for present purposes is Gregory Grossman's point that a command system is "locally stable" on a continuum from command to market institutions.[43]

Especially under taut resource commitments (which, Grossman argues, was the main reason the Soviets adopted command planning in the first place), the introduction of market-type arrangements at selected points will worsen, not improve, economic performance. Further, the effects will be the more adverse, the less adequate are the incentives in the command arrangements (e.g., in rewarding added effort) to begin with. Thus, the central authorities, *out of enlightened self-interest*, must oppose the effects of limited decentralization and, in the end, the decentralization itself as well.[44]

A corollary of Grossman's argument worth noting is that market institutions can replace command institutions, provided the replacement is on a large enough scale (as, for example, in Yugoslavia). The cautious implementation of the Soviet reforms, then, can be explained by an understandable reluctance of the present Soviet leadership to introduce enough decentralization to overcome the dysfunctional effects of combining it with command planning. "Enough" here would of course imply relinquishing the central control over resource allocation that command planning provides.

It is possible to extend the present line of argument a short step further. It is a fact that Soviet-type central planning has "problems" that derive from its inherently awkward, cumbersome mode of operation. Such problems will be a constant source of temptation to attempt to rationalize the system of planning and management by decentralizing —increasing enterprise autonomy, reducing the number of plan success indicators, tinkering with the price structure, and other devices familiar from the experience of the 1965 reforms. Coupled with Grossman's analysis, this point suggests that we should expect oscillations in Soviet planning institutions—relatively brief, desultory flirtations with "reforms," followed by gradual but inexorable retrenchments towards a more straightforwardly centralized system. This hypothesis is consistent with the modern view of Soviet one-party politics in which would-be leaders are ever watchful for substantive issues with which to appeal to party cadres for support. That improvement in planning and management is such an issue is suggested by the slogan for the tenth five-year plan (1976–80): the "Plan for Quality and Efficiency."

IV. Soviet Economic Performance since Stalin

The subject of this section is vast. Alternatively, it is a broad array of subjects grouped loosely under the heading "performance." At the outset, we must specify the criteria of comparison: the Soviets' own goals (growth, equity, well-being)? someone else's goals? the achievements of an earlier period (time-series)? the achievements of other countries (cross-section)? a combination of time-series and cross-section criteria (as when adjusting comparisons for the "stage of development")?

That hurdle crossed, we can then choose quantitative or qualitative measures of performance. The former include aggregate gross national product or national income; the broad components of the aggregates (consumption, investment or saving, government spending); the individual elements of the broad components (housing, autos, telephones; or fixed investment, human-capital investment); and the sectors or branches of origin of the aggregates (industry—heavy or light; agriculture; military). One must not forget total or per capita figures, either. The qualitative measures of performance include demographic characteristics, environmental quality, or simply the "quality of life."

It is clear that, short of writing several monographs on the subject, choice is mandatory. Our focus will be a very narrow one. We will ignore equity and well-being; cross-section comparisons; qualitative indicators of performance—indeed, everything listed above except the aggregate, quantitative measures, with some sectoral or other breakdowns, compared with the record of the Stalin era. Our primary interest will be in Soviet economic growth; we will not be concerned with agriculture. After reviewing the quantitative evidence on Soviet growth since Stalin, we will turn our attention to the dominant feature to emerge from that evidence, namely, the deceleration of Soviet economic growth and its probable or at least possible causes.

We noted above the impressive record of Soviet industrial growth (particularly of heavy industry) during the 1930s. We also noted the cost of that record in terms of reductions in real wages and in real per capita income. A similar pattern existed with regard to gross national product (GNP) and its components: total real GNP increased rapidly (nearly 12 percent a year on the average for 1928–37), as did gross investment (over 19 percent a year for the same period—although this component of GNP actually fell in 1938–40); household consumption, however, grew at only 3.6 percent a year in 1928–37 (although it actually increased to 4.6 percent a year in 1938–40.)[45]

More immediately relevant to the present discussion is the performance record of the early 1950s, just prior to the beginning of the post-Stalin epoch.[46] During 1951–55 industrial output grew at an overall rate of 11.7 percent a year on average, with intermediate products output growing at nearly 11 percent a year and machinery output at nearly 14 percent a year. Interestingly, consumer goods output grew at nearly 10 percent a year during this period. GNP expanded at nearly a 7 percent average annual rate, and gross investment at better than 12 percent, while consumption managed 8.2 percent. Real wages joined in the prosperity, growing at an annual average rate of better than 10 percent. Overall, during the fifth five-year plan (1951–55)—the first such plan following what is conventionally regarded as the postwar recovery period—the Soviet economy can be said to have performed rather well.

The conventional wisdom is that the good growth record of the fifth five-year plan continued into the second half of the 1950s, but that after 1958 the Soviet economy entered a period of secular retardation from which it has not emerged.[47] In actual fact, the slowdown of postwar Soviet economic growth can be seen to have begun earlier than 1958[48] —somewhere around the midpoint of the decade and only a few years after Stalin's death. True, GNP increased slightly faster in 1955–58 than in 1950–55 (7.4 percent per year on average versus 6.9 percent, respectively), and investment expanded substantially faster (14.9 percent a year versus 12.4 percent). For all the other variables cited here, though, as well as for most of the components of industrial output, the growth rates in 1955–58 were below those realized in 1950–55.

Our minor correction of the conventional wisdom on the growth slowdown is corroborated by evidence on revisions in the five-year plans in the mid and late 1950s. The sixth five-year plan (1956–60), which reflected a glowing optimism derived from the banner results of the fifth plan, survived only two years. The annual plan for 1958 was not part of any long-term plan, and the so-called seven-year plan (which itself would be effectively abandoned two years early) began in 1959.

The secular decline in Soviet economic performance, as measured here, is illustrated in Table 1. The table shows average annual growth rates of Soviet GNP and selected components, by sector of origin (A) and end use (B), for five-year intervals from 1951 to 1975. The pattern is not entirely uniform (*vide* "civilian machinery"), and there are some short-term reversals of the trend (especially in 1966–70). Further, most of the annual rates of increase in the most recent five years, 1971–75, are enviable by U.S. standards for the same period. Still, the data in Table 1 indicate clearly not only that the post-Stalin slowdown is real, but also that it is broad in scope and not insignificant in magnitude.

How can we explain the very evident secular retardation of Soviet growth since the 1950s? This question has attracted considerable attention from scholars. The discussion has become spirited, and not all the results are in. There are two main schools of thought, plus a recent "compromise" position that pleases neither school completely.

The first school of thought, which by longevity and numbers of adherents can be termed the orthodox school, grew out of work pioneered by Abram Bergson on estimating Soviet GNP and national income

TABLE 1.

The Slowdown in Soviet Growth, 1951–75

(average annual percentage rates of growth)

A. Soviet GNP by Sector of Origin (Factor Cost), 1970 Prices*

	1951–55	1956–60	1961–65	1966–70	1971–75
Industry	10.3	8.9	6.6	6.2	5.9
Civilian machinery	9.9	11.4	7.9	6.9	8.9
Light industry	11.2	7.0	2.4	8.0	2.6
Agriculture	4.1	4.1	2.4	4.2	−2.0
GNP	5.8	5.8	4.9	5.3	3.7

B. Soviet GNP by End Use (Factor Cost), 1970 Prices**

	1951–55	1956–60	1961–65	1966–70	1971–75
Consumption	5.9	5.4	4.0	5.1	3.8
Fixed investment	12.2	10.3	7.1	6.3	5.4
GNP	6.0	5.8	5.0	5.5	3.8

*Excludes weapons
**Includes weapons
SOURCE: Rush V. Greenslade, "The Real Gross National Product of the U.S.S.R., 1950–1975," in U.S. Congress, Joint Economic Committee, *Soviet Economy in a New Perspective: A Compendium of Papers* (Washington: Government Printing Office, 1966), pp. 272, 276.

according to Western definitions.[49] Focusing on productivity, the orthodox school uses econometric techniques with an assumed simple ("Cobb-Douglas") form of the aggregate production function to obtain estimates of capital, labor, and composite (or "total") factor productivity over time. These estimates for the period since 1950 show a secular tendency for productivity growth to decline. Table 2 shows recent estimates of average annual growth rates of Soviet composite factor productivity for five-year intervals from 1951 to 1975. The declining trend is readily evident for GNP production; however, the decline is dramatic for industrial production, long the highest-priority sector of the Soviet economy.[50]

The decline in estimated factor productivity provides a rationale, but not an explanation, for the slowdown in Soviet postwar economic growth. For an explanation, we must rely on qualitative evidence—for example, inefficiencies in planning (the "defects" discussed in section III above); changes in the structure of production over time; a diminishing rate of decline in the average age of capital goods; and slower rates of increase in human capital formation.[51] With qualitative evidence, of course, we cannot assess the relative importance (or even the empirical significance) of the various factors; hence the explanation is at best conjectural. Further, we have only a qualitative basis for assessing future growth prospects.[52]

The second, "unorthodox," school of thought originated with work by Martin Weitzman.[53] Noting that the capital-labor ratio had changed markedly over time, as a direct result of the Soviet growth strategy, Weitzman used a less restrictive ("constant-elasticity-of-substitution" or CES) specification of the aggregate (industrial) production function. The CES function permits the elasticity of substitution between capital and labor to differ from unity (which it cannot do, by assumption, with the simpler Cobb-Douglas function); this feature in turn permits the shares of output going to capital and labor to vary (which they cannot do under Cobb-Douglas assumptions). As Weitzman puts it (emphasis in the original):

> It is useful to think of the elasticity of substitution as a measure of the rate at which diminishing returns set in as one factor is increased *relative* to the other. A less than unit elasticity of substitution implies eventual difficulty in increasing output by primarily incrementing one factor, because diminishing returns set in strongly and rapidly. Such a situation would have special relevance for the Soviet case because capital has grown so fast relative to labor.[54]

Weitzman's results indicate an elasticity of substitution between capital and labor in Soviet industry that was substantially less than unity—about 0.4. That elasticity implies a reduction in the imputed factor share of capital in total industrial production from an estimated 86 percent in 1950 to only 44 percent in 1969; the share of labor of course moves in the opposite direction. This is in marked contrast to the constant shares required if one assumes a Cobb-Douglas production func-

TABLE 2.

Post-Stalin Trends in Average Annual Growth Rates of Composite ("Total") Factor Productivity in the USSR*

(percentages)

	1951–55	1956–60	1961–65	1966–70	1971–75
GNP production	1.4	1.8	0.9	1.5	−0.2
Industrial production	3.6	3.2	0.6	1.3	1.5

*Includes weapons
SOURCE: Greenslade, p. 279.

tion. Weitzman's findings, if valid, suggest that the declining composite factor productivities found using Cobb-Douglas assumptions, and on which the orthodox explanation rests, are a spurious result of a mis-specified model, not a rationale for the retardation of Soviet growth.

The unorthodox school's rationale for that retardation is that the Soviet Union has encountered diminishing returns to capital because of increasingly limited ability to substitute capital for labor. While Weitzman does not have to resort to a list of conjectures to obtain an explanation from his findings, he does have to try to explain the low elasticity of substitution—that is, *why* the Soviet economy was trans-formed "from a near labor surplus situation in the early 1950s to a position now where labor scarcity is an important fact of economic life."[55] The uncertainty in his own conjectures is of the same quality, if not quantity, as that of the orthodox school. It is possible, though, to infer something about future growth prospects from Weitzman's results. Continued rapid expansion of the capital stock would appear to be an expensive growth strategy. Further, with prospects not good for increasing the rate of growth of the labor force,[56] the only hope for reversing the industrial growth slowdown is technical change.[57] This conclusion is certainly consistent with the strong Soviet interest in expanding trade with the West in order to gain access to modern technology.[58]

Recent work by Stanislaw Gomulka has provided a bridge between the positions of the orthodox and unorthodox explanations of the So-viet growth slowdown.[59] Gomulka finds what he calls the standard (our orthodox) approach unsatisfactory on empirical grounds and of little help in projecting future growth rates. At the same time, he be-lieves Weitzman's model to have been misspecified.[60] Gomulka's paper is too long and involved to summarize here in any detail. In essence, by disaggregating both the time period and the data on labor produc-tivity, he shows that the elasticity of substitution between capital and labor (while it may be less than one) is not an important determinant of Soviet postwar growth. Moreover, he argues that factor productivity has declined since Stalin and therefore helps account for the retarda-tion of growth; however, we should look at three different components of productivity growth. Two of them ("catching up" after World War II and the change in the length of the work year in 1956–61) are tran-sitory; the third is the conventional long-term trend in technical change. An interesting implication of Gomulka's work is that Soviet economic growth is approaching a long-run asymptotic path.[61] Only with a dis-crete parameter shift (which, like Weitzman, he believes can come only, if at all, through technical change) can the Soviets untrack their performance record and return to the higher rates of earlier periods.

V. Conclusions and Prospects

We began our retrospective view of Soviet economic planning and performance since Stalin with two rival hypotheses:

1. Stalin's death caused fundamental changes in the Soviet economy; and

2. Stalin's death, while it may have altered certain specific features, did not effect basic long-term changes in the Soviet economy.

For the first hypothesis to prevail, we should have observed a significant structural change in Soviet command planning and marked changes in both overall economic performance and its components over the past quarter century. Conversely, for the second hypothesis to prevail, the changes since Stalin should be superficial, with the planning system remaining largely intact and trends in performance exhibiting long-run stability in spite of changes in political leadership.

The evidence examined in this chapter could be interpreted as favoring either of the rival hypotheses. On balance, however, our conclusion is that the weight of the evidence is on the side of the second hypothesis: personalities matter, but underlying economic forces matter more, especially in the long term. This conclusion holds for both planning and performance.

In section III, we noted that the death of Stalin had two pertinent implications for the mechanism of central, command planning assembled during the first twenty-five years of the Soviet industrialization effort. First, it opened up the political process within the Communist Party of the Soviet Union, so that emergent leaders sought substantive issues on which to appeal to party cadres for support. The ensuing debates included economic issues, of course, and frustrations about the economy contributed to second thoughts about the planning system. Second, Stalin's death made it possible not only to discuss and analyze planning problems but eventually also to implement a seemingly ambitious program to correct some of the more pressing of those problems.

With the benefit of more than a decade's hindsight, though, we see that the two implications of Stalin's death have in fact been of little real significance. The alterations in planning methods first introduced in 1965 have not changed the basic operation of Soviet central planning; indeed, many of them have been effectively abandoned. Moreover, the best prognosis is that, while there may be further modifications in the future, they will prove to be at most tinkering that will prove disappointing, and, in the end, these modifications will be abandoned, too. The reason is that, over the range of modification the Soviets seem willing to try, tinkering creates problems that can only be alleviated by ceasing to tinker. In short, the system will out, and fundamental change in the system is not in prospect.

We saw in section IV that Soviet economic growth performance has deteriorated rather steadily since the mid-1950s—since, that is, shortly after Stalin's death. It would be misleading, though, to interpret the coincidence of timing as causation. Apart from difficulties of comparing the pre-Stalin period (which included a decade or more devoted to World War II) with the post-Stalin period, one would have to account for the essential similarity of Soviet growth strategy and policies throughout the entire period since postwar recovery was completed in about 1950. For example, it is mostly talk about consumer goods, not output, that has increased more rapidly under Stalin's successors; in fact, consumer goods production grew impressively in the 1951–55 quinquennium.

Skepticism that Stalin's death was a significant cause of the slowdown of Soviet growth is supported by recent empirical work. That work suggests that already in the 1950s, and increasingly since then, the Soviet economy had matured to the point where certain of the early, transitory sources of economic growth were disappearing—e.g., backlogs of modern technology from which to borrow, and reserves of skilled or trainable labor that could be matched with additional machines. Further, barring major advances in technology and ignoring short-run factors such as the sharp increases in world oil prices since 1970, future prospects appear to be for relatively steady growth about a stable trend that is well below earlier achievements. Rapid accumulation of capital will not be the engine of growth it once was, and (at least for some years) increases in the labor force cannot yield much incremental growth.

The thesis that Soviet economic growth is approaching a long-term asymptote has numerous implications. Space does not permit a full rehearsal, but several implications merit brief mention here. First, prospects for consumption standards appear similar to those for overall production: steady growth—but not the dramatic increases that long were presumed to be the rationale for depressing consumption in order to expand investment. Second, military spending may retain its priority status but, with reduced growth expectations, will experience more stringent competition from other claims on resources (including consumer goods output). Third, the current conventional wisdom about Soviet economic growth is consistent with the vigorous efforts in Moscow over the past decade to expand trade with the technologically advanced capitalist countries; those efforts are quite likely to continue so long as the Soviets lag in significant areas of modern technology. A corollary for the capitalist countries is that they should think twice before granting special concessions to attract Soviet orders; the orders may well come of their own accord.

Notes

1. J. Michael Montias, "Comment [on a paper by Jerzy F. Karcz]," in Erik Thorbecke, ed., *The Role of Agriculture in Economic Development* (New York: National Bureau of Economic Research, 1969), pp. 266–74.

2. Alexander Gerschenkron, "A Textbook on the Soviet Economy," *World Politics* 7:4 (July 1955), p. 645.

3. Stanley H. Cohn, *Economic Development in the Soviet Union* (Lexington, Mass.: D. C. Heath, 1970), pp. 30, 42.

4. Alexander Gerschenkron, "Russia: Patterns and Problems of Economic Development, 1861–1958," in Gerschenkron, *Economic Backwardness in Historical Perspective: Essays* (Cambridge, Mass.: Harvard University Press, 1962), p. 149.

5. For convenience, we use the past tense throughout this section without, however, prejudging whether the various aspects of the Stalinist system are still present in the Soviet economy.

6. Note (for later reference) that, both in formulating and in implementing a national plan of this kind, information on who is to do what must not be lost in the process of aggregating to national totals. Otherwise, the central planners will not be able (after adjusting the totals for consistency or optimality) to send back the adjusted figures to the right operating economic agents. Zaleski refers to a national plan of this kind as "an aggregation of administrative dossiers" (Eugene Zaleski, "Planning for Industrial Growth," in V. G. Treml and R. Farrell, eds., *The Development of the Soviet Economy* [New York: Praeger, 1968], p. 68). (This source is a useful reference on Soviet planning systems in different periods.)

7. Robert W. Campbell, "On the Theory of Economic Administration," in H. Rosovsky, ed., *Industrialization in Two Systems: Essays in Honor of Alexander Gerschenkron* (New York: Wiley, 1966), pp. 186–203.

8. Gerschenkron, "Russia: Patterns," p. 149.

9. Cohn, *Economic Development*, pp. 28–29. Naum Jasny, in his *Soviet Industrialization, 1928–1952* (Chicago: University of Chicago Press, 1961), pp. 21 and passim, makes a roughly comparable argument, although he (usefully, in our opinion) divides the Stalin era into periods different from the five-year plans. (In particular, he traces the severe slump in Soviet economic progress in 1938–40 to the purges rather than to war preparation—e.g., pp. 13, 18–19). The following quotation summarizes his interpretation of Stalinist economic performance (p. 21):

In those periods [Three "Good" Years, Stalin Has Everything His Way] when the Soviet machine operated with a reasonable smoothness, when major disturbances were absent, or when the Soviets succeeded in reducing the harmful effects of those disturbances, the large sector of the economy consisting of heavy industry, investment, and transportation made big strides ahead.

10. Reported in Cohn, *Economic Developments*, p. 39.

11. Jasny, *Soviet Industrialization*, p. 9.

12. Alexander Gerschenkron, "Economic Backwardness in Historical Perspective," in Gerschenkron, *Economic Backwardness in Historical Perspective: Essays* (Cambridge, Mass.: Harvard University Press, 1962), pp. 5–30; Gerschenkron, "Russia: Patterns," pp. 118–51; Alec Nove, *An Economic History of the USSR* (London: Allen Lane, 1969).

13. Mischa Gisser and Paul Jonas, "Soviet Growth in Absence of Centralized Planning: A Hypothetical Alternative," *Journal of Political Economy* 82:2, Part 1 (March/April 1974), pp. 333–52.

14. Oleg Hoeffding, "The Soviet Industrial Reorganization of 1957," *American Economic Review* 49:2 (May 1959), p. 65.

15. One example of Western analyses of economic policy issues in the post-Stalin political process is Sidney Ploss, *Conflict and Decision-Making in Soviet Russia: A Case Study of Agricultural Policy, 1953–1963* (Princeton: Princeton University Press, 1964). Useful historical perspective can be gained from Moshe Lewin, *Political Undercurrents in Soviet Economic Debates: From Bukharin to the Modern Reformers* (Princeton: Princeton University Press, 1974).

16. See, for example, Alec Nove, "The U.S.S.R.: The Reform that Never Was," in L. Dellin and H. Gross, eds., *Reforms in the Soviet and East European Economies* (Lexington, Mass.: D. C. Heath, 1972), p. 23.

17. Literally hundreds of references could be cited here. Two examples that are used in this paper are Zaleski, pp. 67ff., and Nove, "The U.S.S.R.," pp. 21ff.

18. Hoeffding, "The Soviet Industrial Reorganization."

19. Robert W. Campbell, "Economic Reform in the U.S.S.R.," *American Economic Review* 58:2 (May 1968), p. 547.

20. Central Intelligence Agency (CIA), *Organization and Management in the Soviet Economy: The Ceaseless Search for Panaceas*, ER-77-10769, December 1977, p. 17.

21. Nove, "The U.S.S.R.," p. 23.

22. An admirable rehearsal and analysis of the issues and proposals in the debate are to be found in Eugene Zaleski, *Planning Reforms in the Soviet Union, 1962–1966*, translated by M.-C. MacAndrew and G. W. Nutter (Chapel Hill: University of North Carolina Press, 1967), pp. 66–121.

23. Actually, Liberman had made similar (though more modest) proposals, stressing similar themes, in the 1950s (Zaleski, *Planning Reforms*, pp. 76ff.).

24. Evsei G. Liberman, *Economic Methods and the Effectiveness of Production*, translated by Arlo Schultz (Garden City, New York: Anchor Books, 1973).

25. This paragraph relies heavily on Zaleski, *Planning Reforms*, pp. 73–77. See also Nove, "The U.S.S.R.," p. 28.

26. Of the numerous references on this subject, the following are used here: Campbell, "Economic Reform," pp. 547–50; Nove, "The U.S.S.R.," pp. 30–31; Zaleski, *Planning Reforms*, pp. 141ff.; and CIA, *Organization and Management*. The last two provide a wealth of detail between them.

27. Actually, this change by itself was more nominal than real, because (as we pointed out in section II) only a few of the myriad indicators under the previous system had really been effective.

28. Zaleski, *Planning Reforms*, p. 153.

29. Campbell, "Economic Reform," p. 549.

30. Martin L. Weitzman, "The New Soviet Incentive Model," *The Bell Journal of Economics* 7:1 (Spring 1976), pp. 251–57.

31. Zaleski, *Planning Reform*, pp. 156–60; CIA, *Organization and Management*, pp. 4–5.

32. Campbell, "Economic Reform," p. 553.

33. No invidious comparison of Soviet politics with U.S. politics is intended, nor would one be justified. Consider, for instance, the fanfare and exhortation that accompanied the announcement of the National Energy Plan in April 1977.

34. CIA, *Organization and Management*, p. 19; Nove, "The U.S.S.R.," p. 30.

35. In addition to the works cited throughout the text, careful studies of the reforms that reach the same conclusion include Marie Lavigne, "Economic Reforms in Eastern Europe: Ten Years After," in Z. Fallenbuchl, ed., *Economic Development in the Soviet Union and Eastern Europe*, Volume 1 (New York: Praeger, 1975), pp. 42–64; Hans-Hermann Höhmann and Hans-Bernhard Sand, "The Soviet Union," in H.-H. Höhmann et al., eds., *The New Economic Systems of Eastern Europe* (London: C. Hurst, 1975), pp. 1–42; and Jan Marczewski, *Crisis in Socialist Planning: Eastern Europe and the USSR* (New York: Praeger, 1974).

36. Zaleski, *Planning Reforms*, p. 141.

37. Campbell, "Economic Reform," p. 550.

38. Nove, "The U.S.S.R.," p. 32.

39. See also CIA, *Organization and Management*, pp. 7–8.

40. Nove, "The U.S.S.R.," p. 33.

41. Deborah Duff Milenkovitch, [Book review of Höhmann et al., *The New Economic Systems*], *Soviet Studies* 28:4 (October 1976), p. 651.

42. Nove ("The U.S.S.R.," p. 34) asserts that "*the major obstacle to change lies in a combination of inertia, habit and self-interest*" (his emphasis). One might agree with this statement of "the" were changed to "a"— but not otherwise.

43. Gregory Grossman, "Notes for a Theory of the Command Economy," *Soviet Studies* 15:2 (October 1963), section VIII.

44. Thus, we find Nove's remark ("The U.S.S.R.," p. 33) that "*the [Soviet] system has an inner logic which defies gradual change*" (his emphasis) to be closer to "the" major obstacle to change than "inertia, habit and self-interest" (see note 42).

45. Abram Bergson, *The Real National Income of Soviet Russia since 1928* (Cambridge, Mass.: Harvard University Press, 1961), p. 217.

46. All figures in this paragraph and the next are from Cohn, *Economic Development*, pp. 28–29.

47. Recall Cohn's reference, cited in section I, to the period 1953–58 as the "bountiful post-Stalin years" (*Economic Development*, p. 42).

48. It is necessary here to violate the proscription on discussing agriculture to point out that 1958 was a singularly good year for agricultural output. Hence, using 1958 as an end point in calculating average annual growth rates imparts an upward bias to data for the period up through 1958, and vice versa for the period after 1958.

49. For example, Bergson, *Real National Income*.

50. Here again, we see that the GNP data support the conventional wisdom that the growth slowdown began only in the late 1950s. The data on productivity in industrial production, though, support our view that it started somewhat earlier.

51. Cohn, *Economic Development*, Chapter 6; Abram Bergson, *Planning and Productivity under Soviet Socialism* (New York: Columbia University Press, 1968); Abram Bergson, "Toward a New [Soviet] Growth Model," *Problems of Communism* 22:2 (March–April 1973).

52. Stanislaw Gomulka, "Soviet Postwar Industrial Growth, Capital-Labor Substitution, and Technical Changes: A Reexamination," in Z. Fallenbuchl, ed., *Economic Development in the Soviet Union*, Volume 2 (New York: Praeger, 1975), p. 4.

53. Martin L. Weitzman, "Soviet Postwar Economic Growth and Capital-Labor Substitution," *American Economic Review* 60:4 (September 1970), pp. 676–92.

54. Ibid., p. 679.

55. Ibid., p. 682.

56. Substantial increases in labor *quality*, however, may be possible. Human capital is generally thought to be measured in the labor, not the capital, variable in empirical work with aggregate production functions.

57. Weitzman, "Postwar Soviet Economic Growth," p. 686.

58. Note that, as Soviet foreign trade expands, the economy of the USSR becomes more sensitive to variations in world economic activity. For example, an article in the *Wall Street Journal* (March 22, 1978, p. 10) bore the title "UN Says Slowing of Western Economies May Be Easing Eastern Europe Growth" [including that of the USSR].

59. Gomulka, "Soviet Postwar Industrial Growth." Gomulka's bridge provides firmer footing than Greenslade's observation ("The Real Gross National Product," p. 279) that "no doubt both these factors [slow growth in total factor productivity and diminishing returns] are at work in the Soviet economy."

60. Gomulka, "Soviet Postwar Industrial Growth," pp. 3–4.

61. This implication is consistent with the orthodox school's suggestion that a diminishing rate of decline in the average age of the capital stock accounts for part of the decline in total factor productivity. The Soviets have been adding rapidly to their capital stock for some forty years now; hence, a considerable fraction of capital is relatively old. Higher and higher rates of new investment will therefore be required just to sustain overall productivity growth rates.

Post-Stalin Agriculture and Its Future

James R. Millar

> The Soviet village is indeed the weakest point of the Soviet system, its Achilles' heel. It will have a great part in the ultimate destruction of Soviet power.
>
> NAUM JASNY,
> *Soviet Studies* (October 1951)

> Agriculture is often described as the Achilles heel of the Soviet economy. But while this is true, it is less often remembered that Achilles could after all walk upon his heel.
>
> PETER WILES,
> *Foreign Affairs* (July 1953)

These statements by Jasny and Wiles illustrate a salient continuity of the post-Stalin period.[1] The Soviet rural village remains the "weakest point" of the Soviet economy. But Soviet society continues to walk upon its Achilles heel. In fact, Soviet agriculture has made greater progress since 1953 than anyone anticipated, and the "Malthusian wolf" is farther than ever from the door. In the twenty-five years since Stalin's death agricultural output has increased at a very respectable annual average of at least 3.5 percent,[2] while population growth has averaged only about 1.4 percent per annum.[3] Compared to the many countries that have had difficulty maintaining a significant growth rate of food products per capita, the USSR is clearly exceptional. Growth and the diversification of Soviet agricultural output since Stalin's death has made possible a significant enrichment of the average Russian's diet. Food consumption per capita, for example, has increased (in constant rubles) 100 percent since 1951, and this reflects eating better quality products more than it does merely eating more.[4] The magnitude of the change since Stalin is measured by the fact that per capita production of agri-

135

cultural products in 1953 had just regained the prewar 1940 level, which was itself only at approximately the 1928 level. And the 1928 level of per capita consumption had probably been less than that of 1913.

The ambitiousness*and high priority of the goal of enriching Soviet diets, rather than policy failure, are responsible for having converted the Soviet Union from a modest net exporter into a regular and significant net importer of agricultural products during the last decade. These large imports of grain, however, reflect only one dimension of the Soviet agricultural problem today—the liability of Soviet field crops, and especially grains, to sharp year-to-year fluctuations. Variability of this sort is not new, of course. What *is* new is the decision to import grains to compensate for harvest shortfalls. It was Nikita Khrushchev who reversed long-standing Soviet policy and ordered imports on a significant scale to offset the otherwise adverse impact that the poor 1963 grain harvest would have had on Soviet livestock herds, which, in turn, would have undermined planned increases in per capita production of animal husbandry products. Although Khrushchev soon fell from power, the precedent has remained. In 1975 the Soviet Union experienced a shortfall of 80 million metric tons of grain—equal to approximately 40 percent of the total and bountiful harvest of 1973, or 80 percent of the best Western estimates of the 1972 year-end grain stock inventory.[5] Imports to compensate for this disaster cost an enormous amount of foreign exchange that in earlier years would have been reserved to import Western technology, and they completely unsettled international grain markets.

The changes that have taken place in Soviet agriculture since Stalin, then, have been of fundamental significance to the Soviet consumer, and they have raised agriculture from the bottom to very nearly the top of the nondefense priority list. In the present chapter we shall examine Soviet agriculture in both historical and world perspectives. The concluding sections attempt to assess the nature of the problems Soviet agriculture faces and the prospects for their satisfactory resolution.

Disappearances and Reappearances: The Historical Record

The contemporary model of Soviet socialist agriculture shares historical features with previous models, but it is very different today from the Stalinist model of the early 1950s. The similarities over time are not so much the result of continuously acting forces as they are of recurring reactions, or historically ingrained responses, to particular types of problems. The concept of "continuity and change" is inadequate for describing the development of contemporary Soviet agricultural institutions, since even the changes that have taken place in recent years provide a certain continuity with the past. Particular solutions tend to reappear over time. Thus, much that once "disappeared" has in fact "reappeared" in contemporary Soviet agriculture.

A recent official history of Soviet agriculture provides a completely new periodization, one that obscures the fundamental contours of the Soviet experience. According to this work, Soviet agricultural history is divided into four periods.[6] The first runs from the revolution of 1917 through 1925, and it therefore mixes war communism with the radically different period of the New Economic Policy (NEP). The second period stretches from 1925 to 1941, which buries 1928, a critical turning point on the road to rapid industrialization; forced, mass collectivization; and the purges. The only virtue of 1925 as a dividing point is that statistics on agricultural output for the 1930s look better with 1925, rather than 1928 as a base year. The only traditional break that these articles provide is 1941, the outset of World War II, but this period is extended beyond Stalin's death to 1964, the year Khrushchev was removed from power. Stalin and the hero of de-Stalinization are obliged to share the same historical period! The final period is Brezhnev's, and the years 1965 through 1976 are represented by myriads of statistics revealing rapid growth rates of both inputs and outputs. Throughout this revision of Soviet agricultural history neither Stalin nor Khrushchev is mentioned by name, and yet each left a clear and easily read mark on the institutional structure of contemporary Soviet agriculture.

The only other figure of comparable significance was, of course, Lenin, who was obliged to use his enormous personal authority to the limit to introduce the NEP early in the 1920s. Money, markets, and normal trade relations had disappeared in the revolution and civil war, and the NEP restored these institutions to the dismay of many Bolsheviks. The NEP also allowed the peasant family farm to flourish, with all that implied in the way of complex production functions, "self-exploitation" of family labor, and smallness of scale in production units.

The NEP was a period of growing pecuniary relations among members of the rural population and urban, industrial, and governmental transactors. By all objective measures NEP agriculture was a success. Prewar output levels were restored relatively quickly, the composition of agricultural output improved markedly, and the peasant producers showed themselves to be highly sensitive to market forces.

Mass collectivization at the close of the 1920s not only put an end to private middle-man activities, it also depecuniarized the rural sector by converting almost all economic transactions into in-kind payments to Machine Tractor Stations (MTS), to members for work performed, and as obligatory deliveries to the state. Collective-farm agriculture was imposed upon the rural population, and administrative measures replaced the market as the primary means for allocation of resources. Peasant resistance to collectivization led ultimately to a compromise that allowed peasant families, on condition of working a minimum number of days on the collective farm, access to tiny plots of land upon which they were allowed to continue private activity—mainly horticulture and animal husbandry. Thus, with mass collectivization there reappeared the "hungry plot" of post-Emancipation Russia, a plot too small to live on, but large enough to provide an effective incentive to get the lord's land worked. Collective-farm agriculture was imposed on the apparent assumption that it would facilitate the extraction of an agricultural surplus to finance rapid industrialization. Nothing of the sort took place.[7] Agricultural output fell in absolute value, the composition of agricultural output deteriorated, and many in the countryside and elsewhere starved.

World War II interrupted recovery from the mistakes and excesses of mass collectivization, and postwar recovery favored the industrial-urban sector once more. By the time Stalin died in 1953, the rural sector was relatively (and perhaps even absolutely) more backward than it had been in 1928. This was the apogee of the Soviet unbalanced growth path, and since 1953 repeated attempts have been made to restore balance.

The first attempts by Stalin's heirs to address the agricultural problems he left to them did not involve significant institutional change. On the contrary, Nikita Khrushchev started out merely tinkering with the system Stalin had created in the 1930s. Agricultural procurement prices were increased and taxes reduced. Farmer earnings increased noticeably as a result, but the fundamental system of collective-farm, team cultivation with residual determination of farmer earnings, along with the MTS system, the four-track agricultural procurement system, and the coexistence of a tiny private agricultural system remained the salient organizational features. What *was* new was a promise by the state to adhere to "socialist legality" in its dealings with farms and farmers, a decision to create material incentives for workers, and a realization of the centrality of agriculture for improvement in the standard of living of urban households.

Farm output did increase appreciably between 1953 and 1957, but the increase was attributable in large part to the concurrent and almost incredible expanded cultivation of marginal lands in the remoter regions of the USSR. The "Virgin Lands" campaign brought into cultivation an area equal to the total cultivated area of Canada. This innovation was structural in only one respect. These lands were opened mainly by the creation of state farms, and the role of the state farm has grown continuously thereafter. Subsequently, the growth of the state farm sector has been a result of the conversion of weak collective farms into state farms. State farms cultivate a larger share of total arable land than collective farms today, and this trend continues.[8] State farms are organized on the model of state industrial enterprises, of course, so that this innovation was both important and costly to the state budget.

The development of the Virgin Lands was in large part a stopgap measure designed to increase total agricultural output rapidly in the expectation that the regularization of the Stalinist model of collective agriculture would soon produce results. The attempt to make Stalin's model of socialist agriculture work failed to meet expectations, however, and it was overturned in 1958. Like Lenin and Stalin before him, Khrushchev broke with previous agricultural policy and introduced radical changes in the institutional structure of agricultural production.

In 1958 the MTS system was abolished, and the old four-channel agricultural procurement system was also abandoned. Both changes substituted pecuniary for in-kind transactions. Since 1958 all taxes on agriculture have been paid in money, and farms have been obliged to purchase capital equipment and farm inputs from state agencies. Brezhnev and Kosygin continued the process of pecuniarization and intensification of Soviet agriculture, but with even greater emphasis upon research and development, mechanization, and the use of mineral fertilizers and pesticides. Financial discrimination against the collective farm has also been abandoned and farmer earnings have been increased and stabilized by a minimum guaranteed annual wage and access to the state pension system. The difference between Khrushchev's policies toward agriculture and those of his successors has been mainly a matter of acceleration and greater consistency. Nowhere is this more evident than in the priority that has been accorded to livestock production under Brezhnev and the consequent very large imports of grain and fodder from the West to support it. Per capita meat consumption has become the primary symbol of agricultural success in the USSR.[9]

A new model for agricultural production has been building therefore since 1958 under Khrushchev and Brezhnev. It has two prominent aspects: intensification of production and pecuniarization of transactions within the agricultural sector, and between it and the other sectors. The farm, whether collective or state, remains very large (although the operational unit is much smaller and has remained about the same throughout the period), which is a legacy both of the Stalinist model and of even more ancient Bolshevik mythology about increasing returns to scale in agricultural production. But the economic context in which Soviet farms operate today is essentially a socialist market environment, a reappearance, in effect, of a prominent feature of the NEP. Dealings with farm workers, with state procurement agencies, with state industrial enterprises on both input and output sides, are all carried out in pecuniary, quasi-market terms. These changes are particularly important as an index of the change in policy makers' attitudes toward agriculture specifically and toward economic problems generally.

It is a shock to return, for example, to Stalin's last official pronouncements on Soviet agriculture. Consider his response to the recommendation of two prominent Soviet agricultural economists to sell the MTS system to the collective farms:

> The outcome would be, first, that the collective farms would become the owners of the basic instruments of production; that is, their status would be an exceptional one. . . . [Would not one] say that such a status could only dig a deeper gulf between collective-farm property and public property, and would not bring us any nearer to communism . . . ?

> The outcome would be, secondly, an extension of the sphere of operation of commodity circulation. . . . What do Comrades Saina and Venzher think—is the extension of the sphere of commodity circulation calculated to promote our advance towards communism?[10]

Twenty-five years later this traditional Bolshevik (and Marxist) animus toward commodity production and exchange has almost completely disappeared. Although still not as prominent as during the NEP, markets, prices, and other pecuniary institutions are playing more significant roles than at any time since. Moreover, trained economists have access to statistical data unavailable prior to 1957,[11] and a reformation has taken place in the interpretation of Marx. Economists, sociologists, and others have had much greater freedom than ever before to find their own citations in the writings of Marx, Engels, and Lenin to support their analyses and reform proposals. As a result, much less nonsense is written these days about agriculture than was the case only a decade or so ago.

Viewed in historical perspective, then, recent developments in Soviet agriculture are clearly favorable to rationalization. A more pragmatic and less ideologically rigid approach has gradually gained ground. Current institutional arrangements are far more conducive to growth and efficiency than at any time since collectivization. Finally, beginning in

1958, the sector has experienced the longest period of organizational stability and of continuous growth in the history of the Soviet regime.

Soviet Agriculture in World Perspective

The performance of Soviet agriculture is ordinarily evaluated in the light of American agriculture. In the first place, this is because analysts are frequently concerned with Soviet strategic capabilities and because such comparisons are thought to reveal something about the superiority of the American economic system. In the second place, although the Soviet Union has inferior natural conditions for agriculture, there remain numerous physical similarities in the practice and potential of agriculture in the United States and in the USSR. Both countries occupy large land masses and contain relatively small populations. Thus, the kind of intensive farming that characterizes most of Asia is not relevant to an assessment of Soviet agriculture. The sort of medium intensity of cultivation that is typical of the United States is suitable for the USSR too. Moreover, both countries have large economies, measured in terms of total GNP, and both also rely upon international trade for only a small proportion of their needs. Even so, an unqualified direct comparison of Soviet and American agricultural performance can be quite misleading with respect to the gravity of Soviet problems. To correct this bias, it is useful to compare the USSR with the typical developing country.

With few exceptions, the situation confronting the developing nations of the world is very different from that confronting Soviet leaders.[12] Although the Soviet Union shares with many developing countries the fact that it has been converted from a regular exporter of grains to the industrial countries into a net importer, this does not mean in the Soviet case a diminution in capacity to feed the population. It reflects instead an enrichment of the diet at a rate greater than can be sustained by domestic production year in, year out, and this itself is a characteristic result of the practice of overcommitment planning in the Soviet economy as a whole. It also reflects a new priority of the household sector of the economy.

Unlike the Soviet Union, the typical developing country is small in size and tends not only to be overpopulated, but to be experiencing very rapid population growth as well. The rate of growth of population in the Soviet Union is not much greater than in the United States. Given that the demand for food products ordinarily grows less rapidly than personal income (that is, that the income elasticity of demand for agricultural products is less than unity) and that this disparity tends to enlarge with economic development, the problem of satisfying the Soviet population's demand for food products is essentially a matter of time and cost and is not problematic in itself.

Unlike most developing countries, the Soviet Union is not a newly independent colonial country and it is not characterized by existing or potentially serious political unrest, problems which tend to inhibit rational agricultural policy making in many underdeveloped countries. Moreover, less than 40 percent of the Soviet population is rural today, and, despite disadvantages, the rural sector is literate and has access to health care unparalleled in the typical developing country. The Soviet Union is no longer primarily an agrarian economy, and the high level of development of the industrial sector and the relatively high degree of education of the rural population are mutually supportive prerequisites for modernization of agricultural production.

Soviet agriculture is, then, in a reasonably favorable position when viewed in the context of the developing economies of the world, and indeed it does not compare unfavorably with many developed economies in many respects. Certainly the agricultural problems and prospects of the island economies of Japan and England are hardly comparable. What the Soviet Union shares with many developed economies is the fact that agricultural production is relatively high-cost and highly subsidized. In fact, a global view reveals a handful of low-cost agricultural producers, notably the United States, Canada, Australia, and Argentina, whose governments are obliged in most years to deal with agricultural surpluses because the high-cost producer countries are sheltering and subsidizing their farmers.[13] The subsidy in the Soviet case is very large, but it stems more from strategic and ideological preferences for autarky than from the political influence of farmers.

A Comparison of Agricultural Performance in the United States and USSR

Soviet agriculture has two very clear disadvantages that need to be dealt with at the outset. The United States economy is more highly industrialized than is the Soviet economy. Partly for this reason and partly for reasons of a different ordering of priorities, modernization of agriculture began significantly earlier in the United States. Climatic and other natural conditions in the Soviet Union are much less favorable to agriculture than is the case for the United States, which has a longer growing season, more uniform and reliable rainfall, smaller year-to-year variations in mean temperatures and other conditions. The north-south temperature gradient is steeper in the United States as well, which permits some year-round growing zones. Nowhere in the vast stretches of the USSR are there to be found agricultural regions as richly favored as those of Iowa or Illinois.

Although these climatic differentials between Soviet and North American agriculture explain a portion of the differential performance of agriculture in each, they ought not be exaggerated. D. Gale Johnson, an authority of long standing, has argued persuasively that he does not "believe that soil and climatic conditions have been a major factor in restraining output growth. Nor do climatic conditions that prevail in the Soviet Union require the large year-to-year variability in total farm output that actually exists."[14]

Long-term comparison, from 1951 to 1975, indicates that growth in total agricultural output in the Soviet Union has outpaced that of the United States. The average annual rate of growth of total agricultural output was 3.5 percent, or a bit better, for the USSR and only 1.6 percent for the United States for these years.[15] As population growth rates have been very similar, the gap in per capita production of agricultural products has clearly been narrowing. The very magnitudes of output changes are quite impressive for the Soviet Union. For example, grain output averaged 88.5 million metric tons annually during 1951–55. By 1971–75 it had climbed to 181.5 million tons (or nearly 190.1 if the very poor 1975 harvest is excluded). The average for the first three years of the tenth five-year plan, 1976–78, has been almost 210 million tons. Similarly, total meat production more than doubled between the early 1950s and the current period, and equivalent increases were obtained for many other desirable food products such as milk, eggs, and vegetables.[16]

When one recalls that per capita production of agricultural products in 1953 was no greater than it had been in 1928, the increase over the past twenty-five years speaks for itself, but closer examination points up several serious problems. First, the average annual rate of growth of agricultural output appears to be slowing down, falling from 4.9 percent per annum in the 1950s, to 3.0 percent in the 1960s, to an average of just short of 1.0 percent during the first half of the 1970s.[17] Although the very poor crop year of 1975 influences this low rate substantially, the trend is not encouraging, and it is highly unlikely that the rapid rates of growth that were obtained in the immediate post-Stalin years can be reestablished.

Moreover, if we apportion the increases in agricultural output since the early 1950s between increases in the physical quantities of the conventional inputs (land, labor, and capital) and the increase in the jointly measured productivity of these inputs, it may be seen that most of the growth is attributable to the growth of inputs rather than to growth in total productivity (see Table 1). By contrast, total factor productivity has apparently increased at a somewhat more rapid rate in the United States. Although these measurements present difficulties and are not entirely reliable, it would appear that the already very large productivity gap that existed at the close of the Stalin period has not been narrowed. The increases that have been obtained in Soviet agricultural output have been purchased mainly by means of increasing the quantity of resources used in production.

In addition to the land resources added by the Virgin Lands campaign, very large investments have been made in Soviet agriculture. Since the late 1960s the share of gross fixed capital formation allocated to agriculture has been in the neighborhood of 25 percent. If investment in all branches of the economy that are supportive of agriculture, such as agricultural machinery manufacture and fertilizer production, is included, the share of investment in 1976 exceeded 34 percent of gross investment in the entire economy.[18] Soviet economists have been distressed to discover that the productivity of capital has been declining precipitously over the years, and the marginal product of capital is low enough now to raise questions about the usefulness of continued heavy

TABLE 1.

Output, Inputs, and Total Productivity in
U.S. and Soviet Agriculture 1951–75*

	Average Annual Rate of Growth (Percent)			
	1951–60	1961–70	1971–75	1951–75
USA				
Output	2.1	1.1	1.8	1.6
Inputs	0.2	−0.1	0.2	0.1
Total productivity	1.9	1.2	1.7	1.5
USSR				
Output (3-year moving average)	4.9	3.0	0.9	3.4
Inputs	2.7	2.0	2.0	2.3
Total productivity	2.2	1.0	−1.1	1.0

*The base year for the calculations shown is the year before the stated initial year of period.

Source: Douglas B. Diamond, "Comparative Output and Productivity of US and Soviet Agriculture," unpublished paper presented to the Conference on Soviet Agriculture, Kennan Institute for Advanced Russian Studies, Washington, D.C., November 16, 1976, Figure 5A.

investment.[19] As a consequence, the enormous investment of recent years has not led to a significant release of labor from agricultural employments, and the Soviet economy remains highly labor intensive despite growing capital intensity.

It is possible to obtain a rough comparison of the manpower requirements of agricultural production in the Soviet Union and the United States. In the United States, 4.6 percent of the total labor force was employed *directly* in agricultural employments in 1975. The figure for the Soviet Union (including those engaged on the private plots) was 25.4 percent.[20] The absolute figures for 1972 were 29.0 million worker years in the Soviet Union and 3.8 million in the United States. Of course, American farmers utilize more farm inputs that have been purchased from other sectors and a larger and more sophisticated distributional network for their output. When all labor inputs are counted, including those incorporated in the inputs farms purchase and those involved in processing, transporting, and marketing food and fiber products, the total labor input in Soviet agriculture was 43.9 million worker years in 1972, as against 12.1 million worker years in the United States that year.[21]

Comparison of Soviet and American agriculture, then, reveals what appears to be an inordinate absorption of current resources of labor, land, and capital in Soviet agriculture to produce a still inadequate and thus very costly output. The comparison raises two questions. First, why has the enormous economic effort of the last twenty-five years yielded so modest and variable a return? Second, what is the current Soviet leadership doing about the productivity gap and how successful are their efforts likely to be?

Problems, Policy, and Prospects of Post-Stalin Agriculture

A survey of informed Western opinion reveals a striking consensus regarding the causes of inefficiency and low productivity in Soviet agriculture today, although each expert ordinarily emphasizes different specific problems. The long list of specific problems may be grouped under four broad headings: (1) undercapitalization; (2) adverse composition of the agricultural labor force; (3) irrational price and wage formation practices; and (4) "systemic constraints," by which I mean certain irrational administrative practices and preferences that have acquired an aura of sanctity by reason of either ideology or simple bureaucratic inertia.

Soviet agriculture is undercapitalized in a relative sense only—relative to the United States[22] and relative to the output targets that have been set for the sector. If one takes into account the need for investment in rural infrastructure, that is, in rural road networks, retail outlets, and so forth, then it is obvious that Soviet agriculture trails far behind levels in the United States. Moreover, the limits set by climatic constraints will require relatively heavy investment in mechanization to speed planting and harvesting, in research and development of hybrids, and in new techniques of cultivation, areas much neglected during Stalin's years. Soviet soils are relatively poor also, and their quality has deteriorated through a general absence of proper soil and grassland management. Continued rapid expansion of livestock herds will require sustained heavy investment in facilities, transport, research, and veterinary medicine. Thus, continued heavy investment in Soviet agriculture is necessary, but it will not be easy to find the funds.[23] Even more troublesome, Soviet agriculture is already quite capital intensive by Western standards. A Western analyst recently described it as "two to three times as capital intensive as countries on a similar level of per capita income but subject to the discipline of market prices."[24] Both the average and the marginal products of capital are low and declining by all reports. For example, the energy capacity of Soviet agriculture doubled and productive capital per worker increased two-and-one-half times between 1965 and 1975, but gross production increased only by a third over the same decade.[25] Additional capital investment can only be justified, therefore, by substantial increases in yields, productivity, and efficiency.

This brings us to the second problem area—the agricultural labor force. Increased mechanization, the use of complex chemical compounds such as pesticides and fertilizers, cultivation of new hybrids, development of adequate soil maintenance programs, and upgrading farm management all require a highly educated and well-motivated labor force. Unfortunately, the age, sex, and educational composition of the agricultural labor force is highly disadvantageous.[26] The rural population has a higher proportion of nonworking-age population (young and old taken together) than the urban, which reflects the departure of able-bodied youth to urban-industrial pursuits. The agricultural population is 65 percent female as well, and the able-bodied woman of child-bearing age is less likely than her male counterpart to devote full time to work on the collective. Women are also less likely to seek to acquire high-level skills, mainly because the burdens of child-rearing, housekeeping, and private plot husbandry occupy much of their time. There is a bitter irony too about the provision of educational facilities for rural youth. Education is *the* primary lever for upward mobility in the Soviet Union generally, and this applies with even greater force in rural areas. Education opens opportunities for nonrural employments and thus tends to promote the exodus of the more talented and ambitious young people—even where the education provided is specific to agricultural job descriptions.

What makes the problem of the agricultural labor force so intractable is the relative backwardness of the rural sector. Though the degree of backwardness has lessened markedly since 1953, it still extends to all aspects of Soviet rural life, from the most private to the most public. Relative backwardness is characteristic of developing economies, but the Soviet experience is extreme. Recent sociological surveys in the countryside reveal not only that the young want to leave for industrial occupations, but that their parents want them to do so as well.[27] Unlike American farm families, who groom one or more of their children to take over the private family farm, the Soviet rural family has only a small personal stake in farming and little motivation other than family cohesiveness to encourage bright, capable young people to stay in farming. As an old woman kolkhoznik put it in one of Savchenko's stories: "Everybody is attracted to the cities. . . . Only old people and women are left. . . . and after we die nobody will be left."[28]

The total rural population, however, remains large, and despite the decline that can be expected, there is no reason for despair if rural employments and rural life can be made attractive enough to slow the decline to a reasonable rate. It would certainly make no sense to attempt to arrest it altogether. Much has been done to improve the quality of rural life, but much more remains to be done.

Although the current institutional structure of Soviet agriculture is much more favorable to efficient production than at any time since the initiation of collectivization, procurement prices paid to Soviet farms, prices charged in state retail outlets for agricultural products, and urban-rural income differentials are still not economically rational— that is, they do not serve as correct indicators of true scarcities and thus do not call forth appropriate producer behavior. However, the very fact that all transactions in the agricultural sector have been put in pecuniary terms makes this irrationality obvious not only to the Western observer but to any concerned Soviet policy maker as well. For example, Soviet agricultural products may be the most highly subsidized in the world.[29] Retail prices on many food products are too low relative to available supplies and therefore relative to nonagricultural goods as well. Wholesale prices (procurement and transfer prices) on a variety of agricultural products have no reasonable relationship either to each other or to retail prices, and so it goes.

Realigning state retail prices would be easier if the leadership had not promised repeatedly since 1954 to hold food prices constant. Thus, any adjustment in relative agricultural prices can take place only by lowering certain prices, and this would be possible only if reductions in the cost of producing these (relatively) overpriced goods could be expected.[30] Recent experience has shown that this is not a reasonable expectation—for prices of most agricultural inputs are in fact inflating. The situation is not promising.

However, the logic of relative prices is very forceful, especially now that the sector has been pecuniarized. Money represents power—purchasing power—in the Soviet Union, as it does elsewhere. And like it or not, managers of state and collective farms cannot but be tempted to bend in the direction prices point. In the absence of a major step backward to Stalinist measures—and this is most unlikely—the pressure to rationalize agricultural prices is inexorable. Since unit costs of agricultural products are not likely to fall, retail food prices will eventually have to rise to permit a more rational structuring of the whole gamut of agricultural prices.

Rural-urban wage differentials present a somewhat different problem, however, and it falls into the fourth category of problems we listed above. There is little question that the adverse wage differential has decreased during the last twenty-five years, but the change has hardly been radical. The wage on state farms has increased from less than 50 percent of the industrial wage to about 80 percent, and earnings on collective farms have increased from about 25 percent to 60 percent.[31] This kind of differential is typical of developed economies, but it is possible that in the Soviet case it ought to be reversed. Solution of the problem of creating an educated, well-motivated agricultural labor force in an economy in which private farming does not exist may require a differential that favors rural employments. But here we run into a "systemic constraint"—the fact that the Soviet Union is unabashedly a workers' state, and this has typically been interpreted to refer primarily to the industrial worker.

This essentially ideological distaste for a differential wage favoring agricultural employments is only one of a number of systemic constraints on progress in Soviet agriculture. A similar constraint, imposed for similar reasons, is the reluctance to permit the private sector of Soviet agriculture to operate at an optimal level. Soviet leadership has come to realize, mainly through Khrushchev's unhappy experience, that there is sufficient interdependence between public and private agriculture for discrimination against the private sector to rebound upon the public. The current leadership has been willing to tolerate the continued existence of private plot agriculture. Although many of the claims that have been made in the West about the greater productivity of private agriculture in the Soviet Union have been greatly exaggerated, it is nonetheless obvious that the current allocation of resources between the two sectors is not optimal. More important than enlargement of the area of individual private plots, which might be useful to some extent, would be the production and sale of small-scale implements, such as small motorized units, and of other agricultural supplies to improve the efficiency and output of private agriculture.

Most Western observers have been highly critical of the scale of Soviet agricultural enterprises, and the fact that so few private agricultural ventures in the capitalist West are of anything like the scale of the typical sovkhoz or kolkhoz is itself a sign that diminishing returns to scale set in early in agriculture. Bolshevik faith in the benefits of scale seem to be unshakable and impervious to experience either there or in the world at large. There is no reason, however, why the actual operating unit, the brigade, for example, could not be of optimal size, with farms remaining as large as they are today for other reasons. The problem is not really the large size of the typical farm, but a failure to delegate sufficient responsibility and decision-making authority to units that are more nearly optimal in scale.

This brings us to three systemic traits that all observers of Soviet economic affairs are familiar with, traits that are not specific to agriculture at all and that are firmly rooted in Stalinist central planning. They are the tendencies to overcentralize decision making, to overcommit resources in the planning process, and to make decisions with a very low time horizon. Taken together, these three mutually reinforcing traits, which have thus far proven resistant to post-Stalin reform attempts, represent the most formidable obstacle to the evolution of efficient agricultural production. Excessive centralization is an even greater problem when it comes to planning and organizing agricultural production than it is for industry, because the variability of conditions of production (soils, climate, terrain, moisture, and so forth) is much greater in agriculture.

Overcommitment of resources is itself largely the outcome of the high degree of centralization of decision making and the mistrust of local adaptation of plans to local conditions. But it has become a sort of Soviet bureaucratic habit as well. The underlying notion seems to be that high targets serve as *means* as well as *ends*. The large grain imports of the 1970s, for example, have resulted from the fact that targets for the growth of livestock herds were set at unattainable levels, given any reasonable projection of sustainable rates of growth of the fodder base. What is unusual in this case is not that the targets were set so high, but that these ultimately consumer-sector targets attained the degree of priority to permit the expenditure of large quantities of precious foreign exchange.

Finally, despite the five-year format of Soviet planning, managerial decision making at all levels ordinarily operates within a much shorter time horizon. The attempt to get results soon, if not immediately, contributes to a failure to optimize in the medium and longer run. It leads to allocation by priority and the consequent neglect of low priority areas. It also contributes to overcommitment planning, for it induces Soviet administrators to set targets that are not attainable on a sustained basis.

The Future of Soviet Agriculture

The problems catalogued above lead most Western students of Soviet agriculture to be pessimistic about the outlook for continued rapid growth of Soviet agricultural production. The agricultural labor force is certain to decline, the rate of capital formation in agriculture and agriculture-related industries cannot increase, and a decrease is more likely judging from the tenth five-year plan.[32] Expansion of the land area under cultivation is most unlikely, and current investment in reclamation and restoration of arable land and pasturage is unlikely to add as much to the total available as long-term neglect and heavy usage will require to be withdrawn from use.[33] Continued growth of agricultural output will necessarily depend, therefore, upon increases in total factor productivity, that is, increases in the productivity of the conventional inputs taken together. Since total productivity has never increased in in the past at the 3 to 3½ percent rate required to match average annual growth of output during the last quarter century, it follows inescapably that the rate of growth in agricultural production over the next five to ten years will be lower. It also follows that Soviet agriculture will remain high-cost agriculture, for it is going to absorb large quantities of scarce resources, especially investment resources.

Meanwhile the Soviet consumer's income continues to grow, and he has come to expect expanding supplies of high-quality farm products such as dairy products, fruits, vegetables, and beef. Failure of food output to grow commensurately with income and the still relatively high elasticities of demand for these high-quality products are going to be very disturbing to consumers and political leaders alike, and there is no feasible way to avoid some enlargement of the gap between the way Soviet consumers would like to divide their income among the various types of farm products and the actual composition of Soviet farm output. Raising prices to ration the scarcer products may indeed prove to be as politically unwise as the current leadership seems to believe. Hence the dilemma for them. Thus, agriculture will remain for the foreseeable future *the* central domestic focus of political and economic attention. It seems safe in the light of these considerations to conclude that the USSR will continue to import from the West substantial quantities of grains, especially fodders (including soybeans), and perhaps of meat products as well.

In many ways and for many reasons the situation of Soviet agriculture is bleak. However, I am not myself prepared to paint the future of Soviet agriculture in too somber a color. Admitting to the problems outlined above, let me stress a few of the offsetting factors for post-Stalin agriculture. First, the current institutional structure of agricultural production is much more conducive to the development of efficiency than has been the case since the end of the 1920s. Second, Bolshevik ideology is an optimistic doctrine because it implies that solutions to all economic problems *do exist*; they need only be found. Third, Soviet leaders from Lenin forward have demonstrated an ability to get results if the goals have sufficiently high priority, and Soviet agriculture has, in my opinion, attained the requisite degree of priority. Finally, it is well to remember that, historically, most Western medium-term predictions of the growth of Soviet agriculture have been wrong, and almost always on the low side. Wishful thinking may be part of the explanation. But an inability to realize just how high a price Soviet leaders have been willing to pay (and impose) to achieve their goals has also been a factor. This might be labeled a "systemic advantage" of the Soviet-type economy.

Long-term comparison of output growth in the United States and the Soviet Union, say from 1913 to the present, which is long enough to wash out a large portion of the effects of short-term variation in growth in each system, reveals a small but significant differential advantage for the Soviet Union.[34] Thus, although a continuation of the rate of growth of agricultural production over the next five to ten years at the 3½ to 4 percent of the last twenty-five years would be unrealistic, a rate of growth in the neighborhood of 2–2½ percent is not impossible or unreasonable, and unexpectedly good weather could lead to an even more favorable outcome. Thus far, the tenth five-year plan is off to a good start, thanks to several good crop years. Finally, in a world in which aggregate demand for food products is expected to grow rapidly, more rapidly, some claim, than can be supplied,[35] it is encouraging to know that the Soviet Union is potentially self-sufficient and is investing heavily in the food sector. It just might prove to be a good investment.

Notes

1. This article is based upon a number of recent studies of Soviet agriculture. Most important are three papers presented at a conference on the future of Soviet agriculture that was held at the Kennan Institute for Advanced Russian Studies on November 16, 1976. These included my own paper, "Models of Soviet Socialist Agriculture"; D. Gale Johnson, "The 10th Five-Year Plan, Agriculture and Prospects for Soviet-American Trade"; and Douglas B. Diamond, "Comparative Output and Productivity of US and Soviet Agriculture." Other significant recent studies of Soviet agriculture include the following: D. Gale Johnson, "Theory and Practice of Soviet Collective Agriculture," The University of Chicago, Office of Agricultural Economic Research, Paper No. 75:28, December, 1975; Jerzy F. Karcz, "Khrushchev's Impact on Soviet Agriculture," *Agricultural History* 40:1 (January 1966); Alec Nove, "Soviet Agriculture Under Brezhnev," *Slavic Review* 29:3 (September 1970); W. Klatt, "Reflections on the 1975 Soviet Harvest," *Soviet Studies* 28:4 (October 1976); Keith Bush, "Soviet Agriculture: Ten Years Under New Management," Radio Liberty, Munich, May 23, 1975; David W. Carey, "Soviet Agriculture: Recent Performance and Future Plans," and David M. Schoonover, "Soviet Agricultural Trade and the Feed-Livestock Economy," both in Joint Economic Committee, Congress of the United States, *Soviet Economy in a New Perspective* (Washington: U.S. Government Printing Office, 1976). See also an earlier article of mine: "The Prospects for Soviet Agriculture," *Problems of Communism* (May–June 1977), pp. 1–16, upon which I have drawn liberally for this essay.

2. Diamond, "Comparative Output and Productivity of US and Soviet Agriculture," Figure 5A.

3. Murray Feshbach and Stephen Rapawy, "Soviet Population and Manpower Trends and Policies," in *Soviet Economy in a New Perspective*, p. 115, Table 1.

4. Gertrude E. Schroeder and Barbara S. Severin, "Soviet Consumption and Income Policies in Perspective," in *Soviet Economy in a New Perspective*, p. 623, Table 2.

5. TsSU, *Narodnoe khoziaistvo SSSR v 1974 g.* (Moscow, 1975), p. 354, and Central Intelligence Agency, *Research Aid. The Soviet Grain Balance, 1960–73*, September, 1975.

6. *Ekonomika sel'skogo khoziaistva* (1977): B. Maniakin and G. Makhov, "Pobeda Oktiabria i vosstanovlenie sel'skogo khoziaistva (1917–1925 gg.)," No. 8; "Pobeda sotsialisticheskogo sposoba proizvodstva (Tsifry i fakty)," No. 9; "Sel'skoe khoziaistvo v Velikuiu voinu i v poslevoennyi period (1941–1964 gg.)," No. 10; and "V usloviiakh razvitogo sotsializma (1965–76 gg.)," No. 11.

7. This point remains somewhat controversial. See, for example, James R. Millar and Alec Nove, "Was Stalin Really Necessary? A Debate on Collectivization," *Problems of Communism* (July-August 1976), pp. 49–66; and James R. Millar, "Mass Collectivization and the Contribution of Soviet Agriculture to the First Five-Year Plan," *Slavic Review* 33:4 (December 1974), pp. 750–66.

8. In 1976 there were 27,300 collective farms working an average of 3,600 hectares of sown area as opposed to 19,600 state farms working an average of 5,900 hectares per farm. TsSU, *Narodnoe khoziaistvo SSSR za 60 let* (Moscow, 1977).

9. The importance of meat production as a symbol of success was first developed, I believe, by Arcadius Kahan.

10. J. Stalin, *Economic Problems of Socialism in the USSR* (Moscow, 1952), pp. 100–101.

11. Official compilations of statistical data were not published after 1938. An official statistical handbook did not reappear until 1957, the first of the *Narodnoe khoziaistvo* series that continues today.

12. Sterling Wortman, "Food and Agriculture," and David Hopper, "The Development of Agriculture in Developing Countries," both in *Scientific American* 235:3 (September 1976). See also, Theodore W. Schultz, *Transforming Traditional Agriculture* (New Haven: Yale University Press, 1964).

13. D. Gale Johnson, *World Agriculture in Disarray* (London: Fontana/ Collins in association with the Trade Policy Research Centre, 1973).

14. Johnson, "The 10th Five-Year Plan, Agriculture and Prospects for Soviet-American Trade," p. 2.

15. Diamond, "Comparative Output and Productivity of US and Soviet Agriculture," Figure 5A.

16. *Pravda*, January 23, 1977, p. 2; *Ekonomicheskaia gazeta*, vol. 6 (1976), pp. 3–6; USDA, *Agricultural Statistics of Eastern Europe and the Soviet Union, 1950–70* (Washington, D.C., 1973); USDA, *USSR Agricultural Situation: Review of 1977 and Outlook for 1978* (Washington, D.C., 1978); speech by Premier A. Kosygin, November 4, 1978, AP Wireservice.

17. Diamond, "Comparative Output and Productivity of US and Soviet Agriculture," Figure 5A.

18. Carey, "Soviet Agriculture: Recent Performance and Future Plans," pp. 586–87.

19. A. Pronin and M. Terent'ev, "Povyshat' effektivnost' ispol'zovaniia proizvodstvennykh fondov," *Ekonomika sel'skogo khoziaistva*, No. 12 (1973), pp. 7–15; Folke Dovring, "Capital Intensity in Soviet Agriculture," unpublished paper presented to the Fifth International Conference on Soviet and East European Agricultural and Peasant Affairs, Oct. 5–7, 1978, University of Kansas, Lawrence, Kansas.

20. Diamond, "Comparative Output and Productivity of US and Soviet Agriculture," Figure 8A.

21. For the complete analysis, see Millar, "The Prospects for Soviet Agriculture," Table 3, p. 9.

22. Fixed capital (excluding land) per worker is actually higher in agriculture than in industry in the United States, which is not the case for the Soviet Union. For a discussion see A. M. Emel'ianov, "Problemy tempov rosta i povysheniia effektivnosti sel'skokhoziaistvennogo proizvodstva," *Izvestiia akademii nauk SSSR: seriia ekonomicheskaia*, No. 6, 1970, pp. 20–33.

23. The share of total net fixed investment that agriculture has absorbed (directly) has increased from 19.6 percent in 1961–65 to the 26.9 percent that is called for in the (current) tenth five-year plan. The latter is only marginally above the rate that was achieved on average annually during the ninth five-year plan, and there would appear to be no way to increase the

share further. Most of the potentially arable land in the Soviet Union is already under cultivation too, and current plans for reclamation and restoration will not be sufficient to do much more than offset the withdrawal of exhausted marginal lands. Carey, "Soviet Agriculture: Recent Performance and Future Plans," p. 590; Hopper, "The Development of Agriculture in Developing Countries," especially p. 199.

24. Dovring, "Capital Intensity in Soviet Agriculture," p. 19.

25. Cited in Dovring, ibid., p. 2.

26. For an excellent general discussion see Norton T. Dodge, "Recruitment and the Quality of the Soviet Agricultural Labor Force," in James R. Millar, ed., *The Soviet Rural Community, A Symposium* (Urbana: University of Illinois Press, 1971). More recently, see Central Intelligence Agency, *Research Aid, USSR: Some Implications of Demographic Trends for Economic Policies* (January 1977), and Stephen Rapawy, "Estimates and Projections of the Labor Force and Civilian Employment in the USSR: 1950 to 1990," U.S. Department of Commerce, Bureau of Economic Analysis, 1976, pp. 19–20 and 61–63.

27. See, for example, V. N. Kolbanovskii, ed., *Kollektiv kolkhoznikov, sotsial'nopsikhologicheskoe issledovanie* (Moscow, 1970), especially Chapters 6 and 7.

28. V. Savchenko, "Pis'mo," *Novyi mir*, No. 4 (1966), p. 118, as cited by Dodge, "Recruitment and the Quality of the Soviet Agricultural Labor Force."

29. The subsidy has been running at about 85–90 percent of the level of explicit Soviet defense expenditures and represents approximately 28 percent of national income originating in agriculture. Constance B. Krueger, "A Note on the Size of Subsidies on Soviet Government Purchases of Agricultural Producers," *ACES Bulletin*, Vol. 16–17, No. 2 (Fall 1974).

30. This was Soviet experience historically with respect to the production of a wide variety of nonagricultural products of mass consumption, and this expectation has informed Soviet price policy for a very long time. For the best general discussion and history, see A. N. Malafeev, *Istoriia tsenoobrazovanniia v SSSR, 1917–1963* (Moscow, 1964). See also the various price indices presented in the standard Soviet statistical handbooks.

31. Based on Norton T. Dodge, "The Soviet Agricultural Labor Force, Recent Trends," Table 11, p. 14, presented to the Fifth International Conference on Soviet and East European Agricultural and Peasant Affairs, Oct. 5–7, 1978, University of Kansas, Lawrence, Kansas.

32. See Carey, "Soviet Agriculture: Performance and Future Plans," especially p. 590.

33. Klatt, "Reflections on the 1975 Soviet Harvest," pp. 489–91.

34. Soviet growth was measured over the period at an average annual rate of 3.4 percent, against 3.0 percent for the United States. This is a very conservative measure of the difference, because the impact of war and depression on the two systems were not really offsetting in all likelihood, as the analysis implies. Herbert Block, "Soviet Economic Power Growth—Achievements Under Handicaps," in *Soviet Economy in a New Perspective*, especially p. 268.

35. See, for example, Food and Agricultural Organizations of the United Nations, *The State of Food and Agriculture 1974* (Rome, 1975).

Soviet Regional Development

Robert N. Taaffe

A fundamental goal of Soviet regional policies since Stalin has been the continuation of earlier efforts to spread out economic development from the old areas of Slavic settlement in European Russia to the peripheral regions of the country and particularly to the lands east of the Urals. In many ways, this avowed aspiration for spatial disperson, as opposed to concentration, corresponds to the conventional policy recommendations derived from the application of Western regional growth theory to the center-periphery issue. The concomitant efficiency-equity tradeoffs of this process are considerably less evident in the Soviet experience, however, because of the persistent preeminence of efficiency notions and also because of a major distinction between the nature of developmental problems encountered in at least two types of Soviet peripheral areas.

The classic example of a densely settled agrarian region with relatively low per-capita income is found in Central Asia and in some of the western and southern margins of European Russia. Considerations of regional inequalities in income and development, although rarely of decisive importance, have been used to bolster arguments in favor of increased regional investment. In the case of the pioneer periphery in sparsely settled Siberia and the European north,[1] the basic barriers to development are related directly or indirectly to the hostile natural environment. The traditional efficiency-equity arguments are replaced by considerations of efficiency based on natural resource potentials, which are cited by advocates of Siberian development, counterposed to the efficiencies derived from human resources and the Myrdal-type economies of cumulative causation in European Russia. The issue of national security and the Sino-Soviet territorial conflict tend to enhance the justification for Siberian development, although a precise assessment of the importance of these variables in Soviet locational decision making would be an imposing task.

Another fundamental regional problem in the USSR is the intraregional equivalent of the national core-periphery dichotomy. This involves the major efforts to lessen the polarization of development in the leading regional growth centers by intensifying the spread of industrial investment to medium and small cities as well as to agricultural-industrial complexes in the countryside. This locational program is motivated by the desire to tap additional reserves of labor in contrast to the developmental thrust in the Siberian periphery. The urban variant of the core-periphery problem is the effort to reduce the relative importance of the central cities in favor of the outer zone of agglomerated settlement groups. These peripheral settlements, including suburbs and other towns in the same metropolitan area, are scheduled to be the major sites of industrial and population growth in the urban agglomerations centered on large cities.

All three types of locational dispersion have been evident in Soviet regional planning and practice since Stalin. However, they are usually treated separately in policy recommendations and, to a considerable extent, they are inconsistent objectives. For example, development in Siberia is affected negatively by the national program to divert industrial investment to the lower levels of the urban hierarchy because Siberia has a relatively undeveloped urban structure in contrast to the dense network of urban settlements in European Russia. At a different level, the industrial growth of small and medium towns in European Russia that are not in the vicinity of large cities is seriously impeded by the expansion of the peripheral zone of urban agglomerations. The peripheral zone not only offers an attractive locational alternative but it also enables the mobile Soviet population to avoid the large-city settlement restrictions, except in the rare instances, such as the Moscow region, where migrational prohibitions extend to areas outside the central city.

The issue of peripheral regional development on a national scale is the most important of these three types of spatial dispersion and will be the primary problem to be examined in the context of the broader question of changes in Soviet regional policies and practices in the post-Stalin era. Before we turn to specific issues in Soviet regional economic development in the last quarter-century, a few comments should be made about the regional goals and problems in the USSR prior to the death of Stalin in 1953.

The Stalin Era

With respect to regional development, the Stalin period was marked by unfulfilled expectations. A surge of interest in regional economic issues was evident in the early 1920s. This could be seen in the GOELRO plan for national electrification and in the imaginative debates concerning the delimitation of Gosplan regions, which were supposed to have had important economic-administrative functions. In the latter 1920s Western location theory, particularly that of Weber and Von Thunen, was infused into Soviet locational debates. The industrial location theory of Alfred Weber played a major role in the national conflict over the Urals-Kuznetsk Combine, which involved the creation of iron and steel complexes in these regions based on the long-haul interchange of coal and iron ore.[2] The use of this transport-oriented theory by opponents of the project contributed to an abrupt demise of Western location theory in Soviet planning. This trend persisted through the Stalin era and was symptomatic of the general intellectual xenophobia of this period. In the 1930s the industrial ministries made locational decisions essentially on an ad hoc basis. Presumably inspired by the virtual ignoring of transport costs in the Urals-Kuznetsk decision, their locational choices tended to focus upon the construction of very large enterprises. Little attention was paid either to diminishing economies of scale or to transport factors.

The absence of usable locational guidelines made it easier for Stalin to introduce a radically different plan on the eve of World War II. The new objective was to make the major Soviet regions more self-sufficient in fuels and raw materials, machinery, and consumer goods. This shift was intended to reduce transport costs in general and long rail hauls of basic commodities in particular. Superficially, this sudden obsession with lowering transport costs appeared to reflect the transport bias of Weberian theory pursued to an illogical extreme, particularly when the transport savings often were more than counterbalanced by higher production costs. However, one should scarcely discount the importance of defense motives prior to the war and the subsequent dislocations in the Soviet energy economy, primarily in the Donets basin and Baku, for the persistence of this program of relative regional autarky until the death of Stalin, despite the difficulty of justifying this policy by comparative cost criteria.[3] Curiously, the "socialist principles of location" that were developed most fully during this period have been transferred into contemporary Soviet theory with only modest changes, even though the planning emphasis clearly has shifted to a focus on regional specialization and on the attainment of economic objectives that are considerably broader than minimizing transport outlays. The durability of these principles seems to reflect their linkage to Marxist-Leninist ideology rather than their relevance for the complexities of locational decision making.

Despite the strong regional component in the Stalinist locational objectives, Soviet economic administration, of course, was sectorally organized and highly centralized. Territorial planning and administration were at their nadir. With respect to specific locational measures, neither the efforts to shift manufacturing to the East nor even the most publicized projects of diffusing growth to the periphery, such as the Urals-Kuznetsk Combine, had succeeded in redressing the pronounced regional imbalances in development. Although scarcely motivated by long-term considerations of regional growth, the most successful major locational changes that occurred under Stalin were the forced evacuation of over 1,300 industrial enterprises and approximately 20 to 25 million people from the path of the German invasion in World War II to the eastern margins of European Russia and to Soviet Asia.[4]

The Response to Changing Resource Constraints

Relatively high priority has been given to investment in the peripheral regions of the USSR during the post-Stalin era, essentially in response to rapidly changing resource constraints on development and, to some extent, international economic and political stimuli. These efforts have been motivated by specific economic needs and guided by sectorally oriented national economic plans rather than consistent and long-term plans of regional development. With some important exceptions, the types of resource scarcities that give rise to a transfer of investment priorities from the center to the agrarian peripheral regions usually are different from those encouraging development in the pioneer periphery; in certain cases, the factors tending to enhance development in one type of peripheral region tend to retard growth in the other type. For example, the shortages of energy enhance enormously the role of Siberia in the national economy and simultaneously reduce the incentives for industrialization in the heavily agrarian and energy-poor western margins of European Russia. Conversely, the scarcities of industrial labor pose a seemingly insurmountable obstacle to diversified economic development in Siberia while providing a strong motive for allocating industrial investments to regions with a labor surplus. It should be noted, however, that the exploitation of petroleum and natural gas in Central Asia represents an exception to this energy-labor dichotomy.

Energy and Raw Materials

In the post-Stalin era a great deal of the investment in the areas east of the Urals has been motivated by a desire to use the abundant raw materials of this zone. This has led to the impressive growth of nonferrous metallurgy (particularly aluminum), ferrous metallurgy, chemical industries, and many other industrial sectors, as well as to costly transport projects, such as the start of construction of the long-delayed Baikal-Amur mainline. However, the most striking economic change in Siberia has been its projected ascendancy to a dominant position in Soviet energy supply. The relative stagnation or impending depletion of the petroleum, natural gas, and coal deposits of European Russia and the utilization of many of its best hydropower sites have transformed the objective of shifting the major energy base to the East, which has about 90 percent of the national energy resources, from a vague aspiration to an immediate imperative. The growing output of petroleum and natural gas in the northern and eastern edges of European Russia will not compensate for the decreased production of these commodities in the remainder of this zone. A major effort is underway in European Russia to reduce the growth rate of energy consumption by restricting the expansion of energy-oriented industries in general and the consumption of petroleum and natural gas in particular; by constructing nuclear power plants in the Ukraine and elsewhere in this zone; by encouraging the exploitation of local, high-cost energy resources; and by replacing petroleum and natural gas by coal in thermal power plants, including those in the formerly oil-rich Volga-Urals region. Conversely, the burgeoning energy economy of the East will account for nearly all the growth of energy output in the USSR during the 1976–80 five-year plan, including all the expansion of oil and gas production and more than 90 percent of the increase in coal output.[5]

Efforts also have been made by Soviet planners to site the new plants of the major industrial consumers of energy and raw materials in Siberia in order to expand the local use of these resources. However, the share of the East in energy consumption has increased at a very slow rate. From 1971 to 1975, the Eastern share rose from 21.6 percent to 23.8 percent or less than one-quarter of national energy consumption.[6]

Neither the constraints on energy consumption in European Russia nor the program to expand energy-based industrialization in the East will retard the massive east-west flows of energy, which are scheduled to increase by an unprecedented amount. The volume of energy that European Russia imported from the East reached the impressive level of 130 million standard tons of fuel in 1970, and this flow nearly tripled to a level of 360 million tons by 1975. The five-year plan calls for the extraordinary magnitude of 700 million tons of standard fuel to be moved from the East to satisfy the voracious energy appetites of European Russia. These flows will involve 240 million tons of petroleum, 120 million tons of coal, and 220 billion cubic meters of natural gas.[7] It seems difficult to imagine that only twenty-five years ago the movement of 10 million tons of coal from the Donets basin to the Moscow region was viewed with alarm as a major example of an economically unjustified long haul. In 1975, the costs of fuel movement in the USSR were three billion rubles. These transport outlays should increase even more than the near-doubling of the fuel tonnage by 1980 because of substantially longer average hauls. Moreover, enormous investments will be needed for energy-related transport construction. The tapping of the energy resources of the East will require the expansion of the oil and gas pipeline network, increased rail capacities, and the completion of transmission lines to move the power generated by the huge dams in the Angara-Yenisey complex and the thermal power plants burning the open-pit coals of Siberia and Kazakhstan. In addition, many of these energy flows will be dependent upon major transport innovations that are still in the experimental stage, including the transmission of electricity at high voltages over long distances; technological changes in pipeline transport of petroleum and natural gas as well as the possible movement of liquefied natural gas; and the ultimate development of massive coal-slurry pipelines to handle the shipments of open-pit coal to European Russia.[8]

In addition to high transport costs, Siberian energy development is impeded by many other problems, such as the underdeveloped productive and social infrastructure of this region, the rigorous natural conditions, the necessity for higher wages to attract workers, a relatively high level of capital investments and low degree of capital productivity, and the apparent need for substantial imports of Western technology. After 1980 the ability of the West Siberian oilfields to increase or even sustain high output levels is uncertain. The major deposits at the huge Samotlor field will soon reach their maximum level of output, and the increments in production will have to come from medium-sized fields in the West Siberian swamplands to the north of existing wells.[9] Nikolai Inozemtsev, director of the Institute of World Economy and International Relations in Moscow, has disputed these gloomy forecasts by asserting that the Soviet Union will continue to be a major net exporter of petroleum by opening up new producing sites in Siberia and, most of all, by restricting the consumption of petroleum.[10] The prospects of either reduced production or reduced consumption offer little comfort to the growing number of energy consumers in European Russia and Eastern Europe, who will have become of necessity increasingly dependent upon Siberian supplies.

Labor

Another resource constraint that will have a profound locational and regional effect is the impending shortage of industrial labor in the USSR. This shortage is indicated by the anticipated decline in the growth rate of the population of labor-force age from 1.9 percent a year in the 1971–75 period to an annual rate of only 0.3 percent by the latter 1980s, with the sharpest decreases occurring among the Slavic population and the greatest gains in the Central Asian republics.[11] The most acute labor shortage is found in Siberia. Since Stalin, the Soviet government has employed a wide range of economic and other incentives to resolve this critical problem which has made the exploitation of vital Siberian resources more difficult and impeded this region from developing a diversified industrial economy and an adequate infrastructure. This imbalanced development, in turn, has retarded migration. Judging by the net migrational loss of 770,000 people in Siberia during the 1959–70 intercensal period, efforts to induce migration have had little success.[12] The problem is not so much attracting people to Siberia as it is keeping them there without coercion. By contrast, some of the greatest interregional migrational gains during this period were in areas planned to have net migrational losses—the Ukraine and the Northern Caucasus. The labor deficits of Siberia have been worsened by the increasing pressure on enterprises in European Russia to prepare for the anticipated shortages of labor by discouraging migration to the East. The developmental guidelines for Siberia apparently have been scaled down to recognize these migrational realities, and serious restraints have been imposed upon labor-intensive industrialization in this region.

By contrast, the industrial attractiveness of the agrarian periphery in European Russia and Central Asia has been enhanced because of a significant rural labor surplus. In the case of Central Asia, this rural population surplus is being augmented at a rapid rate because of the extremely high rates of natural population increase, which are among the highest in the world, and because the high birth rates are accompanied by very low crude death rates of this young population. Population forecasts show that all the growth of the Soviet labor-force age population in the 1980s will be derived from Central Asian populations. By the year 2000 the traditionally Islamic peoples in the USSR (in Central Asia and elsewhere) may constitute as much as one-fourth of the Soviet population as compared to one-eighth at present.[13] However, serious problems are involved in diverting this substantial labor potential to nonagricultural employment. The Central Asian peoples' deep cultural roots in the countryside have made them the most spatially immobile large population group in the USSR. It has been extremely difficult to entice Central Asian men and, even more, women to fill the industrial job openings in local cities. Soviet economic demographers and many Western observers regard as quite unlikely the prospects of major interregional diversions of the Central Asian labor surplus to culturally and environmentally alien regions of the USSR.[14] The most feasible alternative is to increase local urban employment opportunities substantially in the hope that the Central Asian rural population will respond to these economic stimuli as well as to the push factor of increased rural population pressure.

Land

Just as the projected limitations in the growth of the labor force and the constraints on capital investment will impel the USSR to alter its classical growth strategy of reliance on increased factor inputs to one of greater dependence on technological progress, a similar restraint has emerged with respect to agricultural land. The ploughing of almost one million acres of grasslands in the Virgin Lands for grain cultivation was the most ambitious agricultural program undertaken by Khrushchev in the East, paralleling his efforts to create a Soviet corn belt in the south of European Russia. The Virgin Lands usually provide about one-third of Soviet wheat output, but their annual yields are highly variable, and these farmlands are subject to persistent problems of wind erosion and limited soil moisture. The concentration of the Brezhnev regime on increased agricultural investment and monetary incentives has marked the end of the dramatic instant remedies to agricultural problems that were so popular with Khrushchev and even with Stalin, from his introduction of collectivization to his subsequent infatuation with the metaphysical genetics of Lysenko. This shift from the extensive to the intensive in agriculture is motivated in part by the limited possibilities of major additions to the stock of arable land and is aided enormously by the willingness of the present leadership to assign a high priority to investment in the agricultural sector.

Water and Environmental Protection

As is the case with energy and raw materials, enormous disparities in water resources are found between the East, with roughly 82 percent of the surface water runoff, and European Russia, where most of the water is consumed. An even greater dilemma is posed by concentration of water resources in the northern portions of each of these zones, contrasting sharply to water-deficit areas in the southern areas of these regions. The massive water diversion schemes of Stalin's "Great Projects of Communism" in the early 1950s attempted to provide remedies to these interzonal water problems; these schemes were resurrected by Khrushchev in his long-term Communist Party program of 1962. Although most of the water diversion programs, including the transfer of water from Western Siberia to Kazakhstan, Central Asia, and European Russia, and a comparable proposal to shift the waters of the European North to the southern areas of this zone by way of the Volga-Kama system, have been the objects of intensive study for decades and are still being investigated by Soviet scholars and planners, none of these projects has been implemented as yet.[15] One of the most serious consequences of these regional imbalances in water supply is that industries in the heavily industrialized southern areas of European Russia are experiencing shortages of water, and restrictions have been placed on the construction of water-consumptive industries in these regions.[16]

One of the most striking changes in Soviet regional development since Stalin is the increased concern at present for environmental conservation as reflected in the introduction in the current five-year plan of goals for environmental protection at ministerial, regional, and enterprise levels; comprehensive environmental legislation; and the requirement of environmental impact statements for large-scale construction projects.[17] Both Soviet and American experience indicates that it is much easier to write an environmental law than to implement one, particularly when implementation involves difficult choices between environmental and economic objectives. Nonetheless, environmental concerns in Soviet regional development are much more important now than they were during the era of Stalin, who seemed to regard nature as a type of class enemy to be conquered and transformed in order to serve national economic interests.

It is evident that the basic changes in Soviet regional policies and investment shifts between the center and the periphery can be traced in large part to increasing regional imbalances in the demand, supply, and reserves of natural and human resources. A commitment to a specific regional program usually has reflected the urgency of a particular resource need rather than a consistent planning response to long-term issues of comprehensive regional development. In contrast to the Stalinist disregard of regional forecasting, the present Soviet leadership has demonstrated a strong concern for the analysis of regional development as part of a long-term plan for the distribution and growth of productive forces. Although progress has been made toward this objective, a wide range of problems remain to be solved before the projections of long-range regional planning can supplant short-term sectoral objectives in Soviet locational decision making.

Conflict in Locational Decision Making

In addition to planner's evaluations of resources, Soviet assessments of comparative regional advantage in investment decisions also seem to influenced by regional interest groups and particularly by the conflicts between proponents of development in the East and in European Russia. This debate has persisted with varying degrees of intensity from the tsarist era through the heated controversy over the Urals-Kuznetsk project to the present day. Advocates of development in European Russia, particularly the government and party of the Ukraine and many all-union sectoral ministries, feel that a disproportionate share of the income and capital of the western regions of the USSR has been siphoned off through various devices into costly and economically unjustified projects in the East. In their view, these funds would yield substantially higher returns if they were invested in European Russia, which has a relatively large pool of skilled labor, a developed productive and social infrastructure, and proximity to major domestic and international markets. As could be anticipated, the response of the supporters of development in the East, including the Siberian groups, the regional research institutes of Gosplan, and, usually, the leadership and planning institutions of the Russian Republic, has focused on the growing disparities in the resource potentials of the eastern and western zones of the USSR, which they fell ultimately will justify the investments needed for development in the East.[18]

The party serves as the arbitrator of this protracted locational debate, and it frequently decides, in principle at least, in favor of investment in the East. However, the national plan directives usually provide compromise solutions that encompass some of the objectives sought by both of the regional interest groups; advocates of differential directions of regional development normally can find support for their positions in the national economic plans. The national plan stresses massive resource development projects in the East, and high industrial growth rates are usually scheduled for this zone as well. But many other sections of the plan provide even more substantial support for investment in the western regions. For example, one section of the current economic plan demonstrates the priority of the East in new investment by assigning 30 percent of the allocations for new industrial construction to that region, which is considerably in excess of the 20 percent share of the East in industrial production.[19] However, another section of the plan directives indicates that the overwhelming share of industrial growth in the USSR in the 1976–80 period will occur through the modernization and replacement of existing industrial stock, which provides a strong basis for the maintenance of the industrial preeminence of European Russia.[20]

Many of the planning mechanisms have been designed to reduce the competitive disadvantages of Siberia caused by its higher costs of construction, installation of machinery, and transportation. These measures include the use of regional coefficients of normative investment effectiveness, which are applied to ten Soviet regions, four climatic zones, and even one seismic zone.[21] These coefficients compensate for some of the higher regional costs by permitting Siberian projects to be justified at a lower threshold level of investment effectiveness than used elsewhere in the USSR, and particularly in European Russia, to evaluate investment alternatives. Although this approach might be a useful device for encouraging investment in the East, it is scarcely conducive to spatial efficiency. For this reason, the planners of some funded Siberian projects, such as the Baikal-Amur Mainline (BAM), have attempted to increase the effectiveness of allocations within this immense and diverse region by urging the use of "corrective" coefficients of investment which would reflect the real extra costs of construction and development associated with the harshness of the natural environment.[22] Use of these coefficients would help eliminate or defer the most costly and economically dubious industrial or mining projects in this zone. Of course, any call for an accurate assessment of the developmental costs caused by Siberian physical-geographic factors will be supported enthusiastically by proponents of investment priority for European Russia.

As is the case with many other regional incentives, such as migrational and investment stimuli, the relatively low freight rates for the mass exports of bulk commodities from Siberia have negative as well as positive effects. The exploitation of Siberian resources is made more attractive in planning calculations by use of low freight charges.[23] However, the same rates provide a major disincentive to create a diversified industrial base in Siberia compared to the alternative of shipping these commodities to European Russia for higher-level and comprehensive industrial processing.

In recent years, the leadership appears to be more cognizant of the arguments that massive inputs of capital investments, often with very low returns, are needed for economic development in Siberia and for the provision of a level of life which would enable that region to attract and retain migrants. Even the Siberian-oriented planners now cite data pointing out that average construction costs in Siberia are 50 percent to three times higher than in European Russia and that the costs of providing an adequate social infrastructure for each new inhabitant of such pioneer regions as the area served by the BAM amount to 18,000 rubles, compared to 5,000–7,000 rubles for a new settler in European Russia.[24] Apparently, the leadership has become reconciled to the view that in the immediate future, at least, Siberia will remain primarily an exporter of energy and raw materials; it is not apt to become a comprehensively developed industrial society modeled after the older industrial regions of European Russia.

Changes in Territorial Planning Since Stalin

The limitations on Soviet economic growth imposed by the relative scarcities and distributional imbalances of natural resources, labor, and capital, and the regional conflicts over the allocation of investment have generated an urgent need for effective territorial planning. Since Stalin, substantial gains have been made in this area, but many major problems have yet to be surmounted. The fundamental difficulty at present is that of developing territorial planning and administration in a highly centralized economy, which returned to sectorally focused planning after a chaotic experiment with regional economic administration. Despite their enhanced economic role, union republics are clearly subordinate to the central government in planning and administration. The limited access of union-republic planners to national data and central authorities seriously diminishes the prospects of successful regional challenges to the decisions of central ministries and planners, which presumably reflect national rather than "provincial" concerns, although republic-level planners maintain that the central ministries often confuse national interests with "narrow departmental" motives and approaches.

Another impediment to effective regional planning is that the ethnically delimited union republics usually are not meaningful economic regions. For example, the Russian Republic occupies three-fourths of Soviet territory or one-eighth of the land area of the world, but for many economic purposes constitutes a single administrative-planning region as well as an economically meaningless statistical reporting unit in national statistical handbooks. A modest effort was undertaken in 1961 to provide administrative functions for nineteen statistical regions of Gosplan, including ten regions in the RSFSR. But even this program persisted only until 1969, when the last regional planning commissions were abolished.[25]

Most of the locational planning in the USSR is carried out in the center with only limited attention to external economies and diseconomies in specific locational decisions. This problem is moderated, but scarcely eliminated, in some types of production associations and in territorial-production complexes used in long-term forecasts and planning of some integrated energy and resource regions, primarily in the pioneer periphery. The designation of territorial-production complexes is one of the most important contributions to regional analysis and planning in the post-Stalin era.[26] At present, the planning impact of this innovation is impeded by the absence of a formal administrative structure for these complexes and the frequent lack of correspondence and coordination between these spatial production entities and the network of territorial-political administration. In addition, many unresolved methodological problems are associated with the definition and evaluation of the economic effectiveness of the territorial-production complexes.[27]

Some of the major goals of regional industrial development in the Russian Republic and, particularly, in the East are listed in the national economic plan. However, as Pavlenko has pointed out, the industrial ministries are not assigned responsibility for fulfilling these regional objectives in the national plan.[28] Recently, five-year plans for development in selected regions in the East, as well as for the cities of Moscow and Leningrad, have been approved by the central government and the party and have been incorporated into the national economic plan. Effective territorial planning, however, is difficult to implement on a patchwork basis, inasmuch as this approach ignores the interdependencies among regions and the evident need for both horizontal and vertical coordination in Soviet regional planning.

Long-term Territorial Planning

A major effort has been made during the Brezhnev era to introduce long-term regional forecasting and planning on a comprehensive basis to compensate for a major shortcoming in Soviet economic planning. The first major long-range locational and regional plan in the Brezhnev period projected the distribution and development of economic activity by sectors and regions for the 1971–80 period and was devised by the cooperative efforts of 560 research organizations and planning agencies. However, this plan was discarded shortly after its inception because of the crudity of its methods and the limited utility of its prognoses.[29] A plan for the distribution of productive forces for the 1976–90 period was then formulated in conjunction with long-term plans for the national economy, social development, and scientific-technical progress. The sectoral locational plans were prepared by the central ministries; the regional sections, by the research institutes of Gosplan; and the local regional, settlement, and urban plans, by Gosstroy (State Construction Committee) and Gosgrazhdanstroy (State Public-Works Construction Committee).[30] But the old problems seem to be reappearing. According to the deputy director of the RSFSR Gosplan, N. Singur, there is very little coordination in the work of these groups.[31] They are forecasting for different time-horizons and using different methodologies and assumed objectives. The absence of a common methodology has yielded contradictory recommendations for the same problems. For example, many of the industrial projects scheduled for construction by Gosstroy along the route of the Baikal-Amur Mainline have been sharply attacked by the research institutes of Gosplan responsible for regional projections in the long-term plan.

Although clearly needed, it seems quite doubtful that the science of long-range regional forecasting in the USSR, or anywhere else, has advanced to the point where accurate predictions can be made and encompassed in national economic planning with any degree of confidence. A promising alternative is the growing use by Soviet planners of goal programming, in which selected key tasks involving diverse ministries and research institutes are assigned high priority and approached in an integrative manner, often in a regional context.[32] Territorial-production complexes could be considered as a special case of this broad approach, which moderates some of the temporal and institutional constraints of existing planning practices.

Quantitative Approaches to Locational and Regional Analysis

A major advance in regional analysis in the post-Stalin era has been the surge of interest in quantitative approaches. This has had a positive effect on the quality of Soviet locational research and also has helped clarify major issues of regional development in the USSR. For example, production-transportation programming models have transcended many of the most evident limitations of the oft-quoted "socialist principles of location," which represent a combination of Weberian-type transport-minimization objectives, regional equity considerations, and defense motives. The programming approaches have provided an operational form for transport objectives and have substituted the objective of maximizing consumption for the narrow least-cost goals of the socialist principles. In addition, the compilation of regional input-output tables for 1966 and 1972 has provided important insights into the complex development and interdependence of regional economies in the Soviet Union, although the relevance of these approaches for current regional planning appears to be rather limited.

In one sense, the use of these and other quantitative approaches and the computerization of Soviet economic planning would tend to enhance the dominance of the center in locational decision making. This trend would be strengthened by the completion of the long-delayed national automated network of economic information, which would feed in massive amounts of economic data to computing complexes in Moscow. On the other hand, Siberian scholars have pointed out that locational planning from the center often pays little attention to external economies and diseconomies, essential regional socioeconomic features, and environmental particularities. They also note that many scientific-research institutes in European Russia structure their investigations to ensure that the outcomes will favor location in the western regions.[33] For example, the economic models of these institutes often focus on labor outlays and other comparative regional costs and assume that adequate supplies of labor are available. This approach obviously yields results unfavorable to location in Siberia. The Siberian counterattacks, as reflected in their mathematical models of regional development, cite the possibility of creating an optimal national economic plan by combining optimal regional plans (subject to certain national constraints) as an alternative to highly centralized plan formulation.[34] In addition, the Siberian models point out directly or indirectly the dependence of European Russia on Siberian natural resources and emphasize the immense planning potentials of the resource-oriented territorial productive complexes.[35] The Siberian studies invariably forecast a substantially higher rate of growth for Siberia than for European Russia.

These efforts at spatial and regional quantification are exciting intellectual ventures with some important applications, particularly with respect to narrowly defined locational problems, such as the minimization of fuel flows or the location of cement plants in a given region. Unfortunately, these approaches have produced relatively few answers to the more general problems of Soviet regional development, because of the complexity of these regional issues and the substantial lag in

transferring the quantitative methodologies to regional planning. Moreover, there are many specific problems impeding more widespread application of these quantitative approaches such as inadequate information (including the existing price system), unresolved methodological
problems, limitations in computer capacities, and the intricacy of the
task of incorporating essential noneconomic variables.

The Growing Need for Socioeconomic Territorial Planning

One of the most important trends in Soviet regional forecasting and
planning since Stalin has been the increased awareness of the need to
consider a wide range of socioeconomic variables. Many Soviet scholars now stress the inadequacies of economic plans which do not consider population trends, migrational patterns, urban development and
the settlement system as a whole, and the social infrastructure of cities
and regions. Despite this obvious need, only modest progress has been
made to encompass these variables into locational planning.

The most urgent socioeconomic planning task is to guide migrational
flows of labor into directions corresponding to the preferences of planners and, presumably, broader societal interests. This involves diverting
labor from surplus to deficit regions and retaining the labor-force age
population in pioneer regions, in small and medium-sized cities with
an industrial potential, and in agricultural regions with shortages of
young farm workers. However, as noted above, the actual pattern of
migration bears little resemblance to national objectives. One of the
reasons for the pronounced deficiencies in migrational planning is the
reliance on the planning mechanisms of the Stalin era to cope with the
complex problems of a society in which individual locational preferences have become preeminent and in which the pervasiveness of job
opportunities has given migrants a broad range of directional possibilities.[36] This trend is reflected in the precipitous decline of organized
labor recruitment in the post-Stalin era. During the period from 1930
to 1950, 22 million workers were recruited by organized methods,
compared to only 5.6 million between 1951 and 1970.[37] Moreover, the
decline is becoming increasingly evident even within this latter period;
this trend can be seen in the sharp drop in the number of participants
in organized recruitment programs from 2.8 million in the 1951–55 in-
terval to a total of only 571,000 people in the recent five-year span from
1966 to 1970.[38]

Another carry-over from the Stalin era is the neglect of urban development in national economic planning. There is neither a central
ministry handling urban affairs nor a section of the five-year plans

concerned explicitly with the problems of comprehensive urban development. The conspicuous omission of urban policies or effects from the "socialist principles of location" has prompted at least one Soviet regional economist, O. S. Pechilintsev, to urge that the traditional preoccupation of locational planning in the last forty years with transport economies be replaced by a concentration on urban agglomeration economies.[39]

Even the general plans of Soviet cities, with the important exceptions of Moscow and Leningrad, are more similar to architectural documents than to comprehensive socioeconomic plans. As a Soviet urbanologist, M. Mezhevich, has observed, the economic component of these general urban plans essentially constitutes lists of industrial enterprises supplied to city soviets by branch ministries.[40] The regulation of the growth of cities relies on administrative restrictions on migration and new industrial construction. These are the same planning instruments used unsuccessfully during the Stalin era. It is not surprising that the cities in the USSR with more than one-half million inhabitants are growing at a rate substantially in excess of that of small cities, despite the ostensible planning efforts to check the growth of large cities. One of the most positive signs of increased Soviet concern for redressing the imbalance in planning emphasis associated with the relative neglect of the comprehensive socioeconomic planning of urban development is the inclusion of long-term urban and settlement forecasts in the 1976–90 plan. The importance of social and economic variables in these projections, however, is uncertain because this task has been assigned to Gosstroy, which traditionally has adopted a narrow architectural-engineering approach to urban and regional planning.

Siberian scholars, planners, and political leaders have stressed that the basic impediment to migration to the East and, even more, the retention of the population of this region is the inadequate social infrastructure of Siberian cities.[41] This problem is intensified by the nature of the existing investment and planning structure. On a ministerial level, the construction and industrial ministries have been assigned responsibility for the urban expenditures associated with new industrial development in Siberia. Most of their investments, however, are channeled into direct productive activities, and the provision of housing and urban services is seriously neglected. This problem is particularly acute in the new industrial towns of Siberia, which have some of the most critical shortages of labor.

On a national scale, the absence of a general national plan on the quality of life that would guide efforts to equalize living conditions among the regions of the USSR is cited as an important reason why the level of amenities is inversely correlated to regional labor needs.[42] Inasmuch as the higher costs of living in Siberia diminish the effectiveness of the higher wages in this area, which is another deficiency of the regional planning process, the limited availability of urban services and other amenities often is the decisive element in the choices of migrants to leave Siberia. Advocates of eastern development have urged that Siberia be given preferential treatment as part of a policy they term "social-economic protectionism." Implementation of this policy would involve massive investments in the urban social infrastructures of this region and the substantial augmentation of real incomes in order to enable Siberia ultimately to be able to compete successfully for migrants with European Russia.[43] Proponents of development in western regions of the USSR present the counter-argument that the amount of investment in social overhead capital that would be needed to attract and retain the desired number of migrants would be prohibitively high. Moreover, there is no assurance that this investment would attain its objectives, inasmuch as the climate of Siberia would still discourage settlement, particularly in an era when amenity-oriented migration is becoming increasingly important in the Soviet Union.

Thus, as in many other aspects of regional planning, a fundamental improvement has occurred in the post-Stalin era in the level of awareness and analysis of the problems which are the primary concern of socioeconomic territorial planning. But as yet, these migrational, urban, and social-investment variables have been implemented only on a modest scale because of the complexity of this task and the persistence of many of the planning mechanisms that were better suited for the simpler economic assignments of the Stalinist command economy.

Prospects for Regional Economic Development

Despite the major changes in the Soviet regional economy since Stalin, the fundamental geographic disparity between the concentration of resources in the East and the preeminence of the western regions in industrial production and consumption will persist, as will the competing claims of regional interest groups for investment priorities. Because of the intensive and prolonged industrialization of European Russia, the depletion of many of the natural resources of this area has transformed it into a mature industrial zone which will become progressively more dependent on massive imports of energy and raw materials from the East. Nonetheless, European Russia still possesses some enormous labor, infrastructural, and locational competitive advantages over the East. Unless Siberia, in particular, can resolve its chronic shortages of labor and moderate its seemingly insatiable demands for invest-ment capital, it appears to be destined to remain a highly specialized exporter of energy and other forms of natural wealth with an industrial structure dominated by the early stages of the production process. This trend will be reinforced by the transport-cost savings of processing the long-haul and concentrated flows of Siberian crude oil in the western regions of the USSR and shipping the finished products, which have higher freight rates and market prices, over relatively moderate dis-tances to spatially dispersed consumers in European Russia and East-ern Europe. Siberia is apt to retain many of the features of a pioneer periphery rather than become a complex, developed, and balanced re-gional economy.

A new and important element in regional development will be the growing international interdependence of the Soviet economy. The economic growth of the European core and the western peripheral regions will be enhanced by proximity to CMEA and West European markets and suppliers as well as by available labor reserves. Central Asia will benefit less from international contacts, but it will have the largest surplus labor reserves in the USSR. The strong aversion of the Central Asian peoples to interregional migration could very well in-spire large-scale industrialization in this region comparable to that of the other classical-type peripheral regions in the western and southern margins of European Russia. Expanded international linkages will also have a positive effect on economic growth in the East. In addition to the markets which CMEA countries, Western Europe, Japan, and, hopefully, the United States can provide for the exports of the East, the infusion of East European capital and labor in joint investment projects will contribute to the development of Siberia as will the pos-sible investment and technology of Western countries.

Soviet developmental experience since Stalin has demonstrated that the exploitation of the natural resources of the USSR is encountering many of the problems common to industrialized societies, particularly to those of North America. In the near future, the Soviet Union will have to make difficult choices in balancing domestic needs, CMEA commitments, and trade with the West to acquire technology. More-over, many difficult decisions about regional investment priorities will have to be made. The possibilities of making consistent, economically defensible, and enduring choices would be enhanced significantly if substantial progress were made in resolving the problems incurred by the limited role of regional planning and administration, the substantial gap between analytical methodologies and planning practices, and, fi-nally, the lack of conceptually sound, comprehensive, and operationally relevant guidelines for locational choice and integrated regional development. The growing concern with these problems in the USSR provides encouraging indications that major efforts toward a resolution of these complex issues will be a prominent feature of Soviet planning and development in the future.

Notes

1. The term Siberia will be used to denote the Soviet regions of West Siberia, East Siberia, and the Far East.
2. For a discussion of the Urals-Kuznetsk controversy see M. Gardner Clark, *The Economics of Soviet Steel* (Cambridge: Harvard University Press, 1956), and F. D. Holzman, "Soviet Ural-Kuznetsk Combine: A Study in Investment Criteria and Industrialization Policies," *Quarterly Journal of Economics*, 1957, pp. 368–405.
3. This policy did not even reduce the average length of rail hauls or the degree of regional self-sufficiency. See Robert N. Taaffe, "Transportation and Regional Specialization: The Example of Soviet Central Asia," *Annals of the Association of American Geographers*, no. 2, 1962, pp. 80–98.
4. Yu. G. Saushkin, "Khoziaistvennoe osvoenie territorii SSSR posle oktiabria," *Vestnik Moskskovskogo Universiteta: Seriia Geografiia*, no. 1, 1978, p. 6.
5. Ya. Mazover, "Razmeshchenie toplivodobyvaiushchei promyshlennosti," *Planovoe khoziaistvo*, no. 11, 1977, p. 138.
6. Mazover, p. 139.
7. Ibid.
8. Yu. Bokserman, "Puti povysheniia effektivnosti transporta topliva," *Planovoe khoziaistvo*, no. 11, 1977, pp. 99–102, and Robert W. Campbell, "Issues in Soviet R & D: The Energy Case," in *Soviet Economy in a New Perspective* (Washington: Joint Economic Committee, Congress of the United States, U.S. Government Printing Office, 1976), pp. 99–103.
9. Theodore Shabad, "News Notes," *Soviet Geography*, no. 3, 1977, p. 273.
10. As quoted in the *Wall Street Journal*, May 8, 1978.
11. Murray Feshbach and Stephen Rapawy, "Soviet Population and Manpower Trends and Policies," in *Soviet Economy in a New Perspective*, p. 133.
12. B. Urlanis, ed., *Narodonaselenie stran mira* (Moscow: Statistika, 1973), p. 411.
13. Feshbach and Rapawy, p. 120, and a NATO study of Soviet economic development quoted in the *Chicago Tribune*, June 1, 1978. The labor-force population data include Kazakhstan as well as Central Asia.
14. Feshbach and Rapawy, pp. 116–129. Among many other impediments to interregional migration is the ability of only 15 to 20 percent of the Central Asian peoples to speak Russian.
15. Philip P. Micklin, "Irrigation Development in the USSR during the 10th Five-Year Plan (1976–1980)," *Soviet Geography*, no. 1, 1978, p. 20.
16. *Gosudarstvennyi pyatiletnii plan razvitiia narodnogo khoziaistvo SSSR na 1971–1975 g.* (Moscow: Politizdat, 1972), p. 248.

17. P. Poletaev, "Sovershenstvovaniia planirovaniia okhrany prirody," *Planovoe khoziaistvo*, no. 10, 1977, pp. 36–43.

18. Many of these arguments are summarized in Leslie Dienes, "Investment Priorities in Soviet Regions," *Annals of the Association of American Geographers*, no. 3, 1972, pp. 437–454.

19. A. Triakin, "Territorial'nyi aspekt planirovaniia," *Planovoe khoziaistvo*, no. 8, 1977, p. 66.

20. A review of the regional aspects of the tenth five-year plan in relation to the center-periphery issue can be found in Robert Jensen, "Soviet Regional Development in the 10th Five-Year Plan," *Soviet Geography*, no. 3, 1978, 196–201.

21. V. Holubnychy, "Spatial Efficiency in the Soviet Economy," in V. Bandera and Z. Melnyk, eds., *The Soviet Economy in Regional Perspective* (New York: Praeger Publishers, 1973), p. 20.

22. Iu. Skobolev, "Narodnokhoziaistvennaia programma osvoeniia zony BAM," *Planovoe khoziaistvo*, no. 7, 1978, p. 78.

23. Holubnychy, p. 29.

24. Skobolev, pp. 78–79.

25. V. F. Pavlenko, *Territorial'noe planirovanie v SSSR* (Moscow: Ekonomika, 1975), p. 85.

26. *Novye territorial'nye kompleksy SSSR* (Moscow: Mysl', 1977), p. 275.

27. Pavlenko, p. 275.

28. Ibid., p. 178.

29. N. N. Nekrasov, *Regional'naia ekonomika* (Moscow: Ekonomika, 1975), pp. 93–95, and A. G. Granberg, *Optimizatsiia territorial'nykh proportsii narodnogo khoziaistva* (Moscow: Ekonomika, 1973), pp. 27–31.

30. N. Singur, "Planirovanie ratsional'nogo razmeshcheniia proizvoditel'nykh sil RSFSR," *Planovoe khoziaistvo*, no. 9, 1977, p. 107.

31. Singur, p. 107.

32. V. Budavei, "Programmo-tselevoi metod v narodnokhoziaistvennom planirovanii," *Voprosy ekonomiki*, no. 1, 1978, pp. 3–13.

33. O. S. Pechelintsev, "Urbanizatsiia, regional'noe razvitie, i nauchno-tekhnicheskaia Revoliutsiia," *Ekonomika i matematicheskie metody*, no. 1, 1978, p. 14.

34. A. Aganbegyan, K. Bagirovskiy, and A. Granberg, *Sistema modelei narodnokhoziaistvennogo planirovaniia* (Moscow: Mysl', 1972), pp. 286–298.

35. M. K. Bandman, *Modelirovanie formirovaniia territorial'no-proizvodstvennykh kompleksov* (Novosibirsk: Nauka, 1976).

36. A more detailed discussion of this problem can be found in Robert N. Taaffe, "The Migrational Process in Centrally Planned Economies," in J. Odland and R. Taaffe, eds., *Geographical Horizons* (Dubuque: Kendall-Hunt, 1977), pp. 64–84.

37. Iu. Mateev, "Organizovannyi nabor kak odna iz osnovnykh form planogo razpredeleniia rabochey sil," in A. Maikov, ed., *Migratsiia naseleniia RSFSR* (Moscow: Statistika, 1973), p. 65.

38. Mateev, p. 65.

39. Pechelintsev, p. 8.

40. M. Mezhevich, "Kompleksnoe planirovanie krupnykh gorodov," *Planovoe khoziaistvo*, no. 3, 1978, p. 112.

41. Among the most important studies of this problem are V. I. Perve-dentsev, *Migratsiia naseleniia i trudovye problemi Sibiri* (Novosibirsk: Nauka, 1966), and L. Ryabakovskii, *Regionalnyi analiz migratsii* (Moscow: Statistika, 1973).

42. Taaffe, p. 37.

43. P. P. Orlov, *Sibir' segodnia: problemy i resheniia* (Moscow: Mysl', 1974), p. 194.

Part Three / SOCIETY AND CULTURE

The "New Soviet Man" Turns Pessimist

John Bushnell

If a Soviet George Gallup had polled his country's middle class in the 1950s, he would have discovered a resoundingly upbeat mood. The Soviet middle class would have responded with enthusiastic optimism to questions such as, "Are you better or worse off than before?" "What is your outlook for the future?" "Do you think things are getting better or worse?" The results of the poll would have been published in *Pravda*, a spate of self-congratulatory articles would have followed, and opinion surveys would have become an established Soviet science. Had our Soviet Gallup taken a similar poll twenty years later, the results never would have seen the light of day: by then, the Soviet middle class was sliding into an abyss of pessimism. Gallup would have been under a cloud, and opinion surveys would have been disestablished. Something very much like the preceding scenario has in fact been the fate of Soviet opinion surveys. Of course, there have been no Soviet Gallup polls. Nevertheless, if we marshall the impressionistic evidence and fragmentary opinion samples, and if we attempt to do no more than establish roughly the levels of middle-class optimism and pessimism, it is possible to identify some important trends.*

The argument presented here is that during the 1950s the Soviet middle class became increasingly optimistic about the performance of

---

*My own sense of the public mood derives from four years (1972–76) in the Soviet Union as exchange student and translator. Though I was based in Moscow, my contacts were not limited to middle-class Muscovites. For the sake of stylistic felicity, I refer throughout to the Soviet middle class, but these remarks pertain only to the urban middle class in the RSFSR. This is primarily, but not exclusively, a Russian middle class.

the Soviet system and about its own prospects for material betterment, that this optimism persisted through the 1960s, but that in the 1970s it has given way to pessimism. The rise and decline of middle-class optimism can be linked in part to political developments, but the crucial determinant has been the changing perception of Soviet economic performance. The degree of the Soviet consumer's present and anticipated future satisfaction has been influenced by the real performance of the consumer sector. However, since at least the early 1960s the perception of Soviet economic performance has been affected as well by comparisons that the Soviet middle class has been able to make with consumer standards in other, primarily East European, countries. Such comparisons are not to the advantage of the Soviet Union, and the Soviet middle class does not anticipate any narrowing of the consumption gap in the foreseeable future. This pessimistic outlook on future consumption has contributed to mounting skepticism and cynicism about the values and performance of the regime in other areas as well.

"Middle class" is not a term often employed in discussions of Soviet society. It is used here to refer to what most Western studies have called, following Soviet practice, the intelligentsia. My preference for the term "middle class" certainly does not reflect any greater precision. The difficulty with "intelligentsia" is that in addition to its current Soviet use to designate a very large white-collar professional group, it carries a heavy freight of historically conditioned connotations—radicalism, dissent, or at the very least the mildly critical or skeptical attitude toward the existing order characteristic of intellectuals. The discussion that follows has to do with those who are not themselves dissidents, who have had no contact with dissidents, who have not read dissident literature, and who cannot, in their majority, be classified properly as intellectuals.

In terms of occupation and education, the Soviet "intelligentsia" approximates the white-collar middle class in the West. It includes middle-level office functionaries, doctors, dentists, engineers, agronomists, and so on, as well as members of the intellectual professions. It is a middle class, too, in that it occupies a position between the small sociopolitical elite and the very numerous workers, peasants, and unskilled white-collar employees. In the USSR even more than in the West, the defining trait of the middle class is status rather than income. A doctor earning 110 rubles a month is perceived to have a higher social status than a bus driver earning 180 rubles or more a month. Although members of the elite enjoy markedly higher incomes and other perquisites denied to the middle class, these are the consequences, rather than the cause, of elite status: as a rule, special privileges are granted to those chosen for the elite on political or other grounds.

Because middle-class occupations ordinarily entail special educational qualifications, for present purposes the size of the Soviet middle class may be gauged roughly from the number of persons classified in the official economic yearbooks as "specialists with higher or specialized secondary education." Between 1950 and 1974 this group expanded from 3.3 to 21.4 million employed persons (excluding military personnel as well as retirees and students), or from 5 to 18 percent of the Soviet work force. Besides providing access to middle-class jobs, the educational system lends intergenerational stability to the Soviet middle class. While there is considerable upward mobility into the white-collar middle class, middle-class children enjoy preferential access to the higher and special secondary education that ensures access to middle-class jobs; there is little downward mobility out of the middle class. The Soviet middle class has been expanding around a core that is by now as hereditary as any Western middle class.[1]

The Drift from Optimism to Pessimism

A survey of postwar refugees conducted by Harvard's Russian Research Center in 1950–51 found that in Stalin's last years there was a fairly broad acceptance of the Soviet social and economic systems. Soviet citizens—including those in white-collar middle-class occupations —identified with the Soviet Union's military and industrial achievements. They expected the state to provide a wide range of social benefits and services, as well as job security, and they approved of the regime's stated welfare objectives. While there was pronounced hostility to terror and to the methods of Communist Party rule, the regime was judged not so much by its formal and informal political arrangements as by its performance. A major source of low-level but persistent resentment was the regime's failure to deliver on its proclaimed welfare policies. The middle class was unhappy about its low standard of living. However, the leadership, or the regime, rather than the system, was faulted. Indeed, Soviet citizens did not see any acceptable alternative to the Soviet system, and they certainly did not believe that a capitalist system could provide the social benefits they had come to expect. Terror excepted, the existing system was taken for granted. The Harvard project found that acceptance of the institutional parameters of the Soviet system was stronger with each succeeding generation; there is no evidence that this perceived legitimacy of the system has lessened since then among any but the relatively small contingent of dissidents and critically minded intellectuals.[2] Attitudes toward the performance of the system and toward the leadership have fluctuated, but the system has consistently been judged sound in its principles.

Given the wide acceptance of the system found among the postwar refugees in the late 1940s and early 1950s, Alex Inkeles and Raymond Bauer predicted that if terror were reduced and if the system were perceived to be meeting welfare expectations, the regime would tap a large reservoir of popular support.[3] This is precisely what happened. The 1950s saw a surge of confidence and optimism that stemmed from the virtual cessation of Stalinist terror, very real improvements in living standards, symbolic achievements—such as the Soviet space program —that reenforced patriotic pride, and to a certain extent the progress of national liberation in the Third World, which seemed to indicate that Soviet socialism was the high road to the future. During the late 1950s the Soviet leadership promised that the housing shortage would be eliminated within a decade, that by the mid-1960s Soviet citizens would have a standard of living surpassing the West European average, and that the younger generation would live to see true communism. Against the background of perceived (and quite real) gains, middle-class expectations for the future were fully in accord with official projections.

Alexander Werth, who informally sampled the mood of the middle class in the late 1950s and was struck by its optimism, concluded that there was, indeed, a "New Soviet Man." This New Soviet Man was proud of his country's accomplishments, confident that the Soviet Union was *the* rising power in the world, convinced that the Soviet Union's rapid economic advances were being translated into a rising level of personal well-being, and certain that the Soviet system provided unlimited personal opportunities, especially for the young.[4] Not all observers detected the same degree of middle-class optimism as did Werth, himself an inveterate optimist about things Soviet. Nevertheless, almost all reported a widespread middle-class conviction that the system worked well, that economic development was yielding tangible personal benefits, and that the sense of well-being was enhanced by the marked relaxation of the political atmosphere.[5] Soviet survey data, such as they are, are congruent with the observations of outsiders. Seventy-three percent of the respondents to a poll conducted in October 1960 by the Public Opinion Institute of *Komsomolskaia Pravda*, the newspaper of the Communist youth organization, reported that their standard of living had improved in recent years, while only seven percent reported a deterioration. (The questionnaire was distributed by railroad conductors to the occupants of a single carriage on each of sixty-five trains leaving Moscow on a single day. Soviet critics noted that this produced a demographic bias against peasants and towards business travelers; this would, of course, weight the results in favor of the middle class.)[6]

The only deviations from this pervasive optimism occurred among intellectuals and university students (the children and future members of the middle class). Even among these groups, however, it is evident that the disaffection that followed Khrushchev's 1956 "Secret Speech" was limited largely to demands for the further reduction of intellectual regimentation. This kind of dissatisfaction was a minority phenomenon. Many intellectuals, for instance, viewed continued limitations on freedom as a necessary trade-off for economic development that would ultimately make greater freedom possible; in any case, an appreciable minority of intellectuals did not view political freedom as a desirable end.[7] Even among students, who in 1956 and the years immediately following were more inclined than any other group to voice dissatisfaction, the majority were pleased with their own prospects and projected their own satisfaction onto society at large.[8] If anything, in the late 1950s the average student was more optimistic than his middle-class elders. Asked about their chances for acquiring their own automobiles, fifty-two of eighty-five fifth-year students at Moscow University polled by Jerzy Kosinski said they expected to be able to purchase a car within two or three years, another twenty-eight estimated four to six years, while only five believed they would never own an automobile.[9] Given the virtual nonexistence of a market in private automobiles at the time, these students' expectations were wildly unrealistic. Yet there does not seem to have been generational discontinuity in middle-class optimism, only a slight difference in degree—excessive optimism was characteristic of all members of the middle class.

Middle-class optimism apparently peaked by the early 1960s—it could scarcely have mounted higher—and then remained at a constantly high level into the second half of the decade. As before, confidence about future prospects was based on perceptions of present national achievement and personal betterment. Remarkably, this attitude persisted despite economic difficulties in the mid-1960s that led the post-Khrushchev leadership to back off publicly from unrealistic promises. Judging by the comments of most observers, even the return of food shortages in 1962 and 1963 barely dented middle-class optimism. Exchange students who spent those years in Moscow, for instance, do not mention that difficulties in food supply were a matter of concern to their informants. It may be that students continued to be more opti-

mistic than the older generation, for whom the food shortages were
unpleasantly reminiscent of the bad times of the past, and who consequently worried that the recovery of 1965 might not be permanent.
But again, student attitudes differed from those of their elders only in
degree, not in kind. The middle class appreciated the sobriety of the
Brezhnev-Kosygin team that came to power in the mid-1960s and became more convinced than ever that the system was in good hands
and that the standard of living would continue to improve.[10]

The few available opinion surveys suggest that the bulk of the middle class remained reasonably optimistic about the condition of the
Soviet system until the beginning of the 1970s. In 1968, 130 students
at various Moscow universities were asked unofficially about their attitudes toward the future: more than half of the respondents were
optimistic; one-quarter were "optimistic but had a certain amount of
doubt"; 11 percent were "not very optimistic but not pessimistic
either"; only 2 percent were "not very optimistic." Asked about
their evaluation of life at the moment, 5 percent said they were per-
fectly satisfied with life as it was, and 47 percent said it was "good
enough though some things need improving"; only 11 percent felt
life "should be greatly improved."[11] Jewish emigres surveyed in Israel
(1972) and Detroit (1976) reported relative satisfaction with the material side of life in the USSR. Of the respondents in Israel, 90.2 percent claimed that there had been material improvements in Soviet
society in the last twenty-five years (this figure is perhaps not very
meaningful given the time span). More significantly, 67.2 percent of
the respondents in Israel said that the Soviet regime had the interests
of the people at heart.[12] Neither survey breaks down the results by
professional background (or year of emigration), but the favorable
assessment of material well-being was so preponderant that it must have
been typical of middle-class emigres (and nonemigres) of the late 1960s
and early 1970s.

While the above describes what we know of the attitudes of the
great majority of the middle class, by the late 1960s the attitudes of
middle-class intellectuals had begun to diverge from those of nonintel-
lectuals: the minority of intellectuals had become decidedly pessimistic.
The changed mood of the intellectuals can be attributed in large measure to shifts in the regime's stance on de-Stalinization, the not-so-secret
trials of dissident writers and demonstrators, and the invasion of Czechoslovakia. While the tightening of domestic political and economic
controls obviously had the greatest impact on intellectuals, we may
hazard the supposition that symbolically prominent events—trials, the
Czechoslovak affair, and the concurrent resumption of jamming—

caused a quickening of unease in the middle class as a whole. However, for all but intellectuals this apprehension dissipated when it became clear that there was to be no return to pervasive terror, and that there was no political threat to the well-being of those who observed the written and unwritten rules of Soviet society. The political shift of the second half of the 1960s may have left a low residual level of uncertainty, at the most, but we should be careful not to overstress this. The changes in the political atmosphere were certainly not reflected in the attitudes of the Moscow students surveyed in 1968.

Even in the mid-1970s, when there could be no question about the regime's hard line on open expression of dissent, the bulk of the middle class had no fear of political repression. The September 1974 exhibit of modernist art at Izmailovo Park in Moscow illustrates how selective repression has left intact the sense of personal security of the average member of the middle class. Although an attempt to stage an exhibit two weeks earlier had been broken up by force, when the exhibit did open it was attended—despite the highly visible police presence—by thousands of Muscovites from all (but primarily middle-class) walks of life. Even a sprinkling of army officers put in an appearance. Most members of the middle class do not share the intellectuals' political and cultural distress. While the middle class has little expectation of political liberalization, liberalization that goes beyond assurances of personal security—which they feel they already have—is for most simply irrelevant.

Yet after a brief lag the middle class as a whole did pick up the intellectuals' pessimism, not in association with political developments but in association with a perception of economic decline. Not surprisingly, intellectuals were the first to become economic pessimists. By the late 1960s they were speaking of stagnation and even regression not just as a short-term problem but as the long-term outlook for the Soviet economy. For intellectuals, economic pessimism was bound up with the perception of political rigidity: declining growth rates (the extent of the decline was greatly exaggerated) were pointed to as an example of overall systemic stagnation.[13] Since the early 1970s, economic (or consumer) pessimism has spread to the rest of the middle class, and with gathering momentum. As of the middle of the decade, the Soviet middle class had lost its previous certainty that the economic gap with the West would eventually be closed. Furthermore, the middle class no longer believed that even the slower rate of economic growth was yielding any appreciable improvement in the standard of living. In fact, the middle class was beginning to deny that there had recently been any improvement at all in the standard of living.

It should be emphasized that the drift towards economic pessimism was under way before the agricultural disaster of 1975, which threw the Soviet middle class into a state of depression verging on despair. Neither Polish blue jeans nor Japanese umbrellas, then much in evidence, could offset that devastating blow to middle-class confidence in Soviet economic performance. Neither the uncertainties of the weather nor the fact that Soviet agriculture had been overextended by the drive to increase the proportion of meat in the Soviet diet provided solace: these were felt to be poor excuses indeed for a country that claimed to embody "highly developed socialism."

The shock caused by the 1975 crop failure—and the several years' disruption in the food supply that followed—has yet to wear off. Since 1976 pessimism over the state of the Soviet economy has taken on the blackest hues, and there is now near unanimity that "things are getting worse" and will continue to get worse for the foreseeable future.[14] Exaggerated pessimism might seem a natural response to crop failure and so not particularly significant, but it is worth recalling that nothing similar occurred after the crop failures of the early 1960s. Clearly, the underpinnings of confidence in the performance of the Soviet economy had been eroded prior to 1975. In the early 1960s, consumer difficulties were considered deviations from the overall upward movement. In the 1970s, they have been viewed as the norm.

Apprehension about Soviet economic performance has done more than anything else to shape the present mood of the middle class, but the malaise extends considerably beyond that. Not only has Soviet economic performance been discredited, the very direction of economic policy is now suspect. Middle-class Soviets do not now believe that Soviet economic development benefits them; indeed, it is a middle-class commonplace that whatever economic growth may now be occurring is at the *expense* of the Soviet public. Skepticism about official economic policy is but one manifestation of middle-class disengagement from the regime's goals. Civic cynicism and alienation are so pervasive that by comparison post-Watergate America seems a hotbed of utopian optimism: few members of the Soviet middle class will admit that they do more than go through the motions of their professional and civic duties. Antipathy to Third World countries (not to mention Third World nationals in the Soviet Union) is universal. Even the space program, once the object of so much pride, is now met with apathy—perhaps because, as in the United States, it has been playing too long. What was most remarkable about the public reaction to the Apollo-Soyuz mission were not the smallish crowds that gathered in front of TV stores to watch launch, link-up, and landing, but the much larger crowds on the streets who paid no attention whatsoever to these much ballyhooed events. In almost every respect the mood of the middle class in the late 1970s was very nearly the mirror image of the mood twenty years earlier.

Many of the features of the Soviet system that now contribute to middle-class pessimism have been around for a long time, but of course it is the altered perception of them that is at issue. The changing middle-class attitude toward the black (or multicolored) market is of special interest.[15] The black market and bribery to obtain privileged access to scarce goods are certainly not of recent origin, although the size of the black market has no doubt increased in proportion to Soviet economic growth: a larger economy provides a larger base for black-market operations. But again the crucial change is in perception, not scale. In the 1950s participation in the black market was viewed as an unavoidable necessity, but it was a matter of course, not something salient to the middle-class view of the system. In the new perceptual configuration, corruption is salient, while the formal rules of public life and good citizenship are subordinate and are observed only to the extent necessary for survival. At the least, the middle class is indifferent to rampant petty corruption and pilferage, and increasingly, these phenomena meet with approval. This attitude complements the middle-class view of official economic policy: "It's a crime not to steal from them, all they do is steal from us," is the watchword of the Soviet middle class in the 1970s.

Of course, middle-class pessimism and cynicism are not absolute. Neither attitude is easy to sustain, and the Soviet middle class is anyway not wholly preoccupied with economic and civil life. Furthermore, there are eddies of optimism even within the strong tide of pessimism. Far more significant is the fact that underneath the pervasive pessimism of the middle class there is a residue of systemic optimism: there is still a feeling that in the very long run things will turn out all right, because the Soviet socialist system is, after all, better than the Western capitalist system. The shifting attitudes sketched thus far have to do with the perceived performance of the Soviet system, not with the system in principle. Many intellectuals and most dissidents have bridged the gap by rejecting the system as well as the performance, but for most members of the middle class the implicit contradiction remains for the time being unresolved.

Within the ambivalent majority of the middle class, there are certain generational differences in the strength of this residual optimism. As we have seen, there is some evidence that in the 1950s and 1960s students and junior members of the middle class were less restrained in their optimism than were their seniors, whose expectations were tempered by greater experience of stress and strain in the Soviet workaday world. Today, it is the older generation that is marginally the more optimistic, worldly experience again making the difference. Those over forty continue to fall back on the devastation of the war as the explanation of last resort for present deficiencies. This is a clutching at straws, but the war is more than a convenient rationale: to this day the older generation has vivid memories of the war, and measured against that low point, even the presently perceived stagnation marks a significant advance. On the other hand, the memories of young people do not extend back to the really bad times. Consequently, younger members of the middle class are less impressed by advances in the standard of living over the last twenty years—those whose civic memories go back no more than ten years perceive no improvement at all—and so they are more likely to project their present discontents into the future. Some degree of historical optimism is present in all generations, if only because almost all accept the present system in principle. Yet at the same time the distant, optimistic future is abstract; it is the universally perceived stagnation of the present and bleak short-term future that are operative.

Sources of Pessimism

Real economic performance and regime policy. Thus far we have been considering the swing from optimism to pessimism without really coming to grips with its causes. Since middle-class pessimism is so firmly rooted in the perceived performance of the Soviet economy—the consumer sector above all—we should note first that there is much to be pessimistic about. Both the overall rate of economic growth and the rate of increase of consumption have been declining since the late 1960s. Furthermore, sudden and mysterious shortages of even the most basic consumer goods are endemic, the quality of goods available is low, and the assortment is limited. These problems need not detain us: the catalogue of consumer-industry and retail-distribution ills is voluminous and familiar. Surely, shortages are partly to blame for the middle-class consumer's excessive pessimism, since it is the unobtainable good that is uppermost in the consumer's mind. But shortages are nothing new to the Soviet consumer, and in any objective view the Soviet middle class is better off now—allowing for the continuing disruptions caused by the 1975 crop failure—than ever before.

The rise and fall of optimism does not match the real performance of the consumer sector with much precision. When per capita consumption increased by 5.3 percent annually between 1951 and 1955, and by 4.2 percent between 1956 and 1960, middle-class optimism waxed strong; it was not shaken by the precipitous decline in the rate of increase in consumption to an annual rate of 2.5 percent between 1961 and 1965. The rate of increase in consumption rose to 4.7 percent per year between 1966 and 1970—yet it was in the immediate aftermath of this rising prosperity that middle-class optimism began to erode. The plunge itno pessimism in the early 1970s paralleled a real decline in the rate of increase in consumption (3.2 percent per year, 1971–75), but there is no basis for the middle-class view that the standard of living has not risen at all of late, or that it has even declined.[16]

Certainly we have to look beyond real economic performance to explain changes in the mood of the middle class. Nor do changes in the regime's allocation policy, or its failed attempts at economic reform, wholly account for changes in middle-class perceptions. Khrushchev's "goulash communism" did indeed contribute to the optimism of the 1950s, but his successors' proclaimed consumerist policies have not sustained it. Failure to deliver on consumerist promises has without question contributed to middle-class cynicism, as has the collapse of all attempts at structural reform of the economy. Economic slogans are the butt of countless jokes, and over the years the regime's broken promises have tended to produce an effect opposite to that intended. But failures to deliver on promises have not always given rise to cynicism—the early 1960s provide the best case in point—and the middle-class disinterest in politics extends to economic policy: not much attention has been paid to reform programs or to shifts in the regime's economic priorities.

Middle-class materialism. The fact that consumer-goods shortages and policy failures are perceived differently now than they were twenty years ago is due in part—not so paradoxically—to the fact that the middle class is now much better off than before. All observers since the late 1950s have reported a decline in the Soviet citizen's ideological fervor and an ever-more-resolute determination to lead at least a moderately comfortable life. Most commentators have located this development in the student population. Since 1956 regime spokesmen have complained repeatedly that students are ideologically flabby, preoccupied with creature comforts, and unconscionably indifferent to the past sacrifices that made such self-indulgence possible. Even were it true that materialistic inclinations originated in the student population, so many generations of students have come and gone since the 1950s that the materialistic ex-students of the post-Stalin era now make up a majority of the middle class. But of course the longing to enjoy the fruits of economic development was never confined to the younger generation. The late 1950s saw a sudden upsurge of materialism because it was then that the bulk of the middle class had the first opportunity for material indulgence. As noted, this development was largely responsible for the heady optimism of the period—the availability of consumer goods demonstrated how well the Soviet system worked. But during the succeeding decades materialism has become a way of life and it has become increasingly difficult for the regime to meet middle-class expectations. Nothing fails like success: the regime's earlier success, its welcome promise to provide the good life, generated ever greater expectations and contributed to the current perception of failure.

International comparisons: the semi-mythical West. Yet it is unlikely that the present extreme pessimism of the middle class can be explained entirely by factors internal to the Soviet system. If in some imaginary world the Soviet Union were the most advanced nation, and Soviet middle-class consumers were better off than their foreign counterparts, expectations would still—for the reasons given above—be unsatisfied, but consumer dissatisfaction would not be nearly so acute as it is in the real world. What has happened is that the rise in standard of living and expectations has been accompanied by increasing familiarity with the rest of the world.

The Voice of America, the BBC, and the presence of foreign nationals (tourists and others) have been an important source of information about the West (as well as about the Soviet Union itself). The Western information that has had the greatest impact on the USSR has been cultural rather than political. The penetration of the Soviet Union by Western fads and fashions is widely recognized. It is worth noting, however, that the domestic political consequences of mini-skirts and chewing gum have not been properly assessed. While the demand for chewing gum is entirely apolitical, it has produced a political response by the leadership in the diversion of resources to establish a Soviet chewing-gum industry. More generally, the demonstration effect of Western standards has helped to shape Soviet consumer expectations.

However, it is not the Western model by which the average member of the Soviet middle class judges Soviet economic performance. For all the increasing familiarity with Western culture and Western artifacts, to the overwhelming majority of the Soviet middle class the West remains a never-never land: Western material advantages are fabled but dimly perceived; the West is too far removed from ordinary Soviet experience for meaningful comparisons to be made. Moreover, even those most awestruck by what they have heard of the West are ambivalent about the Western system. Every American family may own a car—something in itself so incredible by Soviet standards that the middle class cannot come to terms with its implications—and every Soviet middle-class family may long for a car, but the price the West pays for oppulent self-indulgence is thought, somewhat inconsistently, to be exploitation, unemployment, and job insecurity. (Soviet white-collar professionals value their own secure inefficiency so highly that they have grossly exaggerated notions of the difficulties of finding and retaining employment in the West.) Too, the West is commonly viewed as an intellectual and cultural wasteland—exciting, perhaps, but spiritually empty. The "materialistic" West is a convenient object onto which the Soviet middle class can project and thereby exorcise its own loss of larger purpose. In short, prosperity within the Western system is, to the Soviet mind, the apple of temptation, succulent but fearful. If this description of the Soviet middle-class view of the West seems metaphorically overwrought, it is because for the ordinary Soviet citizen the West *is* largely a metaphor, a symbol to which potent but contradictory meanings have been attached.

International comparisons: the subversive influence of Eastern Europe. Of much more immediate relevance to the Soviet experience is Eastern Europe. Overlooked in the usual "Russia and the West" dichotomy, Eastern Europe is for Soviet citizens an external reference both more meaningful and more accessible than the West. It has often been noted that East European goods are the standard of excellence for Soviet consumers, and that East European magazines (though not the broadcast media) have served as the major source of information on fashion and modern culture.[17] Furthermore, the volume of East European consumer "information"—i.e., goods—flowing into the Soviet Union has been increasing. Between 1960 and 1975 Soviet imports of consumer manufactures from the GDR, Poland, Czechoslovakia, and Hungary tripled, from 631 million rubles to 1,842 million rubles.[18] This sort of consumer and cultural information from Eastern Europe, besides being far more plentiful than similar information from the West, can be evaluated more matter-of-factly, because it is not overlaid with symbolic meaning.

For that matter, information about Eastern Europe is not confined to what can be picked up within the borders of the Soviet Union. For Soviet citizens, to arrive in East Berlin, Warsaw, Prague, or Budapest is to visit their own version of the West, prosperous but prosaic. In the last two decades millions of Soviet citizens *have* traveled to Eastern Europe.

Soviet Tourists Traveling to Eastern Europe[19]

1960	112,000	1969	735,000
1961	164,000	1970	838,000
1962	180,000	1971	920,000
1963	204,000	1972	936,000
1964	296,000	1973	1,160,000
1965	422,000	1974	1,056,000
1966	497,000	1975	1,214,000
1967	650,000	1976	1,324,000
1968	668,000		

Between 1960 and 1976, approximately 11 million Soviet tourists made the journey. Assuming (as a former employee of Intourist asserts) that roughly half of all Soviet tourists are repeaters, we are still left with around 5.5 million different tourists. Data on the number of Soviet citizens who have traveled to Eastern Europe as members of official delegations, athletic teams, and the like are available only for 1960, when approximately 480,000 went, but this suggests that the total number of official travelers over the same period was as large as the number of tourists, possibly much larger (though surely with a higher incidence of repeaters).[20] To this we should add at least 2,500,000 Soviet soldiers who have been stationed in Eastern Europe.[21] While the total number of Soviet citizens who have seen Eastern Europe at first hand can only be approximated, it is likely to be on the order of 12 to 15 million, of which half have been there more than once. And we may presume that the tourists, and especially the official travelers—though obviously not the soldiers—have come disproportionately from urban (and by extension middle-class) Russia.

Whatever the precise figure, by the early 1970s so many Soviet citizens had been to Eastern Europe and had related their experiences to relatives and friends that the Soviet middle class as a whole had a reasonably accurate picture of consumer standards there. For Soviet travelers in Eastern Europe, the key sights are not architectural monuments but department stores and, to a lesser extent, modern cultural attractions. They descend on clothing and shoe stores in packs, wholly displacing native customers. On every train returning from Eastern Europe, Soviet tourists are caught with more goods than they could have obtained with the rubles they were legally permitted to exchange for East European currencies. The aggressive acquisitiveness of Soviet tourists is ample testimony to their appreciation of Eastern Europe's higher standard of living.

The reaction of the middle class to exposure to Eastern Europe—either directly or at second hand—is complex. On the one hand, the superiority of Eastern Europe's consumer standards is unquestioned. On the other hand, the recognition of Soviet inferiority is often accompanied by emotions ranging from anger to depression. Anger stems from injury to Soviet *amour-propre*: the Soviet Union, after all, is supposed to be the "elder brother" of the socialist camp. Depression results from the conclusion that the Soviet Union is fated to remain behind, and from the realization that the consumption gap is great indeed. One set of Soviet parents was overwhelmed by their inability to fulfill the parental function of helping out a newly married son living in East Germany; when they visited him, it turned out that the Germans—and their son—"already had everything." (Indeed, the son had a larger apartment and earned more than his parents: the East German minimum wage far surpasses the Soviet average wage.)

Equally significant is the way in which Soviet citizens do *not* react to Eastern Europe. While middle-class Soviets, except the most sophisticated, exhibit considerable curiosity about life in the West, there is very little overt curiosity about Eastern Europe. This is only partly due to greater familiarity. The entire category of questions aimed at finding out how life is "under capitalism" has no analogue for Eastern Europe. Despite the realization that the East European standing of living is much higher than the Soviet, Eastern Europe is not felt to differ qualitatively from the Soviet Union. Even if they have not been there, Soviet citizens assume they know more or less how the East European system works. Perhaps because of this assumed similarity, the Soviet middle class does not give much thought to the reasons for Eastern Europe's relative prosperity. There is some puzzlement, of course, and when pressed, Soviets attribute it either to the greater manageability of smaller economies (a few are familiar with the East European economic reforms) or, more frequently, to the differential consequences of the war and to postwar Soviet "assistance." By and large, however, the Soviet middle class simply accepts Eastern Europe's higher standard of living as a matter of fact, as though it were in the nature of things for the Soviet Union to lag behind.

Eastern Europe, then, is the principal standard against which the Soviet middle class measures the performance of the Soviet system, and it is a standard with which the middle class is quite familiar. It does not appear to be coincidental that increasing familiarity with Eastern Europe—more broadly, the increasing openness of the Soviet system—has been accompanied by a decline in middle-class optimism. Obviously there can be no single explanation for a phenomenon as complex as a turnabout in the mood of the middle-class Soviet public. Real economic problems, rising consumer expectations, and increasing familiarity with the West have all played a part. But Eastern Europe is closer than the West, and its impact has been greater, if less remarked. No one believes that the Soviet consumer sector is catching up to its East European counterpart, and this alone must erode Soviet middle-class confidence over the long run.

Furthermore, it seems reasonable to suppose that the perceived similarity of the two systems is more rather than less likely to undermine confidence in the functioning of the Soviet system. The Soviet middle class is strongly predisposed to accept a centrally managed socialist economy as the norm. That being the case, it is more likely to draw comparisons invidious to the Soviet system from socialist Eastern Europe than from the less acceptable, capitalist West. Since the Soviet middle class will not become less familiar with Eastern Europe, and the Soviet consumer sector will not in the forseeable future close the gap with Eastern Europe, the current pessimistic mood will almost certainly continue.

Implications

Public opinion in the Soviet Union is not notably volatile. The news media do not focus public attention on persistent inflation (or its Soviet equivalent), corruption, or high taxes; nor is the pulse of public opinion regularly taken and then reported back to the public itself. Certainly, the pessimism currently rampant in the Soviet middle class is not a response to events magnified by the media. Whatever its origins, middle-class pessimism is the product of convictions arrived at autonomously, in opposition to the image of Soviet society projected by the media, and evidently held quite tenaciously. And if pessimism has settled in for the duration, how long can it remain predominantly associated— as it is now—with the perception of poor economic performance?[22]

There is presently no pronounced tendency among any but the intellectuals to draw political conclusions from the differential performance of the East European and Soviet economies. However, because of the perceived similarity of the two systems, the logical conclusion to draw is that it is the management of the Soviet system—that is, the leadership —that is at fault. Most members of the middle class believe that, in theory, the USSR's economic ills can be remedied—but not by the present regime. Because the legitimacy of the Soviet regime, in the eyes of the middle class, rests so heavily on the promise and expectation of material betterment, the perception that the economic system is being mismanaged must inevitably erode the regime's political legitimacy. Erosion of legitimacy is a far cry from de-legitimation, and the deep-rooted support for the system provides the regime with political capital on which to draw. But the regime today enjoys nothing like the middle-class support that Khrushchev enjoyed in the late 1950s.

This is not meant to suggest that a political crisis looms: the continued existence of the regime would not be directly threatened even by widespread political disaffection. Yet even the presently apolitical disenchantment of the Soviet middle class is politically significant, because the middle class occupies a crucial place within Soviet society. Since the 1930s it has been the cement holding Soviet society together. In what literary scholar Vera Dunham has recently called the "Big Deal," the middle class was then endowed with a system of rewards and privileges. In fact, it was the extension of privileges that produced a distinctively Soviet middle class, whose mission was to halt the social disintegration brought on by collectivization and the industrialization drive. Though of modest proportions for all but the elite, the privileges were nonetheless gratefully received as a modicum of relief from the austerity of the period. Moreover, as Dunham has demonstrated, by the 1940s materialistic aspirations were being given ideological sanction.[23]

The price that the regime paid for buying the support of the middle class was the gradual alienation of the working class, which was cut out of the Big Deal. The rewards, privileges, and public esteem extended to the middle class caused workers to feel slighted in their own proletarian state. Judging by the scanty evidence available, the middle-class optimism of the 1950s and 1960s was not shared by the working class. Though the working class in fact benefited from the increasing prosperity, the rising standard of living may have further alienated the workers, who felt that the middle class was receiving a disproportionate share of the benefits. At any rate, all reliable observers have reported that the working class has, since the 1950s, been consistently suspicious of the middle class and antagonistic to the "bosses." Furthermore, working-class discontent is more volatile than middle-class discontent: strikes and other working-class disorders, if not massive or numerous by Western standards, have been endemic since the early 1960s.[24]

In the last decade or so, then, the regime's base of support in the middle class has been eroding without offsetting gains in the working class. In the long run, the Big Deal has failed to achieve its purpose: those dealt out remain dissatisfied; the expectations of those dealt in have not been met. It should be reiterated that discontent is not now

political in nature—we have not been examining the attitudes of dissidents—and that public opinion is not the most important factor in Soviet politics. Nevertheless, it is a factor. At a minimum, the leadership
would like to retain public support. A step beyond that minimum, the
need to cater to middle-class—and other—expectations places constraints
on the Soviet leadership. Serious efforts have been made, for instance,
to improve the consumer sector. The problem for the regime is that
the middle-class perception of economic stagnation is fundamentally
correct: in order to maintain overall growth rates, the promise made
in the early 1970s that the consumer sector would henceforth have
priority has been deferred, but even renewed emphasis on heavy industry has failed to stem the decline in the rate of growth. In neither
the short nor the long run can middle-class expectations be met, and
the pressure of public dissatisfaction will continue to mount. The pressure will probably not be vented violently, but neither is it likely to
dissipate entirely without effect.

Notes

1. The statistics have been calculated from *Narodnoe khoziaistvo SSSR v
1974 g.* (Moscow, 1975), pp. 448, 549, 565. This proportion is approximately
the same as that arrived at by Soviet sociologists attempting to delimit the
intelligentsia as a social group; the relevant literature is summarized in
Mervyn Matthews, *Class and Society in Soviet Russia* (London, 1972), pp.
141–48. L. G. Churchward, *The Soviet Intelligentsia* (London, 1973), pp.
3–8, counts as members of the intelligentsia only those with a higher education and arrives at a figure of 10,676,000 (counting students, retirees, and
officers) as of 1967. My own sense of the situation is that many persons without a higher education do in fact hold junior executive jobs in many institutions, and that they are perceived to be members of the "intelligentsia." It is
also true that many persons with only a specialized secondary education
(which anyway covers a very broad range of training) do not hold middle-
class jobs. My own figures are not meant to be precise, only to establish an
order of magnitude. Churchward's different approach stems from the fact
that he is really concerned with the role of intellectuals and others with
special expertise in the Western sense.
  The literature on the relationship between the intergenerational stability
of the middle class (intelligentsia) and access to education is summarized in
Matthews, *Class and Society*, pp. 296–305, and Murray Yanowitch, *Social
and Economic Inequality in the Soviet Union: Six Studies* (White Plains,
N.Y., 1977), chapters 3 and 4.
  2. Alex Inkeles and Raymond Bauer, *The Soviet Citizen* (Cambridge,
Mass., 1961), pp. 234–95. Stephen White, "The USSR: Patterns of Autocracy and Industrialization," in Archie Brown and Jack Gray, eds., *Political
Culture and Political Change in Communist States* (London, 1977), pp. 25–
65, provides some data on attitudes towards the system since Stalin's death.

3. Inkeles and Bauer, *Soviet Citizen*, pp. 293–95.

4. Alexander Werth, *Russia Under Khrushchev* (New York, 1962), pp. 85–86, 92, 98, 133–35.

5. Louis Fischer, *Russia Revisited* (New York, 1957), pp. 13–18, 62, 81, 107; Markoosha Fischer, *Reunion in Moscow* (New York, 1962), pp. 19, 38, 60–61, 96, 131; Harrison Salisbury, *A New Russia?* (London, 1962), pp. 4–5, 9; Klaus Mehnert, *Soviet Man and His World* (New York, 1961), p. 209; K. C. Mahanta, *Three Years in Soviet Russia* (Hyderabad, 1962), pp. 130, 136; Leonid Vladimirov, *Rossiia bez prikras i umolchanii*, (Frankfurt/Main, 1969), p. 288. Louis Fischer and Klaus Mehnert report a mix of skepticism and optimism, but the only informed strong dissent from the view that the late 1950s witnessed a surge of middle-class optimism is Isaac Don Levine, *I Rediscover Russia* (New York, 1964), pp. 5, 197, and passim.

6. Elisabeth Weinberg, *The Development of Sociology in the Soviet Union* (London, 1974), pp. 85–86.

7. A. Zr., "The Conscience of a Generation," *Problems of Communism*, May-June 1961, pp. 9, 11, 13–14; Mehnert, *Soviet Man*, pp. 215–71; Louis Fischer, *Russia Revisited*, p. 51.

8. Tim Callaghan, "Studying the Students: Between Conformity and Dissent," *Soviet Survey*, July-September 1960, pp. 16–18. Peter Juviler, "Communist Morality and Soviet Youth," *Problems of Communism*, May-June 1961, p. 18, reports that some youths—not necessarily students—did tend to fault the regime for current shortages.

9. Jerzy Kosinski [Joseph Novak], *The Future is Ours, Comrade* (New York, 1960), pp. 199–201. Interestingly, of 85 workers polled at the same time, only 23 saw a car in prospect within 2 or 3 years, 31 believed they would be able to buy a car within 4 to 6 years, while 31 believed they would never be able to buy a car. Kosinski, p. 43, provides some evidence that young people were indeed more optimistic than their elders.

10. On student attitudes in the first half of the 1960s see Joel Schwartz, *Soviet Fathers versus Soviet Sons: Is There a Conflict of Generations?* (Pittsburgh, 1966), p. 14; Ernest Simmons, "The New 'New Soviet Man,'" in C. Faust and W. Lerner, eds., *The Soviet World in Flux* (Atlanta, 1967), p. 34; John Gooding, *The Catkin and the Icicle: Aspects of Russia* (London, 1975), p. 40; William Taubman, *The View from Lenin Hills* (London, 1968), pp. 188, 241, 243. That students may have been more optimistic than adults is indicated by Maurice Hindus, *The Kremlin's Human Dilemma* (Garden City, N.Y., 1967), pp. 69, 97.

11. A picture of continued optimism is presented by the ever-optimistic Alexander Werth, *Russia: Hopes and Fears* (New York, 1970), pp. 14, 163, 166, 329. The survey of Moscow students is reported, without a date, in David Lane, *The Socialist Industrial State* (London, 1976), p. 91. Lane has informed the author that the survey was probably conducted in 1968.

12. Jeffrey Ross, "The Composition and Structure of the Alienation of Jewish Emigrants from the Soviet Union," *Studies in Comparative Communism*, Spring-Summer 1974, pp. 110–14; Zvi Gitelman, "Soviet Jewish Emigrants: Why Are They Choosing America," *Soviet Jewish Affairs*, 1977, no. 1, pp. 31–46.

13. Jonathan Harris, "The Dilemma of Dissidence," *Survey*, Winter 1971, pp. 113–14; George Feifer [An Observer], *Message from Moscow* (New

York, 1971), pp. 314, 321–24; John Dornberg, *The New Tsars: Russia Under Stalin's Heirs* (Garden City, N.Y., 1972), p. 272; Vladimirov, *Rossiia*, pp. 288, 297, 315–24.

14. My own observation of the middle class turn towards pessimism prompted me to attempt to reconstruct the changes in the mood of the middle class. Others in the Soviet Union at the same time noted the same phenomenon. Increasing dissatisfaction over the standard of living is also noted by the emigre economist Igor Birman, "From the Achieved Level," *Soviet Studies*, April 1978, pp. 168, 171. An unsystematic survey of 28 recent Jewish emigres (most left the Soviet Union between 1976 and 1978) in Chicago in early 1978 confirmed my own impressions: 21 of the respondents maintained that conditions would continue to deteriorate; 3 said that conditions would improve, though not soon; 4 said conditions would improve soon. (For what it is worth, 3 of the 4 relative optimists had left the Soviet Union before 1976, when middle-class pessimism had not become as widespread as it has since.)

15. The best recent surveys of the black market are Hedrick Smith, *The Russians* (New York, 1976), chapter 3, and Gregory Grossman, "The 'Second Economy' of the USSR," *Problems of Communism*, September-October 1977, pp. 25–40.

16. Gertrude Schroeder and Barbara Severin, "Soviet Consumption and Income Policies in Perspective," *Soviet Economic Problems and Prospects* (Washington, D.C., 1976), pp. 621–22.

17. Juviler, "Communist Morality," p. 20; Hindus, *The Kremlin's Dilemma*, pp. 52, 64, 66, 87, 385; Dornberg, *The New Tsars*, p. 267; Schwartz, *Soviet Fathers*, p. 6; Mahanta, *Three Years*, p. 130; Mikhailo Mikhailov, *Leto moskovskoe 1964* (Frankfurt/Main, 1966), pp. 6–8.

The interaction of Eastern Europe and the Soviet Union is not confined to the consumer sector. Zvi Gitelman, *Diffusion of Political Innovation: From Eastern Europe to the Soviet Union* (Beverly Hills and London, 1972), pp. 27, 32, 49–53, suggests some ways in which Eastern Europe has exerted an intellectual and political influence on the Soviet Union, although what really emerges from his study is the Soviet leadership's ability to block substantive political influence.

18. *Vneshniaia torgovlia SSSR za 1959–1963 gody* (Moscow, 1965), pp. 200–231, 266–79, 304–21; *Vneshniaia torgovlia SSSR v 1976 g.*, (Moscow, 1977), pp. 124–47, 163–72, 193–202.

19. The figures for 1960–73 are based on data in International Union of Official Tourist Organizations (IUOTO), *International Travel Statistics* (annual). Only for the years 1968–70 did Intourist furnish IUOTO a breakdown of the number of Soviet tourists traveling to East European countries. For the other years, I have derived the figures from the number of Soviet tourists entering East European countries, as reported by those countries, reduced by 20 percent to allow for multi-country visits. (The correction is based on a comparison of East European and Soviet reports on Soviet tourists in Eastern Europe for 1968–70, when both sets of data are available, and on a separate calculation of Soviet tourists in 1960 from Soviet sources by Mary Jane Moody, "Tourists in Russia and Russians Abroad," *Problems of Communism*, November-December 1965, p. 4.) Figures for 1974–76 have been calculated from S. S. Nikitin, "Mezhdunarodnyi turizm i svoboda lich-

nosti," *Literaturnaia gazeta*, 25 June 1975 (for 1974), and Radio Liberty Research Bulletin, RL 204/77, 31 August 1977 (for 1975–76), which provide figures on the number of Soviet tourists to the "socialist bloc." These figures have been reduced by 20 percent to arrive at the East European figure. (This correction is suggested by figures for "socialist bloc" tourism provided by Intourist for 1968 and reported in Zhores Medvedev, *The Medvedev Papers* (London, 1971), p. 267, which can be compared with the figures for East European travel supplied by Intourist to IUOTO for that year.)

20. Calculated from Intourist figures seen by Moody, "Tourists," pp. 4, 6–7.

21. Statistics on Soviet unit force levels and deployment in *The Military Balance* (London, annual), indicate a rise from 300,000 Soviet soldiers stationed in Eastern Europe to about 400,000 over the last ten years. Taking the low figure and multiplying by 9 (allowing for a two-year rotation), we get a total of around 2,400,000 soldiers in Eastern Europe (all in the GDR, Poland, Czechoslovakia, and Hungary) between 1960 and 1976.

22. Walter Connor, "Opinion, Reality and the Communist Political Process," in Walter Connor et al., *Public Opinion in European Socialist Systems* (New York, 1977), pp. 185–86, also suggests that consumer dissatisfaction may become politicized, although he further suggests (ibid., p. 176)—mistakenly in my view—that Soviet consumer expectations have thus far remained within a "domestic-historical" framework and as yet present no problem for the regime.

23. Vera Dunham, *In Stalin's Time: Middleclass Values in Soviet Fiction* (Cambridge, England, 1976).

24. The most informed account for the 1950s is Jerzy Kosinski, *The Future is Ours, Comrade*, pp. 86–99 (cf. note 9 above, which indicates that workers did not share student optimism about the prospects for acquiring an automobile). See also A. Zr., "The Conscience of a Generation," pp. 12–13; Klaus Mehnert, *Soviet Man*, p. 104; Ernest Simmons, "The New 'New Soviet Man,'" p. 20; Alexander Werth, *Russia: Hopes and Fears*, p. 113.

There are surveys of the known strikes and other worker disturbances in Albert Boiter, "When the Kettle Boils Over....," *Problems of Communism*, January-February 1964, pp. 33–43, and M. Holubenko, "The Soviet Working Class: Discontent and Opposition," *Critique* (Glasgow), Spring 1975, pp. 5–25. In addition, I learned in the first half of 1976 of worker protests associated with food shortages in Sverdlovsk, Volgograd, and the Siberian coal fields; no doubt there were others as well.

Georgia and Soviet Nationality Policy

Ronald Grigor Suny

Seldom has the death of an individual, even that of a great tyrant, so definitively marked the end of one political era and the beginning of another as did the passing of Joseph Stalin. The Soviet system, in so many essentials the creation of his peculiar understanding of Russia's needs and his personal requirements for the maintenance of a monopoly of power, almost immediately began a process of gradual change which, however incomplete, has left a society significantly less terrorized, considerably more prosperous, and much more open to the rest of the world. In the twenty-five years since Stalin's death, the central political question facing the Soviet leadership has been: in reforming the Stalinist political and economic order, how much of what had become the Soviet system had to be dismantled? Within the ruling party, and in society as well, two conflicting tendencies can be observed: one committed to change leading to a more flexible social order, and the other dedicated to preservation of the status quo. As we have seen in the preceding chapters, this reform-preservation conflict has been reflected in a number of contradictory movements: decentralization of political and economic decision making versus conservation of the Stalinist command economy; intellectual tolerance versus repression of deviance and dissent; openings to the West versus maintenance of traditional xenophobia; greater liberty for national and ethnic expression versus the containment of such expression within the Stalinist formula "national in form, socialist in content." The result of these erratic shifts in government policy and the apparent loss of direction by the political elite has been increasing frustration on the part of many groups within

Soviet society, an erosion of commitment to the regime and its ideals, and the partial replacement of the official Marxist-Leninist ideology by patriotism and nationalism.

The enormous changes in Soviet society and political practice since Stalin should not obscure the elements of continuity that run from the stormy years of social reconstruction, through the years of moderate reform under Khrushchev, to the present period of conservative retrenchment. While most of the change in the last twenty-five years has occurred on the political and cultural level, much of the continuity can be located in the fundamental social, economic, and demographic trends initiated under Stalin. Urbanization, industrialization, and the spread of education and technology were affected only superficially by the change in political leadership. It is undeniable that the reduction of police terrorism and the decentralization of political power have to a degree shaped social developments, but the basic contours of the extrapolitical tendencies had been well-established by the Stalin revolution.

All of the constituent peoples of the Soviet Union have been affected by the social revolution of the Stalin years as well as by the political changes since Stalin; still, the emphasis of most analysts of the recent Soviet past has been, understandably, on the center and at the top, that is, on the Russian heartland and the ruling communist elite. When attention has been turned to the non-Russian periphery, it has usually been to look at the treatment of the minority nationalities as a separate aspect of Soviet policy, as "nationality policy" or the "national question." Such an approach, while illuminating the vacillations in policy arising from the reform-preservation conflict within the central leadership, usually neglects to examine the underlying indigenous social developments taking place in the ethnic areas. A study of nationality policy emanating from the center tells us little about the implementation or effectiveness of that policy among the various nationalities. Only an unquestioning acceptance of the outdated totalitarian model of the USSR would permit a researcher to conclude that the writ of the Kremlin always runs without resistance in outlying areas. The newest work on Soviet nationalities has already indicated clearly that their recent history has been sufficiently diverse to preclude many all-inclusive generalizations about the non-Russian half of the Soviet population. Thus, before a complete picture of post-Stalin development can be drawn, individual studies of each major nationality are required.[1]

Indeed a careful look at the history of Soviet Georgia during the last twenty-five years demonstrates that the experience of that republic has not been shaped to any great extent by the turns and twists of official nationality policy. Rather, Georgia's development, while evolving under the influence of general Soviet policy, has been primarily the product of indigenous social and political trends and local resistance to imperatives from the center. The picture that emerges from Georgia is complex and at times indistinct, but available evidence indicates that modernizing forces from beyond the Caucasus and nationalizing forces within Georgia itself have been engaged in an intense struggle since the heavy hand of Stalinist police rule loosened its grip. In order to evaluate the changes in Soviet Georgian society since Stalin's death, the interplay between the reform-preservation vacillation on the part of the leadership and the contradictory social forces pitting modernization against "renationalization" must be carefully investigated.

Nationality Policy since 1953

In the 1950s state policy toward the nationalities was articulated only occasionally, and then always incompletely. But in the new party program adopted by the Twenty-second Party Congress in 1961, Khrushchev elaborated the official theory of national development: Soviet nationalities were to continue to evolve through the "flourishing" (*rassvet*) of their ethnic culture, but this process would lead dialectically to a "drawing together" (*sblizhenie*) of these nations until their "complete merger" (*sliianie*) was achieved with the creation of a new Soviet people.[2] These pronouncements flew in the face of the tendencies that had been evolving during the preceding decade and seemed to signal a political attempt to reverse certain "objective" developments.

With the fall of Khrushchev in 1964, some slight changes were introduced into Soviet nationality policy. Among the minor concessions made to national sensibilities was the elimination of the assimilationist term *sliianie* from official statements about the future of Soviet minorities. The term *sblizhenie* was retained, but party leader Leonid Brezhnev emphasized that rapproachement among the nationalities would occur as the result of the play of "objective" social forces and not as the result of artificial prodding by the party.[3] In 1965, as if to underline the sincerity of this new approach, the government once again began to publish the laws of the Supreme Soviet and its Presidium in the national languages of the republics, something that had not been done since 1960.[4] Chairmen of republican supreme soviets, councils of ministers, republican supreme courts, and planning committees became, ex officio, members of the corresponding all-union institutions.

Essentially, the new party leadership adopted a policy of "benign neglect" of the nationalities, a policy that soon proved inadequate.

Within a few years it became apparent that two developments were occurring which were undesirable from the Kremlin's position: first, local national elites with a base of support in their republics were acquiring independent attitudes and practices with nationalist implications; second, a new nationalism with oppositional overtones was being articulated more and more openly.

The state's current nationality policy can be seen most clearly in the final draft of the new Soviet constitution adopted in 1977. Affirming the successful construction of socialism in the USSR, the preamble to the document claims that a "new historical community of people, the Soviet people, has emerged" as part of that process.[5] At least one Western analyst has argued that this formulation "aims at total deprivation of the Soviet nations of their separate national identities," but the Soviet leadership has been quite circumspect in its statements concerning the meaning of this concept.[6] Three days before the constitution was ratified by the Supreme Soviet, Brezhnev declared,

> The Soviet people's social and political unity does not in the least imply the disappearance of national distinctions. . . . The friendship of the Soviet peoples is indissoluble, and in the process of building communism they are steadily drawing ever closer together and their spiritual life is being mutually enriched. But we would be taking a dangerous path were we artificially to step up this objective process of national integration. That is something Lenin persistently warned against, and we shall not depart from his precepts.[7]

The new constitution reaffirmed the right of union republics to secede from the Soviet Union, though there had been much discussion in the early 1960s among the drafters of the constitution about doing away with this largely fictitious right. However, other prerogatives formerly held in law by the union republics have been lost in the new constitution. Republics no longer have the right to possess their own armed forces as they did in the 1936 constitution. Nor are they permitted to enter into direct relations with foreign states.[8] Most importantly, the administrative functions of the union republics are no longer as clearly demarcated in the constitution as they had been in the past, and the central government retains the right to decide on the republics' competence in policy matters.

Although these constitutional clauses simply affirm in law what has been usual practice, some observers in the West fear that they mark a diminution of ethnic autonomy.[9] Yet it can also be argued that the provisions in the new constitution, the result of long discussions and many political compromises, actually represent concessions toward the nationalities as well as some aggrandizement of authority by the central government. In his speech to the Supreme Soviet, Brezhnev noted that there had been proposals "to introduce into the constitution the concept of one Soviet *nation*, to abolish the union and autonomous republics, or to limit drastically the sovereignty of union republics by depriving them of the right of secession from the USSR and of the right to enter into foreign relations. The proposals to liquidate the Council of Nationalities and to establish a one-house Supreme Soviet would have moved in the same direction."[10] These more drastic assaults on the ethnic minorities were rejected by the leadership, and the official recognition of the multinational composition of the Soviet people was written into the document. Thus, twenty-five years after Stalin's death, the tensions between assimilationist and nationalizing trends have been tentatively resolved in a fragile compromise.

Georgia: Modernization and Renationalization

The fluctuations of official policy seem to have had less effect on the development of Georgian society in the recent past than the long-term, underlying dynamics which began in the Stalin years and even earlier. In the most general way one can describe the last 150 years as a period of the "reformation" of the Georgian nation. With the Russian annexations of Georgian lands (1801–29), most Georgian-speaking peoples were united under a single political authority for the first time since the fifteenth century. Although the autonomous monarchies and principalities were abolished by the Russians and their territory administered in conformity with other tsarist provinces, the Georgians benefited from Russian protection in several ways. The destructive invasions by the Muslim powers to the south, Persia and Turkey, which had nearly annihilated the Georgian states, were brought to an end, and in time the danger from raids by the mountain peoples in the North Caucasus was eliminated.[11] The security provided by the Russians permitted the reestablishment of the agrarian economy and the rebirth of urban life. The Georgian nobility, who at first resisted Russian rule, were pacified and integrated into the Russian nobility, and by the mid-nineteenth century were loyally serving the tsarist state as civil administrators and military officers. Thus, the advantages brought by Russian administration to Georgia diluted the recurring efforts to resist the new foreign authority. Ambivalence toward Russia has remained part of Georgian national consciousness to the present.

Georgia was just beginning to modernize when the revolution of 1917 made it possible for Georgians to break free of Russian control and establish an independent Georgian state. Run by Menshevik Social Democrats, the Georgian republic lasted three years (1918–21), during which the first cautious steps were taken to create a unified nation-state out of the antagonistic elements in Georgian society. The process of national integration was far from complete when the Red Army overthrew the Menshevik republic in February 1921.[12]

The destruction of political independence and the forced integration of Georgia into the Soviet Union ended the first period of Georgian national reconstruction. Even as political autonomy and local initiative were reduced for Georgians, two general developments were transforming the life of all nationalities in the Soviet Union: modernization and renationalization. Initiated in the early Soviet period and accelerated during the Stalin revolution, these two trends have had a strong influence on the life of Soviet ethnic minorities to the present.

Modernization refers to the complex processes associated with industrialization, urbanization, and, in the USSR, with the state-directed assault on the peasantry which reduced the weight of agriculture in economic life and ended the isolation of the peasants as it integrated agricultural laborers into the new urban working class. In Georgia industrialization had been quite modest before the revolution, but by 1940 industrial output had increased 670 percent over 1928. Even considering Georgia's low base, this marked a tremendous growth. Between 1940 and 1958 Georgia's industrial output grew by 240 percent, and from 1958 to 1965 by 157 percent.[13] Whereas in 1913, industrial production in Georgia amounted to only 13 percent of the value of total production, by 1970 industry, construction, and transportation-communications accounted for 53 percent of Georgian national income.[14]

The urban population of Georgia has grown steadily during the Soviet period, from 666,000 in 1913 to 2,241,000 in 1970. Georgian urbanites have in the sixty years of Soviet power increased from just over a quarter of the Georgian population to nearly half by the mid-1970s. Yet Georgia has not urbanized as rapidly as many other parts of the USSR and, unlike the country as a whole, does not have a majority living in cities. Only 44 percent of Georgians were urbanized by 1970, and Armenians and Russians still made up a disproportionately high percentage of Georgia's urban population.[15]

More significant in terms of modernization are the figures for the percentage of the total working population engaged in industry, building, and transportation-communication in contrast to the percentage engaged in agriculture. In 1939 the figure for industry was 19.4 percent of Georgia's working population, with 61.9 percent in agriculture. Twenty years later the figure for industry had increased to one-quarter of the working population while that for agriculture had fallen to one-half. By 1970 34 percent of the work force was in the industrial sector while 38 percent was in agriculture and lumbering.[16] It is clear that Georgian economic development has been aided by its link to the USSR and by the official Soviet industrialization ideology and policy.[17] However incomplete Georgian industrialization and urbanization may be, the society in which Georgians live today is vastly more interconnected with cities, factories, and economic growth than was the society into which Iosif Dzhugashvili was born a hundred years earlier.

The achievements of the communist leadership of the Soviet Union in expanding the economic power of their society are well enough known to Western readers not to require detailed defense. But less easily ascertained is the effect of the modernization process on the minority nationalities as cohesive ethnic groups. Most Western writers, while recognizing the assimilationist pressures that accompany modernization, would agree with Richard Pipes that the expectations of nineteenth-century liberals and socialists that nationalism would "dissolve in the acid bath of modernity" have proven utopian.[18] Soviet analysts as well have noted that the "construction of socialist nations" in the USSR has not led to the elimination of national differences. Indeed, in recent years there has been an increase in national consciousness and open expression of nationalism in the Soviet borderlands. This phenomenon is difficult to explain, for the expectation remains that in modernizing societies traditional allegiances to ethnic identifications would become less relevant.[19]

To explain the development of the new nationalism in the wake of modernization, it is necessary to look at another process that occurred simultaneously with industrialization and urbanization in the USSR—renationalization. The social transformation of Soviet society entailed much more than economic development. Along with the shift from agriculture to industry and from village to city, there was an expansion of mass education and welfare services and the creation of a modern multinational army and civil service as well as a technical intelligentsia. New modern institutions had the dual effect of opening the advances of Western and Russian learning to the Soviet minorities and of raising the literary abilities of these peoples in their own languages. For some nationalities renationalization meant the creation of an alphabet and a written language. For others it involved the initial establishment of a political framework. For Armenians it meant a fundamental demographic shift, as thousands migrated from other parts of the Soviet Union and the world to reoccupy a small piece of their

ancient territory. For Georgians it involved the gradual reestablishment of their political control and ethnic dominance over their historic
homeland, a process which had barely started during the brief period
of independence.

Before the revolution, Georgians had not exercised political power
in the territories that now make up the Soviet republic of Georgia.
Besides Russian officials, Armenian businessmen held the most important posts both in government and in the economy. Still primarily a
nation of rural nobles and peasants, the Georgians remained on the
fringe of the emerging urban society both politically and culturally,
and a desperate reaction to the displacement of their language and traditions led to the assertion of a new nationalism directed against both
Russians and Armenians. With the revolution and the brief period of
Menshevik rule, the Georgians began to displace the Armenian middle
class and to establish their own demographic and cultural hegemony in
the towns of Georgia, especially in the capital, Tbilisi, where they had
long been second-class citizens. In the early Soviet period Georgian
and non-Georgian cadres coexisted in the party and government apparatus, but the policy of developing "national cadres" (*korenizatsiia*)
steadily led to the Georgianization of the local government. At the
same time Armenians who had not already fled from the new communist republic migrated from Georgia to the Armenian Soviet republic, thus further consolidating the Georgian hold on the Georgian
republic.

The demographic consolidation of the Georgian nationality faltered
in the Stalin years but has accelerated since 1953. By 1970 Georgia's
population had grown to 4,686,000 from 4,044,000 in 1959. In 1959,
64.3 percent or 2,601,000 were ethnic Georgians; by 1970 that figure
had grown to 66.8 percent or 3,131,000.[20] This increase in the relative
weight of Georgians in Georgia's population is notable for two reasons.
First, it marks a reversal of the trend evident during the 1930s of a fall
in the percentage of Georgians (see Table 1).[21] Second, in comparing
the relative growth of Georgians in their republic to that of other titular nationalities in their home republics, the Georgians, despite their
modest birth rate, show greater increases than other republics, with the
exception of the Muslim republics with their high birth rates. In the
last several decades, as the weight of Georgians was rising, the corresponding weights of Armenians and Russians in Georgia were falling.
Georgia is the only union republic in which there has been an absolute
fall in the number of Russians.[22] The number of Armenians in Georgia
rose insignificantly between 1959 (443,000) and 1970 (452,000), but

TABLE I.

Ethnic Composition of Georgia by Percentage of Total Population

Nationality	1897	1926	1939	1959	1970
Georgians	66.3	66.8	61.4	64.3	66.8
Armenians	9.2	11.5	11.7	11.0	9.7
Russians	—	3.6	8.7	10.1	8.5

their percentage in the population of the republic fell. This Georgian-ization of the republic is primarily the result of out-migration of Russians, Armenians, and Jews.[23]

Yet another demographic datum is worth noting: the Georgians are much more likely than any major Soviet nationality to live within the confines of their national republic. In 1970 97 percent of Georgians in the USSR lived in Georgia, whereas their neighbors, the Armenians, had the lowest percentage (60) of any titular ethnic group living its home republic, and the Azerbaijanis had 86 percent of their ethnic group living in their republic.[24] That Georgians seem content to remain in Georgia appears to argue for the cohesiveness of the Georgian nationality.

The cohesiveness of the Georgians is also supported by evidence on intermarriage and bilingualism. Soviet statistics are silent on the question of intermarriage, but an American scholar has managed to discover some figures for 1969, when 93.5 percent of Georgians who married did so endogamously and only 6.5 percent intermarried.[25] As for bilingualism, Georgians showed high percentages in the population with no fluency in Russian. According to the 1970 census and the calculations of a Western observer, 91.4 percent of rural Georgians and 63 percent of urban Georgians were not fluent in Russian.[26] Even in Tbilisi, only 42.6 percent could command fluency.[27] The percentage of Georgians in the capital city unable to express themselves fluently in Russian (56.4) is higher than that for any of the other titular nationalities in the capital cities of their republics, with the single exception of the Armenians in Erevan (63.1 percent of whom are not fluent in Russian).[28] These figures show little tendency toward the assimilation of Georgians through the acquisition of Russian; indeed, a quite clear resistance to learning Russian is evident.

Besides demographic changes and political nationalization, Soviet Georgians also experienced a cultural revival, essentially a continuation of the rebirth of Georgian culture that had taken place in the late nineteenth and early twentieth centuries. That part of the old intelligentsia which remained in Georgia after 1921 was complemented by a new Soviet-educated intelligentsia. State-supported arts and publishing nourished an expanding creativity, though strictly within the framework of Soviet socialist norms. Most importantly, there was now a Georgian university, founded under the Mensheviks in 1919, and subsidized scientific research could be carried on in Georgian. Georgian theater, opera, and film flourished, as a new audience was exposed to culture in the native language. Folk music and dance became part of officially supported art and were promoted in the towns and cities among people who otherwise might have lost contact with the art of their village past. Ethnicity was actively fostered by the state, even to the extent of forcing the use of ethnic motifs on modern architects, painters, and sculptors. Under Stalin the national and traditional in the arts were preferred to Western, cosmopolitan modernism.

As must already be apparent, a fundamental contradiction existed between the processes of modernization and renationalization. Modernization was creating an industrial, urban society with increased mobility and material wealth and with greater opportunities for education and integration into general Russian and European life; at the same time renationalization was generating a new national culture, preserving and revitalizing local traditions, and in a variety of ways preventing the assimilation of the Georgians into an interethnic conglomerate. These contradictions went unresolved in official nationality policy and were reflected in the very formula designed for the arts—"national in form, socialist in content"—and in the confusion over whether the goal of Stalinist policy was to solidify the nation or to assimilate the minorities. These contradictions were not articulated during Stalin's rule; only in the more tolerant period after 1953 did the tensions developed during the process of modernization surface in a new nationalism.

Political Change After Stalin

One of the most striking changes in the last twenty-five years has been the decentralization of political and, to a degree, economic decision making. During the Stalin period, Georgia was directed almost completely from the center. After the great purges destroyed the last vestiges of local political initiative, Georgia was ruled by Stalin's lieutenant Lavrenti Beria, who operated through hand-picked cadres in Tbilisi. Economically, the industrial machine was almost entirely controlled by all-union ministries, and the threat of police intervention kept local party officials in line and prevented the emergence of any resistance to Kremlin authority.

Beria's brief ascendancy after Stalin's death was brought to an abrupt end when his fellow Politburo members in Moscow arrested him in June 1953 and brought him to trial. The elimination of Beria's supporters in Tbilisi was completed in September 1953, when V. P. Mzhavanadze, who had long served in the Ukrainian party apparatus under Khrushchev and as political commissar in the army, was elected first secretary of the Georgian Party. The Beria-sponsored Central Committee was dismissed, with the exception of two members.[29] Purges continued through the next few months, and by the Sixteenth Congress of the Georgian Communist Party in February 1954, the first secretaries of the Abkhazia, Adzharia, and Tbilisi regions had been replaced, new elections had been held in nearly nine thousand party cells, more than two thousand secretaries had been removed from these cells, and over one thousand candidate members of the party had been expelled.[30] The new party leadership that took power in September 1953 proved to be remarkably stable, and Mzhavanadze was to dominate Georgian politics for the next nineteen years.

The fall of Beria can be interpreted as a reassertion of the power of the party over that of the police with the aid of the army. It represented a reversal of the situation under Stalin, when the police had been the dominant political force by which the will of the Kremlin leadership was imposed on the regional parties. From 1953, the new authority of the party, combined with Khrushchev's policy of economic decentralization, increased the power of local parties in the national republics. Under Khrushchev the central party seemed willing to take the risk of somewhat reduced control over the national republics in hopes that these local parties would be able to gain local sources of support and provide stable government in the peripheries. A policy of indirect rule through dependent local elites replaced the old Stalinist system of direct control from Moscow. In Georgia the long tenure of Mzhavanadze aided the establishment of entrenched local authorities, who developed their own ethnic political base from which they could "negotiate" with central authorities.

In the first post-Stalin years, central political interference in the economy of Georgia was notably reduced. The aim of the central government appeared to be the gradual reform, rather than the preservation, of Stalinist practice. The number of administrative personnel was sharply reduced, as political operatives in many industries were eliminated. Many industrial firms in Georgia were transferred from all-union ministries to the republic's control; by 1958, 98 percent of industrial output in Georgia was produced by enterprises under the republic's management.[31] In all probability the motivation for this industrial decentralization was the poor showing in industry in the last years of Stalin's life. Industry in Georgia was not growing as rapidly as it had in the prewar period, and much of the debate at the Sixteenth Congress of the Georgian Party exposed the inadequacies of the country's largest enterprises—the Rustavi metallurgical complex, the Zestafon ferroalloy plant, and the Kutaisi autoworks.[32]

Georgia's problem with industry seemed to be chronic. In July 1955 a plenum of the Central Committee of the CPSU further criticized the performance of Georgian industry.[33] At the same time Georgian peasants benefited from the policies of Khrushchev which raised state prices for agricultural produce, reduced the amounts of compulsory deliveries, and left a greater area of decision making to the collective farms. However, these reforms reduced the comparative advantage that Georgian fruit and vegetable farmers had had over northern grain farmers during Stalin's time, for grain prices rose considerably.[34]

The political de-Stalinization and cultural "thaw" of the early post-Stalin period raised hopes for more far-reaching reforms and caused much confusion in Georgia. The party congress planned for May 1953 was delayed, and in the interim local party meetings were held to debate past policies and future plans. The official party history reports that about fifty thousand communists engaged in this critical and self-critical exercise, and it can be imagined that this period created expectations about the extent of political change that would soon be frustrated.[35] Within Georgia a few measures were taken to improve the situation for non-Georgians living in the autonomous regions. The school systems of the Abkhaz ASSR and the South Osetin region were reorganized; new Abkhaz, Osetin, and Armenian schools were opened; and a sector for Abkhaz language and literature was established in the Sukhumi Pedagogical Institute. Radio programs in Armenian and Azeri were revived, and newspapers in Russian, Abkhaz, Azeri, and Georgian were issued.[36]

The costs and limits of reform within the system left by Stalin became apparent within the first few years after his death. Khrushchev's experiments with decentralizing power led to the explosion of long-latent tensions. One of the most violent manifestations occurred in Tbilisi in connection with the third anniversary of Stalin's death, March 5, 1956. No official ceremony marking the occasion was held in the USSR. Just a few weeks earlier Khrushchev had made his famous "secret speech" denouncing the "cult of personality" and the crimes of the Stalin era. While this new turn in Soviet policy was hailed by the Russian intelligentsia and by reformers within the ruling elites, it had a peculiar resonance in Georgia. On March 5 an unofficial demonstration took place at the monument to Stalin that stood on the bank of the Kura in Tbilisi. Each day thereafter crowds of students and onlookers gathered at the statue to listen to poems and speeches commemorating the deeds of Stalin. On March 9 Georgian officials permitted a celebration of the anniversary, but as students moved through the central streets of the capital they were fired upon by police and the army. Dozens of young people were killed and hundreds were wounded.[37]

The response to the peaceful protest was extreme, and it deepened local resentment against the central government. Many in Georgia held Khrushchev personally responsible for ordering the army to fire on the unarmed crowd. In July the Central Committee in Moscow issued a resolution critical of the Georgian Central Committee, and in August the second secretary in Tbilisi was replaced by a Russian.[38] Yet the Georgian leadership managed to weather the storm. Party leader Mzhavanadze and university rector Viktor Kupradze attempted in interviews to play down the number of victims of the shootings, and a campaign of lectures was organized to spread party views.[39] For his success in pacifying the Georgians, the first secretary was raised to candidate membership in the Presidium of the Central Committee of the CPSU in June 1957.

The demonstrations in Tbilisi were seen by many as a revival of Stalinism and by others as the first open expression of Georgian nationalism in forty years. So little of the essential evidence needed for meaningful generalizations about this event is available to Western scholars that one must be cautious about attempting an analysis of its causes and significance. Georgia, like the other republics in the Soviet Union, had emerged from the Stalin years as a fundamentally changed society, more urban, more mechanized, with its traditional village life confined to an ever-decreasing part of the population. Yet this new, incompletely modernized society had been imposed on the Georgians by an alien political elite working through local Georgian cadres. At the same time, Georgian national culture had been revitalized through Soviet sponsorship. By 1956 the growing national awareness, coupled with anxiety about loss of ethnic uniqueness in the face of modernization, had led to a strong resurgence among young people of a commitment to Georgian ethnic identity. For young Georgians not fully acquainted with the darker side of Stalin's reign, his memory was still sacred, and his career represented a great achievement of one of their nation. Stalin's denigration was an appropriate symbol for the treatment of Georgian national consciousness at the hands of the Russian (Soviet) rulers. Patriotic pride was mixed with political protest in March 1956, but the response from the Soviet government, swift and brutal, illustrated starkly its inability to resolve the dilemma of a reformist leadership over how much of the Soviet system to change and how much of Stalin's authoritarianism to preserve. The answer to the government's confusion in Tbilisi was a bloody sign that reform was to be limited by the party's determination to preserve its essential monopoly of power.

Georgia for the Georgians

In the years after the Tbilisi demonstrations the government made some concessions to Georgian national pride and loosened cultural controls on Georgian art and literature. In March 1958 a festival of Georgian culture was held in Moscow, and later that year the 1500th anniversary of Tbilisi's founding was celebrated. But much more important than these gestures in the realm of culture was the gradual consolidation of a national communist elite ruling in Georgia with a significant degree of greater autonomy. The loosening of political controls from the center and the growing ethnic consolidation and consciousness locally merged in a combination dangerous both to the leadership in Moscow and to non-Georgians living in the republic. In the late 1950s, the Georgian party elite increased its hold over political, economic, and cultural institutions in the republic, and while ruling in Moscow's name, actually offered a low-level resistance to policies from the center that attempted to drive the Georgians too fast in economic development or cultural assimilation.

Local political control and ethnic favoritism manifested itself economically in the growth of a vast network of illegal operations and exchanges which produced great private wealth for some Georgians, while the republic's economy grew insignificantly according to official statistics. Despite Khrushchev's campaigns against speculators and "privatism," a degree of "capitalist restoration" took place in Georgia and was carried out by people in the government or close to it. Between 1960 and 1971, Georgia's national income grew by 102 percent, the third lowest rate in the USSR.[40] Yet in 1970, the average Georgian savings account was nearly twice as large as the Soviet average.[41] At the same time the educational system was turning out large numbers of specialists who avoided work assignments yet managed to live quite well. By the early 1970s Georgia had the highest percentage of the population in institutions of higher education of any major nationality.[42] Yet continually the press reported that thousands of graduates of high schools and of the university in Tbilisi were unwilling to accept work.[43]

Higher education in Georgia had become the prerogative of Georgians, and other nationalities found it difficult to enter schools of higher learning. In 1969–70, Georgians, who made up about 67 percent of the republic's population, accounted for 82.6 percent of the students in higher education, while Russians, with 8.5 percent of the population, made up only 6.8 percent of these students; Armenians fared even worse: with 9.7 percent of the republic's population, Armenians accounted for only 3.6 percent of the students in advanced courses.[44] Georgian control of the local party and republican institutions was resulting, not in an egalitarian application of Leninist nationality policy, but in officially sanctioned discrimination against minorities within the republic. Thus, the efforts of the early Khrushchev years to reverse such discriminating practices fell victim to the decentralization of political authority, which permitted a reassertion of national control now manifested in the inequitable treatment of local minorities. National autonomy in Georgia had come to mean, on the one hand, resistance to central Russian authorities and, on the other, the exercise of local power against the unrepresented local minorities.

The concern with growing nationalism was reflected in the party program of 1961, which asserted that "Communists consider it their primary obligation to educate the working people in the spirit of internationalism and socialist patriotism, and [to struggle against] any manifestation of nationalism and chauvinism."[45] In the years between the Twenty-second Congress and the fall of Khrushchev, efforts were directed toward nurturing a "spirit of socialist internationalism" among party cadres in Transcaucasia. Links between the three republics were strengthened by the creation of a Transcaucasian Bureau of the Central Committee of the CPSU, by the operation of the Transcaucasian economic administration, and by a variety of interrepublican organizations.[46] The central leadership was particularly concerned about the selection of party cadres on the basis of nationality and was determined to avoid national favoritism in the union republics. In the party program "any kind of manifestation of national isolation in the education and employment of party workers of different nationalities in the Soviet republics" was declared "impermissible."[47]

Despite these efforts to end ethnic favoritism in Transcaucasia, such practices persisted and in some ways grew worse. The Transcaucasian Bureau complained that areas inhabited by minorities did not receive adequate films or radio broadcasts in their native languages.[48] At the Twenty-second Congress of the Georgian Party, it was noted that Georgian scholars were still carrying on heated polemics among themselves and with scholars in other republics on historical questions with national implications: "Out of absolute trivia they are trying to inflame what could become a national catastrophe."[49]

"Temporary Soviet Power"

The fall of Khrushchev in October 1964 made little difference in the national development of the Georgian republic. The Mzhavanadze leadership remained in power for another eight years, and corruption, inefficiency, and discrimination against minorities continued to mark Georgian economic and political life. The beginning of the end for the Mzhavanadze regime was signaled by an article in *Pravda* on March 6, 1972. A resolution adopted by the Central Committee of the CPSU criticized the organizational and political work of the Tbilisi City Committee.[50] Corruption, "liberalism" in personnel matters, and failure to meet economic targets were noted. While the tone of the resolution was markedly restrained, it had an immediate galvanizing effect on the party organization in Georgia and initiated an intense internal examination and renewal of party leaders. In the next few months a series of rapid changes occurred in the most important party offices. The first secretary of the Tbilisi Committee was replaced by E. A. Shevardnadze, the forty-four-year-old minister of internal affairs, and Shevardnadze was made a member of the Bureau of the Georgian Central Committee. For a brief time it looked as if the purge of the Mzhavanadze machine might end with these lower-level maneuvers, but Moscow soon promoted the fortunes of Shevardnadze, and on September 29, 1972, he replaced Mzhavanadze as first secretary of the Georgian Communist Party.

The major reasons for this change in leadership were the widespread corruption in the administration of the republic, which, in turn, had caused poor economic performances by Georgian industry and agriculture, and the tolerance of nationalist tendencies within the party and intelligentsia. In terms of the growth rate of industrial production, Georgia held twelfth place among the union republics with a rate of 0.2 percent for 1972 instead of the projected 6 percent.[51] Total income for an average worker or office employee's family had declined by twenty rubles from 1971 to 1972.[52] Agriculture too, particularly in Abkhazia, was not meeting planned targets, except in certain specialized crops such as tea, sunflower seeds, and fruit.[53] On collective farms "instances of embezzlement, report padding, bribery, extortion, deception and hoodwinking were uncovered."[54] The procurement operation was particularly subject to fraud, since state collectors paid farmers in cash and frequently cheated them. While collective farmers' incomes had increased by ninety-nine rubles between 1971 and 1972, most of their income had come from outside the collective sector. In 1970, for example, farmers received three times as much income from their private plots as from the collective farms.[55] Much produce never reached the state or collective farm markets but was sold illegally. Only 68 percent of fruits and vegetables produced in Georgia in 1970 was marketed, compared to 88 percent in Azerbaijan and 97 percent in Armenia.[56]

The corruption, black marketeering, speculation and bribe taking in Georgia have their counterparts throughout the Soviet Union in what is referred to as the "second economy."[57] But as one observer of this all-union phenomenon has noted, when it comes to illegality and venality, "Georgia has a reputation second to none."[58] "In form this activity may not differ greatly from what takes place in other regions, but in Georgia it seems to have been carried out on an unparalleled scale and with unrivaled scope and daring."[59] In Georgia uninterrupted power for nineteen years had given the post-Stalinist clique an almost completely free hand within the republic. This, combined with the Caucasian reliance on close familial and personal ties in all aspects of life and the reluctance to betray one's relatives and comrades, led to an impenetrable system of mutual aid, protection, and disregard for those who were not part of the spoils system. "Business as usual" in Georgia meant, in the words of an official report, "favoritism, parochialism, cronyism and careerism flourishing on the basis of family ties and corruption, as well as a broad field for malicious talk and tale bearing; wives and other family members begin to usurp the positions of their high-ranking husbands and state problems begin to be solved in the narrow circle of relatives, the family or close friends."[60]

Such an internally reinforcing system of favors and obligations could not be reformed from within, and it was only with Moscow's backing that Shevardnadze was empowered to purge the worst offenders of the Mzhavanadze regime. In a speech to the Georgian Central Committee in July 1973, he warned those assembled, "There will be no mercy for bribetakers and extortionists."[61] One of the first officials to be dismissed was the notorious Gelbakhiani, the rector of the Tbilisi Medical Institute, who, along with the party secretary of the Institute, was discovered to have tampered with entrance examinations, excluding qualified students and admitting those who paid bribes or had proper connections.[62] Not surprisingly, Soviet statistics showed that Georgia had the highest number of doctors per ten thousand persons in the population of any country in the world.

Not only corruption but also officially condoned nationalism—or what Teresa Rakowska-Harmstone has called "orthodox nationalism"—became the target of attack in the public statements of Shevardnadze.

In one of his earliest speeches the first secretary complained that under Mzhavanadze "a half-baked nationalism raised its head in some places in the republic; things came to such a pass that attempts were made to rehabilitate emigre writers who are hostile to us. In those years the public psyche, man's inner world and his faith in bright ideas suffered more than the economy."[63] In other speeches the party leader condemned "national narrow-mindedness and isolation," and particularly the reluctance of many Georgians to study Russian. Artists, writers, and film makers were attacked for exploiting themes with nationalist overtones, but the strongest attacks were reserved for that most ideological of sciences, the study of history.[64]

The chauvinism both of Georgians toward ethnic minorities within Georgia and of the minorities themselves came under fire. The Abkhaz, Adzhar, and South Osetin regions had for years resisted both Russian and Georgian intervention into their internal operations. At a meeting of the Georgian party organization in April 1973, it was reported that "in Abkhazia a half-baked 'theory' according to which responsible posts should be filled only by representatives of the indigenous nationality has gained a certain currency. . . . No one has been given the right to ignore the national composition of the population or to disregard the continual exchange of cadres among nations and the interests of all nationalities."[65] At the same meeting it was noted that Adzharian officials had discouraged the development of tourism, for fear that this would lead to migration from other republics. Yet, the party organization was told, such instances of national isolation were understandable as a form of self-defense against the sometimes high-handed and insensitive treatment of minorities by the Georgians.[66]

The Shevardnadze purges continued for several years, and hopes were aroused that fundamental changes were taking place in Georgia. But resistance to reform was great and sometimes violent. As investigators moved closer to exposing a ring of speculators in Tbilisi who operated out of the opera house, a mysterious fire in that historic building destroyed the evidence. Suspicions of arson were directed at the police themselves.[67] Disillusion soon set in, and, as one acquaintance in Tbilisi expressed it to me: "We had temporary Soviet power!" Removing the most flagrant offenders could not change a system so deeply imbedded that the great mass of the party was involved, a system which in fact benefited a large part of the population. Shevardnadze's plaintive remarks about the psychological effects of the corruption are very revealing. In the experience of a whole generation of Georgians, the Soviet system has in actuality come to mean, not the establishment of

a just and egalitarian society, but rather the creation of a new, privileged elite which has been able to amass private wealth through control of the levers of political power.

The New Nationalism

The dual developments of modernization and renationalization in
Georgia have not been accompanied by a significant democratization of
the political superstructure. Despite the reforms of the Khrushchev
years, the preservation of Stalinist authority patterns has limited the
development of legitimate forms of criticizing the status quo. New
generations of educated young people with broad intellectual interests
have come up against the immovable restrictions on the exercise of
power and on expression. The resultant frustration has led many young
Georgians to adapt to the prevailing norms of personal acquisition and
easy-going hedonism, while others have placed their hopes either in an
idealized version of their own national past or in anticipation of a nationalist solution in the future. The failure of political reform under
Khrushchev to challenge fundamentally the old elites and the perceived immobility of the present government have encouraged an
extralegal expression of political and ethnic discontent both in Georgia
and throughout the Soviet Union.

In the 1970s Georgia witnessed the appearance of an "unorthodox"
or dissident nationalism. Its most articulate and active advocates were
a small group of students and professional people stimulated by their
aversion to the all-encompassing corruption that they saw around them.
Zviad Gamsakhurdia, the son of the prominent Georgian writer, Konstantin Gamsakhurdia, was a lecturer on American literature and the
English language at Tbilisi State University when he began to complain
to authorities about the treatment of various Georgian architectural
monuments. In 1972 he and his associates became aware of the theft of
religious treasures from the Georgian Patriarchate in Tbilisi. Gamsakhurdia phoned Shevardnadze, then still minister of internal affairs, and
an investigation was begun. The threads of the investigation led to the
wife of First Secretary Mzhavanadze, and though he soon lost his post,
an official cover-up of the thefts was maintained. Gamsakhurdia soon
publicized his claims and made contact with the Russian dissident movement and the Western press. In mid-1974 Gamsakhurdia and others
formed a Human Rights Defense Group in the Georgian capital. Pur-
suant to the Helsinki accords of August 1975, a "watch committee" to
observe human rights violations was set up in Tbilisi in January 1977.
Until his arrest in April 1977, Gamsakhurdia wrote numerous articles

complaining about the poor condition of Georgian national monuments and the illegal deportation of Georgian Muslims (the Meskhians) to Central Asia, and defending his arrested colleagues.[68] After more than a year in prison, Gamsakhurdia was tried and sentenced to three years in prison and two in exile.[69]

While this type of dissident nationalism is not widespread in Georgia, and while Gamsakhurdia and his associates were easily isolated from the population, their activity illustrates developing tendencies within the Georgian intelligentsia. Besides the desire for rights of free expression, the Georgian nationalist dissidents manifest a revival of religious enthusiasm, anxiety about the demoralization of the Georgian people, and a clear dislike for Russians and Armenians. Their attitudes are expressed in less extreme form by many Georgian intellectuals. At the Eighth Congress of Georgian Writers in April 1976, Revaz Japaridze angrily opposed suggestions by the Georgian minister of education that history, geography, and other subjects should be taught in Russian. He was outraged by an order from Moscow that all textbooks for higher educational institutions be published in Russian and that dissertations and their defenses be translated into Russian. Japaridze's speech was greeted by nearly a quarter hour of applause, and the audience would not permit the minister of higher education to answer him. When Shevardnadze spoke, he was interrupted by shouts as he tried to allay fears of Russification.[70]

In the spring of 1978 the potency of Georgian nationalism was revealed dramatically when the government made an ill-advised attempt to remove a clause from the draft of the new Georgian constitution which affirmed Georgian to be the state language of the republic. On April 14 an estimated five thousand people, primarily university students, demonstrated in the streets as the Supreme Soviet met to consider the draft. Shevardnadze, jeered by the crowd when he first tried to speak to them, returned later to announce to the demonstrators that the disputed clause would be retained.[71] This was a highly unusual concession to an open expression of opposition to state policy, a clear indication of the uneasiness and caution of government policy toward the new nationalism.

One nationalism furthers other nationalisms. As one people develops ethnic consciousness and the sense of exclusiveness and pride that accompany it, other peoples living near or among the first group often react with their own counternationalisms. In Georgia the growth of Georgian nationalism, both institutional and dissident, has stimulated nationalism among the local minorities—Russians, Armenians, Jews, Adzharians, Abkhazs, and Osetins. Georgian Jews, for example, a group

which historically had not suffered from anti-Semitic persecutions from
the dominant community, have, nevertheless, begun in recent years to
emigrate to Israel and the United States. After decades of hearing propaganda about the Soviet motherland (*rodina*) and the Georgian fatherland (*samshoblo*), the Jews of Georgia now seek their own homeland
and national future outside the Soviet Union.

The Abkhaz people have reacted against what they contend is Georgian interference in their national life and Tbilisi's failure to foster
Abkhaz cultural and economic development. In December 1977, 130
Abkhaz intellectuals signed a letter of collective protest and circulated
it widely. In May 1978, twelve thousand people gathered in the village
of Lykhny to support the signers of the letter and to demand that
Abkhazia be allowed to secede from Georgia and join the Russian republic (RSFSR). Deluged with letters and telegrams in favor of secession, Moscow dispatched I. V. Kapitonov, secretary of the Central
Committee, to Sukhumi and installed a new party leader in Abkhazia.
Gently but firmly, Kapitonov told the local party organization that
secession was impermissible. Shortly afterward, the government acknowledged the seriousness of Abkhaz complaints by decreeing a
costly plan "for further development of the economy and culture of
the Abkhaz ASSR."[72]

Official responses to the new and more open expressions of Caucasian
nationalism are most striking in their relative tolerance and flexibility.
Twenty-five years earlier such expressions would have been dealt with
by brutal police repression. Perhaps this policy of conceding to demands which cost little to the existing structure of power is the clear-
est indication of the degree of political change since the death of Stalin.

Continuity, Change, and Nationalism

At the end of the first quarter century of post-Stalinist evolution the
contradictory developments of the Soviet past, the simultaneous drive
toward modernization and the creation of revitalized nationalities within
the Soviet federal structure, have not brought about either Russification or assimilation in Georgia. Instead two kinds of nationalism now
exist: a pervasive and growing national consciousness that operates
within the system to maximize the benefits to the Georgian people
themselves; and an illegal, dissident nationalism still characteristic only
of a miniscule minority of the Georgian population. Official nationality policy, with its avowedly assimilationist goals, has had little real
effect on the Georgians, who have moved steadily toward consolidation of their ethnic separateness. The unresolved tension between the

assimilationist tendencies of modern society and the reconsolidation of Geórgian ethnicity has produced an increasingly potent nationalist mood in all parts of Georgian society and counternationalisms among the ethnic minorities within the republic.

The new nationalism is related both to the continuing social trends carried on from Stalinist times and the freer political atmosphere of the last quarter century, which marks the most fundamental change from the past. More specifically, four major reasons for the appearance of this nationalism can be elaborated.

First, the reduction in political penalties with the relaxation of the Stalinist terror has made it easier for people to express long-latent national feelings. Whereas other forms of political action and expression were more strictly prohibited, in Georgia the state made significant concessions to the population's national feelings. Thus, nationalist expression may be an outlet for a variety of discontents—political, economic, intellectual, and cultural—a kind of political sublimation for activity and ideas that are otherwise too dangerous to articulate.

Second, the national elite in Georgia used the opportunity offered by the Khrushchev years to consolidate local power. With the backing of the local ethnic majority, it legitimized its rule and gained support vis-a-vis Moscow. The autonomy permitted by Moscow, which now chose to rule indirectly through local cadres, gave the national elite the chance to cultivate popular support through the exploitation of national feelings. Ethnicity, in turn, became an important criterion for success, as the Georgian leadership patronized members of their own nationality to the exclusion of others. The percentage of Georgians in the party increased from 73 percent in 1952, already higher than the percentage of Georgians in the population of the republic, to over 76 percent in 1970.[73] Ethnic consolidation both in the republic as a whole and in the ruling institutions further contributed to the rise in national identification and pride. Nationalism was expressed in culture, in cadre favoritism, and in the economic "exploitation" of the Soviet system.

Third, nationalist expression has been a genuine indicator of the historic fear of small nations that they will be swallowed up by larger nations in the process of modernization. Georgian nationalists fear the loss of their language and its replacement by Russian, the destruction of their ancient monuments, and the elimination of their unique customs, traditions, and way of life. Built into nationalist fears are a deeply rooted conservatism and apprehension about what the future in a multinational state holds for the minorities. There is also a positive side to this anxiety. Not only does it work to preserve ethnicity in the face of modernizing pressures, it also provides an alternative to the model of development imposed by the dominant Soviet nationality. Georgians, in their national pride, have come to feel that their further evolution is hindered by the restraints placed on them by the Russians. It is widely believed among Georgians that left to themselves, they would more quickly realize their historic potential.

Finally, the erosion of Marxist ideology within the Soviet Union has cleared the way for its replacement by patriotism and nationalism. Ironically, the Soviet government itself has aided in this process by transforming Marxism from its original purpose—a critical and revolutionary tool of the working class against the status quo—into a rigid, dull rationalization of the existing order. Nationalism, on the other hand, holds out a hope for a better future with reference constantly to great moments in the national past. The romanticism, irrationality, and utopianism of nationalism at least provide an alternative to the mundane reality of a slowly modernizing society with all its inadequacies.

Notes

1. A recent though not wholly successful attempt to examine the indigenous development of Soviet nationalities is the collection of essays edited by George W. Simmonds: *Nationalism in the USSR & Eastern Europe in the Era of Brezhnev & Kosygin: Papers and Proceedings of the Symposium held at the University of Detroit on October 3–4, 1975* (Detroit: University of Detroit Press, 1977).

2. *XXII s"ezd KPSS: Stenograficheskii otchet*, vol. 3 (Moscow, 1962), p. 314.

3. Teresa Rakowska-Harmstone, "The Dialectics of Nationalism in the USSR," *Problems of Communism* 22:3 (May-June 1974), pp. 18–19.

4. *Vedomosti verkhovnogo soveta*, 1965, no. 36, p. 839.

5. A. Shtromas, "The Legal Position of Soviet Nationalities and their Territorial Units according to the 1977 Constitution of the USSR," *The Russian Review* 37:3 (July 1978), p. 267.

6. Ibid.

7. *Izvestiia*, October 5, 1977; translation in E. Bagramov, "A Factual Survey of the Soviet Nationalities Policy," *Reprints from the Soviet Press* 27:5 (September 15, 1978), p. 49.

8. Shtromas, p. 271.

9. Ibid.

10. *Izvestiia*, October 5, 1977; translation from Shtromas, pp. 271–272.

11. The historian of this period, David Marshall Lang, writes: "By the year 1800, the process of disintegration of the Georgian state had reached a critical stage. . . . Left to itself, it is doubtful whether the Georgian nation would even have been assured of physical survival." *The Last Years of the Georgian Monarchy, 1658–1832* (New York: Columbia University Press, 1957), pp. 282–283.

12. The revolution in Georgia and the controversy over Georgian autonomy after 1921 is discussed in Richard Pipes, *The Formation of the Soviet*

Union: Communism and Nationalism, 1917–1923 (Cambridge, Mass.: Harvard University Press, 1964), passim. See also, Firuz Kazemzadeh, *The Struggle for Transcaucasia (1917–1921)* (New York: Philosophical Library, 1951).

13. Alec Nove and J. A. Newth, *The Soviet Middle East: A Communist Model for Development?* (London: George Allen & Unwin, 1967), p. 40. Of the least-developed republics in the USSR, those of Central Asia and Transcaucasia, Georgia has in the post-Stalin period been growing slower than most. From 1940 to 1958 only Azerbaijan and Turkmenistan grew at a slower rate than Georgia, and in the period 1958–65 Georgia was next to last, with only Turkmenistan behind.

14. Richard B. Dobson, "Georgia and the Georgians," in Zev Katz, ed., *Handbook of Major Soviet Nationalities* (New York: The Free Press, 1975), p. 162.

15. Rakowska-Harmstone, p. 6.

16. Dobson, p. 162.

17. This argument is made by Nove and Newth, passim.

18. Richard Pipes, "Introduction: The Nationality Problem," in Katz, p. 3.

19. The contradiction between modernization and ethnic revival was recently explored by V. Stanley Vardys in an excellent short study of Baltic nationalism and modernization, but his conclusion that modernization has been ineffective in eroding nationality begs the question of why this paradox exists. "Modernization and Baltic Nationalism," *Problems of Communism* 24:5 (September-October 1975), pp. 32–48. A partial answer is provided by Teresa Rakowska-Harmstone, who argues that the "powerful integrative forces" of modernization, which one would expect to work against the preservation of ethnicity, have been modified somewhat in the national republics "where the retention of a federal administrative framework safeguarded the territorial loci and formal ethnocultural institutions of most minorities, thereby preserving the bases for potential manifestations of national attitudes" (p. 2). Trond Gilberg, in an interesting article on modernization in Romania, demonstrates the limits of Karl Deutsch's modernization model, which predicts cultural assimilation of minorities. "Romania: Problems of the Multilaterally Developed Society," in Charles Gati, ed., *The Politics of Modernization in Eastern Europe: Testing the Soviet Model* (New York: Praeger, 1974), pp. 117–159.

20. J. A. Newth, "The 1970 Soviet Census," Soviet Studies 24:2 (October 1972), p. 215.

21. Dobson, p. 168.

22. The number of Russians in Georgia fell from 408,000 in 1959 to 397,000 in 1970. Newth, p. 216.

23. The number of Armenians in Georgia rose by only 2 percent, while the number of Armenians in Azerbaijan rose by 9.5 percent and those in Armenia rose by 42.3 percent between 1959 and 1970. The number of Azerbaijanis in Georgia, a group which is largely rural, has a high birthrate, and apparently does not migrate, rose in the same period by 41.6 percent. Newth, p. 218.

24. Ibid., p. 215; Teresa Rakowska-Harmstone, "The Study of Ethnic Politics in the USSR," in Simmonds, p. 24.

25. Wesley A. Fisher, "Ethnic Consciousness and Intermarriage: Correlates of Endogamy among the Major Soviet Nationalities," *Soviet Studies*

29:3 (July 1977), p. 398. These figures are for marriages within the Georgian republic.

26. Brian D. Silver, "Methods of Deriving Data on Bilingualism from the 1970 Soviet Census," *Soviet Studies* 27:4 (October 1975), p. 596.

27. Ibid.

28. Ibid., pp. 592–597. Erevan is a special case because of the large number of immigrants from outside the Soviet Union who usually do not speak Russian.

29. John Ducoli, "The Georgian Purges (1951–53)," *Caucasian Review*, 6, 1958, pp. 58–59.

30. *Zaria vostoka*, October 4, 1953; Ducoli, p. 59.

31. *Ocherki istorii Kommunisticheskoi Partii Gruzii*, vol. 2 (Tbilisi, 1963), p. 252.

32. *Ocherki istorii Kommunisticheskoi Partii Gruzii, 1883–1970* (Tbilisi, 1971), p. 686.

33. *Ocherki*, vol. 2 (1963), p. 262.

34. Nove and Newth, pp. 59–60, 62–63.

35. *Ocherki* (1971), p. 684.

36. *Ocherki*, vol. 2 (1963), pp. 250–251.

37. G. Charachidze, "The Riots at Tiflis—an analysis," *Caucasian Review*, 3, 1956, pp. 99–104.

38. *Zaria vostoka*, August 9, 1956.

39. *Ocherki*, vol. 2 (1963), p. 270. Professor Yaroslav Bilinsky has suggested to me that Khrushchev's patience with Mzhavanadze might in part have been due to their close acquaintance, dating back to the 1940s when both worked in the Ukrainian party.

40. *Narodnoe khoziaistvo SSSR 1922–1972: Iubileinyi statisticheskii ezhegodnik* (Moscow, 1972), p. 515ff.; Dobson, p. 163.

41. Dobson, p. 163.

42. Ibid., p. 177.

43. *Zaria vostoka*, March 24, 1956; *Ocherki*, vol. 2 (1963), p. 269.

44. Dobson, p. 177.

45. *XXII s"ezd KPSS, Stenograficheskii otchet*, vol. 3 (Moscow, 1962), p. 245.

46. K. B. Udumian, "Iz opyta partiinykh organizatsii Zakavkaz'ia po internatsional'nomu vospitaniiu trudiashchikhsia," *Voprosy istorii KPSS*, 1964, no. 12 (December), p. 17.

47. *XXII s"ezd KPSS*, vol. 3, p. 315.

48. Udumian, pp. 25–26.

49. *Zaria vostoka*, February 2, 1964.

50. *Pravda*, March 6, 1972: "V tsentral'nom komitete KPSS: Ob organizatorskoi i politicheskoi rabote Tbilisskogo gorkoma Kompartii Gruzii po vypolneniiu reshenii XXIV s"ezda KPSS." An English translation of this resolution is available in *Current Digest of the Soviet Press* (henceforth, *CDSP*), 24:10, April 5, 1972, pp. 7–9.

51. *Zaria vostoka*, February 28, 1973; *CDSP* 25:13, April 25, 1973, p. 1.

52. *Zaria vostoka*, July 31, 1973; *CDSP* 25:31, August 29, 1973, p. 5.

53. *Zaria vostoka*, November 25, 1972; *CDSP* 24:50, January 10, 1973, p. 5.

54. *Zaria vostoka*, February 28, 1973; *CDSP* 25:13, April 25, 1973, p. 2.

55. *Zaria vostoka*, July 31, 1973; *CDSP* 25:31, August 29, 1973, p. 5.

56. *Izvestiia*, March 23, 1973; *CDSP* 25:12, April 18, 1973, pp. 9–10.

57. Gregory Grossman, "The 'Second Economy' of the USSR," *Problems of Communism* 26:5 (September-October 1977), pp. 25–40.

58. Ibid., p. 34.

59. Ibid., p. 35.

60. *Zaria vostoka*, February 28, 1973; *CDSP* 25:13, April 25, 1973, p. 5.

61. *Zaria vostoka*, July 31, 1973; *CDSP* 25:31, August 29, 1973, p. 6. For an interpretation of the causes of Georgian corruption, see David Law, "Corruption in Georgia," *Critique*, 3 (Autumn 1974), pp. 99–107.

62. *Zaria vostoka*, November 3, 1973; *CDSP* 25:44, November 28, 1973, p. 4.

63. *Zaria vostoka*, February 28, 1973; *CDSP* 25:13, April 25, 1973, p. 6.

64. Two historians who wrote about the period 1917–24, U. Sidamonidze and A. Menabde, were taken to task for their less than total condemnation of the Mensheviks and Georgian autonomists. In a speech to the Tbilisi party organization, Shevardnadze said: "There have recently been manifestations of a politically dangerous tendency, under the guise of restoring historical objectivity, to depart from a Party appraisal of N. Zhordania, the Menshevik leader, double-dyed national chauvinist and inveterate enemy of Soviet Georgia, and others. . . . We take a realistic view of the need for a scientific study of the historical past. However, this should help us to make better predictions of the future. One should look at the past through the eyes of the future, or the study of the past becomes an end in itself." *Zaria vostoka*, February 8, 1974; *CDSP* 26:8, March 20, 1974, p. 3. Even the official history of the Communist Party of Georgia, published in 1971, was attacked for being "unfree of subjectivism," especially in dealing with the period 1952–70. The writing of history was a way to promote "nationalist prejudices," and the party leaders warned the academic establishment to beware of "a certain infatuation with antiquity." *Zaria vostoka*, April 27, 1973; *CDSP* 25:16, May 16, 1973, p. 5.

65. *Zaria vostoka*, April 27, 1973; *CDSP* 25:16, May 16, 1973, p. 5.

66. Ibid., pp. 5–6.

67. These rumors were reported to the author in Tbilisi. In *Arkhiv samizdata*, document no. 2109, which can be found in *Materialy samizdata* 2/76, January 23, 1976, Georgian nationalists claim that those arrested for the fire were Jews and Armenians but that only Jewish names were released. This document claims that Vasken I, the Catholicos of the Armenians, inspired this arson (p. 4).

68. Gamsakhurdia's writings have been published in *Materialy samizdata*, AS 2581 in MS 28/76, August 25, 1976; AS 2444 in MS 16/76, May 14, 1976; AS 2580; AS 2757 in MS 42/76, December 31, 1976; AS 2809; and in other issues.

69. *New York Times*, May 20, 1978. For reporting that Gamsakhurdia's televised expression of remorse might have been fabricated, two American journalists, Craig Whitney of the *New York Times* and Harold Piper of the *Baltimore Sun*, were ordered to retract their articles and were fined by a Moscow court.

70. A Russian translation of Japaridze's speech was published in AS 2583 in MS 23/76, July 14, 1976.

71. *New York Times*, April 15, 18, 1978; *Zaria vostoka*, April 16, 1978.

On April 14 a similar clause was restored to the new constitution of the Armenian SSR.

72. *New York Times*, June 25, 1978; *Zaria vostoka*, May 26; June 7, 1978. For more on the conflict in Abkhazia, see Roman Solchanyk and Ann Sheehy, "Kapitonov on Nationality Relations in Georgia," *Radio Liberty Research*, RL 125/78, June 1, 1978; and Ann Sheehy, "Recent Events in Abkhazia Mirror the Complexities of National Relations in the USSR," ibid., RL 141/78, June 26, 1978.

73. *Kommunisticheskaia Partiia Gruzii v tsifrakh (1921–1970 gg.) (Sbornik statisticheskikh materialov)* (Tbilisi, 1971), pp. 171, 265.

The Soviet Family in Post-Stalin Perspective

Peter H. Juviler

A leading Soviet women's advocate recently quoted to her readers a letter from the spouse of a field geologist.[1] The geologist was away on expeditions much of the time, leaving her husband at home to raise their eight-year-old son. The couple became estranged and subsequently divorced. The situation just described is symptomatic of some current trends in Soviet family life. The family is small, with only one child. The marriage has ended in divorce. The divorce came about because of tensions created by the wife's independence and by conflicts of roles and of authority between the spouses.

Low birth rates, high divorce rates, and parental neglect of children caused the Soviet regime concern as early as the 1930s. These concerns remain today. But since Stalin, new conflicts have come to the fore in family life, brought on by massive social changes. The regime has been seeking new ways of responding to family needs and shortcomings. Some of the social and policy changes affecting Soviet families (outside of the most traditionalist areas of the country) are the subject of this chapter.

Parental choice about how many children to raise continues to affect the demography and the labor-force availability in the USSR. The birth rate, in turn, is closely connected with other crucial aspects of change: a growing legal freedom and personal assertion of *marital choice*—especially choices to stay single and to divorce; the drawn-out growing pains of *women's liberation* in the face of persistent women's

Mrs. Ida Zilius rendered valuable assistance. Professor Wesley Fisher kindly made available to me some materials that would otherwise have been unobtainable.

inequality in the home; and the slow drift of *authority in the family* from patriarchal to more democratic patterns.

This account touches on rural as well as urban, non-Russian as well as Russian, families. Generalizations about trends in freedom of choice since Stalin refer both to regime policy and to the actual behavior of family members, for families typical of the great mass of outwardly conforming Soviet citizenry. Deviance from party-approved norms in family life, such as delinquency, parental misconduct, and religious dissidence, and the regime's efforts to repress such happenings, I have treated elsewhere.[2]

Parental Choice

Had the original Marxist and Bolshevik expectations for the family and its "withering away" been realized, there would be no such issues of family life and policy. After the Stalinists restored the family to honor, the watchword became not the eventual "withering away" of the family but its "strengthening." Now, roughly 94 percent of Soviet people live with some form of residential or budgetary tie to the 60 million families they form.[3] Nuclearization of these families into units of no more than two generations was on the rise in tsarist cities.[4] Increasing urbanization since then has multiplied the number of nuclear families. City families today average only 3.5 persons. Not only nuclearization but falling birth rates account for their small size, as well as for the small size of rural families, which now average 4.0 persons for the USSR. Indeed, live birth rates have been steadily dropping during this century: 45.5 (per thousand population) in 1913; 31.2 in 1940; 24.9 in 1960; and only 18.1 in 1977.[5].

If this trend keeps up, families will not even be reproducing themselves in the fairly near future. The population will then level off and decline, and the shortage of labor power will become ever more serious, according to many Soviet demographers.[6] Basic to this present trend is the drastically declining fertility of women—not their capacity to have children but their desires, their choices as to how many children to raise.[7] Some changes associated with this diminishing fertility have not yet run their course by any means.

First, the fertility of rural women is dropping toward that of city women in many parts of the USSR.[8] Second, urbanization has long been associated with smaller families; the USSR, today 62 percent urban, will be 75–80 percent urban by the year 2000.[9] Third, as Appendix A shows, seven union republics already have very low birth rates, ranging from 13.6 to 18.2; the birth rates of four other union republics, though high in 1950, are now falling toward the low levels of the first seven republics. Only the four Central Asian republics still have high average birth rates. There, much of the indigenous population holds to traditional ideals of large families. Whereas only 3.5 percent of women questioned in the western USSR expect to have five or more children, a *third* of the women questioned in Central Asia expect to have *eight or more* children![10] If and when the proportion of Central Asians living in villages goes down, one may expect average birth rates in Central Asia to fall as well.[11]

Soviet women must have two or three children each in order to guarantee an adequate labor force, according to the prevailing opinion of demographers.[12] But women stubbornly choose to have only one or two, on the average, for the whole of the USSR.[13] Their exercise of parental choice confronts the demographers and the Communist Party, all the way up to the general secretary, who expressed strong concern, with the prospect of an aging population and a labor shortage.

Yet unlike Stalin, the present regime has turned aside suggestions that it return to the compulsive legislation of parental and marital choice in order to increase birth rates and preserve the family.[14] Under Stalin, nontherapeutic abortions were banned in 1936 and divorce fees were raised. Wartime losses in people and births prompted new laws to protect the family as a childbearing unit and to raise the disastrously low wartime birth rate. The decree of July 8, 1944, barred paternity suits and forbade the recognition of a nonhusband's paternity, even when he voluntarily acknowledged it. The decree was meant, on the other hand, to encourage unmarried women to have children, in a situation where there were only two men for every three women of childbearing age, owing to the loss of 20 million men in the war. Thus, though only registered marriage gave rise to paternal rights and obligations under the 1944 decree, the state undertook to give unmarried mothers a grant for every child born to them out of wedlock and to care for such children in state homes. Family allowances for all mothers went up, and more nurseries and kindergartens were ordered. But sharp cuts in allowances in 1947 took the noncompulsive heart out of the severe new family law. The 1944 decree included other intended protection for the family based on registered marriage: a new, complicated, and expensive divorce procedure in two courts.[15]

Buttressed by such a restrictive law, the Soviet family came to be seen by the ideologues as an essential replenisher of labor power and a psychological bulwark of Stalin's authoritarian system, a "microcosm of the new socialist order," alongside the redisciplined school and the mass youth organizations.[16]

More and more women reacted inarticulately to Stalin's compulsion
by having illegal abortions. Couples circumvented the divorce barriers
through de facto divorces and marriages unprotected by law. As for
advocates of women's rights and interests, their voices had long been
stilled by the abolition of the Zhenotdel, the Women's Department of
the Central Committee, in 1930, and then, by the climate of conformity and terror under Stalin.

By 1954, less than a year after Stalin's death, an articulate movement
began pressing for family law reform, especially for equality of extramarital children, easier divorce, and an easing of women's conditions
of life. The revival of research and a limited leeway for the discussion
of sensitive social issues opened up channels of public debate on matters of family life (excepting the political ones such as freedom of
religious upbringing). Out of the debates and party decisions have
come measures reducing the compulsion on parents to have more children, while continuing to try to hold parents responsible for the proper
upbringing of their children.[17] The party leadership considers "an effective population policy" to be a matter of some urgency. Lawyers
and demographers have considered the possibility of compulsive "demographic legislation," such as a new abortion ban, to reverse the lifting
of the old abortion ban in 1955, but the party, apparently, has sided
with the majority view that a new set of compulsive laws would not
serve the party purposes.

The family law reform of 1968 permitted the voluntary acknowledg-
ment of extramarital paternity. It opened up a narrow field for paternity suits in some cases of noncasual liaisons, removed the documentary
stigma of illegitimacy by no longer crossing out the father's name in
the old birth certificate and permitting the mother to enter a patro-
nymic and her own last name as the father's, for a child born out of
wedlock. The partial restoration of women's rights and equality was
furthered by prohibiting husbands from divorcing wives during preg-
nancy or less than a year after childbirth, and by more extensive spouse
support and property division clauses.[18]

Instead of compelling parental choice, the regime is trying to raise
the incentive to have more children by easing the financial and child-
care burdens of parenthood.[19] Much remains to do, as our discussion
of women's liberation will remind us.

When it comes to parental choice as to how to raise children, the
state has become, if anything, less permissive since Stalin. Part of the
regime's concern is with the role of faulty upbringing in aggravating
the persistent problems of juvenile delinquency and crime. Central

Committee secretary M. S. Solomentsev said of the 1968 family law reform, when introducing the law for passage, that its purpose was "to increase the responsibility of citizens to the family and society," as well as to further the goals of women's equality and the encouragement of motherhood.

Criminologists cite failures of the family as educator as "a leading cause" of juvenile lawbreaking. Hence, while the post-Stalin regimes have liberalized juvenile punishment in courts and labor colonies, they have also increased the range and severity of the criminal and administrative responsibility of parents who neglect, abuse, or contribute to lawbreaking by their children.

New since Stalin, also, is the effort to mobilize a whole network of nonjudicial social agencies such as the commissions on juvenile affairs, comrades' courts, social counselors, and committees in work places to help the family and the school. The intervention of these amateur agencies is uneven in reach, effectiveness, and sensitivity to the needs of individual juveniles and their families. But whatever the impact, work places are involved in influencing wayward parents more than they are in most other countries.[20]

In short, the authority of the state over the family has not faded since Stalin. Rather, it has assumed new forms—in some ways more compulsive than they had been, in some ways less so. The attempt to compel fertility has been abandoned, at least for now. The complex social changes helping to lower birth rates touch many sides of family life, from marriage and divorce to women's liberation and equality.

Marital Choice

Marriage formalities in the USSR made the institution of marriage seem a casual affair indeed until recently. After years of experimentation with "wedding palaces" and new ceremonials even in humbler surroundings, secular ceremonials, complete with bridal gowns and wedding parties, are again becoming popular in Soviet cities. Since the 1968 reform, there has been a one-month waiting period between application and registration. Sometimes, that period may be lengthened to up to three months.

Yet the tide of legal divorces flows unabated. As marriage became a bit more difficult, the regime gave up on legal attempts to stem the tide of family breakup. A simplified divorce procedure, involving only one court, went into effect January 1, 1966. The 1968 reform added a provision for the simple registration of divorce without court trial on the condition of payment of a fifty-ruble fee and a three-month waiting period, when there is mutual consent and when there are no minor children of the marriage.[21]

By 1977, 902,000 families were dissolving by divorce annually. As Appendix B shows, this is one divorce for every three marriages on the average for the USSR; much higher divorce rates prevail in major cities of the European USSR, and in big cities generally.[22]

Divorces directly reduce fertility, since couples avoid having children when they feel divorce coming on. They may remain unmarried for years after divorce. Less than half of divorced women remarry, and a half-million children of broken marriages remain fatherless.[23]

Unmarried Soviet men and women, both divorced and single, form a huge untapped "reserve" of increased fertility. One in five men over twenty are unmarried as are nearly two in five women (38 percent). Younger unmarried men far outnumber younger unmarried women because of marriage-age differences. But older unmarried women far outnumber older unmarried men because of the latters' preference for much younger mates.[24] The drop in marriage rates over the last twenty years from 11–12 per thousand inhabitants to about 10 is one cause of the fall in women's fertility rates. This helps explain the recent effort to resume earlier experiments with get-acquainted services and marriage bureaus and to open marriage counseling offices, still at a very early stage.[25]

Students and sexually segregated workers constitute other "reserves" of fertility. About 5.7 million students were enrolled in day technical high schools and colleges in the 1977–78 school year. These people are in their otherwise most fertile years—a larger population than in any Soviet city except Moscow. Yet schools are not in the business of promoting baby booms. They have not done "everything possible to help create prerequisites for combining family life and above all motherhood with getting an education," such as alloting special dorm space (there is none to allot except at Moscow University) and liberalizing stipends for pregnant students.[26] The partial separation of men and women in "cities of bachelors" near heavy industry and "cities of women" near light and textile industry had economic but not demographic rationality.[27]

A large jump in divorce rates (see Appendix B) occurred after the liberalization of divorce procedures in 1965, effective January 1, 1966. Officials of ZAGS, the civil registry office, with whom I spoke in 1968 maintained that the 1966 rise was caused by a backlog of divorces that had piled up under the old Stalinist legislation. But something else besides the law must account for the rises in rates since then. There is little doubt that recent rises are related to urbanization and to social and economic change in the USSR.

Chances are that a divorce will be initiated by the wife rather than by the husband. The husband's alcoholism, and the drunken bedlam and violence to wife and children accompanying his drinking, is the most frequent cause given by wives to the court to explain the breakup of the marriage. It is the top reason in nearly half the cases. Incompatibility, a rubric including all kinds of problems from sex to fights over housework, is the second reason. Infidelity is the third most frequent reason given for petitioning for divorce.[28]

Experts tend to dismiss these reasons as clues to what really accounts for the rush to divorce these days. Drunkenness is hardly new in Russia. Neither are the side effects of urbanization. Family ties have been loosening, rather, because the family is losing functions that kept it together. Spouses spend so little of their total time on their children's upbringing that even one ideal time budget allots only seven percent to this.[29] Upbringing is transferred increasingly to other agencies: schools, youth organizations, and informal peer groups. The family has also been losing its functions of economic production. The restraints of religion, extended family influences, community mores, and the former victorianism of the Stalinist regime, whereby divorce was a blot on the career of a party member, have all eroded.

The marriage union has become more fragile, more dependent on mutual accommodation, respect, attraction of the spouses, an arrangement more of pleasure and less of necessity. Ironically, this approach toward the socialist ideal of "finally cleansing family relations from material calculation,"[30] though not fully achieved, has already helped destabilize the family, increase divorces, and lower the birth rate.[31] After considering marital choice as it affects the rural family, I will return to another basic reason for the unwanted opposite trends in divorce and birth rates.

The Soviet socialist transformation of the countryside has been at the heart of the de-economization of the family unit. First came the violent, costly collectivization of private peasant farm households in 1929–34. Private peasant households had made up some 70 percent of the population. This shifted a share of farm family income outside the family to the communal sector of the kolkhoz, or collective farm. The collective farm household, or *dvor*, remained as a unit of property ownership (of small farm inventory, some livestock, the house and auxiliary structures, and garden plot products). The dvor also retained productive functions based on the private plot. Despite punitive taxation after World War II, the household farming economy yielded the family, or more correctly the dvor, twice the income it received from the work of its members on the collective farm. Khrushchev saw to it that collective farms paid better wages and moved to curtail private-plot farming. Although the Brezhnev regime reversed the latter policy, the shift in sources of household income continued, as Table 1 shows.

The garden plot still absorbs many hours of toil[32] and puts on the table most of the farm household's meat, milk, eggs, potatoes, melons, and vegetables.[33] But it is no longer central to the household livelihood in many cases. Moreover, the prominence of collective-farm family life in the countryside is a thing of the past. In 1953, 57 percent of the population was listed as collective farmers. This proportion fell to about one-third in the late fifties, as Khrushchev promoted the more communalized crop factories—the sovkhozy or state farms; it reached a low of 15.7 percent in 1977.[34] This trend has direct demographic consequences because collective farm families tend to be more fertile than are families in other economic sectors. Economically, too, the shift to state farming is significant, because state farmers (officially included in the category "workers") have smaller garden plots than do kolkhozniki and rely less on private farming income—21 percent of the total according to one older estimate.[35]

Because a better life and an urban outlook have trickled into the villages, farm couples today are likely to be bound less than they were twenty or thirty years ago by economic necessity and common toil and more by ties of companionship and affection and by the rearing of one, two, or three children.[36]

Western Belorussia, reabsorbed into the USSR during World War II, was fully collectivized by 1952. Young people there are reported today to be marrying mainly for love. Their marriages have become a matter of individual choice and affinity rather than the result of parental pressure. Economic considerations no longer enter into family

TABLE 1.

Weight of Household Farming Income in the
Total Collective Farm Budget, USSR, 1958–74, Percent

Year	Income from Collective Farm	Income from Household Farming	Other Income
1958	39	45	16
1970	45	36	19
1974	44	26.6	29.4

choices, especially parental choices. But the officially desired and, in some lesser ways, the actual trend in Belorussia, as in many other Soviet areas, is for the loosening of economic bonds (at whatever cost in stability). The official ideal is that Soviet socialization of farming "will clear marriage and family relations once and for all of material calculations and increase the role of factors such as a person's outlook, his ideals and aspirations, his moral and esthetic feelings."[37]

Rural divorce patterns are coming to resemble those in the cities. Wives initiated half of the 637 divorce cases studied in seventeen rural areas of Grodnensk province, Western Belorussia. Again, the number one reason given (see Appendix C) was their husbands' alcoholism and brutality. These spouses do not yet seem to have reached the high "moral and esthetic level" of the ideal Soviet husband. In the old days, it is said, a peasant woman would hang on to a bad marriage because she was bound into a time-honored and essential village division of labor between the sexes, inhibited from divorce also by religious beliefs, socialization, and the whole way of life, which taught patience and resignation. The married peasant woman of today is much more likely to break off the marriage and divide the property of the dvor.

It is hard to imagine that Stalin's regime, with its disapproval of and stricter restraints on divorce, would have tolerated the following citation, with obvious approval, by a present-day researcher of a petition for divorce by mutual consent from Zhdanov kolkhoz, Volkovyskii district, Grodnensk province:

> Having discussed our relationship, we have reached the conclusion that it makes no sense for us to prolong our marital state. Although we have been married nine years and have two children, we have no feeling or affection for one another. Given such indifference it will be better for us to dissolve the marriage. It would also be better for our children. We are dividing our property voluntarily.[38]

The extensive materials consulted and the findings selected here, as well as personal observation in the USSR over a span of years beginning in 1955, all seem to support the opinion that rising divorce rates in the USSR reflect a "desire for more choice in every area of life."[39] The chaos of "revolution from above" subsided more than forty years ago. The blood purges and then the war that broke up families are long since past. The era of strong official disapproval of divorce has ended. Alternative housing is increasingly available for divorcés. People are becoming more self-centered, more absorbed by hope and striving for a happier and more comfortable personal life. They defer less than their grandparents did to the authority of church, state, morality, or tradition in their choices of when to marry and divorce. They act in ways familiar to urban families in other industrialized countries—at least, their expectations run in roughly the same direction, though less trammeled by tradition. Without trying rashly to attribute a specific share of cause to the women's liberation movement, one must add that in its Soviet form, too, it has probably contributed to divorce rates, and it has certainly led to falling birthrates.

Women's Liberation

The term "women's liberation" heads this section to indicate that in the Soviet Union, as well as in the West, the question of changing sex roles, of greater female equality, has been a burning issue, both before the late thirties and after Stalin.

Women's emancipation may be a better term to use for this development, in the sense that it was initiated from above, not from below. Barely in power, the Bolsheviks hastened to legislate women's full equality of family, economic, and civic status, *in the law*. Bolshevik leaders saw this as a blow to the old authoritarian social order and a way to right a historic wrong to women. "Liberation" implies a feminist movement. Feminism had always been a minor aspect of the Russian revolutionary movement and its Marxist segment. (For a while the Women's Department of the Communist Party Central Committee, the Zhenotdel, served both as women's advocate and as a political mobilizer for the party. Impatient with this ambivalence and excluding any priority except industrialization, Stalin abolished it.)

The Bolsheviks disagreed about how quickly they could dispense with the family and about whether free love was preferable to the sober "proletarian marriage based on love" espoused by Lenin. The family existed in Soviet family law and policy as a relic to be used for child rearing and mutual support of its members until the society at large could find resources with which to take over the motherly, housewifely, and welfare functions of the family. The family code of 1926 actually increased the economic claims of family members on each other, in the face of the growing unemployment of women. The proletarian-toned first five-year plan of 1928–32, with its collectivization of peasant households and attacks on parental authority, probably undermined family stability more than did any conscious family policies of the Bolsheviks.

Constituting nearly half the industrial labor force by World War II, women took much of the home-front effort on their shoulders; these are the people about whom *Pravda* had run a discussion in the late twenties, questioning whether a woman could stand at a lathe! Today 51.5 percent of workers and employees are women.[40] Women make up 49 percent of the industrial working force and substantial or majority proportions of virtually every other occupational category.[41]

Some women work because they have to in order to supplement the family income. Others work because they want to. The more skilled the worker category and the more creative the work they do, the more likely women are to rank work satisfaction first, satisfaction of being with other workers (a typical office worker's reason) second, and material considerations last.[42]

Work fulfills an original Bolshevik aim: it makes women more independent. The peasant woman in the Belorussian divorcing couple quoted earlier earns over 100 rubles from the kolkhoz. With that and her house and garden plot she can easily get by.

The rub is that the Bolsheviks envisaged a woman fully independent of the family, emancipated "from kitchen and frying pan." Instead, women still work a "double shift" and encounter many other costs in their division of roles, work, and authority with men. As a Soviet expert has pointed out, "Women's emancipation is a great achievement of our epoch. But a price must be paid for that great achievement. The price includes complications of relations between the sexes."[43] These complications often involve conflicts over the nature of femininity, over the division of labor in the family, and over authority in the family. One of the reasons there are so many Soviet expert sources to quote on this problem, aside from the greater post-Stalin possibilities of discussing social problems openly, is that the regime has been virtually forced to give attention to women's role-conflict because of its toll in divorce, reduced fertility, and neglected children.

The wider question of feminism and femininity in the USSR falls beyond the range of this inquiry into the status of the Soviet family. Suffice it to say that many men, and some women too, lament the alleged passing of the tender, modest, motherly "keeper of the hearth" and resent the "masculinity" of the younger generation of hard-swearing, smoking, drinking, promiscuous women, whose strong aggressiveness is concealed by the svelte new superficial image beaming attractively out of the TV set, movie screen, and magazine cover. The crisis of sexual identity is exacerbated by the fact that a man's mentors are mainly his mother and female teachers. It reaches into families to cause divorce.

Larisa Kuznetsova, a leading publicist and women's advocate, cautions women not to be ashamed of the new strength they have gained as a natural adaptation of their old femininity to changed social circumstances. However, she also sees the danger of a woman's losing all of the feminine difference so important to men. As an example, she cites the woman geologist frequently away on expeditions, whose situation was described at the beginning of this chapter. She and her husband divorced by mutual consent because her manliness, her absence of feminism, he wrote, created in him "an insatiable emotional craving, even an obsession . . . Who is 'he?' Who is 'she?' Who has the strength? Who the masculinity? My male essence could not endure this."[44] For all it may cost in both sexes learning to adjust, Kuznetsova concludes, "In no way can we assert that men maintain the same position of preeminence—social, economic, and therefore psychological, that they did a century ago. In other words, the very 'stuffing' of femininity is changing its ingredients."[45]

Femininity but with shared authority—that is the demand of the new Soviet woman whom Kuznetsova represents. Can one imagine such an outlook under Stalin? The only possible public image then resembled the heroine of Panferov's novel *Bruski*, who said at a Kremlin meeting in 1937: "Our hearts are overflowing with emotions, and of these love is paramount. Yet a wife should also be a happy mother and create a serene home atmosphere, without, however, abandoning work for the common welfare. She should know how to combine all these things while also matching her husband's performance on the job." "Right!" said Stalin.[46]

Division of labor in the family was not a simple question even then. It has now become the central family issue. The "double shift chronically overburdens women, making them nervous and destroying their femininity, youthfulness and beauty."[47] But today Soviet women are farther than ever from the illiterate, dependent drudges of old. Working women are as educated as their male coworkers,[48] whose further on-the-job training and greater advancement they subsidize with the liberation of their husbands from most housework.[49] Again and again, surveys by Soviet researchers record women's expectations from marriage: love, respect, trust, common interests, companionship, consideration, sexual fulfillment, and help with the housework.[50] Yet women end up doing two to three times as much housework as men. This well-known statistic and the findings behind it have been presented many times.[51] It remains only to give some additional examples, so as to convey the present state of the problem.

When, in an experiment, mothers working in an Odessa construction organization received a daily hour off, they spent it on more housework. Husbands of these women shared housework evenly in only 8.6 percent of the families and helped to raise the children in 28.4 percent.[52]

This is a small help because Soviet parents spend on the average only six hours a week on upbringing, perhaps a fifth of the time spent on all domestic duties.[53]

A recent survey of 4,000 working youths and married couples with and without children in Taganrog shows what happens to women's free time after marriage and motherhood. The appearance of children spells the end of free time for the wife. For example, on "cultural" activities at home unmarried men spend 9.0 hours a week and women, 9.4 hours. Married men spend 11.15 hours and married women, 13.5. But after children appear, married men spend 15.4 hours at "cultural" pastimes in the home, while married women spend only 5.3. The mother reads on the average 1.65 hours; the father, 5.6 hours. Mother watches TV 3.15 hours a week; father, 9.25 hours.[54] While the wife is cleaning, washing clothes, cooking, and changing diapers, the husband is either out somewhere or, if at home, comfortably lying on the couch, reading or watching television.

As in this country, there are many women who put family and home ahead of work.[55] They do not resent being one of the many women holding disproportionately low-paid or low-ranked posts within their trades and professions.[56] Nor do they mind that their children's grade-school readers brim with sex-role stereotyping of women and little girls, and that the females do the housework in the stories.[57] It is probably a matter of indifference to these nonliberated women that many of the proposed solutions for their double burden promise simply to reduce it, or to remove them from production and pay them to tend their babies, rather than shift some of that burden to their husbands.[58]

But for the well-educated working woman, the "second shift" grows intolerable. She will *not* assume the duties of a servant, as she is expected to do, while her husband turns to drink or outside social life and self-improvement. "The husband and wife often determine domestic duties virtually in open combat, the wife taking the offensive and the husband defending himself—supported by the traditions that say housework degrades a man." Until this conflict is resolved, the number of divorces will not drop, nor will the depression of birth rates.[59]

As many Soviet sociologists see it, the basic demographic problem is created not by divorces, but by the unwillingness of most women to pay the "price" of large or even medium-sized families. Women are "in rebellion." New interests crowd out home, children, and family. Women feel, increasingly, the need for "self-expression, personal improvement, equality with other people in all spheres of life, for respect for their person, for freedom of behavior and choice." There are not enough grandmothers and child-care facilities, despite the enormous expansion of nurseries and kindergartens. Besides, parents are unprepared to cope with family difficulties and to raise children. Divorces are producing millions of single-parent families along with additions to the 20 million bachelors and unmarried women twenty to forty years old. Annually, 700–800,000 children appear to be raised only by their mothers, owing to illegitimate births, divorces, and husbands' deaths. Husbands' indifference also raises the "price" of a second and third child. The response of women is simply to stage a slowdown in childbearing.[60]

Together, divorces and drops in birth rate help bring women's "second shift" to the level of a major national issue for the government, the major issue in family policy.[61] The "second shift" adds up to 180 billion person-hours a year, only 18 percent less than person-hours expended at regular work—for women, a second, thirty-hour work week. The level of employment among women has reached 94 percent of that among men.[62] Virtually the whole country's growing urban population is caught up in this issue.

Authority in the Family

It is hard to imagine a Stalinist regime allowing its experts to write about "women in rebellion" and demanding equality. No less hard to imagine under Stalin would have been serious inquiry into the final determinant of choice among family members: the division of authority in the family, a large topic that can be dealt with only briefly here.

Under the 1977 Soviet constitution, the division of authority within the family is equal, as it has been since 1917 but with a very important difference. Family law proclaims the equality of men and women in family relations. The constitution speaks of the full equality of "spouses" in family relations. Women tend to be less than equal in nonregistered conjugal relationships because of limitations on claiming the paternal support of the father of a child when the father does not voluntarily acknowledge his paternity. In sum, spouses may claim legal protection of equality in family relations only where the law says such relations exist. The law enforces woman's freedom of choice to give her body to her husband or to withhold. A husband who forces his attentions on an unwilling wife is liable to prosecution for rape—if she brings charges.[63] The law does recognize one element of inequality in the family: the position of head of the collective-farm household, who is responsible for the fulfillment of tax and certain other household obligations to the state. Otherwise, the government has ignored suggestions that it recognize a head of every family.[64]

The census takers, on the other hand, insist on naming a head of every household: the one whom family members name as head, whether or not the family actually has an active single holder of more authority than others. Only 28.5 percent of all families in 1970 listed women as heads. Moreover many such women heads are widows or unmarried mothers. Frequencies of female headship give just a rough idea of division of authority. It is known, for example, that the lower the percentage of women heads in a region, the higher the birth rate (because local traditionalism and patriarchalism accompany high birth rates).[65]

The conflicts over doing housework involve not simply a particular division of labor but also perceptions of authority in the family. Husbands and wives often give different answers on questionnaires asking them who is the head of the family. The discrepancy seems to increase as one goes to older couples and to couples with less education. In one survey, 88 percent of young nonspecialist husbands thought they were family heads, but only 52 percent of their wives agreed with them; 66 percent of husbands with higher and specialized secondary education considered themselves to be family heads, and only 44 percent of their wives agreed with them. Less than one-fifth of the wives in these two groups of families considered themselves to be family heads. Grown children tend to support the perception of their fathers. No more than five percent of husbands, regardless of age group (younger or older, over 35) or educational level (specialists or ordinary workers) considered their wives to be heads of the family. The discrepancy in perception of the wives' headship far exceeded that in perception of the husbands'.[66]

Family heads in the sociological sense have the right of giving orders and making decisions. Other family members have the obligation to carry out the head's decisions and to minister to family needs. Soviet researchers see the family in transition from the autocratic type, with one head of household, to the biarchic type (spouses share authority), or the democratic type (either spouses share all authority or they decide together with the children).[67] The proportion of autocratic families diminishes and the proportion of democratic families increases, as the survey moves from a small town to a medium city and to a metropolis like Moscow.[68]

Some headships are purely formal. They are recognized and the head is listened to, but nobody carries out his orders and the wife is actually in control. In any event, the younger and better educated the family, the less likely it is to have a head. When a head is recognized, men are accorded the authority of head because they are "breadwinners," while the most frequent reason for according headship to a woman is that she cares for the family (the last consideration in recognizing a man's headship). To earn her authority, the woman must work in the family; to earn his, the man must be the main earner, in many cases.

Regardless of headship, the wife will generally play a larger role than the husband in spending money, even large sums of money, for the family, and in the upbringing of children. Many parents have little time for children. And a recent survey prompted the conclusion that parents pay "insufficient attention to the upbringing of children in a majority of cases, especially the father."[69] Just as the post-Stalin Soviet state has not solved the problem of division of labor, so it has not been able to prevail on or encourage the majority of parents to exercise effective authority over their children.

One would like to see more data to test one Soviet conclusion that Soviet families are moving slowly from traditional authority (with deference to a head, regardless of function or quality), which has become a relic, to charismatic authority (they do not use the term "charismatic"), based on the recognition of real functions for the family and personal qualities, to formal headship—symbolic authority—and ultimately to the equalitarian family without headship.[70] The present division of authority in the Soviet family, to the extent that one can generalize about it, supports the appraisal that women's freedom of choice has increased faster in education and employment since Stalin than it has in areas less susceptible to state control such as decision making and authority within the family.[71]

Conclusions

The nature of the state's interaction with the family has changed considerably since Stalin. State involvement with the family continues to be intense. But the compulsion has shifted from women to men, as freedom, or relative freedom, of parental and marital choice has been restored in post-Stalin reforms of abortion rules, laws on marriage and divorce, paternity, and birth registration.

Watching the present trend toward zero population growth and ever smaller families, the Soviet regime has decided, for now at least, to avoid renewing compulsive efforts at birth stimulation and to increase parental incentives to choose to have a second or third child.

There are virtually no signs yet of legal or educational support for the idea that men should take on at least a share of domestic chores, if not an equal one. The trend in Soviet state policy has been to try to lighten women's double burden of outside and domestic work without shifting some of the burden on to men's shoulders, the latter a step many deem essential to the final liberation of women.

Women are seeking and exercising greater social freedom; they evince a "desire for more choice in every area of life." That choice must be exercised at the expense of the past authority of the state and of their spouses. Women's changing view of the meaning of femininity, where it crops up, tends to exacerbate family conflicts. These conflicts often begin not in unequal burdens alone, but in women's new resistance to the double burdens. The conflicts originated in the very growth of equality and independence envisaged by Bolshevik (and other Russian) revolutionaries.

Divorce is one way for women to assert their freedom. Divorce is not mainly a man's game any more. Registered divorces have risen to new heights of one for every three marriages in the USSR, two for every three marriages in the big cities. Soviet sociologists may no longer cite low Soviet divorce rates, as they once did, to show the superiority of the socialist over the bourgeois way of life.

Another act of choice and independence by women has been to desist from having more than one or two children. This "rebellion" by women in the family is what has created the government's sense of crisis and has drawn its attention to women's double burden and the need to lighten it. The fall in birth rate, the smaller family size, and increased freedom of choice have had an ambivalent impact. Soviet believers in large families lament that this assertion of choice produces families too small for proper upbringing and too many self-centered only children. The chauvinists among Soviet men find the new claims of women to be an unsettling nuisance, if not a serious threat to their sense of their own identity and sex roles. Other people, especially females, have welcomed the new family trends as signs of transition to an era in which women will take their lives and choices into their own hands, approach full equality, decide family size along with their husbands on the basis of a couple's wishes, and not because of spontaneous nature or reasons of state. That women are in rebellion is all to the good for these observers, both male and female.

Division of authority in the family is hard to define and measure. From the little information available, it seems that Soviet families are in transition from (1) the traditional authoritarian structure of a single male head (or female when the male is missing), to (2) personal authority based on contributions and individual qualities or merely formal male authority and much participation, to (3) a democratic structure of decision making and work sharing. To complicate the picture, women hold considerable power, even under male headships, by spending the family money. A family may make decisions democratically but will still leave much of the housework to the wife.

In all three regards—equality, choice, and authority—the post-Stalin course of Soviet families and their interaction with the state authority over them, as well as the position of women in the families, seem to indicate that Soviet society is slowly becoming less repressive and relationships more equalitarian.

APPENDIX A.
Union Republic Birth Rates, 1940–77

Union Republic	1940	1950	1977
USSR	31.2	26.7	18.1
Group I			
RSFSR	33.0	26.9	15.8
Ukraine	27.3	22.8	14.7
Belorussia	26.8	25.5	15.8
Georgia	27.4	23.5	17.8
Lithuania	23.0	23.6	15.5
Latvia	19.3	17.0	13.6
Estonia	16.1	18.4	15.1
Group II			
Kazakhstan	40.8	37.6	23.9
Azerbaidzhan	29.4	31.2	25.2
Armenia	41.2	32.1	22.5
Moldavia	26.6	38.9	20.3
Group III			
Uzbekistan	33.8	30.8	33.7
Kirgizia	33.0	32.4	30.2
Tadzhikistan	30.6	30.4	36.5
Turkmenia	36.9	38.2	34.2

SOURCE: *Narodnoe khoziaistvo SSSR za 60 let* (Moscow: Statistika, 1977), p. 73; *Narodnoe khoziaistvo SSSR 1977 godu* (Moscow: Statistika, 1978), pp. 24–25.

APPENDIX B.
Marriages and Divorces per 1,000 and
Their Ratios, USSR, 1940–77

Year	Marriages[a]	Divorces[a]	Div/Mar[b]
1940	6.3	1.1	17.6
1950	11.6	0.4	3.4
1955	11.5	0.6	5.2
1960	12.1	1.3	10.7
1965	8.7	1.6	18.4
1966	8.9	2.8	31.5
1967	9.0	2.7	30.3
1968	8.9	2.7	30.0
1969	9.4	2.6	28.9
1970	9.7	2.6	26.8
1971	10.0	2.6	26.0
1972	9.4	2.6	27.6
1973	10.1	2.7	26.7
1974	10.3	2.9	28.2
1975	10.7	3.1	28.9
1976	10.1	3.4	33.7
1977	10.7	3.5	32.0

SOURCE: [a]*Narodnoe khoziaistvo SSSR v 1977 godu* (Moscow: Statistika, 1978), p. 26. [b]Estimated from other figures, percent.

APPENDIX C.

Reasons for Divorce in the Opinion of Husband,
Wife, and Judge, Grodnensk Province, Western Belorussia,
1972–73 (637 divorce cases), Percent

Reason for the Divorce	According to the Opinion of		
	Judge	Wife	Husband
Alcoholism	38.7	44.3	10.6
Incompatibility	15.1	6.7	22.2
Infidelity	9.4	12.6	15.3
Casual marriage	8.5	2.0	4.5
Long separation (owing to circumstances)	5.4	3.8	3.1
Loss of feeling for unknown reasons	5.3	8.6	12.3
Cruelty	3.6	5.6	0.6
Sentencing to deprivation of freedom for three or more years	3.3	2.6	2.1
Physical and mental illness	2.1	1.7	2.6
Interference of parents and relatives	1.5	4.4	11.3
Infertility	0.8	0.7	1.0
Physiological mismatch	0.3	0.3	0.5
Other reasons	6.0	6.7	6.0

SOURCE: V. T. Kolokol'nikov, "Brachno-semeinie otnosheniia v srede kolkhoz-nogo krest'ianstva," *Sotsiologicheskie issledovaniia*, no. 3 (1976), p. 82.

Notes

1. Larisa Kuznetsova, "Zhenskaia kar'era," *Literaturnaia gazeta* (hereafter *LG*), March 15, 1978, p. 13.
2. Peter H. Juviler, "Law and the Delinquent Family: Reproduction and Upbringing," in Donald D. Barry, George Ginsburgs, and Peter B. Maggs, eds., *Soviet Law after Stalin*, Part II, *Social Engineering through Law* (Leyden: Sijthoff, 1978), pp. 213–28; Peter H. Juviler with Brian E. Forschner, "Juvenile Delinquency in the Soviet Union," *The Prison Journal*, 58, 2 (Autumn-Winter 1978), pp. 18–28.
3. *Itogi vsesoiuznoi perepisi naseleniia 1970 goda*. Vol. VII (Moscow: Statistika, 1974), pp. 4, 186, 238; B. Urlanis, "Sem'ia i problemy demografii," in D. I. Valentei, ed., *Molodaia sem'ia* (Moscow: Statistika, 1977), p. 5.
4. A. G. Kharchev, *Brak i sem'ia v SSSR: opyt sotsiologicheskogo issledovaniia* (Moscow: Mysl' 1964), pp. 215–16.
5. *Itogi*, pp. 4, 238–39; *Narodnoe khoziaistvo SSSR* (hereafter *NK SSSR*) *v 1977 godu* (Moscow: Statistika, 1978), p. 71.
6. V. Perevedentsev, "Edinstvennyi v sem'e," *LG*, March 16, 1977, p. 12; A. Ia. Kvasha, ed., *Upravlenie razvitiem naseleniia v SSSR: Problemy i perspektivi* (Moscow: Statistika, 1977), pp. 90–110; D. Valentei and A. Kvasha, "Sotsial'no-ekonomicheskie problemy narodonaseleniia SSSR v dolgosrochnom perspektive," in D. Valentei, ed., *Demograficheskaia situatsiia v SSSR* (Moscow: Statistika, 1976), pp. 1–6; *NK SSSR 1922–1972* (Moscow: Statistika, 1973), p. 9.
7. Urlanis, p. 11.
8. *Itogi*, p. 4; P. I. Simush, *Sotsial'nyi portret sovetskogo krest'ianstva* (Moscow: Izdatel'stvo politicheskoi literatury, 1976), pp. 252–53.
9. "Rod liudskoi: Skol'ko nas budet?" *LG*, January 28, 1976, p. 13.
10. Sh. Amanashvili, "Model' i real'nost'–slishkom malo skhodstva," *LG*, April 21, 1976, p. 13; G. A. Bondarskaia, "Differentsiatsiia rozhdaemosti po etnicheskim gruppam," Darskii, pp. 26, 31.
11. G. A. Bondarskaia, "Etnicheskaia differentsiatsiia rozhdaemosti v SSSR i ee sushchestvo," Darskii, p. 119; *NK SSSR za 60 let*, p. 44.
12. Iu. B. Riurikov, "Deti i obshchestvo," *Voprosy filosofii*, No. 4 (1977), p. 121; V. A. Belova, *Chislo detei v sem'e* (Moscow: Statistika, 1975), p. 93.
13. Valentei and Kvasha, p. 6; Urlanis, pp. 5–7.
14. Juviler, "Law and the Delinquent Family," pp. 205–40; and Peter H. Juviler, "Whom the Law Has Joined: Conjugal Ties in Soviet Law," in *Soviet Law after Stalin*, Part I, *The Citizen and the State* (Leyden: Sijthoff, 1977), pp. 119–57.
15. Donald D. Brown, ed., *The Role and Status of Women in the Soviet Union* (New York: Teachers College Press, 1968); Stephen P. Dunn and Ethel Dunn, *The Study of the Soviet Family in the USSR and the West* (Columbus, Ohio: AAASS, 1977); Beatrice Brodsky Farnsworth, "Bolshevik Alternatives and the Soviet Family: The 1926 Marriage Law Debate," in Dorothy Atkinson, Alexander Dallin, and Gail Warshofsky Lapidus, eds., *Women in Russia* (Stanford: Stanford University Press, 1977), pp. 138–65; H. Kent Geiger, *The Family in Soviet Russia* (Cambridge, Mass.: Harvard University Press, 1968); Fannina W. Halle, *Women in Soviet Russia* (New

York: Viking Press, 1933); Peter Juviler, "Marriage and Divorce," *Survey*, No. 48 (1963), pp. 104–17; Gail Warshofsky Lapidus, "Sexual Equality in Soviet Policy: A Developmental Perspective," in Atkinson et al., *Women in Russia*, pp. 115–38; William Mandel, *Soviet Women* (Garden City, N.Y.: Anchor Books, 1975); Bernice Glatzer Rosenthal, "The Role and Status of Women in the Soviet Union: 1917 to the Present," in Ruby Leavitt, ed., *Women Cross Culturally: Change and Challenge* (The Hague: Mouton, 1975), pp. 429–55; Rudolf Schlesinger, ed., *The Family in the USSR: Documents and Readings* (London: Routledge and Kegan Paul, 1949); *The Emancipation of Women: From the Writings of V. I. Lenin*, Preface by Nadezhda K. Krupskaya, with an Appendix, "Lenin on the Woman Question," by Klara Zetkin (New York: International Publishers, 1966); George St. George, *Our Soviet Sister* (Washington: Robert B. Luce, 1973).

16. Lapidus, "Sexual Equality," p. 130.
17. Peter Juviler, "Soviet Families," *Survey*, no. 60 (1966), pp. 51–61; Juviler, "Law and the Delinquent Family."
18. Juviler, "Whom the Law Has Joined."
19. Bernice Madison, "Soviet Services for Women: Problems and Priorities," in Atkinson et al., *Women in Russia*, pp. 307–22.
20. Juviler, "Law and the Delinquent Family"; USSR Constitution of 1977, Article 35, on "creating conditions that permit women to combine labor with motherhood, legal protection, material and moral support of motherhood and childhood, including paid leaves and other benefits to pregnant women and mothers, gradually shortening the working day of women with small children."
21. Juviler, "Whom the Law Has Joined."
22. V. P. Tomin, "Vsesoiuznyi simpozium po demograficheskim problemam sem'i," *Sotsiologicheskoe issledovanie* (hereafter *SI*), no. 2 (1976), p. 189; S. Golod, "Sotsial'no-psikhologicheskie i nravstvennye aspekty tsennosti sem'i," in Valentei, *Molodaia Sem'ia*, p. 48; G. Naan, "On, ona i vtoroi zakon termodinamiki," *LG*, September 15, 1976, p. 12.
23. V. Perevedentsev, "Commentary on Statistics: Incompatibility?" *Current Digest of the Soviet Press*, no. 7, March 15, 1978, p. 1, from *LG*, February 15, 1978, p. 13.
24. Urlanis, "Semia i problemy demografii," pp. 9–11.
25. *NK SSSR za 60 let*, pp. 72, 73; M. Sonin, "Demograficheskii aspekt 'sluzhby braka,'" in Valentei, *Molodaia sem'ia*, pp. 74–75; A Rubinov, "Schast'e tak vozmozhno," *LG*, March 8, 1978, p. 12. See also *LG*, November 30, 1977, p. 12; February 8, 1977, p. 12; December 22, 1976, p. 13.
26. Urlanis, "Sem'ia i problemy demografii," p. 11; A. Vishnevskii, "I uchit'sia i zhenit'sia," *LG*, January 12, 1977, p. 3; Otdel sotsial'no-bytovykh problem *LG*, "Studentka s rebenkom," *LG*, December 1, 1976, p. 12; *NK SSSR v 1977 godu*, p. 495.
27. V. Perevedentsev, "Goroda zhenikhov," *LG*, February 16, 1977, p. 13.
28. Ibid., L. V. Chuiko, *Braki i razvody* (Moscow: Statistika, 1975), p. 162.
29. L. A. Gordon, E. V. Klopov, "Ratsional'nvi biodzhet vremeni: podkhod k probleme i opyt nachal'nogo rascheta," *SI*, no. 1 (1977), p. 29.
30. Preamble, Fundamental Principles of Legislation on Marriage and the Family of the USSR and Union Republics, June 27, 1968.
31. Paul Hollander, *Soviet and American Society: A Comparison* (New

York: Oxford University Press, 1973), pp. 256–57; Golod, "Sotsial'no-psikhologicheskie," p. 47.

32. V. P. Kolokol'nikov, "Brachno-semeinye otnosheniia v srede kolkhoznogo krest'ianstva," *SI*, no. 3 (1976), p. 14.

33. Ethel Dunn, "Russian Rural Women," in Atkinson et al., *Women in Russia*, p. 183.

34. *NK SSSR za 60 let*, p. 8; *NK SSSR v 1970 godu* (Moscow: Statistika, 1971), p. 7.

35. Dunn, "Russian Rural Women," p. 183; *Itogi*, pp. 252–53; V. P. Tomin, "Regional'nye osobennosti vosproizvodstva i migratsii naseleniia," *SI*, no. 2 (1977), p. 203.

36. Simush, *Sotsial'nyi portret*, pp. 249–70; Tomin, "Regional'nye osobennosti," p. 187.

37. Kolokol'nikov, "Brachno-semeinye otnosheniia," p. 81.

38. Ibid., p. 83.

39. Hollander, *Soviet and American Society*, pp. 277–78.

40. Larisa Kuznetsova, "Zhenskaia kar'era," *LG*, March 15, 1978, p. 13.

41. *NK SSSR za 60 let*, p. 469.

42. Z. A. Iankova, "Razvitie lichnosti zhenshchiny v sovetskom obshchestve," *SI*, no. 4 (1975), p. 43; Colette Shulman, "The Individual and the Collective," in Atkinson et al., *Women in Russia*, pp. 375–84; M. G. Pankratova and Z. A. Iankova, "Sovetskaia zhenshchina: Sotsial'nyi portret," *SI*, no. 1 (1978), p. 20.

43. Naan, "On, ona i vtoroi zakon."

44. Rezanons, "O mode i staromodnosti," *LG*, November 24, 1976, p. 11; Larisa Kuznetsova, "Zhenstvennost'," *LG*, January 25, 1978, p. 12.

45. Ibid.

46. Quoted by Lapidus, "Sexual Equality," p. 131.

47. Iurii Riurikov, "Liubov' i sem'ia segodnia: Ostrye i spornye voprosy," *Molodoi kommunist*, no. 10 (1975), quote is from pp. 93–94; L. A. Gordon and E. V. Klopov, *Chelovek posle raboty* (Moscow: Nauka, 1972), p. 136; V. N. Pimenova, *Svobodnoe vrem'ia v sotsialisticheskom obshchestve* (Moscow: Nauka, 1974); and Dunn and Dunn, *The Study of the Soviet Family*, pp. 12–13, 26–33.

48. *NK SSSR za 60 let*, pp. 477–78.

49. Gordon and Klopov, *Chelovek posle raboty*, pp. 200–201.

50. Iankov, "Razvitie lichnosti," pp. 43, 46; Golod, "Sotsial'no-psikhologicheskie," pp. 49–54.

51. See note 47.

52. E. V. Porokhniuk and M. S. Shepeleva, "O sovmeshchenii proizvodstvennykh i semeinykh funktsii zhenshchin rabotnits," *SI*, no. 4 (1975), pp. 104–5.

53. Gordon and Klopov, *Chelovek posle raboty*, p. 29.

54. L. Gordon and E. Gruzdeva, "Byt molodoi sem'i," in Valentei, *Molodaia sem'ia*, p. 41.

55. Porokhniuk and Shepeleva, "O sovmeshchenii," p. 105.

56. Iankova, "Razvitie lichnosti," p. 43; Barbara Jancar, "Women in Soviet Politics," in Henry W. Morton and Rudolf L. Tökés, eds., *Soviet Politics and Society in the 1970s* (New York: Free Press, 1974), pp. 118–60; Joel C. Moses, "Women in Political Roles," in Atkinson et al., *Women*

in Russia, pp. 333–53; Jerry F. Hough, "Women and Women's Issues in Soviet Policy Debates," ibid., pp. 355–73.

57. Mollie Schwartz Rosenhan, "Images of Male and Female in Children's Readers," in ibid., pp. 293–305.

58. Lapidus, "Sexual Equality," pp. 132–36.

59. Perevedentsev, "Commentary on Statistics."

60. Riurikov, "Deti i obshchestvo," pp. 115–21.

61. Alexander Dallin, "Conclusions," in Atkinson et al., *Women in Russia*, p. 393.

62. Iankov, "Razvitie lichnosti," p. 47.

63. A. F. Gorkin, *Nastol'naia kniga sud'i* (Moscow: Iuridicheskaia literatura, 1972), pp. 583–84.

64. A. L. Pimenova, "Novyi byt i stanovlenie vnutrisemeinogo ravenstva," *SI*, no. 7 (1971), pp. 34, 38–45.

65. E. K. Vasileva, *Sem'ia i ee funktsiia* (Moscow: Statistika, 1975), pp. 76–77; *Itogi*, pp. 202–3.

66. Vasileva, *Sem'ia i ee funktsiia*, pp. 78–80; A. Antonov, "Izmenenie struktury i zhiznedeiatel'nosti sem'ei," in Valentei, *Molodaia sem'ia*, pp. 28–31.

67. Pimenova, "Novyi byt," pp. 35–36.

68. Z. A. Iankova, "Sotsialisticheskii obraz zhizni i sem'ia," in M. N. Rutkevich, ed., *Problemy sotsialisticheskogo obraza zhizni* (Moscow: Nauka, 1977), pp. 189–91.

69. Pimenova, "Novyi byt," pp. 40–44.

70. Ibid., p. 45.

71. Hollander, *Soviet and American Society*, p. 263.

New Aspects of Soviet Russian Literature

George Gibian

When we speak of "literature under Stalin," the strange-sounding phrase really makes good sense: the condition of culture (writing, theater, art, architecture) was indeed determined to an important degree by Stalinist policies. The periodization of the history of Soviet literature followed closely that of political developments—War Communism, NEP, the five-year plans, World War II, Zhdanovism, the Thaw. It would be odd to speak of "American literature under Nixon," or "the President Ford cultural period." In Soviet Russia, however, the political leadership has taken literature and culture very seriously and made sure its preferences and prohibitions left their mark.

The pressures on writers were extreme; the system was murderous. The literary world lived under the threat of an author disappearing because of a poem or novel. Writers were sent to camps or were shot because of what they wrote or were accused of having said.

Some excellent works were produced under Stalin, but for the most part, literature dealt routinely and monotonously with prescribed or favored topics and avoided proscribed ones. The method or style of "socialist realism," vague and changeable as that term was, urged optimistic, lucid, highly didactic writing. The chief subject matter was production: the focus was on problems in industrial development (at times, in collectivized agriculture), which would be identified, dramatized, attributed to culprits, and then gloriously surmounted.

Stalinist literature was written overtly and stridently for the masses —for their uplift, edification, indoctrination—and against "bourgeois ideology." It was highly formulaic, simple, public (i.e., not personal,

252

subjective, complex). Russian writers were cut off from the Western world with its artistic and ideological developments; at the same time their connections with some of the roots of their own Russian literature, with the generations of the 1920s and just before, with Russian modernism, as well as with that twin branch of Russian literature, the post-1917 emigration (Nabokov, Remizov, Khodasevich, Bunin, and many others), were also severed.

If some readable, craftsmanlike, professional, and even highly artistic works nevertheless resulted, it is a tribute to the resilience and irrepressibility of Russian literary talent, and perhaps also to sheer good luck.

The death of Stalin in March 1953 was followed by a lightening of the pressures we have been summarizing. When we compare the various post-Stalin restrictions on writers with the oppression of the Stalin era itself, we must not lose sight of one basic and huge difference. In the last twenty years, some writers have been arrested and imprisoned, but the main worry of most of them has been whether their works would be published, how they would be cut, edited, or rewritten, and whether they would be criticized or rewarded by various favors. Under Stalin, their concern had been whether they would be put in a labor camp or executed.

Literature of the Thaw and of the Khrushchev and post-Khrushchev eras was marked by several developments which were fairly predictable, given the removal of Stalinist autocracy; the general outlines of these can be fairly easily summarized. Before examining the various categories of changes, however, we should emphasize that what we call "literary politics" or "literary organization" continued to play an inordinately large role in Soviet writing. Seldom has there been a literature so organized, with so many congresses, "union" organizations, meetings, and other formal structures aiming both to control and to aid it—a literature which at its best, paradoxically, is most concerned with the unorganized, uninstitutionalized individual.

This bureaucratization of literature has continued undiminished since the death of Stalin. One often has the impression that actual literature —the novels, stories, plays, and poems themselves—are talked about and written about far less in Soviet Russia than are discussions at the Union of Writers, expulsions from it, threats by political figures, trials and sentencings, and praise and dispraise in articles based on social and other nonliterary considerations. For the authors, the major concern is still: Will it get through? Will they print it? Russian writers stress that this question is a perennial and destructive consideration in their minds as they write. Not censorship in the sense of an institutionalized structure with civil servants perusing literary works and formally passing on what can and cannot be printed (even though such offices do exist and function), but other subtler forms of censorship and self-censorship constitute the ubiquitous atmosphere of post-Stalin as well as of Stalinist literature: awareness of who was criticized for what in the press and of what has been printed and what has not; the lure of trips abroad; repairs done or not done to one's summer house in Peredelkino (the literary colony outside of Moscow); the request to sign an attack on Solzhenitsyn or someone else; receiving prizes; being asked to serve as secretary of the Union of Writers or to support a motion to expel a fellow writer; and many other forms of guiding and controlling how one actually writes and changes material submitted for publication.

While this basic feature of Soviet literary life has continued even after the diminution or disappearance of Stalinist terror, many other features have been altered, and we shall now turn to an examination of the various changes which have taken place since 1953.

We can divide post-World War II Soviet literature roughly into four periods: Zhdanovism and the last years of Stalin (1947–53); the Thaw (1954–56); the pendulum or see-saw period, from about 1957 to 1970 (with swings of alternating liberalizations and freezes); and the present stabilization or post-Solzhenitsyn period—a plateau, without sudden changes, but with protrusions of fascinating concerns and investigations.

At times, especially in the early period of the Thaw, it seemed as if the basic structure of some works remained the same, while the component elements had been switched: black replaced white and vice versa, or the negative photograph replaced the positive print. Whereas, under Stalin, for instance, the "collective," the "group," often the party organization, were ultimately upheld and lauded, in the literature of the Thaw the "loner," the split-off, alienated individual, was apt to be the hero. In addition to preoccupation with industrial production, and sometimes instead of it, writers now paid attention to private, individual concerns: to emotions, personal relations, the concrete particulars, even the trivia, of daily individual life.

The most marked change from Stalinist literature has been the progressive decrease of the long list of previously taboo topics. It was as if white spaces on the literary map of the world—the unexplored areas of untouchable subjects—were gradually being filled in; literature could now spread beyond its limits and explore previously forbidden or delicate subjects. These included, step by step, the following formerly hush-hush areas: the dangers of having relatives abroad; premarital or extramarital love affairs (without automatic explicit censure); high officials' abuse of their power; the poverty of the countryside in comparison with the cities; the privileges of high officials; the existence of anti-Semitism; the fact of denunciations; the existence of labor camps; illegal "repression" in Stalinist days; the various mistakes, abuses, and finally crimes, of Stalin; the horrible conditions inside labor camps (first, in the past, and later, in recent days); Soviet unpreparedness at the time of Hitler's attack in 1941; ways in which Stalinism trickled down through Soviet society; the existence of pro-Stalinist people and ideology in Russia today; the moral decay of Soviet people; and many other subcategories of the above subjects. (Still unexplored are the two most important intellectual categories of this century outside of Russia —Freudian, Jungian, and other dynamic and depth psychology and Marxism. Paradoxically but understandably, these have not been seriously, fully, and freely taken account of in Soviet literature.)

Parallel to the extension of possible subject matter was the series of "rehabilitations" of writers who had become unpersons and, in part, the publication of their works. Some of the authors were still alive; others had died or been killed. The list is very long, and the degree to which they were rehabilitated (and the dates when this occurred) varied widely. Some were rehabilitated only to the extent that an encyclopedia might now carry a short article about them (perhaps with a negative evaluation, the charge of some ideological error, such as having been excessively subjectivist, formalist, or modernist). Others were favored with the republication of once-vanished works, or the first publication of a work written "for the drawer," from a manuscript in the possession of a widow, a friend, or the secret police. The latter group included Bulgakov, Olesha, Babel, Mandelstam, Zoshchenko, Platonov, Tsvetaeva, and many others.

"Formalism" and "modernism" did not become favorites in conventional Soviet evaluation, but at least these concepts no longer constituted sufficient cause to expunge a work from Soviet print. A tolerated seat, somewhere in the back of the bus, was now available to such writers as Mandelstam.

Similarly, certain emigré writers were no longer automatically condemned to unperson oblivion merely because they had left Soviet Russia. Particularly authors who were safely dead could be referred to, some of them even praised, printed, and thus "repatriated." (The once virulently anti-Soviet Ivan Bunin, ironically, is one of those who have been re-imported into the USSR particularly widely.)

At the time of the first stage of the Thaw, around 1956, the overthrow of the first taboos created a wave of excitement in Russia. Such works as Vladimir Dudintsev's *Not By Bread Alone* (1956) and Ilya Ehrenburg's *The Thaw* (1954) caused a tremendous stir. Soviet readers and writers were exhilarated to see such attitudes as these works embodied, in print, in the Soviet Union. When we read these works a quarter of a century later, they no longer have the power which novelty and the crossing of limits gave to them at the time. They seem interesting, readable, but of historical interest rather than gripping. Since 1956 others have gone beyond the lines which they had reached; the borders of the permitted have been extended. We see it demonstrated once more that literary values—insights into character, power of the phrase, skills of patterning literary compositions—are needed, in addition to the interest of the subject, to give enduring appeal to a literary work.

The excitement in the air of Russia in the years 1954–56 was also based in part on expectations: the sense that one was at the threshold of a new era—that the old bastions were falling and the future held the promise of continuous improvement. This hope was fulfilled only to a small degree. Fundamentally, it has been frustrated. Soviet literature has moved beyond the point of 1956, but there have been backward oscillations of the pendulum, too, and, still more important, the Soviet authorities have demonstrated that the process would not inevitably move toward complete freedom. The Hungarian revolt of 1956, the persecution of Pasternak after *Doctor Zhivago* received the Nobel Prize in 1958, and the silencing and exiling of a number of writers in the 1970s showed that the party considered the cultural liberalization process almost complete by the end of the 1970s. Still more important, the leadership was willing and able to place clear limits on it (just as the military invasion of Czechoslovakia had proved that the Soviet government was willing and able to use its armed forces outside of its borders—something which various optimists in the West and inside Russia considered unimaginable).

By the end of the 1970s, Soviet writers had made a variety of gains. Communications with foreign countries, while still highly restricted, had become far freer. The most established writers (Evtushenko, Voznesensky, Granin, Nagibin, Trifonov) visited the West and Japan fairly frequently. Foreigners in turn were able to travel to the USSR—as participants in cultural exchange programs, tourists, or personal visitors to fellow writers. Various forms of information about Western literature and culture had become available, more extensively than at any time since 1928. Western magazines, theatrical performances, and art works, while still restricted, came in with foreign visitors.

Moreover, many writers as well as outstanding musicians, painters, and dancers such as Brodsky, Rostropovich, Neizvestny, Baryshnikov, Nureyev, and of course, Solzhenitsyn, emigrated in the 1970s or were "exported." Some of them then served as focal points for still further contacts between the USSR and the West, by letter, telephone call, and personal visits. The possibility of visiting the West as a tourist, or of emigrating (coupled with the sizeable Jewish emigration, which was taken advantage of by some non-Jewish participants, and which included writers), and the numerous visits to Moscow and Leningrad by foreigners immeasurably increased the international awareness, the sense of participation, of being "in touch," on the part of Soviet writers, critics, and some readers.

As the extreme forms of Stalinist terror were lifted, *samizdat* (unofficial circulation of works in typed, mimeographed copies), *tamizdat* (publication of Russian literary works in the West, without official consent, by writers still living in the USSR), and *magnitizdat* (unofficial taping of songs by Soviet authors) expanded greatly. While such forms of quasi- or semi-publication reached only a relatively small fraction of the Soviet population, their importance in giving access to works either unpublishable, or not desired by their authors to be officially published, was far greater than one might conclude from the relatively small number of people who actually read or owned the various *spiski* (collections of typed *samizdat* works) or smuggled copies of *tamizdat*.

Finally, the years of Solzhenitsyn's residence in the Soviet Union, when he spoke his mind freely to foreign correspondents, wrote challenging open letters to Soviet authorities, was attacked but stood his ground unafraid, constituted a tremendously important factor of Soviet literary life in the 1960s and 1970s. It was a dramatic ideological duel between an individual, heroic, martyrdom-bent, on the one hand, and a powerful, gigantic modern state, on the other.

Solzhenitsyn's two large novels, *The Cancer Ward* and *The First Circle* (both published abroad in 1968), considered purely as works of literary art, apart from their ideas, are composed in stylistic and narrative forms quite compatible with the dominant official literary modes of Soviet Russia. However, they are so thoroughly hostile to official Soviet ideology and institutions that it would have been unthinkable under Stalin for such works to have been submitted to a Soviet publishing house, and for their author to continue to reside at liberty, as a declared oppositionist. Solzhenitsyn's long survival within the country (a thorn in the side of the officials, an encouragement to the opponents) demonstrated to what extent the partial opening of the USSR to foreign journalists and to world public opinion had undermined its power to use extreme repressive measures.

Despite the various favorable developments in Soviet literature, however, the mood at the close of the 1970s was glum. The ability of the party to keep the lid on; the basic fact of the continuation of fundamental controls over culture by the party, despite relaxations here and there; the lack of hope for any significant further improvement in the future, near or remote—all these factors caused the decade to end without any of the exhilarating vigor and without the feelings of freshness and youthfulness that had marked Soviet culture in the mid-1950s. Paradoxically, while the general spirit was depressed and stagnant in 1979, actual conditions (the limits of the permitted) were freer than they had been twenty-five years earlier, at the outset of the Thaw. But the intense hopes for radical liberalization that had arisen after Stalin's death had now given way to resigned acceptance of a stable, or at best, a slowly and unevenly improving cultural situation. This seemed not to be enough. The end of high hopes may be the chief fact of all, which seeps like a gas into the nooks and crannies of Soviet cultural endeavors, and pervades the intangible milieu, and hence affects all that is being written, spoken, and felt in Soviet Russia today.

Let us now turn from the general characterization of post-Stalin literary conditions, and from comparisons with pre-1953 conditions, to an examination of the chief trends and groupings of post-Stalin literature.

The many shifts in Soviet Russian literature of the last quarter century, heterogenous as they are in scope and in quality, can be understood as various ways in which writers have been trying to do something new—as moves in new directions. Soviet authors, consciously or unconsciously, have been making an effort to create a different literature from what had existed under Stalin. The difference or originality of post-Stalin literature stems from a variety of thematic and formal innovations and preoccupations.

Literature of the Countryside

One literary category with emphases very characteristic of the late 1960s and of the 1970s consists of works embodying a search for simple, ancient, Russian rural ways. Mainfold expressions of this theme have swept Russia, have taken the hearts of intellectuals by storm, and enjoy the support of some of the most powerful men in the Soviet Union, including, it is said, members of the Politburo.[1]

The authors of this literature of the *derevnia*, the village or countryside, known as *derevenshchiki*, the producers of *derevenshchina*, bear names ranging from Abramov and Astafiev through the B's (Belov), and the time-hallowed Russian name Rasputin, to the beloved Vasili Shukshin, film actor, director, writer of stories and novels. Despite the vast differences among these writers or even among several works by the same author, one can sum up their chief orientation. The village writers stress the differences between countryside and city. Although they deplore the dehumanization caused by urban, technological civilization, they also point up the backwardness of life in the villages. They exalt the values of the Russian country dweller, but at the same time they refuse to gloss over his backward features. Salvation, they imply, lies in a return to the ethics and folkways of primeval, or as they would say, "patriarchal" survivors in the Russian provinces—who, neglected by the central authorities, preserve to this day those old, native, national qualities of heart and mind which deserve to be saved, redeveloped, and re-applied.

The typical plot of these rural works is a return—to one's infancy, to one's roots. In Belov's story *Behind Three Portages*, written in 1963, for instance, the hero, a major in the army, has made a career in the army, i.e., in the Soviet establishment, and is returning after many years to revisit his native village. He takes buses, hitches rides in trucks, walks; he runs into his old sweetheart, sees with amazement the poverty of the countryside. Yet he is also astounded by the beauty of the landscape, the birch trees, the folk songs, the folksy characters. In the end, when he arrives at the site, he finds the village is not there: it was abandoned and destroyed during the collectivization of agriculture.

The founding father of this massive school of writing is an author not likely to be given credit for his achievement within Soviet Russia —Alexander Solzhenitsyn. His story *Matryona's House* appeared in *Novyi mir* in 1963. The narrative structure is typical: this time the returning hero-observer is not an officer, but an intellectual who had been imprisoned in camps. After his release, he deliberately settles in a remote village, and takes a room in the house of Matryona, an old peasant woman. The story relates his quest to discover ever deeper qualities in Matryona's character. The sadness of her life, as well as the marvelous traits of her character, are gradually revealed to the narrator —the outsider, the intellectual, the stranger—and through him, to us, the readers.

Matryona stands in contrast to everyone else in the village. Its inhabitants are greedy, materialistic, brutal. Matryona is selfless, delicate, tactful, happy. The manner of her death is significant—she is helping relatives move a portion of her house, which she consented to let them have, when a train smashes into the load at a railroad crossing. Only at that moment does the narrator fully perceive her great qualities, connected with ancient Russia (feeling for true folk songs, Russian rural place names, primeval situations—such as her marriage to a brother of her missing fiancé, who then returns and avenges himself) and with the tradition of glad martyrdom. Matryona refused to seek her own advantage, did not keep a pig, worked for others without pay, allowed herself to be robbed, would not defend herself or demand her due. The narrator concludes on a religious note, with a biblical reference and a litany—to the effect that she was "that very just person [*pravednik*] without whom . . . the village will not stand. Nor the city. Nor our whole land."

The rural nationalism displayed by Shukshin, Rasputin, and many other writers is an important phenomenon, and some of their stories and novels are fine works of literary art. Yet we should be missing a significant part of the Russian mentality if we assumed that Russian nationalism is only rural. Nostalgia for the rural past, indignation over cruelties wreaked in the Russian countryside by the Soviet regime and by modern technology, admiration for the wisdom and resilience of the simple rural population—all of these must be fully appreciated and analyzed. But there are also excellent writers who present us with descendants (children or cousins) of rural inhabitants, now transported into an urban setting, into the modern world of research institutes and factories (Baranskaia's *Week Like Any Other Week* [1969], Syomin, Trifonov), who base themselves on Dostoevskian-Turgenevan-Tolstoyan traditions, and express an urban Russian nationalism which may be more complex, more serious, and in the long run, more enduring and significant.

Documentary Prose

A similar urge to create literary works that would be more truthful than those written before 1953 explains the popularity of another substantial category of Soviet nonfiction or semifiction—*dokumentalnaya proza*, or documentary prose. If village prose is the quantitatively largest outpouring of Russian literary energy today, then documentary prose follows close behind. The shift to documentary prose—found in pure form and in various mixed subgenres—is directed toward gaining hold of something one can trust—fact, truth, objectivity. A reaction against insincerity and lies, it grows out of distrust of phrases and falsehoods that have been officially and massively propagated.

Notable examples of documentary prose are Andrei Bitov's reflective travelogue about his visit to Armenia, *Travels to Armenia* (1972), and *The Wheel* (1972), something on the order of Tom Wolfe's New Journalism in the United States. *The Wheel* features interviews and descriptions of the city of Ufa, the world capital of motorcycle racing on ice, a town apparently obsessed with fanaticism for this rare sport. Bitov's long article is reportage at its best—factual, psychological, entertaining.

Literature of Moral Probing

Several of the most interesting recent works analyze the minutiae of the moral dilemmas faced by individuals living in the Soviet Union today or at crucial times in the past, such as the Civil War or the 1930s. Some of the finest stories in this category are by Yuri Trifonov. They do not make sweeping attacks on the "system"; they do not contain generalizations criticizing official ideologies or established Soviet institutions. Instead, they present, in great psychological detail, situations in Soviet life in the last quarter century which contain subtly revealed examples of moral turpitude. In the story *Exchange* (1969), for instance, a family welcomes a mother, who has cancer, as an addition to their household, because this increase in their number will entitle them to a larger apartment, which, when she has died—as they expect will happen soon—they will still be able to keep. But the raw bones, the plots of his works, do not adequately convey either his mastery or the subtlety of his moral diagnosis. Trifonov has the finest eye for the particulars of the concrete material setting of Soviet social life, and for their symbolic and psychological significance—all the cactuses, pictures, and other furnishings—as well as for the shadings of moral decisions to be made or evaded.

Trifonov's stories usually deal with the life of urban, well-situated intellectuals (theater people, the privileged, the elite). They almost always present a person who is revealed to us gradually and delicately as someone with moral decay at the heart of his being, but not before we have seen him quite neutrally, sympathized with him, understood him, and watched him act or, more often, not act, for sins of omission are more frequent than those of commission for Trifonov's characters. Usually we have the firm impression that we might have acted as Trifonov's character did, or at least, that we can sense in ourselves the compulsion, the force, of his temptations, of the pressures exerted on him. We do not feel at all distanced from or superior to Trifonov's frail, destructive, and destroyed characters. Only late in his stories do we realize, with a start, that what we have witnessed, with full understanding but without any explicit condemnation, has really been the process of utter ignominy rehearsed for us through time, in its development, and displayed without name calling yet also without the slightest apology.

Trifonov's most powerful work to date is *House on the Embank-ment* (1976), the story of two friends from schooldays, spanning a quarter of a century, which presents in the most poignant manner the processes by which boys in secondary school, and later grown men in learned institutes for the study of literature, were brought to persecute, denounce, and betray individuals to whom they owed a great deal, as if this were the most natural, understandable, reasonable, proper thing to do. Trifonov strips away historical layers and interweaves the personal and professional lives of several characters—primarily two, an upwardly mobile, weak young man, and the descending son of privileged governmental officials. Trifonov's journey into the past focuses, like most of his tales of the last decade, on analysis of moral corruption. How men slip slowly into betrayal is the chief inner action of Trifonov's work.

Trifonov's short novel demonstrates that innovation and quality are not necessarily directly related. *House on the Embankment* is a conventional Soviet prose work with respect to construction and theme. The pressure to denounce, to conform, the seeping of Stalinist denunciations from the highest to the lowest levels of society, professional and personal intermingling of concerns—all these topics have been used over and over in Soviet literature since 1954, but the complexity, subtlety, and power of Trifonov's ways of dealing with them in this novel surpass Soviet parallels, and make us wonder if we could not think of him as the Henry James of today's Russia.

In 1978 Trifonov published another astonishing work, *The Old Man*. In this short novel he explores the enthusiasms as well as the dubious purges of the Civil War. Survivors of the era, the former participants in its battles, search in the Russia of today, through correspondence with friends, in their own memories, and in archives, for the truth about the so-often romanticized past. In this work Trifonov dares to put in question Leninism itself, one of the last remaining shibboleths of Soviet published literature.

A predecessor of Trifonov in treating ethical questions was Daniil Granin. In 1956, in *Opinions of One's Own*, this fine Leningrad writer narrated in one flashback the story of a man who all his life believed himself to be an advocate of the downtrodden, an independent soul, a courageous enemy of privilege and injustice. However, when as a young worker he had once spoken up for a just cause, an older colleague warned him that junior people such as himself, "they swallow without chewing"; he would be better advised to wait until he rose in the hierarchy before disagreeing with his superiors. He backed down

—and in the present moment of Granin's story, when he fails to resist the pressures exerted on him by people whose support he needs and abandons a young rebel to his fate, he realizes that he will never rise high enough, that he will never turn courageous, that he is and will always be not a brave person with "opinions of his own," but an abject conformist. The story was one of the key works of the Thaw. It embodied its central moral, psychological, and artistic concerns better—more concentratedly and poignantly—than Ilya Ehrenburg's novel, *The Thaw* (1954), which has given that period its commonly accepted name.

Trifonov, Granin, and others show, through the deterrent example of their morally decayed protagonists, the shamefulness of yielding to social pressure; the great power of that pressure; and the demands of one's place of work, industrial or academic. Inversely, these writers deplore the absence of independent thinking, talking, acting. The conduct that Granin's narrative suggests the heroes should have engaged in, but did not, is not at all specifically Russian, nor is it very novel. It is the old-fashioned, Hellenic-Roman, Hebraic-Christian virtue of manliness: the courage to stand up for one's own opinions, and to challenge the majority, the powers that be. Granin's and Trifonov's ethics is the traditional morality of the truthful, daring minority; their literary techniques are not novel either—they are the scrupulous, moral-psychological analysis of the Tolstoyan fictional tradition.

Solzhenitsyn

The overt, broad-gauged, multilevel attack on the Soviet system by Alexander Solzhenitsyn should be mentioned at least briefly, even if it is already widely known and voluminously described. His three main targets are clear: the leader of the revolution that started it all, Vladimir Lenin; the most repulsive and most hated institution of the state, the concentration camps; and Soviet Marxist ideology in all its ramifications.

The genres or literary modes that Solzhenitsyn has used are numerous: polyphonic dialogues in his large novels, *First Circle* and *Cancer Ward*; mixed rhetorical elevation, personal reminiscence, and historical documentation in the multivoiced work *Gulag*; historical fiction, in *August 1914* and *Lenin in Zurich*; and a brief twentieth-century hagiography, in *Matryona's House*. Solzhenitsyn's corpus is artistically and structurally so broad ranging that it almost constitutes an encyclopedia of literary modes by one author alone. He is aflame with dedication to his task. We can think of him as a conscious Anti-Lenin who intends to pillory and undo what Lenin had built with an analogous energy and sense of mission.

Fantasy and the Bizarre

Several Russian writers have resorted to techniques entirely different from the socialist realist mode: they have explored, among others, fantasy; surrealistic, bizarre humor; the vision; and black humor. In their manner, often accompanied by an equally clear hostile ideological orientation—these important authors are going in a direction at least tangential, and sometimes 180 degrees opposed, to the earlier dominant, approved Soviet literary styles.

The rationale for such writing was best stated by Andrei Sinyavsky, in his essay *On Socialist Realism*, published in the West in 1960:

> I put my hope in a phantasmagoric art, with hypotheses instead of a Purpose, an art in which the grotesque will replace realistic descriptions of ordinary life. Such an art would correspond best to the spirit of our time. May the fantastic imagery of Hoffmann and Dostoevski, of Goya, Chagall, and Mayakovski (the most socialist realist of all), and of many other realists and nonrealists teach us how to be truthful with the aid of the absurd and the fantastic.

Sinyavsky's own stories, such as *The Trial Begins* (1960), illustrated what he had in mind. Many other writers of various generations have also turned to experiments with fantasy and the absurd. Vasili Aksenov came close to it in the bitter story *The Overstocked Tare of Barrels* (1968). Valentin Kataev, an older author famous for works written in the 1920s and 1930s, mingled memories and dreams in *The Holy Well* (1966) and *The Grass of Oblivion* (1967).

Younger writers (Vladimir Maramzin, Yuri Mamleev) were quite at home in this genre. In the 1970s, it became the major literary manner of "dissonant" writers, equally of those who remained in the Soviet Union and those who left. The chief recent works of this school, and in the opinion of many, the outstanding works of the last few years, were Venedikt Erofeev's *Moscow Roosters* and Alexander Zinoviev's *Yawning Heights*, which circulated widely in *samizdat* and were published in Western Europe in 1976 and 1977, respectively.

In 1979 an attempt was made to publish jointly both unofficial and official writers, in one collection. A large anthology of works in various genres, with the title *Metropol*, was submitted to the Union of

Writers. It contained stories and poems by famous, established writers, such as Voznesensky, Aksenov, Iskander, and many others, as well as by unknowns and *samizdat* writers. The volume was resoundingly rejected and denounced by the Union of Writers and was promptly published in the United States. Its introduction stressed the desire to expand the limits of literature and criticized the cautious narrowness of published Soviet writing. While *Metropol* contains many different styles and types of writing, works of bizarre subject matter and grotesque literary manner are most strikingly prominent in it.

Recent Soviet works of fantasy are a clear move away from the heritage of socialist realism and towards the grafting of the manner of Western writers of the grotesque and absurd (from Jarry and Kafka to Beckett and Vonnegut) on to native, Russian roots of nonrealistic writing (Remizov, Bely, Zamiatin, Mayakovsky and other Futurists, and Kharms.)

The "Little World" of Personal Concerns

A very large and elusive group are those who do not openly show discontent with officially urged Stalinist modes, in either substance or literary manner, but who just walk away and look in the other direction. We cannot be sure if they are intentionally and consciously evading, or if it just happens that their artistic interests are different. These authors, predominantly short-story writers, deal with emotions and the small events of private lives. They include Kazakov, Granin, Nagibin, Bitov, Grekova, Makarova, and many others. They may tell of the life, love, and singing of a drunken renegade (Kazakov's *Outsider*, 1959); or they may write a long novel with self-conscious literary art, self-reflexive, reminding us of Gide, or Joyce, or Barth, rather than of Sholokov and Simonov. (An example is Bitov's *Pushkin House*). These writers do not express dissent; instead, they demonstrate their interest in a world remote from "social command." From their works we can deduce their view of the role of literary art. The themes and the literary manner they choose emphasize the individual's spiritual and emotional life and avoid the powerful, the political, the public. They concentrate on showing how emotional life, as we know it from the Russian nineteenth- and early twentieth-century classics (Turgenev, Tolstoy, Bunin, Prishvin), far from having vanished from the earth, has survived in the Soviet Union, in modified form, yet as intense as ever.

In answer to a questionnaire in *Problems of Literature* (*Voprosy Literatury*, no. 9, 1962) on the subject "What are Your Themes?" Kazakov answered: "Happiness and its nature, suffering and its overcoming,

the moral duty to the people, love, finding a purpose for oneself, relationship to work, the vitality of dirty instincts, these are some of the
problems which now interest me. These same problems, phrased in
different ways, I keep meeting constantly in the works of all of our
most talented prose writers and poets." He delights in shocking his
readers by attacking, or seeming to attack, Soviet platitudes: "I don't
think that literature immediately and right away influences people's
lives and their moral condition. That is evidenced by many unjust,
unclean critics, who of course have read Tolstoy and Chekhov and
Hemingway—have read them and learned nothing." Or: "I do not
make a point of studying life and do not collect material, except when
I go somewhere on instructions of the editors. I altogether fail to understand that phrase 'studying life.' One can throw light on life, one
can reflect about life, but to 'study' it is no use. One must simply live."[2]

Return to the Past

Various writers have been saying something new or have moved
forward in new ways, paradoxically, by returning in some sense to
the past.[3] On the level of literary form and convention, they have
returned to the past by working within, or alluding to, and following,
or reworking, literary conventions of past periods. Such regressions
can under certain circumstances constitute an innovation, a forward
movement away from the current dominant literary manner.

On the level of subject matter, writers have returned to the past in
several ways, for example: by recreating historical material or events
from the author's or the character's childhood or youth (in a way
that emphasizes the pastness of the past); by making the past an object
of inquiry and probing its significance for the present; or by focusing
on survivals of the remote past (for example, archaic, premodern ways
of behaving, thinking, and talking) as objects of literary representation. The various ways of looking backward are a distinctive feature
of Soviet Russian writing in our time. Literature about the past embodies new kinds of feelings about what in the past is worthy of being
dwelled upon, and about what constitutes the nature of time.

Vitali Syomin's work is an apotheosis of the survival, into our days,
of the vitality and toughness of unintellectual, traditional Russian people. Syomin was an exception among Soviet Russian authors in not
being an inhabitant of either Moscow or Leningrad; rather he was
very much at home in his native Rostov-on-the-Don until his death
in 1978.

Vitya, the narrator of Syomin's tale *Seven People in One House* (1965), is an educated person, a former teacher, now a journalist, who married into the family, but everyone else in the story belongs to the working class and is of peasant origin. The heroes of the book are, so to speak, first, the setting itself—the house in which the family lives, and second, Mulya, the widowed mother-in-law. (Vitya is married to her daughter Irka.) The story consists of incidents in the lives of members of the family and their friends. Drinking, swearing, and slang dominate the action.

Mulya's family, as the story reveals them, and above all Mulya herself have a clear cut code of behavior: one is loyal to the family and respected according to one's know-how, primarily as applied to building and maintaining a house (mixing mortar, repairing fences and shutters). The predominant virtue is vitality: self-assertiveness, energy. The characters are far from saints. Not only hard-working laborers, they are also, on occasion, crooks, drunks, and even murderers. Their amorality is astonishing to Vitya, the intellectual outsider:

> Ninka always amazed me, because she was through and through at home in the world against which I, according to my profession, was obliged to fight. If I should say, "People steal in all the stores," this would be a tragic acknowledgement of the fact that all the exertions of teachers, newspapermen like myself, writers, the highest state authorities, all those who teach what is good and what is bad, had been in vain. When Ninka asserted, "People steal in all the stores," she did not feel either bitterness or disillusionment. She lived in that world. No better and no worse than the others. That is all.

The characters like everything to remain set and traditional. A gypsy is expected to act like a gypsy, a worker like a worker—along lines set down by folk stereotype and tradition. They do not gloss over things but look straight at them and accept them, whether it is the promiscuity of one character, or a stabbing by another.

A struggle for power is clearly going on between the women and the men. Mulya evidently is the most powerful person in the house. The narrator has only admiration for her female superiority in strength. Vulgar and amoral as she is, Mulya deserves to stand alongside Solzhenitsyn's hagiographic portrait of the spiritual and selfless Matryona, the heroine of *Matryona's House*.

The conduct of Syomin's characters is guided not by consciousness and reason but by tradition and instinct. Syomin shows them to be motivated by ingrained patterns of behavior based on ancient Russian peasant ways, transported by the fundamentally unchanged rural population to the fringe areas of urban life. Proverbs are cited for guidance; the behavior of others is noted but not dissected. Colorful, metaphoric advice is given: "Don't shit steam, you'll burn your legs," is the peppery admonition given to a character who has lost his temper. Syomin places us in a world of graphic thinking and folk formulas.

The modern age, technology, politics, and intellection are ignored in Syomin's *Seven People in One House*. Perennial concerns—animal, instinctual—remain. Surviving and feeling at home in one's house are the chief values. A very old woman, Manya, remember the Tsars Nikolay and Alexander III, but "the point was not in Alexander and Nikolay. What was important was that Manya survived them. That was understandable to all. Uncle Petya felt it, and I felt it. I looked at the yard, the house, I recalled it as it used to be in those days, and more and more felt that I belonged here. I liked that feeling, to be at home, in this shack, in this street."

Syomin shows us the survival of ancient Russian *byt*, the details of how simple people live in this world, in almost animal, instinctual traditional ways. There is nothing modern about his narrative form. His manner of story telling could be from the middle of the nineteenth century; the folkways of his characters are still older. By going back to those particular aspects of the past, told in Leskovian fashion, Syomin stood out among the other writers of the last couple of decades. He was interested in that past which is embodied in national, folksy characters like an anthropological calque right into his own days.

Our next example, Daniil Granin, is in many ways antithetical to Syomin—in subjects, attitudes, and forms, for instance—yet he shares Syomin's fascination with time and the past. Granin has written so much and so well, and the themes and forms of his works are so varied and rich, as to make him an author of exceptional importance in trying to understand what has been happening in Soviet Russian prose today.

Granin has been a prominent Soviet published author for over twenty years and has served as secretary of the Leningrad Union of Writers. Granin's works reveal thematic and artistic concerns the significance of which extends beyond the writer himself to the Russian intellectual and literary climate of our time. Granin's writings mark a shift in the *Zeitgeist*—a change in Russian sensibility since the start of what we have termed the stabilization period; he is one of its best morally and artistically questing published writers.

In *The Return Ticket* (1976), which is part story and part essay, Granin turns toward the interrogation of the past. Granin presents the past as surviving in living connections with, and as influences over, the present. The work discusses, for example, the Dostoevsky historical preserve—the "memorial" in the town of Stara Russa—but it is itself another, verbal memorial to Dostoevsky, whom Granin cites as the exemplary creator of novels about memory and the preservation of the past among the living. The narrator recalls his visit to Dostoevsky's house in Stara Russa, his talks with the Dostoevsky scholar and museum director Georgi Ivanovich, events in the history of Stara Russa, and his visits to places where the action of *The Brothers Karamazov* is supposed to have taken place. He reflects on many subjects, such as the reasons why writers locate their works in real places. He cites passages from Alyosha Karamazov's speech about memory; he dreams of his father, thinks of his father's life (his second marriage and his work as a forester), recalls former friends and Stara Russa as it had been during NEP, converses about the length of time it takes forests to become established and about holding on to the past and things as they used to be versus the desire for change and improvement. Among the topics of his meditations are relations between fathers and their children: Dostoevsky's relationship to his father and to his characters; Andrian's tyrannical father's relations to him as a child. The last page of *The Return Ticket* links an illustration in a volume of *The Brothers Karamazov*, of Alyosha speaking to children surrounding him, with the desire of the post-World War I generation to remove prewar photographs and other objects from their lives and concludes by emphasizing the influence of childhood memories on the formation of those people who persevere in remaining human and good despite all the blows that life has dealt them.

This very brief and incomplete summary of the topics which Granin takes up, in the order in which he does, inevitably will seem disjointed; the text does jump from one topic to another. Yet there is order and unity under the surface heterogeneity.

The Return Ticket, confusing as it may seem when examined in its twists and turns, is quite lucid in its general direction, when we look at its point of departure and conclusion. The first page states, "The country of my childhood had been destroyed, my childhood had perished." The last page ends with the affirmation of the enduring positive influence of good childhood memories (one's parents in real life, Alyosha Karamazov's sermon to the children in the novel) on the entire subsequent life of an individual. Taken out of context, this conclusion perhaps sounds excessively moralistic and uplifting, but the story is not at all jarringly didactic. Between the two points, the melancholy beginning and the encouraging ending, Granin meanders among many different forms of narration. What starts as a short story (first person narration, dialogues) soon shifts to travelogue (descriptions of a village, a small town, a large town, Leningrad), to reminiscences, essays of reflection and speculation, social comment, character sketches, conversations. There is constant movement, from one narrative mode to another. There is no stasis, no rest; all is in flux and eternal movement. For Granin, all things flow.

The range of reference is extremely broad. Granin weaves into his work allusions to Gorky, to Zoshchenko's quasi-psychoanalytical quests into his youth, to the scholar Mikhail Bakhtin. He gives historical statistics about Stara Russa, deplores the dearth of Soviet studies of religious literatures, cites *Eugene Onegin* and *Crime and Punishment*. Many places, events, and literary details are included. Granin's loose, all-embracing form opens the door to all experience and many possible stances toward it. The story is kept from flying apart centrifugally by the author's centripetal questioning. Throughout, there is an unusually high proportion of interrogation, addressed by the narrator to his material, in a persistent effort to find and give it significance.

Nothing in *The Return Ticket* is unilinear and direct. The story is richer in questions than affirmations and answers. What are the reasons for Granin's abundant range of heterogeneous references? He seems obsessed with the instability of our world, aware as he is of change all around him: the destruction of an old town or region (due to wear and tear, or to war), and the aging and passing of individuals, and of whole historical epochs. He is fascinated with the spectacle of this phantasmagoria not for its own sake but because he is searching, in the chaos of life, for a stable point.

Granin finds this stability only in connections. All things, taken alone, by themselves, shift, change, and perish in this story, but they also stand in a relationship to other things, and in this system of links, there is enduring comfort. This comfort has to do with the moral formation of human individuals—Granin's focus and conclusion. These seemingly separate elements are not really isolated but exist meaningfully in their connections with, and effects on, other factors. The connections between the various places, things, and characters to whom Granin refers are those of moral effects, interwoven in memory.

Granin's way is to look at various successive aspects of each relationship. He does not view human beings as completed or stationary but sees them in process, being made. In Granin's scheme, there is no teleology, no progress-oriented, unilinear or dialectical time, Hegelian or Marxist. We are in a world of coexistence, where past and present, in eternal change, nevertheless are linked, through memories. Fathers and sons, history and the present, die, yet live and continue to affect life.

In 1956, in *Opinion of One's Own*, Granin had presented as the climax of his story the hero's moment of *anagnorisis*, his perception of his life-long self-deception and cowardice. In other works, he probed a variety of intellectual, moral, and even practical, bureaucratic problems of the lives and careers of engineers and industrial managers.

Granin represents a sophisticated mingling of attitudes towards historical and intellectual Russian legacies as something to be treasured and used in the moral shaping of future generations. His nationalism, while implicit or even covert, is complex and deep and exemplifies an important current within present-day Russian consciousness—literary and otherwise—which should not be ignored when trying to understand contemporary Soviet Russia. His work deals with urban situations. He presents perennial Russian emotions, but in their new, Soviet, urban, yet still very Russian incarnation. Granin perceives life as a thick network of relationships cutting through time, a tapestry which seems to have its center of gravity, or its focal point, inside a mind. *The Return Ticket* belongs to the history of Russian spirituality as much as it does to the history of belles-lettres.

Fascination with time and returns to the past have not been rare in the history of Russian literature. The critic Tynianov, in a famous collection of essays, showed how the archaizers of the early nineteenth century were really innovators. Reprises of the picaresque tradition, for example, are strewn over the history of Russian as well as Western literature (Thomas Mann's *Felix Krull*, Saul Bellow's *Augie March*, and many others). Soviet prose writers today have their particular ways of being original by returning to some aspects—thematic or formal—of the past. The variety as well as the frequency of works in which they attempt this is striking. It has been one of the ways in which they have recently found it most natural to move out along new lines: by taking backward glances. In the Soviet context, this represents a marked shift away from stereotypes of progress, forward movement, unilinear time, which mark official thought—away from all teleology and towards a sense of time as simultaneity.

Young Prose

A situation peculiarly appealing to twentieth-century readers is that of the young person "trying to find himself." The vague and trite phrase "finding oneself," so frustratingly familiar to us today, can mean finding a vocation (literally a profession or a job) or discovering what one values in life, what one wants to look for, or it may mean finding some basic truth—a philosophy of life. It is always a quest for a discovery connected with the self. This search is as old as Oedipus and Aeneas, or Pierre Bezukhov and Konstantin Levin. The contemporary Soviet Russian version of literature that treats this theme is called *molodaia proza*, young prose. Vasili Aksenov has been the chief author in this category, but he has many comrades, among them Gladilin. There are several variants in approach to, and orientation of, the quest, and even more in the texture and dominant literary qualities of the stories.

Aksenov's short stories and novelettes (*Colleagues* [1960], *Starry Ticket* [1961], *Oranges from Morocco* [1963]) established this subgenre. Aksenov's heroes sometimes work out their finding of themselves in remote places—Siberia, or islands, towns, and beaches of the Baltic—but they are urban dwellers, formed by the big city, imbued with its sophisticated, confusing, value-destroying milieu. The city is where the action is, even if, as in the short story *Half Way to the Moon*, the hero is a truckdriver who only gets a whiff of cosmopolitan and metropolitan culture, at a distance, from the airport and on board an airliner, shuttling between eastern Siberia and Moscow.

An important characteristic of the Aksenov-Gladilin school is the flippancy and cleverness of the heroes' language. The protagonists of these stories are suave, slick, cool, intelligent, educated, ironic. In their sophistication and disillusionment, they contrast sharply with the generation of their fathers. The heart of Gladilin's little masterpiece, *First Day of the New Year* (1963), lies in the contrast between the son (at a point of crisis in his life) and the father (dying of cancer in a hospital), and in the effort at communication across a huge gap. The two speak to each other haltingly in different languages, from different sides of the barricades, albeit about the same issues.

The popularity of the young prose genre ran its course rather quickly. The stories seemed novel and fascinating, and to some readers, even sensational, but they have not aged or traveled well.

When reflecting on published, "official" Soviet Russian literature,[4] we must keep in mind a consideration which may seem so obvious that we might lose sight of its import. It is the fact that in the Soviet Union responsibility for what is printed is shared by the author with many anonymous editors, editorial committees, party and magazine officials, censors, and others. Self-censorship by the author has already eliminated some of the possible variant forms of the work being written. Nobody will ever know how many vague ideas for entire works (and *a fortiori* particular scenes, characters, dialogues) never resulted in even one line being written, since the writer knew the whole project was hopeless.

When we read something in a Soviet magazine or book, we must realize it may be far from what the author would have liked to have written or from what he actually wrote. When we study Soviet literature, we are doing so in a great cloud of ignorance, far beyond what we should assume to be the case if we were studying another contemporary literature, for example, the French, the Japanese, or the Brazilian. Sometimes we do obtain some corrective information, later on, when a Nekrasov or a Kuznetsov or a Solzhenitsyn moves to the West and becomes free to speak about his past experiences as a writer, and perhaps brings with him unedited, original texts of his works (an exceptional occurrence).

It has happened to me (and I am sure to other students of Soviet literature) when I was visiting writers in Russia whose works I had been following and studying that I was startled, and abashed, to find how misinformed I had been about the circumstances of the composition of their works and their literary activity, from published sources and correspondence. Works which we had taken to be short stories (since that is how they had been published in Soviet magazines) turned out to be fragments of an ambitious, large novel, excerpted for publication, since the work as a whole had been rejected. No mention of the novel had been made in the Soviet press. Another writer, among whose works one particular long story stood out as a hard-to-explain freak, had actually written five or six similar works in that genre, none of which had been published. Knowledge of these works would lead one to interpret quite differently the entire direction of that writer's work. Many authors write historical works or film scenarios, or do translations, because the literary works they would like to write (and sometimes have written "for the drawer") are not acceptable for publication.

The basic ideological stance of some writers is far more critical toward the status quo in the Soviet Union than one would surmise from their published writings. Moreover, some of those observers who through personal meetings, obtain the kind of information which I have been describing are then inhibited from incorporating their full findings in what they write or say about Soviet literature, since they do not want to cause harm to authors or critics whom they had met (or perhaps to their own chances of receiving a visa the next time they would like to return to the Soviet Union to do more research).

Many Soviet works do exist in published form exactly as their authors wished them to be. But we must remember the cautionary warning that whatever works of Soviet literature we are studying may be the composite products of writers and editors. They result from a cooperation not always voluntarily entered into, in fact very often enforced and reluctantly accepted only as a last resort, as the alternative to not being published at all. The writer and the editorial board observe the tacitly understood limits of that which may not be written and yield to the demands for educating the people, uplifting its ideological level, and serving a didactic purpose.

We are certainly not dealing with literature created freely as a pure art form. What is before us is something which is not exactly "literature" in the sense of French or English or U.S. literature—it is a hybrid. A great hesitancy, a modest tentativeness, a sensitive readiness to withdraw and modify one's conclusions ought to be omnipresent in all our discussions of Soviet literature.

Another circumstance differentiating Soviet literature from others is that its meaning and its qualities grow immeasurably, more than those of other literatures, the more we read of it. The more we know of Soviet literature, the more it speaks to us, the more we see in it. Understanding of any one work gains much from the reader's previous acquaintance with other Soviet works. Soviet Russian literature must be placed in its whole native context. One must immerse and saturate oneself in it; it is an acquired taste. If one takes a story by Trifonov or Aksenov or Granin, no matter how good it may seem to a seasoned reader of Russian literature, and gives a translation of it to a very literary English or American reader who is not familiar with Soviet literature, the reader will most probably think much less well of the story than would a veteran reader of Soviet writing. The appreciation of a Soviet work depends unusually heavily on familiarity with other Soviet works and with its conditions, conventions, and circumstances, more than is necessary for other literatures.

Soviet works have less autonomous appeal, less value immediately perceptible to a foreign reader. Much of the pleasure of reading them derives from sensing where the story or novel is just like others, where it differs a little, where the author is stretching conventions, slightly modifying and recombining familiar elements of existing genres or subgenres. A new novel by a Mexican novelist—*The Hydra Head*, by Carlos Fuentes, for example—can be appreciated far more fully by an American reader who knows nothing of either Mexico or Mexican literature, than can a new Soviet work by a reader ignorant of Soviet writing.

Some of these problems of understanding Soviet Russian literature are related to its impurity as an art. It is intimately involved with Soviet Russian thought and society—a literature highly intermingled with nonliterary elements, with politics, culture, daily life. Behind it stretch the great artistic traditions of Pushkin and Tolstoy. The difficulties and limitations of studying it are worth tackling and overcoming for the sake of the insights which, even in adversity, it can give us into a fascinating society and culture.

Notes

1. This account is based on a longer version given at the Biennale Conference in Venice, Italy, in December 1977.

2. Although this chapter is limited to prose, one should mention in connection with the lyrical prose writers, the parallel interests of a series of poets who emerged after Stalin's death—the public figure Evtushenko, the more complex Voznesensky, the reflective Brodsky, the lyrical Akhmadullina.

3. The account which follows is based on a longer version entitled "Forward Movement Through Backward Glances," given at the Conference on East European Drama and Fiction, UCLA, March 1978, to be published in a forthcoming volume edited by H. Birnbaum and T. Eekman, as well as on the article "The Urban Theme in Recent Soviet Russian Prose," *Slavic Review*, March 1978, pp. 40–50.

4. An excellent survey of the entire range of recent Soviet writing is available in Deming Brown's *Soviet Russian Literature Since Stalin* (New York: Cambridge University Press, 1978).

Part Four /FOREIGN POLICY

The Stalinist Legacy
in Soviet Foreign Policy

Charles Gati

Introduction to the Argument

Since Stalin's death in 1953, many Western students of Soviet foreign policy have tended to emphasize "change" rather than "continuity" in the international orientation of the Soviet Union—change for the better, evolution towards moderation and restraint. Their conclusion, it seems, is that Soviet foreign policy—responding both to a new external environment and to different internal circumstances—has successfully shed its Stalinist past. Having substantially reduced its revolutionary commitments, the Soviet Union is said to have begun to transform itself into an essentially status-quo power—steady and ambitious but not reckless, at times assertive but not adventurist, and invariably pragmatic. Not the aggressive revolutionary power it used to be and hence not unlike other major powers, the Soviet Union is thus seen as primarily, if not exclusively, interested in protecting its own security and achievements in an atmosphere of relative international stability.[1]

Is such a general appraisal of post-Stalin Soviet foreign policy—and the cautious optimism it has produced in the West—really warranted? Did de-Stalinization in foreign policy accompany Soviet domestic de-Stalinization?

I think not. The year 1953, it seems, was not a watershed in Soviet foreign policy.[2] When post-Stalin Soviet foreign policy patterns are compared and contrasted with Stalinist behavior from 1928 to 1953, it appears to this writer that there was far more "continuity" than "change." As a basic approach to the outside world, Stalin's conduct of foreign policy was calculating and circumspect, and his historic mix of expansion-and-accommodation, or revolutionary assertiveness-and-peaceful coexistence, which served the Soviet state so well for so long, has remained deeply ingrained in the Soviet political mind. On balance, Stalin cannot be said to have placed more emphasis on revolution making than his successors have on upholding or maintaining the status quo. Essentially cautious and opportunistic, the Soviet leaders from Lenin to Brezhnev have displayed revolutionary assertiveness when and where it seemed safe to do so, while favoring the status quo and peaceful coexistence when and where it seemed necessary or useful to do so. All of them, and perhaps especially Stalin, consistently refused to risk the security of the Soviet Union for distant, revolutionary goals; after all, it was Stalin who as early as the mid-1920s had already advocated, and subsequently implemented, a largely inward-looking posture for the emerging Soviet state ("socialism in one country") against Trotsky's more radical, outward-looking alternative of "permanent revolution." Stated another way, if one were to make use of the conservatism-reformism dichotomy developed by Stephen F. Cohen elsewhere in this book, Stalin's foreign policy—taken as a whole from 1928 to 1953—must be seen as conservative.

It is true, of course, that the *scope* of Soviet foreign policy has changed; Stalin did not develop a coherent policy towards the colonial areas of Asia and Africa, for example, while his successors have certainly done so towards what is now the Third World. It is also true that some of the *issues* on the Soviet agenda are new—such as the current preoccupation with and the management of nuclear weapon systems so destructive as to make wars more dangerous and the consequences of nuclear wars unthinkable. And it is true that it remained for Stalin's successors to cope with such *problems* as the rise of new communist party-states and to define the meaning of "socialist internationalism" and "international relations of a new type." Yet, important as some of these changes in the scope, issues, and problems of Soviet foreign policy may seem, they do not appear to be so far-reaching as to assume that Stalin himself could not or would not have made them. Indeed, if Stalin could now survey the achievements, strategies, and methods of Soviet foreign policy since 1953, would he not endorse its general thrust, offering heartfelt congratulations to his successors for their skillful adaptation of his approach to new international circumstances?

Furthermore, even if one were inclined to dismiss as political rhetoric Khrushchev's own remark—to the effect that, when it comes to foreign policy towards the West, he and his colleagues did regard themselves as Stalinists[3]—the fact remains that Stalin's foreign policy has never been subjected to extensive criticism in the Soviet Union—not even during the height of the domestic de-Stalinization campaign in the mid-1950s. In point of fact, Stalin was criticized for only two foreign policy errors or shortcomings: the country's military unpreparedness on the eve of World War II and his unduly harsh, and ultimately counter-productive, treatment in 1948–49 of Marshal Tito's Yugoslavia (and, by implication, the rest of Eastern Europe). Compared to the charges leveled against him for his "crimes" in domestic affairs, Stalin's foreign policy record was not found wanting. He was not accused of excessive aggressiveness or adventurism, nor did his successors ever promise to de-Stalinize Soviet foreign policy and indeed place it on new foundations.

The reason for the apparent gap between the promise and early pursuit of domestic de-Stalinization on the one hand and the lack of de-Stalinization in foreign policy on the other is self-evident. While his successors believed that Stalin's domestic policies—particularly the intimidation and terror aimed against the Soviet elite—began to threaten the cause of socialism within the Soviet Union, his foreign policy record, by contrast, spoke well of Stalin's skills in promoting Soviet security and hence the cause of socialism abroad. After all, when Stalin became *primus inter pares* in 1928, the Soviet Union was weak and vulnerable, an essentially second-rate power; yet twenty-five years later, by 1953, it could claim to have become one of the two super-powers. His successors, having inherited a tested and successful approach to the outside world, had no reason either to criticize or to change the basic orientation of Stalin's foreign policy.

Thus, the central arguments of this essay are that Stalin's foreign policy was less aggressive and revolutionary than is commonly assumed; that his successors' foreign policy has been more aggressive and revolutionary than is commonly assumed; and therefore that there has been more continuity in the conduct of Soviet foreign policy than is commonly assumed.

Stalin's Foreign Policy Revisited

The emphasis in Western studies on "change" rather than "continuity" in Soviet foreign policy since 1953 stems in part from an undue emphasis on Stalin's foreign policies from the end of World War II to the Korean war. Admittedly, this was an era of expansion and unprecedented aggressiveness in the Soviet conduct of foreign relations, beginning with the imposition of Soviet domination on Eastern Europe, the provocation of the Berlin crisis of 1948-49, the unnecessary and avoidable conflict with Marshal Tito's Yugoslavia, all coupled with intransigent statements and undiplomatic posturing. While some of these policies were indicated by the geopolitical opportunity World War II had created, Stalin—no doubt dizzy with success—probably did push too hard during the early years of the Cold War. His aggressiveness provided glue for Western unity against the Soviet Union—as expressed by the Truman Doctrine, the establishment of NATO in 1949, and the consideration of such radical countermeasures as the use of atomic weapons against Moscow during the Berlin confrontation (recommended by Churchill, but quickly rejected by both the British and U.S. governments). To the extent that Stalin's postwar policies led to the mobilization of the West and the containment of further Soviet advances, therefore, these policies were not only unduly assertive, but —from the perspective of long-term Soviet interests—probably quite counterproductive.

It should be stressed, however, that aggressive Soviet behavior in the early Cold War years was only one aspect of the Stalinist pattern in foreign policy. Stalin was also at the helm when a pragmatic Soviet Union first sought to ally itself with Hitler's Nazi Germany and then ended up forming a grand coalition with such bastions of imperialism as England and the United States. Stalin was at the helm when communists fought shoulder to shoulder with noncommunists in the Spanish Civil War. Stalin was at the helm when, in the early 1930s, the Soviet Union concluded a number of treaties and cooperative agreements with such bourgeois states as France, Poland, Czechoslovakia, Finland, Estonia, and Latvia. Stalin was at the helm in 1935 when the Seventh Congress of the Communist International, reversing the dicta of the Comintern's 1928 Sixth Congress, issued a rather differentiated analysis of complex trends in the capitalist world—an analysis which justified the broad, flexible, coalition-seeking approach—the "Popular Front" strategy—adopted by communist parties everywhere. Stalin was at the helm when, throughout the 1930s, the Soviet Ministry of Foreign Affairs was headed by Maxim Litvinov, a cultivated man who knew how to treat Western diplomats and statesmen, disarming them with the kind of charm and eloquence such modern-day imitators as Foreign Minister Gromyko or Ambassador Dobrynin can only envy. And Stalin was at the helm when certain features of Marxist-Leninist ideology pertaining to international relations were repeatedly modified to accommodate the immediate foreign policy needs of the Soviet Union.

Stalin's thinking in nonideological, power-political terms—meaning that he recognized both the uses to which Soviet power could be put and the limitations of that power—was even demonstrated during the expansionary postwar era. A reluctant supporter of uncertain revolutionary causes abroad, Stalin denied extensive assistance not only to his comrades in the French Communist Party, but to Mao's revolutionary forces in the Chinese civil war as well. A master of *Realpolitik*, he wanted to be on the winning side and hence kept the door open to Mao's enemy, the Kuomintang's Chiang Kai-shek, as long the outcome of the civil war was in doubt. Even in Eastern Europe, in the fall of 1945, when Stalin thought that he might need Western cooperation for the time being, he dramatically reversed previous decisions and as a gesture of goodwill ordered competitive elections in Bulgaria and then agreed to free elections in Hungary.[4] Moreover, and despite the apparent contradiction, at a time when Stalin was proceeding with the widespread purge of Jews in the Soviet Union, he was also supporting the Zionist cause for the establishment of a Jewish state in Palestine— no doubt calculating that such a state would weaken the British in the Middle East. And, finally, it was Stalin who around 1950 gave new emphasis to the old concept of "peaceful coexistence" and who subsequently initiated the coalitionary "peace campaign" of the early 1950s.[5]

Although a brief summary of this kind cannot do justice to the complexities of Stalin's conduct of foreign affairs, it does suggest that Stalin was a rather cautious guardian of Soviet interests in international life. During his last years, as Adam Ulam notes, his policies "created an air of tension which, apart from being a source of danger to Russia, was largely unnecessary."[6] Moreover, the language he used to assess international developments and explain Soviet goals abroad contained more ideological referents than can be found in his successors' pronouncements. But Stalin's actual policies invariably reflected his sensitivity to the international balance of forces; as a result he made all the necessary compromises in order to gain time and hence, he thought, to gain strength.

The Sources of Soviet Conduct

Of all the contemporary explanations of the Stalinist pattern in Soviet foreign policy, George F. Kennan's 1947 "X" article turned out to be the most influential.[7] Dealing with motivation—the issue that has always fascinated analysts of Soviet behavior—he identified the two main sources of Soviet conduct as Marxist-Leninist ideology and what he called the "circumstances of power" in the Soviet Union. Kennan, it will be recalled, found the Marxist view of capitalism and the Leninist view of imperialism quite germane to understanding and evaluating Soviet behavior abroad; he concluded that insofar as the Soviet leaders thought that capitalism contained the seeds of its own destruction and that imperialism would lead to war and revolution, they had to expect and promote the collapse of the noncommunist world. As to the "circumstances of power"—a struggling economy, succession problems, generational conflicts, and the like—their cumulative effect, Kennan thought, was a sense of insecurity which served to reinforce the leaders' ideological disposition to seek appropriate foreign outlets for their revolutionary zeal, beliefs, commitments, or goals.

While Kennan emphasized the internal sources of Soviet foreign policy, more recent analyses fall into two broad categories. "Microanalytic" studies, like Kennan's, stress the changing domestic environment of Soviet conduct; "macroanalytic" explanations emphasize the changing external environment as the primary factor in determining, and limiting, Soviet behavior in international life.[8] As we shall see, both schools of thought have successfully identified a number of important changes in the "environments" of Soviet foreign policy. What remains unclear, however, is whether such "environmental changes"—the inputs into Soviet policy—have actually caused changes in the course of Soviet behavior itself. At issue, therefore, is the influence of the internal and external environment on policy.

Internal Influences on Soviet Foreign Policy

The *first*, and by far the most important, change in the internal environment of Soviet foreign policy has been the substantially increased relative power of the Soviet Union since Stalin's reign. Although its economy remains uneven and technologically quite inferior to that of the West, the diverse and steadily growing military capability of post-Stalin Russia testifies to its new status in world politics. If Stalin's foreign policy had in part stemmed from a sense of weakness and insecurity—from what Kennan had called the "circumstance of power"—what policy change would follow enhanced Soviet domestic strength?

To answer this question, one should assume for the moment that the Soviet leaders do feel confident about their achievements and that they therefore believe some or most of the self-congratulatory messages they so often deliver about the momentous successes of the Soviet state. Would it follow that the new Soviet leaders' confidence about internal strength should help them *overcome* their often-noted historic sense of inferiority vis-à-vis the outside world, especially the West? In policy terms, does it follow that their self-confidence about domestic strength would lead them to pursue a more accommodating foreign policy?

Alternatively, one may suppose that, despite their remarkable achievements, the post-Stalin leaders still lack sufficient confidence in the viability of the Soviet domestic order. Perhaps they measure their accomplishments against more ambitious ultimate objectives or against the power of the United States, and thus find these accomplishments lacking. In that case, their self-congratulatory messages may be no more than New Year's resolutions—the sort of official optimism and wishful thinking so characteristic of political discourse everywhere. Would it follow then that the Soviet leaders' apparent lack of self-confidence about the internal health of the Soviet Union should *reinforce* their historic sense of inferiority vis-à-vis the outside world, especially the West? In policy terms, does it follow that such lack of self-confidence about domestic strength would prompt them to compensate for perceived weakness at home by pursuing an assertive or even aggressive foreign policy?

Because of the widespread belief that Stalin's putative "intransigence" stemmed from a desire to overcome domestic weakness and insecurity and because his successors' putative "moderation" is said to stem from the country's newly acquired domestic strength, the question goes to the heart of the controversy about "change" and "continuity" in Soviet foreign policy. Alas, the evidence—either about Stalin or his successors—is far from conclusive.

In his analysis of the interwar period—an era of considerable Soviet weakness, of course—Alexander Dallin, for example, at first offered this conclusion, suggesting that Soviet weakness led to accommodation: "More than once the response of the [weak] Soviet regime to potential foreign threats was one of reluctant accommodation, retrenchment, and even appeasement—from the Treaties of Brest-Litovsk (1918) and Riga (1920) to the Litvinov Protocol and the effort to propitiate Japan in 1931–32. . . . The reluctant alliance with France and Czechoslovakia in 1934–35 responded to a similar defensiveness born of a quest for time in which to improve the relative power position of the Soviet state." But in a carefully worded footnote, Dallin added this qualification: "It is well to note, however, that perceived weakness need not always produce a conciliatory mood in Moscow; nor does the willingness to seek a detente or compromise need to stem from weakness alone."[9] More recently, Dallin has reiterated his earlier observation (". . . historically a good deal of Soviet policy in the early years of the regime can be shown to have been the product of keenly perceived inferiority compared to the 'capitalist' environment"), but he has come to reject more emphatically the "domestic-weakness-leads-to-foreign-policy-moderation" hypothesis: "It would be a serious error to equate weakness, as perceived in the Kremlin, with willingness to compromise or yield, and the perception of [domestic] strength with inflexibility or intransigence in Soviet foreign policy."[10] In Stalin's time, then, the relationship between real or perceived domestic weakness, on the one hand, and foreign policy accommodation, on the other, remains essentially unclear.

As for the post-Stalin era, Morton Schwartz has explicitly identified the two contradictory interpretations. On the one hand, noting that Moscow's "greatly enhanced military power and prestige may tend to encourage a policy of increased assertiveness and even aggressiveness toward the outside world," he offers the following observation: "The USSR's recent achievements, therefore, may tend to reinforce Russia's historic sense of hostility toward the outside world, and lead to a more assertive policy, one which will now strive for a decisive shift in the world balance of forces. Convinced of their superiority—a conviction strengthened by their vast military power—the Kremlin leaders may be anxious to flex their new muscles. Thus, in the years ahead they may probe for ways to expand Soviet influence around the world." On the other hand, however, Schwartz seems to find the opposite interpretation somewhat more plausible: "The Kremlin leaders' . . . increased sense of physical security . . . will tend to reduce Soviet anxieties about the outside world. It also might, over time, exert a moderating influence on some of the historic traits—suspiciousness, nervous aggressiveness, xenophobia—which have made the USSR so difficult to deal with in the past. A secure Soviet leadership has already become a somewhat more relaxed Soviet leadership. . . . To the extent such judgments can be accurately gauged, Russia seems to have overcome its historic sense of inferiority."[11]

These tentative and carefully worded analyses suggest that no causality can be documented, that none of the four possible hypotheses is necessarily valid:

Domestic weakness – – – – – – – – –→ Foreign policy accommodation
Domestic weakness – – – – – – – – –→ Foreign policy assertiveness
Domestic strength – – – – – – – – –→ Foreign policy accommodation
Domestic strength – – – – – – – – –→ Foreign policy assertiveness

If we could validate any of these hpyotheses, the answer would have considerable implications for Western policy. It would indicate whether the West should try to encourage, to the extent it can, a strong and confident Soviet Union, or whether it should try to keep Moscow, to the extent it can, weak and uncertain of its relative power position. But since we do not have an answer, our advice about "keeping" Russia strong or weak has to be prudent and qualified. Perhaps the situation is analogous to child psychology, where it is assumed that (a) a child's *good* behavior may stem either from his self-confidence ("he is well-behaved because he feels confident about himself") or from his lack of such self-confidence ("he is well-behaved or meek because of his fear of retribution"), but it is also assumed that (b) a child's *bad* behavior may stem either from his self-confidence ("he is arrogant because he is over-confident") or from his lack of self-confidence ("he is arrogant because he is compensating for his insecurity"). And so it is with the Soviet Union: we simply do not know the influence of its newly acquired domestic strength on Soviet foreign policy.

The *second* frequently discussed change in the post-Stalin domestic order has been the apparent decline of ideological rigidity. The reason given for a more pragmatic and more flexible Soviet approach to the outside world is that the new leaders did not experience the early, prerevolutionary days and that their "mind-set" was thus formed during the years of socialist construction. Party bureaucrats, managers, soldiers, and engineers, they have devoted their lives to the solution of practical tasks, not to the making of revolution. While they have certainly participated in political intrigues, most of them did not take part in prerevolutionary conspiracies.

Moreover, the new Soviet leaders have repeatedly modified Stalin's ideology of international affairs. Wars were once said to be inevitable; now they are not. Revolutions were also once said to be inevitable; now there is peaceful transition to socialism too. The international class struggle used to be the major dogma of foreign policy; now it receives less public emphasis than peaceful coexistence. Autarky was to exclude devious foreign influences; now it is the international division of labor and even interdependence that pave the road to socialism and communism. Automation used to show capitalist inhumanity; now computers (often imported) are the new signposts of the scientific-technological revolution. At Lenin's grave, Stalin pledged to uphold the sacred and unshakable unity of the international communist movement; now his successors have yet to find an ideologically adequate explanation for Soviet military contingency plans against China. To be an ideologist in Moscow today is like being a White House spokesman for Richard Nixon, with all the pleasure that can be derived from making yesterday's facts inoperative today.

Yet, it remains doubtful whether Stalin's successors have actually
been less influenced by ideological precepts than Stalin was supposed
to have been. After all, ideological innovation and foreign policy flexibility, not doctrinal rigidity, were Stalin's traits, and his successors have
only outperformed him in ideological gymnastics. But even if one were
to assume otherwise, does the professed decline of ideological rigidity
amount to flexibility, and then does more flexibility necessarily translate into an accommodating or moderate foreign policy? It may well
be, instead, that neither of the two possible hypotheses is valid:

Rigid ideological environment – – –→ Foreign policy assertiveness
Decline of ideological zeal – – – – –→ Foreign policy accommodation

Without denying the steady erosion of faith since Lenin's days and
the far-reaching, though only long-term, implications of this process
for the future of Soviet political culture, what should be emphasized,
therefore, is that the necessity of legitimizing every twist and turn in
foreign policy by ideological incantation is hardly a novel phenomenon in Soviet history. After all, Stalin offered an equally eloquent ideological rationale for the "hard" line adopted in 1928 as for the "soft"
line in 1935; his successors presented an ideological explanation for
their 1968 military intervention in Czechoslovakia (the "Brezhnev
Doctrine") and for their more recent detente policies towards the
West ("peaceful coexistence").

    Furthermore, consider the difference between Stalin and his succes-
sors with regard to the potentially most important ideological issue—
the "inevitability of war" controversy. Given the unbridgeable antagonism between the forces of socialism and imperialism, Stalin saw no
way to avoid either small or large confrontations between the two sides.
In 1953–54, however, Malenkov revised Stalin's assessment, stating that
—because of the destructive quality of atomic weapons and because of
the increasing might of the Soviet Union—an all-out war with imperialism was no longer inevitable—it could be avoided. This was, and
remains, good news, of course, but one must still observe that (1) Stalin's belief in the inevitability of war did not propel him to begin such
wars (as he always sought to enhance Soviet power and influence gradually, indeed incrementally), and that (2) his successors have not, of
course, denounced "small" or "just" wars: the so-called wars of national liberation (Cuba, Vietnam, Cambodia, etc.) and military intervention in their sphere (Hungary and Czechoslovakia).

    In international life—where actions speak louder than words—it does
not make much difference that Stalin professed to believe in (but did
not start) an all-out confrontation with the West, while his successors

neither profess to believe in nor have started such an all-out confrontation. It should also be recalled that the "peace campaign" began in the late 1940s at Stalin's initiative. In the final analysis, Malenkov's revision of Stalin's dogma merely signifies the acceptance of, and the concurrent ideological rationalization for, what Stalin had practiced. Moreover, the same can be said about other changes in the "ideological environment" of Soviet foreign policy since Stalin's time. After all, *Pravda* still holds, for example, that "there are essentially no neutrals in the struggle between the two world systems."[12] And according to the authoritative Soviet *Diplomatic Dictionary*, peaceful coexistence "is a specific form of class struggle between socialism and capitalism." *Plus ça change, plus c'est la même chose.*

The *third* change in the domestic environment of Soviet foreign policy has been identified as the broadening of the decision-making process since Stalin, including the rise of elite factions and competing interests. Vernon V. Aspaturian, for example, has noted that the armed forces, the managers of heavy industries, and party bureaucrats tend to benefit from and hence support a more aggressive Soviet foreign policy stance, while a number of other groups, elite and especially nonelite—such as the state bureaucracy; managers of light industries, consumer goods, and agriculture; cultural, professional, and scientific groups; and much of the population at large—tend to benefit from and hence support the relaxation of international tension.[13] As a minimum, we know enough to say that foreign policy alternatives are debated more openly among a wider circle of advisers and decision makers, and it is also quite likely that resource allocation between military and nonmilitary uses is a particularly lively issue.[14]

Concurrently, the Soviet view of international life has become more differentiated. As William Zimmerman reminds us,[15] the field of international relations could develop only after Stalin's death, with specialists now covering all conceivable aspects of foreign-policy analysis and international-relations theory from the classical balance of power to simulation and beyond. As any recent visitor to the Institute on the USA and Canada or the Institute of World Economy can tell, a new generation of competent international relations specialists has been produced during the last two decades, who are no longer expected merely to supply such "information" as the leadership wants to hear and read. The more prestigious among them are surely heard, even if their influence is probably not much greater than that of Western academics on their governments.

The surfacing of a variety of interests and the apparent competition for resources and influence within the bureaucracy—combined with the availability of more knowledge about the outside world—strongly suggest a decision-making process characterized by compromises and political deals. Such compromises and deals at times may produce a "soft" line on foreign policy in exchange for a "hard" line on some domestic issue, while at other times it could be the other way around. (With respect to foreign policy alone, a "soft" line in one region of the world might necessitate a "hard" line in another.) Thus, speaking of the early 1970s, Marshall D. Shulman observed: "The net result of these conflicting domestic pressures has been that Brezhnev has won a free hand to implement his policy of 'peaceful coexistence' abroad, while the apparatus of orthodoxy and control has been given a free hand to tighten the lines of ideological vigilance at home and to prosecute the 'ideological struggle' between capitalism and Soviet socialism with renewed vigor."[16]

Once again, the controversial issue here is less the existence of such "conflicting domestic pressures" and factional political struggle (which had been particularly evident during the two succession crises of 1953–56 and 1964–68) than their consequence for foreign policy. For the apparent necessity of political deals and compromises in the Kremlin need not always lead to an accommodating foreign policy; the deal could also produce the opposite—"relaxation" at home and "vigilance" abroad. In other words, the mere existence of divergent interests, needs, views, perceptions, and approaches cannot be said to ensure any consistent pattern in Soviet foreign policy—conciliatory, centrist, or belligerent; the fact that competing interests have been compromised does not require a foreign policy of restraint.

Nor can one necessarily expect moderation from the post-Stalin foreign policy elite, even if it is better informed and more sophisticated. True, as Triska and Finley have shown, those in the elite who regularly deal with foreign policy use fewer ideological stereotypes when discussing international politics than do their colleagues whose primary preoccupation is party work or economic affairs.[17] But does more expertise mean more caution? Did the Soviet leaders establish large institutes and request more information on foreign policy in order to learn how to cope better with the outside world, or to learn how best to outmaneuver an increasingly complex outside world? Since we do not know how incoming information is processed, what the parameters of the policy debates are, and, in particular, what political benefits or penalties are derived from the transmittal of "bad news" and the offering of new ideas, it seems that we cannot be sure about the validity of any of the following hypotheses:

Narrow (Stalinist) decision making – – – – – – –→ Foreign policy
                                                 assertiveness
Broadening of decision-making process – – – –→ Foreign policy
                                                 accommodation
Limited knowledge of international life – – – –→ Foreign policy
                                                 assertiveness
Expanding knowledge of international life – – – –→ Foreign policy
                                                 accommodation

External Influences on Soviet Foreign Policy

The apparent lack of causality between domestic inputs and foreign policy makes it particularly apposite to explore the external environment of Soviet conduct. Is that environment, or could that environment be, a source of change for the better in Soviet foreign policy?

To begin with a few simple assumptions, we may take it for granted that members of the international community engage in activities which have a bearing, direct or indirect, on the Soviet Union. States engage in generally self-serving activities: they do what is advantageous for their own interests (though not necessarily disadvantageous to the Soviet Union). Under all circumstances, however, given the military might, economic power, political influence, and global reach of the Soviet Union—in short, its preeminent position in the international system—most states have reason to seek to alter some aspect or feature of Soviet foreign policy. In turn, as the Soviet Union does not operate in a political, military, or economic vacuum, it has to respond to at least some of these attempts at influencing its behavior.[18]

The primary external demands on the Soviet Union are (1) for foreign policy "moderation" (i.e., demands on Moscow to help *maintain* the status quo by refraining from war and intervention) and (2) for "assistance" (i.e., demands to help *change* the status quo by extending political support, and economic as well as military aid). Since these two broad categories of demands are mutually exclusive, the Soviet Union—taking into account domestic needs, pressures, and preferences as well—must evaluate and respond to such contradictory external demands, trying to satisfy as many of its more important or more powerful foreign audiences and constituencies as possible. Should it endanger detente by transporting Cuban troops to Africa? Should it support the confrontationists or the moderates in the Middle East? Should it encourage, to the extent it can, the French Communist Party's drive for power, or should it acquiesce in the perpetuation of a French bourgeois government whose independent policies may exacerbate tension within NATO?

Such, we may presume, are Moscow's agonizing choices, with no option offering only benefits, and hence decisions have to be made in each case with due consideration of the likely costs and benefits. Simply stated, the Soviet Union is linked to too many external causes, issues, and audiences whose demands on and expectations of the Soviet Union greatly differ. To the extent that the Soviet Union has become a vital nexus in the international system and to the extent that the international system has become more complex and atomized, Moscow can satisfy some of these demands and expectations some of the time; it cannot satisfy all of them all of the time.

The international environment in which Soviet foreign policy operates has dramatically changed since Stalin's reign. The international communist movement has disintegrated. The communist bloc Stalin built after World War II has all but ceased to act as a more or less united entity. Almost one hundred new, often radical states have been born, of which the resource-rich developing states have come to present a major challenge to the Western industrialized world. Interdependence is a new economic fact of international life. The "leading role" of the United States in the Atlantic alliance has eroded. Such issues as German reunification and the "liberation" of Eastern Europe are no longer on the Western agenda. The extraordinarily rapid modernization of weapon-systems, spearheaded by the United States, has led to fundamental revisions in the concepts and strategies of warfare.

These and many other developments signify the transformation of the international system since Stalin's time. Some of them—such as the development of new weapons—seem to constitute demands on Moscow for caution and accommodation; others—the rise of new states, for example—may mean opportunities for the expansion of Soviet influence. Considering, for the moment, only the more hopeful of these external influences—those which seem to call for Soviet "moderation"—it seems that the Soviet Union can respond to them in one of two ways. First, its responses can be a tactical reaction—an essentially limited adjustment to external demands. It is the well-known "one step backward," the postponement rather than the cancellation of policy implementation, a temporary concession whose primary purpose is to gain time. We need not concern ourselves very much with this type of response. It originated with Lenin, of course, and it has long been recognized as part of the repertoire of Soviet diplomacy.

The other kind of reaction, as Zimmerman suggests, is far more complex—and seldom recognized. It can begin, perhaps, as a tactical adjustment to international reality, but over time—if properly stimulated and reinforced—it would evolve towards and indeed transform itself into a *learned* response. Learning from the benefits of experience and subjected to carefully orchestrated external stimuli, the Soviet "organism" would thus become capable of genuine and presumably lasting, if not permanent, attitude-modification and "structural adaptation."[19] If the Soviet Union does have the capability of producing such a response, as Zimmerman argues, the implications would be far reaching indeed. It would signal a major opportunity—and responsibility—for the outside world to influence the outcome of debates within the Soviet foreign policy elite and to do so with the objective of contributing to durable change. The United States, for example, could act and speak in such a way as to reinforce the position of "moderates" in the Kremlin; we could attempt to show, by words and deeds, the benefits of detente and cooperation for both sides.

Zimmerman's intriguing hypothesis rests on his critique of American foreign policy toward the Soviet Union during the early years of the Cold War. He argues that the United States was quite insensitive to foreign policy debates—the Varga debates—then taking place in the Kremlin, noting that Stalin's objectives were more fluid and tentative than we had assumed—including, until 1947, his plans for the "people's democracies" of Eastern Europe. But since the United States had assumed that Stalin was determined to establish satellite regimes in that region and then reach Western Europe as well, we responded by a policy of *threatening* military and political mobilization, as if the Soviet Union had no alternative but to do what it eventually did.* The inference to be drawn from Zimmerman's analysis is that if the West had only been less "threatening" and more "reassuring," postwar Soviet foreign policy might have been less assertive, more accommodating. Moreover, Stalin and his colleagues would have *learned* at that time that peaceful coexistence with the West was a genuine and rewarding option.

Putting aside the historical illustration, there is reason to be skeptical about the possibility of achieving "lasting adaptation" in Soviet foreign policy as a consequence of external influences. For one thing, there is the practical problem of policy coordination by the outside world. Neither now nor in the future can we expect to know the parameters

---

*My own research essentially confirms Zimmerman's conclusion about the tentativeness of Stalin's goals, except that I find that Moscow's pre-1947 ambivalence applied probably to Hungary and definitely to Czechoslovakia rather than all of Eastern Europe.

of internal debates on foreign policy in the Kremlin. (Was the Varga debate, for example, about policy or timing?) But assuming that we could make a good guess at the choices discussed, can the outside world then coordinate its policies in such a way as to bring about the desired result? After all, while the United States is the most closely watched and surely the most important single external input, it is not the only one, and even if we could develop a set of finely tuned policies aimed at properly "educating" and influencing the Kremlin, wouldn't other foreign policies from other sources tend to cancel out or at least mitigate the impact of what we would be trying to accomplish?

Even more fundamental is the problem of conceiving the appropriate mix of external inputs. It is not at all clear whether the outside world should be or should appear to be weak or strong, reassuring or threatening, in order to generate "moderation" in Soviet foreign policy. Could Soviet strategic superiority, for example, help the Soviet leaders *overcome* their historic sense of inferiority vis-à-vis the West—a possibly valid but rather risky assumption—and thus produce a more accommodating Soviet foreign policy? Alternatively, should the United States aim at strategic superiority, following our long-held belief that only from a position of strength can we influence and moderate the Soviet Union? But if that approach only tends to *reinforce* a sense of inferiority in the Soviet leadership, wouldn't the concessions likely be only tactical or short lived?

Accordingly, unless we have some reasonably accurate assessment of the impact of external "strength" versus external "weakness" on the Soviet foreign policy debates—in other words, unless we know what combination of external incentives and prohibitions may pave the way to a lasting tendency towards foreign policy moderation—we cannot be confident about the international environment producing such moderation in Moscow. This is not to deny the import of what the non-Soviet world does or is, or how it goes about conducting its relations with the Soviet Union; it is only to suggest that external environmental influences entering into the calculations of the Soviet leadership will not by themselves generate enduring change in Soviet conduct. In the final analysis, it is not a set of often conflicting demands, conditions, or policy inputs that make for change; only *the balance of perceived needs* will do so: the Soviet leaders themselves must judge external developments to be such as to necessitate policy reassessment.

The Balance of Perceived Needs: Key to "Change"?

So far, this essay has focused on the *logic* of assigning change to Soviet foreign policy on the basis of analyzing the internal and ex-

ternal environments of Soviet conduct. Yet, fascinating as it is to spec-
ulate about changing influences on Soviet behavior, the proof of the
pudding is not in the kitchen but in the eating, and hence the ultimate
criterion by which a judgment can be rendered has to be the *record*
—the output—of Soviet foreign policy itself.

Looking at the record, what "new departures" stand out in the history of Soviet foreign policy and how can we account for them?

(1) The Soviet Union discarded the early ideal of "revolutionary
diplomacy" almost immediately after its establishment in 1917. Accepting the practice of what it had once regarded as "bourgeois" diplomatic
intercourse with the outside world, the Soviet leaders promptly decided
to enter into regular negotiations with other states and generally observe diplomatic protocol. Mainly because of his desire to make peace
with Germany and thus cement his shaky regime at home, Lenin did
not hesitate to tell Trotsky that the very survival of the Soviet state
required the adoption of "old" diplomatic practices.

(2) The Communist International's "exclusionary" strategy of the
1920s—better known as the "United Front from below"—was replaced
in the early 1930s by the "inclusionary" or Popular Front strategy.
Sanctioned at the Soviet-dominated Seventh Comintern Congress in
1935, the new approach encouraged all Communist parties to cooper-
ate with the noncommunist left in order to form a united front against
the rise of fascism. Inherent in this fundamental shift was the danger
of reducing the once-sacred "leading role" and ideological purity of
Communist parties. Yet Stalin accepted the potential danger of ideological erosion by socialists, social democrats, and others because he
assumed that only a broader left coalition could ensure the security of
the Soviet Union and defeat the greater danger—Nazi Germany and
its allies.

(3) Compared to the cautious, quasi-isolationist posture in the interwar period, Stalin initiated an expansionary phase in Soviet foreign
policy after World War II. With the establishment of pro-Soviet
regimes in Eastern Europe, "socialism in one country" gave way to
"socialism in one region," as the prewar revolutionary rhetoric could
now be translated into policy. As noted earlier, the change was due
to the opportunity created by World War II and the lack of counter-
vailing power in the international system.

(4) Around 1950–51, in the aftermath of the Berlin crisis and the
Korean war, the confrontationist strategy of the postwar years was
replaced by the peace campaign in Europe and the sudden opening to
the Third World. Unable to break the European impasse and unwilling
to risk a military showdown with the United States, Stalin—and subsequently his successors—shelved the rigid "two-camp" doctrine of

1946-47, resuscitated the "peaceful coexistence" line, and shifted to a rather low-key, low-tension policy towards the outside world. Clearly, the lesson of Berlin and Korea was that the confrontationist strategy had failed to advance Soviet interests and should therefore be modified. For years to come, the Soviet Union was to look beyond the old world for new gains, relying less on the military than on the economic instrument of foreign policy.

(5) Since the mid-1950s, Stalin's successors have come to accept, however grudgingly, a degree of experimentation in Eastern Europe. Khrushchev's overture to Tito in 1955 marked the beginning of greater Soviet tolerance towards national traditions and characteristics in Eastern Europe. Despite subsequent interventions aimed at curtailing far-reaching liberalization in the region, Stalin's insistence on strict uniformity was altered—no doubt because it had created chronic and dangerous instability.

(6) Having learned during the Cuban missile crisis that its inferior military posture vis-à-vis the United States had been a major political handicap, the Soviet Union initiated a massive program of military investments in the 1960s to catch up with, and possibly surpass, the United States in the arms race. An estimated 12 to 15 percent of the Soviet GNP has since been devoted to military procurements, presumably in order to avoid the kind of humiliation Moscow suffered in 1962.

These are among the more important new departures—some accommodating, some assertive in character—in the history of Soviet foreign policy. They suggest three conclusions.

The *first* is that in each case the Soviet leaders embarked on a new course either when the previous policy had failed to produce the desired end or when a new opportunity for the expansion of Soviet influence had presented itself. Irrespective of whether the new course was initiated under or after Stalin, it was usually the Soviet leaders' perception of policy failure that prompted the adoption of new approaches and solutions. In the case of Tito's rehabilitation in 1955, there was the additional factor of Khrushchev using the issue as part of his political struggle against those who, like Molotov and Malenkov, had been implicated in the early anti-Tito campaign under Stalin. On the whole, however, the perceived needs of the Soviet state rather than political infighting can be said to have produced new departures in Soviet conduct—traditional needs as intangible as security, power, influence, or prestige and as tangible as economic and military progress.

The *second* conclusion is that the record of Soviet foreign policy indicates tactical adjustments rather than lasting adaptations. While it may be premature to make a definitive judgment about the most recent period, it is quite clear that, as Zbigniew Brzezinski and others have noted, Soviet policy toward the outside world has been characterized by a cyclical pattern—"by alternating offensive and defensive phases."[20] On the same point, Henry Kissinger is worth quoting at greater length: "Peace offensives, of course, are not new in Soviet history. Peaceful coexistence has been avowed since the advent of Communism in Russia. It was stressed particularly between 1934–1939; between 1941–1946; at the time of the Geneva Summit Conference of 1955; again on the occasion of Khrushchev's visit to the United States in 1959; and following the Cuban Missile Crisis in 1962. . . . On each occasion the period of relaxation ended when an opportunity for expanding Communism presented itself."[21] Given the cyclical pattern of the past, it would require excessive optimism, if not naivete, to emphasize aspects of lasting change in Soviet foreign policy since Stalin.

Third, the record both under and after Stalin suggests neither a rigid "master plan" for global conquest nor a conservative policy aimed at the maintenance of the status quo. If there has been a basic pattern in Soviet foreign policy from Lenin to Brezhnev, it is characterized by the persistent, though cautious, pursuit of opportunities abroad—"persistent" because the overall objective of advancing Soviet influence has not changed and "cautious" because the Soviet leaders have sought to promote Soviet influence so gradually as to make strong and concerted Western countermeasures unjustifiable.

In the final analysis, post-Stalin Soviet foreign policy reflects a curious paradox. For while the internal and external environments in which it operates are different now, the Soviet leaders—under conflicting pressures and impulses and facing demands for both change and continuity—have nonetheless continued to rely on the old, historic mix of assertiveness-and-accommodation. Stalin's heirs must assume that this mix has served the Soviet Union well—that it has been a success, not a failure—and hence they perceive no need for the kind of change de-Stalinization has signified in the domestic realm.

Afterword

In his response to this chapter, William Zimmerman accurately reviews and, in my opinion, mistakenly rejects my skepticism about "lasting change" in Soviet conduct. Our differences, I believe, have to do with Western perceptions of continuity and change in Soviet history and with the extent of Western influence on the long-term evolution of Soviet foreign policy.

With regard to the question of continuity and change in Soviet history, it should be recalled that since the 1920s—and thus well before the post-Stalin era or detente—it has been fashionable in the West to discover a "new" Russia or a "new" Soviet foreign policy. In 1933, for example, Michael T. Florinsky, the historian, noted, "The former crusaders of world revolution at any cost have exchanged their swords for machine tools and now rely more on the results of their labor than on direct action to achieve the ultimate triumph of the proletariat." In 1943, Senator Tom Connally of Texas observed, "Russians for years have been changing their economy and approaching the abandonment of communism and the whole Western world will be gratified at the happy climax of their efforts." In 1956, even Secretary of State John Foster Dulles greeted the post-Stalin "thaw" and the 1955 "spirit of Geneva" by concluding, "The Soviet leaders are scrapping thirty years of policy based on violence and intolerance."[22]

Thus, whenever there is a new Soviet emphasis on "peaceful coexistence" or a new Soviet peace offensive, we are told that the Soviet leaders' priorities and attitudes have undergone substantial alterations. As Henry A. Kissinger put it,

> There is a measure of pathos in our continued effort to discover "reasonable" motives for the Soviet leaders to cease being Bolsheviks: the opportunities to develop the resources of their own country, the unlimited possibilities of nuclear energy, or the advantages of expanding international trade. The Kremlin has been able to exploit this attitude by periodically launching policies of "peaceful coexistence," which have inevitably raised the debate whether a "fundamental" shift has occurred in Soviet purposes, thus lulling us before the next onslaught.[23]

I also find George F. Kennan's 1947 comment most appropriate and instructive:

> When there is something the Russians want from us, one or the other of these [negative] features of their policy may be thrust temporarily into the background; and when that happens there will always be Americans who will leap forward with gleeful announcements that "the Russians have changed," and some who will even try to take credit for having brought about such "changes." But we should not be misled by tactical maneuvers. These characteristics of Soviet policy . . . will be with us, whether in the foreground or the background, until the internal nature of Soviet power changes.[24]

On the question of how much influence the West has had, or can have, on Soviet foreign policy, Zimmerman provides an interesting insight. While he does not demonstrate by specific examples his contention that post-Stalin policy has come to differ significantly from Stalin's conduct, he implies that post-Stalin Soviet behavior *would have* changed for the better if only the United States or the West had acted more wisely (or patiently, or consistently, or in a less threatening way). Hence the new twist: if little or no actual change is manifested in Soviet foreign policy—if, in other words, Moscow has not lived up to our expectations—it must be our fault and thus *we* are responsible for *their* assertive conduct.

This argument, like so many others about the rise of a "new" Russia, stems from an unwillingness to come to terms with the challenge to our liberal values inherent in continuity in Soviet politics and indeed in the permanence of conflict in international life.

Notes

1. As Robert C. Tucker has written, for example, the Soviet "commitment to world Communist revolution, while still intact ideologically, has become very weak as a political motivation and has ceased to be a mainspring of Soviet initiative in world affairs." See his "United States-Soviet Cooperation: Incentives and Obstacles," in Vernon V. Aspaturian, *Process and Power in Soviet Foreign Policy* (Boston: Little, Brown, 1971), p. 904.

2. Marshall D. Shulman was the first to call attention to "significant changes in [Soviet foreign policy] outlook and behavior which began to be manifested before the death of Stalin." *Stalin's Foreign Policy Reappraised* (New York: Atheneum, 1965).

3. Khrushchev was reported to have said, "The imperialists call us Stalinists. Well, when it comes to fighting imperialism, we are all Stalinists." Thomas Whitney, ed., *Khrushchev Speaks* (Ann Arbor: University of Michigan Press, 1963), p. 2.

4. Stalin's pragmatism in Bulgaria was witnessed by the British representative to the Allied Control Commission in Sofia:

> In August, 1945, the Allied Control Commission in Bulgaria was discussing the advisability of the Bulgarians holding a general election on a single list. The British and American delegates on the Commission opposed a single list as being "undemocratic," while the Russians supported it as the only "democratic" method of holding an election. Since Stalin always worked at night, all other Soviet officials also had to work at night, so the sessions of the Commission began at 8:00 P.M. and lasted until 4:00 A.M. On this occasion the discussions started on a Wednesday evening and the elections were due to be held the following Sunday. The discussions on Wednesday, Thursday, and Friday proved fruitless, and we assembled again, much dispirited, on Saturday evening at 8:00 P.M. to listen once more to the Soviet argument in favor of a single list. The Russian side of the negotiations was conducted by the Soviet Commander in Chief in Bulgaria, Colonel-General (later Marshal of the Soviet Union) S. S. Biryuzov. He was obviously trying to drag out the discussions until the polling booths opened at 7:00 A.M. on Sunday morning so that nothing could be done about the matter, be-

cause the population would already be voting for or against the single list of candidates. But at 1:30 A.M. the telephone rang in the anteroom of the Russian general's office, and he sent his aide, a major, to answer it. When the major lifted the telephone to his ear, he stood there, as though struck dumb. The general thought his aide had become ill, so he strode over in a masterly fashion to the phone and seized it. Immediately he came smartly to attention, and stood upright for about five minutes while we could hear a voice crackling over the line. Then he said, "Yes, Comrade Stalin," and came back to us to declare: "As is well known, the Soviet government has always opposed the holding of general elections on a single list. The elections will be postponed until a more democratic method can be found." The Bulgarian prime minister was then sent for, told that the elections were to be put off, and the polling booths to be closed.

Malcolm Mackintosh, "Stalin's Policies towards Eastern Europe: The General Picture," in Thomas T. Hammond, ed., *The Anatomy of Communist Takeovers* (New Haven: Yale University Press, 1975), pp. 229–43. (The quotation appears on pp. 239–40.)

5. See Shulman, *Stalin's Foreign Policy Reappraised.*

6. Adam B. Ulam, *Expansion and Co-existence* (New York: Praeger, 1968), p. 543.

7. X [George F. Kennan], "The Sources of Soviet Conduct," *Foreign Affairs*, 25, 4 (July 1947), pp. 566–82. For one of many critiques of Kennan's essay, see Charles Gati, "X Plus 25: What Containment Meant," *Foreign Policy*, 7 (Summer 1972), pp. 22–40.

8. See Alexander Dallin, "Soviet Foreign Policy and Domestic Politics: A Framework for Analysis," in Erik P. Hoffman and Frederic J. Fleron, Jr., eds., *The Conduct of Soviet Foreign Policy* (Chicago: Aldine-Atherton, 1971), pp. 36–49; Alexander Dallin, "The Domestic Sources of Soviet Foreign Policy," in Severyn Bialer, ed., *The Domestic Context of Soviet Foreign Policy* (Boulder: Westview Press, 1980); Morton Schwartz, *The Foreign Policy of the USSR: Domestic Factors* (Encino & Belmont, California: Dickenson Publishing Company, 1975); Marshall D. Shulman, "Toward a Western Philosophy of Coexistence," *Foreign Affairs*, 52, 1 (October 1973), pp. 35–58; William Zimmerman, "Elite Perspectives and the Explanation of Soviet Foreign Policy," in Hoffmann and Fleron, pp. 18–30; William Zimmerman, "Choices in the Postwar World: Containment and the Soviet Union," in Charles Gati, ed., *Caging the Bear: Containment and the Cold War* (Indianapolis: Bobbs-Merrill, 1974), pp. 85–108; Robert Legvold, "The Nature of Soviet Power," *Foreign Affairs*, 56, 1 (October 1977), pp. 49–71.

9. Dallin in Hoffmann and Fleron, pp. 41–42.

10. Dallin, "Domestic Sources."

11. Schwartz, pp. 89–91.

12. April 30, 1969.

13. Aspaturian, "Internal Politics and Foreign Policy in the Soviet System," in Aspaturian, *Process and Power*, pp. 491–551.

14. For a dissenting view, see William E. Odom, "Who Controls Whom in Moscow," *Foreign Policy*, 19 (Summer 1975), pp. 109–23.

15. William Zimmerman, *Soviet Perspectives on International Relations, 1956–1967* (Princeton: Princeton University Press, 1969).

16. Marshall D. Shulman, "Trends in Soviet Foreign Policy," in Michael

MacGwire, Ken Booth, and John McDonnell, eds., *Soviet Naval Policy* (New York: Praeger, 1975), pp. 8–10.

17. Jan F. Triska and David D. Finley, *Soviet Foreign Policy* (New York: Macmillan, 1968), pp. 124–25.

18. Like Shulman (note 2 above), William Zimmerman has emphasized the "reactive propensity" of the Soviet Union. For a full and by far the most discriminating treatment, see his chapter in Gati, *Caging the Bear*, pp. 85–108.

19. Ibid.

20. Zbigniew Brzezinski, "The Competitive Relationship," in ibid., pp. 157–99, esp. pp. 186–87.

21. Henry A. Kissinger, *The Troubled Partnership: A Reappraisal of the Atlantic Alliance* (Garden City: Doubleday Anchor Books, 1966), pp. 189–90.

22. All quotes cited in ibid, pp. 190–91.

23. Henry A. Kissinger, *Nuclear Weapons and Foreign Policy* (Garden City: Doubleday Anchor Books, 1958), p. 7.

24. George F. Kennan, "The Ideology of Containment: The X Article," in Gati, ed., *Caging the Bear*, p. 15.

RESPONSES

The Soviet Union and the West

William Zimmerman

One of the enduring preoccupations of students of Soviet foreign policy has been their emphasis on the theme of continuity and change. Charles Gati has aimed a number of broadsides, largely intended to assert that continuity with Stalin's foreign policy, rather than change, ought to be emphasized in assessing the quarter century since Stalin's death. Like most broadsides, some hit a target (though not necessarily the intended one), some fall short, and some explode in the cannon.

I believe the following is a fair characterization of Gati's position. First, elements about Soviet foreign policy in the 1960s and 1970s sometimes pointed to as distinctive turn out on several occasions to have had their counterpart during Stalin's rule. In other words, Stalin's foreign policy is closer to current Soviet foreign policy than is often assumed. Second, on reflection, Soviet foreign policy in the quarter century since Stalin's death has not been as different from Stalin's foreign policy as is commonly asserted. Current Soviet foreign policy, therefore, is closer to Stalin's foreign policy than is widely assumed. Third, because in fact there has not been as great a change as has sometimes been claimed, it is inappropriate to assume that there has been, or is likely to be, a change for the better in Soviet foreign policy. Those who see a moderation in Soviet foreign policy over the past quarter century are thus in error.

Fourth, those students of Soviet foreign policy—and Gati includes me in this category—who argue that the United States should act to strengthen the hand of the moderates in the Soviet ruling group do not in practice have any substantive advice to give to American decision makers about how best to moderate Soviet behavior. In the brief commentary that follows, I will address each of these propositions.

On Reconsidering Soviet Foreign Policy and the Stalin Period

Some elements of continuity between Stalin's foreign policy and the contemporary foreign policy of the USSR should be emphasized. It is important, for example, to point out that Stalin was capable of remarkable ideological gymnastics and flexibility in foreign policy. It certainly bears stressing that Soviet foreign policy has always been typified by a tendency to minimize risk. It is also appropriate to stress that cavalier attitudes toward leaders of nonruling parties were characteristic of Stalin as well as his successors. "Proletarian internationalism" for Stalin, as for Brezhnev, have been code words for the primacy of the interests of the Soviet Union. Similarly, there is some validity to the argument, first made by Marshall Shulman, that Stalin's peace offensive was a harbinger of the post-Stalinist policy of peaceful coexistence. In this sense "post-Stalinist" foreign policy began while Stalin was living. And, one can argue, as I have elsewhere,[1] that there are many parallels between the perspectives on the West adopted by Khrushchev and his successors and those which were entertained by Eugen Varga and his colleagues in the last years of World War II and immediately afterward.

Even in view of these similarities, however, the distinctive features of Stalin's overall approach to international politics should be emphasized. Stalin viewed politics, especially international politics, almost exclusively in terms of mobilization—mobilization here having both political and military connotations. His world view was bi-polar, and he perceived international politics as a zero-sum game, in the spirit of the formula *kto-kogo*—who does in whom? For Stalin, capitalist encirclement was an attribute of international politics that was not altered by the security afforded by the communist takeovers in Eastern Europe and Asia after World War II. Being surrounded by countries "democratic and friendly to the Soviet Union" was not enough assurance for Stalin; in the last years of his life he considered capitalist encirclement a political, not a geographical, concept. (Capitalist encirclement, it should be remembered, served also to legitimate the practice of "permanent purge," even as the USSR progressed toward communism.) Stalin persisted in believing in the inevitability of war between capitalist states. He placed great stock in economic autarky for the Soviet Union and regarded such a policy as essential to Soviet security. Finally, because of Stalin's absolute monopoly over the interpretation of doctrine, the possession of policy-relevant expertise by individuals was often dangerous.

Stalin's postures stand in stark contrast to the general outlook of his successors. The mobilization rhetoric—the vocabulary of "struggle," "front," "rotten compromise"—has been replaced by the rhetoric of "problems," "complexity," "reasonable compromise." The inevitability-of-war doctrine has been scrapped, as has the doctrine of capitalist encirclement. In light of these and other changes, a discussion of Stalin's ideological gymnastics which fails to note the dogmatisms to which he clung, and which his successors have systematically abandoned, is misleading. Similarly, it bears noting that Stalin's siege mentality, which manifested itself most clearly in his insistence on autarky, has been abandoned, even at a time when the capitalist world has shown, for the first time in a long while, the boom and bust characteristics that Marxists-Leninists have traditionally insisted are essential features of capitalism.

Finally, I am persuaded that the "post-Stalinist" features of Stalin's last years were largely not his doing but were the result of initiatives by others who were in direct challenge to Stalin. In 1952 Stalin was adamantly opposed to those in the Soviet Union who were advocating concessions to the West, and he reiterated the inevitability-of-war doctrine in his last major statement, *Economic Problems of Socialism in the USSR*, just prior to the Nineteenth Party Congress. At the Nineteenth Congress, however, Malenkov was careful to assert merely that the danger persisted that war *might* break out between capitalist states. It may be that the 1952 turn to the right was made in spite of Stalin rather than at his behest; if so, that may explain why, at the time of his death, Stalin was preparing another major purge, one victim of which almost certainly would have been Malenkov.

Post-Stalin Continuity in Soviet Foreign Policy?

With regard to Gati's second point, I am skeptical about the utility of describing the foreign policy of Stalin and his successors toward the West in more or less the same breath. To be told that one can describe Soviet foreign policy under Stalin and under his successors as a "mix of assertiveness and accommodation" is to be told very little. I seek from Gati a more substantive discussion of how the USSR's mix of assertiveness and accommodation under either Stalin or Brezhnev differentiates Soviet behavior from, for instance, American foreign policy under Roosevelt, Truman, Nixon, and Carter, or German foreign policy under Hitler, Adenauer, Brandt, and Schmidt. At the same time, characterizing Brezhnev's, Khrushchev's, and Stalin's foreign policy as an undifferentiated mix of assertiveness and accommodation obscures differences in, for example, the nature of Soviet-American relations in 1950 and as we begin the 1980s.

"Peaceful coexistence" as practiced under Khrushchev and Brezhnev has been different from the Cold War. Peaceful coexistence entails a blend of cooperation and conflict, to be sure—"assertiveness and accommodation," perhaps—but to remind us of the persistence of U.S.-Soviet conflict is not the same as to assert a basic continuity of Soviet foreign policy under Stalin and his successors. Among the major features of Soviet-American relations twenty-five years after Stalin's death that distinguish them from relations in 1948–53 are the following. (1) While elites on each side regard the other side as expansionist, there is much less disposition to believe that the other side is bent on destroying its opponent. (2) Each side recognizes the importance of creating an environment in which the pursuit of narrow "possessive" interests can be undertaken at less risk. (3) The American-Soviet conflict has become routinized and expressed in ways that were inconceivable while Stalin lived.

By lumping Stalin's foreign policy and the foreign policy of his successors together, Gati has tended to obscure fundamental changes after 1953. Consider, for instance, two major turning points. In 1955 Khrushchev accomplished a major reorientation in Soviet foreign policy. The Soviet Union signed an Austrian State Treaty and pulled out of Austria; the Soviet leadership undertook a major expedition to Asia; relations with Finland were "normalized"; and the Soviet Union advanced a major disarmament proposal. Together, these developments represented a dramatic reversal in Soviet foreign policy. It strains credulity that Stalin would have undertaken this package of moves. Similarly, in the 1970s the USSR has made a commitment to participation in world trade, in sharp contrast to Stalin's autarky.

Measuring Moderation

If Soviet foreign policy has changed more than Gati suggests, then we must examine the nature of the change in Soviet behavior to assess whether it is in the direction of moderation. Two points are in order. First, moderation is a value-laden term; one might define moderation in such a way as to mean a situation, to recall an apt image by Walter Lippmann, in which Soviet children are born singing "God Bless America." Some critics of detente seem to imply this definition when they fault the Soviet Union for pursuing interests opposed to American or Western interests—for engaging in activities of any kind in Africa, for example. Second, moderation needs to be evaluated against capabilities and opportunities foregone as well as against past behavior. Immediately after World War II, the Soviet Union extracted immense resources from Eastern Europe. The Soviet Union took from Eastern Europe about as much as the United States, via the Marshall Plan, put into Western Europe.[2] By that standard, the USSR's behavior in Eastern Europe since the 1950s has certainly been more moderate. Even in the aftermath of the 1973 energy crisis, similarly, the USSR has shown its willingness to restrain its economic demands on the East European states in order to increase the political viability of the Warsaw Pact.

The difference between these standards of moderation should be kept in mind in thinking about U.S.-Soviet relations. The Soviet Union has become a world power in the last twenty-five years; it is no longer merely the continental power it was when Stalin died. As a result, Soviet interests and American interests now clash in places where there was little or no Soviet presence twenty-five years ago. In one sense this implies decreased moderation since Stalin's death. (Moreover, a somewhat more moderate but greatly more powerful Soviet Union might be said to constitute a greater threat to U.S. interests than did a more aggressive but weaker USSR in Stalin's time.) However, the fact that Soviet-American clashes tend to be over peripheral values, to involve conflicts between surrogates, and, often, to be played out in rather stylized ways suggests a considerable moderation in Soviet behavior from the days when "push to the limit" was offset by "know when to stop."

Influencing Soviet Adaptation

Can the West, and the United States in particular, influence Soviet behavior significantly so as to produce "structural adaptation"? On this score, Gati is skeptical. My own view is that there is much evidence that adaptation reflecting changes in values has occurred. There has been a genuine evolution of Soviet elite perspectives on the international system in the past twenty-five years.[3] If nothing else, as Gati has pointed out, the USSR has immensely increased its research capacity with respect to the outside world. This itself is a form of institutional adaptation—a recognition that Stalin's policies were inadequate partly because they were uninformed. The Soviet elite seems to have realized that low-information systems are low-performance systems. In general, much of Soviet behavior in the 1960s and 1970s suggests an analogy with the automobile industry: In a world where the United States remains the General Motors of international politics, what is good enough for General Motors is often good enough for the Ford Motor Company of international politics, the USSR. This is not an argument that structural adaptation produces moderation, but merely that competition generates structural adaptation in order better to compete.

The somewhat tougher question, then, is whether in the 1980s the United States can do anything to moderate Soviet behavior. Again Gati is skeptical. He correctly points out there are various external factors which could influence Soviet behavior in different ways. (It is not, however, an assertion which effectively challenges an approach emphasizing macroanalytical variables.) One should bear in mind how difficult it is to induce desired behavior in rivals, allies, or even clients in the recalcitrant realm of world politics.

Nevertheless, something can be said about what kind of behavior by the United States is likely to elicit relatively more moderate Soviet behavior. Inadvertently, Gati provides some guidance on this score when he comments: "It is not at all clear whether the outside world should appear to be weak or strong, reassuring or threatening, to generate 'moderation' in Soviet foreign policy." I read the two pairs—weak-strong, reassuring-threatening—as different continua and not, as Gati seems to imply, more or less similar notions. In my estimation, the best American stance is one that is strong and reassuring; the least preferable American course is to act weak and threatening. In general, the United States should act to reinforce the views of those in the Soviet elite who are prone to emphasize the complexities and difficulties inherent in any effort to foster revolution, and who see that social and political progress is possible within capitalism. The United States should try to strengthen those in the USSR who believe that linkage to the international economic system constitutes an advantage for, not a threat to, Soviet interests. American elites should also be mindful of the role of style and timing in affecting Soviet behavior. There have been instances in recent years when American elites have behaved as if they failed to distinguish between acting forcefully toward the USSR—a course which often has moderated Soviet behavior—and acting provocatively—a course which will never moderate and which will almost always exacerbate Soviet behavior.

Let me illustrate each of the above propositions by citing the United States involvement in Vietnam. Fifteen years after the event it is still stupefying that the United States responded to the Vietcong's attack on Pleiku—itself doubtless a provocation[4]—by bombing North Vietnam while Soviet Premier Alexei Kosygin was in Hanoi in February 1965. How inclined the post-Khrushchev leadership was to aid North Vietnam prior to this episode is subject to dispute. But it is hard to imagine any act which would have been more calculated to drive the USSR to aid Vietnam. It is equally difficult to imagine an act more likely to undermine the position of those Soviet commentators who in 1964 and early 1965 had been arguing that the nature of American imperialism had changed. Hence the United States, by its actions, managed to ensure (the previously shaky) Soviet commitment to North Vietnam's war of national liberation and at the same time to affect negatively the internal dialogue in the USSR. Such evidence of the U.S. capacity to influence Soviet behavior externally and Soviet internal evolution negatively should give us pause before we assume that our actions are not likely to influence the propensity of Soviet elites to adapt, and indeed to moderate, Soviet foreign policy behavior.

Notes

1. Charles Gati, ed., *Caging the Bear* (New York: Bobbs Merrill, 1974), "Choices in the Post-War World," pp. 85–108.

2. Joint Economic Committee, 93rd Congress, 2nd Session, *Reorientation and Commercial Relations of the Economics of Eastern Europe* (Washington: Government Printing Office, 1974).

3. William Zimmerman, *Soviet Perspectives on International Relations, 1956–67* (Princeton: Princeton University Press, 1969).

4. The United States had decided not to bomb the North while Kosygin was there but did so in response to the attack on Pleiku.

The Soviet Union and Eastern Europe

Roger E. Kanet
and
John D. Robertson

The question of change and continuity in Soviet policy toward the East European communist states since Stalin's death is integral to an understanding of the evolution of Soviet foreign policy generally. At the time of Stalin's death the USSR maintained a dominant position over the countries of Eastern Europe—with the clear exception of Yugoslavia. By the late 1970s the role of the Soviet Union in the region had been challenged on numerous occasions by the smaller communist states. Yet the USSR remains the dominant power in the area and exerts substantial influence over the domestic and foreign policies of its smaller neighbors. The remarks that follow will examine the major developments in Soviet policy toward Eastern Europe, excluding Albania and Yugoslavia, since Stalin's death in an attempt to assess the factors that explain both the changes and the continuity in that policy.

Soviet Relations with Eastern Europe under Stalin

The primary characteristic of Soviet relations with Eastern Europe in the late Stalin era was domination based on coercion. As Seton-Watson, Brzezinski, and others[1] have amply documented, the Soviet Union imposed upon the new communist states in Eastern Europe a political-economic system modeled almost exactly on its own. Soviet policy, which aimed at gaining complete control over Eastern Europe, ignored completely the historical and cultural differences that divided the various countries of the region.

In the political sphere the Soviets imposed a system based on police terror and the dictatorship of the Communist Party to insure the direct dependence of the new regimes on the Soviet Union itself. In the economic area the communist regimes introduced programs focusing on high investments and the development of heavy industry at the expense of other sectors of the economy. Foreign trade was reoriented toward the USSR on terms generally very unfavorable to Eastern Europe. Reparations payments and the creation of joint stock companies facilitated the transfer of resources from Eastern Europe to the Soviet Union.

By 1953 Stalin had created an international system based on Soviet hegemony. In Eastern Europe, with the exception of Yugoslavia, the Soviet Union not only controlled broad political and economic developments but also dictated specific policies. East European leaders were unable to initiate policies that deviated from those determined by Moscow. The relationship was truly imperial and the Soviet position in Eastern Europe seemed invincible. However, there were a number of indications that the policy of direct and virtually complete Soviet domination was not totally successful. Most important was Tito's success in maintaining his political power in Yugoslavia in spite of Soviet opposition and efforts to undermine his political and economic position. In addition, riots occurred soon after Stalin's death in East Berlin and Pilsen and, somewhat later, in Poznan. The Soviet government's failure to take into account local differences and its refusal to invest in consumer-related sectors of the economy resulted in widespread disaffection on the part of the local populations.

Among the most pressing problems were a growing fear among East European leaders of widespread popular opposition; resentment among many in the working class of their relative impoverishment despite promises of improved living standards; indications that concentration on heavy industry and disregard for national economic conditions were having serious negative effects on economic growth; and growing nationality problems in some of the countries, particularly hostility toward Soviet advisers among the lower ranks of the leadership.[2] In part, these problems emerged as the result of modifications in the relationship of the Soviet Union to Eastern Europe that occurred after 1953. To a significant degree Stalin's death represented a watershed in Soviet-East European relations. By 1956 events in both Hungary and Poland demonstrated that the Soviet position was not nearly so secure as it had appeared.

Continuity and Change in Post-Stalin Relations

In the past quarter century Soviet relations with Eastern Europe have undergone substantial change, even though the basic characteristic of Soviet hegemony has remained. Although the Soviets have maintained a "hard sphere of influence,"[3] the degree to which they attempt to intervene in and dictate local developments has lessened. The mechanisms of Soviet control have changed, even though the ultimate resort to military coercion still looms as a distinct possibility and provides part of the background to all Soviet-East European contacts.

In addition to the modfied relationship between the Soviets and their East European "allies," which has introduced a degree of bargaining that did not exist in 1953, the Soviets have lost their unique position within the international communist system. The defection of Albania and China, the development of Eurocommunism, and the splintering of minor communist parties into various factions have meant that the Soviets are no longer the sole interpreters of Marxism-Leninism. These developments have enabled the post-Stalin leaderships of a number of East European countries to gain a modest degree of political autonomy. By the mid-1960s Romania, for example, was using the Sino-Soviet split as a lever to lessen its dependence on the Soviet Union.

Khrushchev and the New Course

Soon after their rise to power, Khrushchev and his associates introduced a number of major domestic reforms that eliminated some of the most reprehensible elements of the Stalinist system. Most important, the role of the internal security policy was reduced, and the indiscriminate use of terror among the Soviet population was substantially eliminated. In addition, the Soviet leadership reassessed the Stalinist economic model, which focused exclusively on the development of heavy industry at the expense of other sectors of the economy. This process culminated in Khrushchev's 1956 secret speech denouncing some of the worst aspects of the Stalinist system.

In Eastern Europe comparable changes in policy were introduced under the aegis of the New Course. Former leaders such as Gomulka in Poland were released from prison and others were posthumously rehabilitated. Ultimately, even though the Soviet Union was playing the major role in modifying the socioeconomic-political system that had been created in the Stalin years, the changes in policy were to have a profound effect on the Soviet-East European relationship itself.

The rapprochement with Yugoslavia, including the Soviet acceptance of the idea of separate paths to socialism, and the denunciation of Stalin and Stalinism in February 1956 added to the growing unrest in a number of East European countries. The Soviet Union was faced with serious challenges in Hungary and Poland in 1956 and, although Soviet troops "resolved" the problem in Hungary in November, the old Stalinist system of terror and coercion was not reestablished.

In the wake of the suppression of the revolution in Hungary and the reorganization of the regime in Poland, the Soviet Union attempted to reorient its relationships within Eastern Europe. Emphasis was now placed on the development of mutually beneficial relations between the Soviet Union and its allies that would reduce the role of overt military force and direct Soviet intervention. Ties were to be created that would bind the East Europeans to the Soviet Union "voluntarily," and economic reconstruction in Eastern Europe was to be stressed. By 1956–58 the exploitative economic policies of the Stalin era had largely been eliminated. Reparations payments ceased, the joint stock companies were disbanded, and the Soviet Union began to provide some economic assistance to Eastern Europe. The Council for Mutual Economic Assistance (CMEA) was revitalized in order to initiate a process of integrating the economies of Eastern Europe with one another and with that of the Soviet Union.

Throughout the Khrushchev era, even though the Soviet Union continued to play the dominant role in relations with Eastern Europe, a number of important developments substantially loosened that relationship. First, the boundaries of acceptable behavior were broadened, and East European leaders were afforded the opportunity to operate without the direct and immediate intervention of the Soviet Union, so long as their activities remained within the newly defined boundaries of acceptability. Throughout Eastern Europe, but most importantly in Hungary, Poland, and Romania, deviations from the Soviet model developed—in Hungary and Poland these modifications occurred primarily in the domestic area, while in Romania they occurred, after the open Sino-Soviet split, in foreign policy. East European countries were able to resist Soviet demands—for example, on the question of branch-based economic integration to be introduced through CMEA. On the whole, the Khrushchev era represented a gradual reduction of the all-pervasive role of the Soviet Union in Eastern Europe, even though it remained the hegemonic power.

Elsewhere, the challenge to the Soviet position within international communism was far greater and more destructive. The "defection" of

Albania and China and the failure of the Soviet Union to bring them back into line were largely the result of the Soviet inability to bring military power to bear on these two countries—as had also been the case with Yugoslavia in the late 1940s. The beginnings of polycentrism within the communist parties of Western Europe—particularly within the Italian party—also represented a new challenge to the Soviet Union's dominant position within the international communist movement.

It is important to note that changing conditions within Eastern Europe, as well as developments within the Soviet Union, were probably more important than the death of Stalin in influencing the modifications in the Soviet-East European relationship. By 1953 implementation of the policy of communization and forced industrialization had increased the stresses placed on the East European regimes. The drive to create miniature "Soviet Unions" had displaced a substantial portion of the local populations and had ignored local economic and political conditions. If Stalin had lived beyond 1953, it is likely that these problems would have surfaced and that he would have had to deal with them. This does not deny the important role of the post-Stalin Soviet leadership—in particular the rapprochement with Tito and the de-Stalinization campaign—in accelerating developments in Eastern Europe. The New Course policies deemphasized to some extent the role of heavy industry and gave greater weight to agriculture, housing, and basic consumer needs.

De-Stalinization, by questioning the ideological foundations of the system, added to the challenges faced by the Soviet Union. The attempt by Khrushchev and his associates to reestablish Soviet control after 1956 focused on "cooperative" and "mutually beneficial" relations. A substantial degree of policy choice—especially in domestic economic matters—was permitted to the East European leaders; this development, in turn, undercut the dominance of the Soviet Union in Eastern Europe.[4] When Khrushchev was forced to resign in October 1964, the Soviet Union's position in Eastern Europe was far weaker than it had been a decade earlier. Albania had withdrawn from the Soviet camp entirely, and Romania refused to follow the Soviet lead on relations with China and on the question of economic cooperation within CMEA. In the economic realm the Soviet position had also weakened; not only had a number of countries introduced substantial degrees of economic decentralization, but trade with the capitalist West had also begun to increase appreciably. These developments reduced the economic dependence of Eastern Europe on the USSR. The empire that Stalin had created seemed about to disintegrate in the face of expanding pressures for increased autonomy from several of the East European states.

Brezhnev and the Politics of Standardization

The first few years of the Brezhnev-Kosygin era witnessed a continuation of the erosion of Soviet dominance within the communist movement. Between 1964 and 1968 the Soviet leadership was concerned primarily with its own problems and demonstrated little decisiveness in coming to grips with the emerging polycentrism within the communist world. Not only were the Soviets unable to reestablish their influence over the Chinese and Albanians, but Soviet authority continued to be challenged in Eastern Europe as well. Efforts to integrate the economies of the region virtually ceased in the face of persistent opposition. Romania openly defied Soviet foreign policy initiatives, and the economic reform movement seemed to be resulting in a gradual increase of polycentric tendencies within the core of the Soviet "empire." These developments culminated with the Prague Spring in Czechoslovakia in 1968 and what the Soviets viewed as a direct challenge to the very basis of communist power. In 1968, as in 1956, the outer limits of Soviet tolerance were reached, and once again the Soviet Union resorted to its ultimate weapon of control—the military power of the Soviet Army—in order to reassert its position. In addition, the ideological basis of Soviet-East European relations was reformulated in the Brezhnev Doctrine, which stated clearly the limits on East European attempts at experimentation.

The Brezhnev Doctrine, which was first expounded in *Pravda* a month after the Soviet invasion of Czechoslovakia, emphasized the absolute necessity of unity within the communist world and the unacceptability of nationalist deviation.[5] The Soviet Union alone retained the right to determine the acceptability of political or economic reform. In addition, however, the Soviets set out to revitalize the efforts toward economic cooperation and integration and the development of a more unified policy toward the West.[6] Although they faced serious opposition within CMEA to their plans for integration, by 1971 the Soviets were successful in gaining agreement to the Complex Program on Economic Integration. While the program emphasized production specialization and plan coordination, it also referred to the eventual introduction of some currency convertibility, as advocated by the Hungarians.[7]

In negotiating the program for economic integration within CMEA, Soviet leaders had to keep in mind two important factors in their overall policy toward their East European allies. First, a growing demand in most of Eastern Europe and the Soviet Union for improvement in living standards required a more balanced program of economic growth.

Rising "consumerism" challenged the relationships that had evolved within the communist states and demanded increased capital investment in areas underfunded in the past. The Polish riots of 1970 gave special attention to the tensions that had arisen between the governing elites and substantial portions of the population. Political stability depended increasingly upon the ability of the communist regimes to provide their populations with improved living standards. In addition Soviet leaders had to take into account the growing economic cost of "subsidizing" the East European economies as a result of the low cost of the primary products that they exported to Eastern Europe and the high prices that they paid for imports.[8]

At the beginning of the 1970s the Soviet Union was confronted with conflicting East European conceptions of CMEA integration, the need for increased imports from the West to meet the technological requirements of continued economic growth, and mounting political pressure for improved living standards. The Comprehensive Program provided for a substantial increase in the coordination of national plans and multilateral consultation concerning both domestic and foreign economic policies. It also set the framework for the expansion of bi-lateral economic relations among the CMEA members and furthered the drive toward specialization and cooperation within Eastern Europe. The East European countries committed themselves to assist in the expansion of major new sources of Soviet raw materials in return for the long-term Soviet commitment of increased deliveries of these raw materials.

The Soviet Union also exerted pressure on its East European partners to improve the quality of the machinery and consumer goods exported to the USSR—thereby encouraging them to seek additional Western technology as a means of upgrading the quality of their own produc-tion. Overall, the program and other developments within CMEA in the early 1970s represented a victory for the Soviet position on integra-tion and began to tie the economies of Eastern Europe more closely to the Soviet economy—in spite of the continued growth of East-West commercial relations.

The mid-seventies also witnessed a number of developments which tended to enhance the economic position of the Soviet Union vis-à-vis its East European partners. In 1975 it was announced that prices in intra-CMEA trade would be revised immediately. The Soviet Union had long sought a revision of prices employed in intra-CMEA trade, as evidence of the deterioration in the terms of trade for raw materials exporters became clearer.[9] However, even though the price changes resulted in a substantial improvement in the relative economic position of the USSR, the Soviet leaders have been aware of the need to mitigate the impact of these changes on the economies of Eastern Europe. Soviet concern for the potential destabilizing effects of the price increases in Eastern Europe was indicated by the relative moderation of the increases and by the provision of Soviet credits to modify their immediate negative impact.

The continued development of specialization and cooperation agreements in industrial production, as well as the joint investments in the exploitation of Soviet raw materials, have strengthened the Soviet economy vis-à-vis the economies of Eastern Europe. The Soviet Union no longer expends as much of its own resources to subsidize East European economic growth as it did in the late 1960s and early 1970s, even though its position in the area depends in part on continuing economic and political stability. The Soviet position has also been strengthened by the increasing dependence of the East European economies on raw materials. Finally, the world energy crisis and the recession in the West, which undermine the East European countries' ability to expand their hard currency export markets, have also worked to the advantage of the Soviet Union in its relationship with Eastern Europe.

In addition to the stress on expanded economic cooperation and integration within the CMEA community, the Soviet Union has also emphasized the need for a greater degree of coordination in the political, cultural, and military-security areas. Regular consultation—usually in the Soviet Union—between party and governmental officials is oriented toward an increase in interdependence among the countries of the area. As Christopher Jones has pointed out, in most of the East European countries promotion within the military depends largely upon personal loyalty to the Soviet Union and prior training in Soviet military academies.[10]

During the 1970s the Soviet Union also reemphasized the organic links between the struggle of the capitalist and socialist social systems, on the one hand, and the international proletarian movement, on the other. This theme has served as the ideological underpinning for efforts to justify increasing central control over such supranational organizations as CMEA and the Warsaw Treaty Organization, standardization of social and economic plans throughout Eastern Europe, and the growing importance of interstate organizational cooperation for the future development of the "socialist commonwealth."[11]

Overall, the Soviet Union still maintains its dominant position in Eastern Europe, and, in some respects, the degree of influence and control has probably increased during the past decade. Nonetheless, tendencies towards polycentrism plague the communist world and affect Soviet policy toward other communist states. The Sino-Soviet split and the development of Eurocommunism are among the most important challenges to the Soviet claims for leadership in the international communist movement. These challenges also impinge upon the relationship of the Soviet Union to Eastern Europe by undermining Soviet claims concerning the universal applicability of their model of socialist development. Although the Soviet Union continues to dominate Eastern Europe, a number of countries enjoy a degree of autonomy in domestic affairs that would have been unthinkable in the early 1950s. In spite of increased efforts to standardize political, economic, and social policies within the CMEA community, the Soviet Union is unable to impose its will with the impunity that characterized the Stalin years. While Soviet policy under Stalin was based largely on coercion, it is now implemented through a combination of persuasion, economic inducement and pressure, consultation, and even negotiation—although more coercive instruments are still available.

So far we have spoken of Eastern Europe as if it were a single unit with a single relationship to the USSR. It is also important to note the diversity within the region and the differences in the Soviet relationship to individual countries. First of all, Romania is much less dependent economically on the Soviet Union than are most of the other countries. The relative abundance of raw materials in Romania and the decisions made in the mid-1960s to push forward domestic development outside the context of Soviet plans for CMEA cooperation have provided the basis for a degree of economic independence from the USSR not shared by the other CMEA members. In addition, the absence of Soviet troops and Ceausescu's effective use of Romanian nationalism have permitted the Romanian leadership to pursue policies in the area of foreign affairs that deviate substantially from those of the Soviet Union. Since the mid-1960s the Soviet Union has been unable to impose its policies on Romania in regard to such questions as the Sino-Soviet dispute, economic integration with CMEA, the invasion of Czechoslovakia, and the broader issue of the leading role of the CPSU in the world communist movement.[12]

Poland and Hungary have also deviated to a substantial degree in their internal policies from the model preferred by the Soviets. In both countries experimentation with economic decentralization, the admission of various forms of dissent, and the relative ease in gaining permission to travel abroad are among developments that would not be acceptable within the Soviet Union. Even the German Democratic Republic has opposed the Soviet Union on a major foreign policy issue considered crucial to GDR interests—namely, detente with the Federal Republic of Germany in the late 1960s.[13]

In spite of these evidences of deviation from Soviet policy[14] we must be careful to recognize that on most major issues the Soviet Union is still able to impose its will on its smaller "allies," if it so chooses.

Conclusions

The internal and the external environments within which Soviet policy is formulated have changed substantially during the past quarter century. De-Stalinization and the reduction of the role of terror in Soviet domestic politics in the mid-1950s had an important impact on political developments in Eastern Europe, and the expansion of Soviet relations with the West in the 1970s has permitted the East European states to increase their interactions with noncommunist states. Since the late 1940s Soviet policy toward Eastern Europe has moved through a number of periods of review, reassessment, and readjustment. On each occasion the Soviets found themselves faced with changed circumstances that made such a reassessment mandatory, if they were to accomplish their primary purpose of maintaining control over the countries of the region.

If we compare the situation of the Soviet Union in Eastern Europe at present with that in 1953 we note that the basic Soviet purposes have remained virtually unchanged. Soviet control over Eastern Europe is viewed as a crucial component of Soviet security policy, since it provides the opportunity to station an estimated half a million Soviet troops in Central Europe.[15] In addition, Eastern Europe still represents a legitimation of Soviet claims to leadership of a worldwide communist revolutionary movement, which is gradually superseding the international state system dominated by the capitalist West. In spite of the similarity in overall Soviet goals vis-à-vis Eastern Europe and the continued Soviet ability and willingness to employ military coercion to maintain its position, the Soviet-East European relationship has undergone substantial changes over the course of the past twenty-five years. Both the degree and the nature of Soviet domination have been modified, and even a decade of Brezhnev's efforts to "standardize" the social-political-economic systems of the region has not succeeded in reestablishing the virtually absolute control exercised in the Stalin period.

Notes

Kanet wishes to express his appreciation to the International Research and Exchanges Board (IREX), the North Atlantic Treaty Organization Faculty Fellowship Program, the Office of External Research of the U.S. Department of State, the American Council of Learned Societies, and the Research Board of the Graduate College of the University of Illinois for financial support for a much larger project upon which the present chapter is based.

1. Hugh Seton-Watson, *The East European Revolution* (London: Methuen, 1956), and Zbigniew K. Brzezinski, *The Soviet Bloc: Unity and Conflict* (rev. ed.; Cambridge: Harvard University Press, 1967).

2. Brzezinski, pp. 140–44.

3. For a discussion of the concept of "spheres of influence" and its applicability to Soviet-East European relations see John P. Vloyantes, *Spheres of Influence: A Framework for Analysis* (Tucson: University of Arizona, Institute of Government Research, Research Series no. 5, 1970), and *Silk Glove Hegemony: Finnish-Soviet Relations, 1944–1974, A Case Study of the Theory of the Soft Sphere of Influence* (Kent, Ohio: Kent State University Press, 1975).

4. Ghita Ionescu wrote in 1965 that the Soviet position within the international communist movement had deteriorated so far by late 1964 that the CPSU was forced to "sign the death warrant of its own former ideological hegemony and leadership," at the European Communist Party conference called primarily to deal with the problem of China. See Ionescu, *The Break-up of the Soviet Empire in Eastern Europe* (Baltimore: Penguin Books, 1965), p. 151.

5. See Sergei Kovalev, "Suverenitet i internatsional'nye obiazannosti sotsialisticheskikh stran," *Pravda*, September 25, 968, p. 4. For an excellent discussion of Soviet views on relations with other communist states see Teresa Rakowska-Harmstone, " 'Socialist Internationalism' and Eastern Europe–A New Stage," *Survey*, 22, no. 1 (1976), pp. 38–54, and no. 2 (1976), pp. 81–86.

6. In December 1968 the director of the Soviet Institute of Economics of the World Socialist System proposed integration that would eventually lead to a "single world communist economy with a single economic plan." G. Sorokin, "Problemy ekonomicheskoi integratsii stran sotsializma," *Voprosy ekonomiki*, no. 12 (1968), pp. 77–86.

7. For an excellent discussion of the politics of integration within CMEA prior to the approval of the Complex Program see Henry W. Schaefer, *COMECON and the Politics of Integration* (New York: Praeger, 1972).

8. See Paul Marer, "Has Eastern Europe Become a Liability to the Soviet Union?" in Charles Gati, ed., *The International Politics of Eastern Europe* (New York: Praeger Publishers, 1976), pp. 59–81.

9. See, for example, O. Bogomolov in *Mirovaia ekonomika i mezhdunarodnye otnosheniia*, no. 5 (1966), summarized in R.R.G., "USSR Exploited by COMECON?" *Radio Free Europe Research, Communist Area, USSR*, 2 June 1966; N. N. Bautina, "The Economic Integration of the COMECON Countries," *Ekonomika i organizatsiia promysh'lennosti* (Siberia), no. 1 (1972), pp. 19–30, summarized in R.R.G., "Moscow's Efforts to Rig COMECON Prices," *Radio Free Europe Research, Communist Area, USSR*, no. 1389, 20 April 1972.

10. Christopher D. Jones, "Soviet Hegemony in Eastern Europe: The Dynamics of Political Autonomy and Military Intervention," *World Politics*, 29 (1977), pp. 216–41.

11. See R. Judson Mitchell, "A New Brezhnev Doctrine: The Restructuring of International Relations," *World Politics*, 30 (1978), pp. 366–90; Nish Jamgtoch, Jr., "Alliance Management in Eastern Europe (The New Type of International Relations)," *World Politics*, 27 (1975), pp. 405–29; and B. Kozin, "The Drawing Together of the Socialist Countries—An Objective Regularity," *International Affairs* (Moscow), no. 10 (1976), pp. 14–21.

12. For an excellent discussion of Romanian foreign policy see Aurel Braun, *Romanian Foreign Policy since 1965: The Political and Military Limits of Autonomy* (New York: Praeger Publishers, 1978).

13. See N. Edwina Moreton, *East Germany and the Warsaw Alliance: The Politics of Détente* (Boulder, Colorado: Westview Press, 1978).

14. For a recent discussion of the similarities and differences in the foreign policy orientation of the communist states see Jeffrey Simon, *Comparative Communist Foreign Policy, 1965–1976* (Santa Monica: The Rand Corporation, P-6067, 1977).

15. International Institute for Strategic Studies, *The Military Balance, 1976–1977* (London: IISS, 1976), pp. 8–14.

The Soviet Union and the Third World

Alvin Z. Rubinstein

In Charles Gati's thoughtful essay, too much is perhaps made of the continuity in Soviet foreign policy in the generation since Stalin's death, and too little of the elements of change. This may have been a result of his absorption in what motivates Soviet policies and shapes Western interpretations of them, rather than in what have been the actual policies pursued by the post-Stalin Soviet leadership. Whatever the reason or reasons, several striking new dimensions to Soviet foreign policy since 1953 cannot easily be subsumed under the homogenizing and distorting rubric of "continuity." One of the most important of these has been Soviet policy toward the Third World.

Stalin's successors charted their course in the Third World initially with largely defensive purposes in mind, but more recently primarily for ambitious imperial ends that have to do with the USSR's immanent global rivalry with the United States.

To search for the roots of Soviet policy toward the Third World in the tsarist period would not be particularly rewarding, though some of the tsars occasionally dabbled in Palestine, Ethiopia, Persia, and Afghanistan; nor would compilations of quotations intended to demonstrate the interest of Lenin and Stalin in the Afro-Asian world go very far toward explaining the present forceful and extensive projection of Soviet military power in such places as the Arab East, Cuba, Angola, and the Horn of Africa, because the actual policies adopted by the post-1953 Soviet leaders in promotion of Soviet state interests are qualitatively different from the ideological and propagandistic statements and taxonomic formulations of Soviet officials at the time when Moscow was the center of a beleaguered, weak, defensive-minded state; nor was Soviet truculence during the height of the 1947 to 1953 Cold War a harbinger of subsequent policy. Whereas the speech making and ideological pronouncements of the Comintern and early post–World War II periods had negligible effects on the actors and events that they were supposed to affect in the Third World, the policies adopted since the mid-1950s have had a profound impact upon the general strategic environment within which the USSR has pursued concrete objectives in the Third World. To argue that current Soviet foreign policy in the Arab East, Southern Asia, Africa, and Latin America has its roots in the tsarist, Leninist, or Stalinist periods would, it seems to me, distort what we know of the past, confuse what we know of the present, and prejudice how we think about the future of the Soviet Union in these areas. Moreover, speculations about what Stalin would or would not have done were he still alive are really irrelevant. We do know that the domestic and external environment within which Soviet policy is formulated has prompted major changes. What we need to do is to evaluate the pressures and aims that drive Moscow's multifaceted effort to project power, establish a presence, and exercise influence in the Third World.

The most far-reaching change in Soviet foreign policy since the death of Stalin has been the shift of Soviet policy from a continental-based strategy to a global one. Years ago, Richard Lowenthal highlighted this qualitative change, observing that Stalin viewed the effective range of his foreign policy in terms of the range of his artillery; Khrushchev, in terms of the range of his rockets. Since the mid-1950s, the Third World has been an essential concern of Soviet foreign policy. For an increasingly confident and powerful Soviet elite, ambition has dovetailed with strategic considerations and with the plethora of possibilities for building influence and advancing Soviet state interests to generate a "forward policy" whose most recent manifestation is Soviet involvement in the Horn of Africa, Southern Africa, and Afghanistan.

The rapidity and verve with which the post-Stalin Soviet leaders moved into the Third World suggest that the reasons for the new policy were compelling, and that, in general, they enjoyed "bipartisan" support in the Kremlin among the major contestants for political power in the succession crisis of the 1953 to 1957 period. Possibly the new look in Soviet foreign policy would have been adopted even had Stalin lived. Nonetheless, his death did come providentially for his successors, enabling them to introduce a new flexibility into Soviet diplomacy at a propitious time. In the period since then, Soviet leaders have shared a basic consensus over the objectives and general tactics to be pursued in the Third World. Such disagreements as there have been by and large remained secreted in the interstices of the Kremlin, and policy seems not to have been affected by the outcome of top leadership struggles or domestic economic difficulties. Certainly, Soviet policy in the Third World does not appear, not even in the explosive Middle East, to have created serious splits in the party leadership.

Strategically, in the early years, the Soviet courtship of Third World countries was designed to offset the U.S. policy of ringing the USSR with military bases from which nuclear strikes could be directed against the Soviet heartland. What the Western powers conceived of as a plan for assuring deterrence, the USSR perceived as a threat to its national security. The polarization wrought by the globalization of containment facilitated Moscow's entry into the Third World. It ran counter to the thrust of the forces of nationalism in the Third World that aimed at discarding all traces of former Western overlordship and at steering an independent course in world affairs. Politically, Soviet overtures were intended to overcome the suspicion of the USSR inherent in the attitudes of ruling non-Communist nationalist elites in the Third World. Ideologically, a "forward policy" suited the optimistic outlook of Khrushchev and his associates. To them, a powerful and economically expanding Soviet Union was a natural ally of the new nations, which basically shared Moscow's anti-imperialist, anticapitalist outlook. Of least importance to Moscow were economic considerations. The raw materials and markets of the developing countries could be utilized by the Soviet economy, but they were not of critical importance.

The polarization of South Asia and the Middle East wrought by the U.S. policy of military "pactitis" facilitated the Soviet entry into these two crucial areas. In 1955 the Soviet move into the subcontinent was sealed by Moscow's readiness to build a major steel mill in the public sector for India, and the entry into the Mediterranean and the Arab world, by the arms deal with Egypt. In both instances, the USSR took advantage of Western shortsightedness to register a stunning diplomatic breakthrough.

Economic assistance helped to establish Soviet respectability in the Third World. The first indication that the post-Stalin leadership was interested in significantly improving relations with non-Communist developing countries came on July 15, 1953, at the Sixteenth Session of the U.N. Economic and Social Council, where the Soviet delegate announced a contribution of one million dollars to the U.N.'s Expanded Program of Technical Assistance. This offer reversed Moscow's previous policy of opposing all U.N. programs for helping developing countries, allegedly on the grounds that they were dominated by Western countries and designed to perpetuate Western investments. Soviet leaders sought to convince Third World countries that the aid would not be used to subvert existing governments or to promote Communist activities within the recipient country.

The Soviet aid program made its debut in Afghanistan. In March 1954, the Soviets undertook to build several grain elevators, a petroleum pipeline, and a cement factory. In February 1955, the USSR concluded an agreement with India under which it was to construct a one-million-ton steel mill in the public sector in the Bhilai region of central India; in September, it provided Egypt with arms, thus dramatically entering the mainstream of Arab-world politics. In all three cases a concatenation of circumstances contributed to Moscow's auspicious entry into the aid-giving field: the difficulty encountered by developing countries in obtaining large-scale credits from the West for public sector projects or military purchases; the disenchantment of developing countries with the limited funds for development available from U.N. agencies; the readiness of the Soviet Union to agree promptly to whatever projects the prospective borrowers proposed; and the determination of the non-aligned countries to find alternative sources of support as a consequence of the Western policy of establishing military pacts, whose effect was to place unaligned countries at a decided military and economic disadvantage.

Between 1954 and 1977 the Soviet Union made commitments of approximately $40 billion to noncommunist developing countries. Of these credits, which are commonly but misleadingly referred to as "foreign aid," approximately $13 billion was assigned for economic projects; of this total about fifty percent was actually utilized by the recipients. By contrast, the developing countries have taken relatively full advantage of Soviet offers of military assistance, the total of which is in excess of $26 billion.

The Soviet Union has given economic assistance to more than forty countries, concentrating on a few key countries in each major region of the Third World: Afghanistan, India, and Pakistan in Southern Asia; Egypt, Syria, Algeria, Turkey, and Iran in the Middle East; Cuba in Latin America; and Ethiopia, Somalia, Ghana, Guinea, and Angola in Africa. Soviet economic assistance has concentrated on politically and strategically important Third World countries and, in recent years, on countries possessing a valuable resource, such as oil, natural gas, bauxite, or phosphates, with which to repay Soviet credits. Moscow does not give grants. Accordingly, since Soviet loans have relatively short maturities, debt repayments by resource-poor recipients have started to exceed actual Soviet outlays, thus creating frictions between the USSR and some Third World clients, such as Egypt, Ghana, and Indonesia. As payments on their debts mount, as the process of arranging for large-scale Soviet projects becomes more complicated and the Soviets more demanding in what they want, and as the performance of many Soviet projects leaves much to be desired, the Third World countries have grown more businesslike in evaluating the advantages and disadvantages of accepting tied Soviet credits.

It is as a major purveyor of arms that the Soviet Union has had an enormous impact on Third World developments. In contrast with the relatively static level of economic assistance, Soviet arms transfers have expanded significantly, especially in the past decade. Wherever regional rivalries exist, the Soviet Union has supplied arms to local actors whose aims are antithetical to Western interests or who are opposed to Western-sponsored military pacts. Over the years, India, Egypt, Indonesia, Ghana, Syria, Somalia, Ethiopia, Iraq, and Angola were prime recipients. All held geo-strategic and political significance in their own right, quite apart from their role in the Soviet-American rivalry.

Shrewd opportunism, not ideology, has been the impelling force behind Soviet behavior. Perceiving openings for penetrating the Third World and for undermining the Western position, Soviet leaders dispensed with the niceties of ideological principles and supplied arms to clients on a lavish scale. The more closely one examines Soviet diplomacy in the Third World, the more one is impressed by the flexibility and opportuneness of its responses to the potentialities of each situation. Soviet achievements have not always been proportional to Soviet outlays, or to the risks Moscow has run on behalf of Third World clients. But Moscow cannot be faulted for diffidence or niggardliness.

Soviet inroads into what had been an exclusive Western preserve have fallen far short of initial Western presentiments of the late 1950s and early 1960s: there has been no notable swing to Soviet-type institutions or practices. With the possible arguable case of Cuba, and of Cambodia (1975), no Third World country has gone communist since 1955. Despite the close ties many developing countries have with the Soviet Union, their Communist Parties remain weak, functioning mainly on sufferance from the dominant noncommunist nationalist groups, who continue to view local communists with suspicion. Soviet gains in the Third World have not always been at the expense of Western interests; for example, Iraq relies heavily on the USSR for arms but looks to the West for its technology and industrial equipment. Moscow has not been able to acquire or retain a secure system of military facilities from prime clients, such as Egypt, India, Somalia, and Iraq. Finally, protracted exposure to Soviet ideas, techniques, and personnel seems not to have generated any widespread belief in the inherent superiority of the Soviet product.

Nevertheless, though Moscow has not found the going easy and has few tangible military-political dividends to show for its efforts, it can derive satisfaction from three achievements. First, the Soviet Union has effectively weakened the Western alliance systems; CENTO in the Middle East and SEATO in Southeast Asia are now defunct, thereby enhancing the security of its southern tier. Through astute diplomacy and economic assistance, it has improved relations with Turkey, Iran (prior to the overthrow of the Shah in 1979), and Pakistan and induced a creeping nonalignment into the once solid phalanx of pro-Western allies. Some of this has been the result of Washington's ineptness and of internal upheavals, but a great deal has been due to Moscow's astuteness. Second, Moscow has become, for the first time in its history, an important factor in the politics of the Middle East, South Asia, and Africa. No longer can decisions affecting the strategic status of these areas be taken without due regard for Soviet views and interests. This achievement is testament to Moscow's impressive capability to project military power into Third World arenas. Third, by aiding such countries as India, Syria, Iraq, Libya, Angola, and Ethiopia, as well as a dozen lesser ones, the Soviet Union reinforces their policy of nonalignment. In strategic-political terms this means the denial of bases to the West; the curtailment, if possible, of Western economic hegemony; and the cultivation of closer ties with the Soviet bloc. These are substantial achievements, and they should be more than enough to command continued support in the Kremlin for the Soviet policies that have been followed in the past generation.

In general, Moscow has courted three categories of developing countries: first, those that adhere to nonalignment and maintain friendly, even dependent, relations with the Soviet Union, often with a tinge of anti-Westernism congenial to Moscow (for example, India, Iraq, Afghanistan, and Ethiopia); second, the swing states that are formally nonaligned but that have shifted, as a result of the vagaries of domestic leadership upheavals, from an obviously pro-Soviet leaning to one more pleasing to the West, and which presumably can one day swing as quickly back to Moscow (for example, Indonesia, Ghana, Burma, Egypt, and Somalia), and third, those countries that are formally aligned to the West but whose alignment has weakened in ways assiduously encouraged by Moscow (for example, Turkey and Pakistan). In this ongoing courtship, Soviet diplomacy has been distinguished generally by a keen appreciation of local opportunities, the dilemmas inherent in trying to establish close ties with regional antagonists, the relationship between regional issues and the superpower rivalry, and the constraints on its own behavior. It has adapted skillfully to regional developments, to changing Soviet strategic aims, and to Moscow's increasing readiness for greater risk taking.

What of the future? In speculating on Soviet policy towards the Third World in the years ahead, we can make the following assumptions about the behavioral imperatives underlying the Kremlin's outlook.

First, there are no isolationists in the Kremlin. The urge to acquire influence and play a global role is not peculiar to the Soviet Union; it is a trademark of any powerful, ambitious imperial system. The Soviet Union has paid dearly for its newly acquired status as a superpower: two generations have sacrificed and suffered to modernize the USSR, to expand its borders in search of strategically secure frontiers, to ensure that decisions affecting its national security would never again be taken without its full participation. Having driven itself to the center of the world stage, Moscow is not likely to retire to the wings soon or gracefully. In its determination is implicit a willingness to bear the cost of an imperial policy in the Third World.

Second, Soviet initiatives will be undertaken in response to concrete opportunities for gain and strategic advantage and not in consequence of any fundamentalist ideological impetus or prepackaged military blueprint. Contrary to the generally accepted view, Soviet leaders are flexible, adaptive, and alert to "contradictions" in the noncommunist world. As befits the operational style of a calculating, tough-minded, sober elite, they will continue to respond pragmatically to events and opportunities, weighing the risks and rewards, the difficulties and dilemmas, careful to minimize the danger of a direct confrontation with the United States but increasingly resolved not to forego prospects for improving their global position and weakening that of the United States. Notwithstanding economic difficulties at home, the Kremlin has the military wherewithal and the will to make such commitments to ventures in the Third World as are required in promotion of the forward Soviet position there. Thus, an interest in Black Africa, though low-keyed in the early years of Moscow's activism in the Third World, has assumed greater prominence in recent years. In the past, Soviet leaders were constrained by limited capability, more pressing priorities elsewhere, and U.S. power. The Soviet involvement in Angola and the Horn of Africa suggests that these constraints are far less operative today. Like the Chinese ideographic character for crisis, which is a combination of the symbols for opportunity and danger, detente combines, for Moscow, a quest for coexistence in Europe and stabilization of the superpower relationship with intense competition in the gray areas lying outside of each superpower's core security community. And Africa is a vast uncommitted, promising political preserve.

Third, whereas the United States has become an essentially status-quo power, the Soviet Union has not. It prizes the political utility of incrementalism, that is, the belief that marginal gains, if sustained and expanded over time, can seriously undermine the alliances and essential relationships of its major adversary, the United States. Being patient, it is prepared to absorb setbacks; having decided that improvement of the strategic environment within which it operates in the Third World is a goal worth pursuing, it is willing to pay the price.

Finally, the Soviets are in the Third World for the long haul. They take a long view of the situation, and are not pressed to show immediate results each time they act. No domestic constituency challenges the essentials of Soviet foreign policy. The Soviets see conflict as endemic in the Third World. Unmistakable to them is the greater control that regional actors have acquired over their own affairs and the lessened ability of the United States, as the leading capitalist power, to intervene and control developments in the Middle East, Africa, Latin America, and Southern Asia.

These assumptions imply continuation, at a high level of interaction and intensity, of the Soviet policy of "competitive coexistence" with the Western world. There are no reasons for assuming that Moscow will not push its ambitious "forward policy" in the Third World. The signs of Soviet engagement are widespread and unambiguous. Still very much a subject for speculation and disagreement, however, are the motivations that prompt this imperial outreach, the achievements to date, and the lengths to which the Soviet Union is prepared to go to pursue its objectives in the Third World.

THE CONTRIBUTORS

George W. Breslauer is Associate Professor of Political Science at the University of California at Berkeley. He is the author of *Five Images of the Soviet Future* and coauthor of *Political Terror in Communist Systems* and *Soviet Politics and Society*.

John Bushnell is Assistant Professor of History at Carnegie-Mellon University. He is completing a study of military revolution in Russia, 1905–1907.

Stephen F. Cohen is Associate Professor of Politics and Director of the Russian Studies Program at Princeton University. His publications include *Bukharin and the Bolshevik Revolution: A Political Biography, 1888–1938*.

Charles Gati is Professor of Political Science at Union College and Visiting Research Fellow at the Research Institute on International Change, Columbia University. A specialist on Soviet foreign policy and the international politics of Eastern Europe, he is coauthor of *The Debate over Detente* and editor and coauthor of *Caging the Bear: Containment and the Cold War*, *The International Politics of Eastern Europe*, and *The Politics of Modernization in Eastern Europe*.

George Gibian is Goldwin Smith Professor of Russian Literature at Cornell University. He is the editor and translator of *Russia's Lost Literature of the Absurd: Selected Works of Daniil Kharms and Alexander Vvedensky* and coeditor of *Russian Modernism: Culture and the Avant-garde*.

Erik P. Hoffmann is Associate Professor of Political Science, Graduate School of Public Affairs, State University of New York at Albany. He is an Associate of the Research Institute on International Change, Columbia University, and Coordinating Editor of *Soviet Union*. He is coeditor of *The Conduct of Soviet Foreign Policy* and coauthor of *In Quest of Progress: Soviet Perspectives on Advanced Society* (forthcoming).

Peter H. Juviler is Professor of Political Science, Barnard College, Columbia University. He is the author of *Revolutionary Law and Order: Politics and Social Change in the USSR* and of many studies of Soviet family and criminal policy. He is completing a book on Soviet delinquents and authority.

Roger E. Kanet is Professor of Political Science, University of Illinois at Urbana-Champaign. He is editor of *The Soviet Union and the Developing Nations* and coeditor of *Politics and Policy in Gierek's Poland*.

Roy A. Medvedev is a nonconformist historian and political thinker who lives in Moscow. His major writings published in English include *Let History Judge: The Origins and Consequences of Stalinism, On Socialist Democracy, On Stalin and Stalinism*, and (with his brother Zhores A. Medvedev) *Khrushchev: The Years in Power*.

James R. Millar is Professor of Economics, University of Illinois at Urbana-Champaign and former editor of the *Slavic Review*. His publications include *The Soviet Rural Community*, which he edited, and many articles on various aspects of the Soviet economy.

Alexander Rabinowitch is Professor of History and Director of the Russian and East European Institute, Indiana University. He is the author of *The Bolsheviks Come to Power: The Revolution of 1917 in Petrograd* and *Prelude to Revolution: The Petrograd Bolsheviks and the July 1917 Uprising* and a coeditor of *Revolution and Politics in Russia: Essays in Memory of B. I. Nicolaevsky*.

John D. Robertson, Assistant Professor of Political Science at Texas A&M University, has recently completed a study of post-industrialism and public policy.

Alvin Z. Rubinstein is Professor of Political Science at the University of Pennsylvania. He is the author of *Red Star on the Nile, Yugoslavia and the Nonaligned World*, and *The Foreign Policy of the Soviet Union*.

Robert Sharlet is Professor of Political Science at Union College and an Associate of the Research Institute on International Change, Columbia University. He is the author of a number of studies on law, politics, and political justice in the USSR and Eastern Europe. His recent publications include *The New Soviet Constitution of 1977* and (with coeditor Piers Beirne) *Pashukanis: Selected Writings on Marxism and Law.*

Ronald Grigor Suny is Associate Professor of History, Oberlin College. He is the author of *The Baku Commune, 1917–1918: Class and Nationality in the Russian Revolution* and is writing a book on the modern history of Georgia.

Robert N. Taaffe is Professor of Geography and Chairman of the Department of Geography, Indiana University. He is the author of *Regional Development in the Soviet Union* and coauthor of *An Atlas of Soviet Affairs.* He has published many articles on transportation, urbanization, and regional development in the USSR and Eastern Europe.

Arthur W. Wright is Professor of Economics and Department Head, University of Connecticut. His publications include studies of Soviet agricultural and energy policies and also of U.S. energy and tax policies.

William Zimmerman is Professor of Political Science at the University of Michigan. He is the author of *Soviet Perspectives on International Relations, 1956–1967.*

INDEX

Abkhazs, in Georgia, 217, 219, 220
Abortions, 229, 230, 242
Adzharians, in Georgia, 217, 219
Afghanistan, 324, 325, 327, 329
Agayan, Ts., 45
Agitprop, 71
Agriculture: under Stalin, 1, 53, 71, 137–39, 140, 146, 162; since Stalin, 3, 32, 53, 74, 135–36, 137, 138–51, 162, 163; performance of, 41, 141–51, 186, 188; and diet, 135–36, 141, 186; collective and state farms, 137–39, 140, 148–49, 233–35, 240. *See also* Grain imports; Livestock
Aksenov, Vasili, 264, 265, 272
Alcoholism, 83, 233, 235, 247, 314, 316, 317, 327
Angara-Yenisey complex, 160
Angola, 324, 327, 328, 329, 330
Antonov-Ovseenko, Vladimir, 33
Armenians, in Georgia, 205, 206–8, 214, 219
Aspaturian, Vernon V., 289
Austria, 4, 308
Azerbaijanis, 208

Babel, Isaac, 255
Baikal-Amur Mainline (BAM), 159, 165, 166, 168
Bauer, Raymond, 182
Belorussia, 234–35, 247
Belov, Vasili, 259

Bergson, Abram, 125–27
Beria, Lavrenti, 3, 33n, 35, 37, 209–10
Berlin crisis (1948–49), 2, 282, 295
"Big Deal," the, 195–96
Birth rates, 227, 228–31, 232, 233, 239–40, 241, 242, 243, 245
Bitov, Andrei, 260–61, 265
Black market, 187
Bolsheviks, and the role of women, 236–37, 243
Bondarev, Yuri, 47
Breslauer, George, 75
Brezhnev, Leonid I.: economic policies of, 5–6, 18, 24, 77; political policies of, 6, 7, 17–19, 51, 59, 62–67, 76–89, 97, 105–6, 117–18; and foreign policy, 6, 280, 288, 290, 306, 307–8, 317; and the 1977 Soviet constitution, 94, 97, 99, 101, 106–7; agricultural policies of, 137, 139, 162, 234; and nationality policy, 202, 203, 204
Brezhnev Doctrine, the, 288, 317
Brzezinski, Zbigniew K., 296–97, 312
Bukharin, Nikolai, 19, 39, 117
Bulgakov, Mikhail, 255
Bulganin, Nikolai A., 37, 40, 117
Bulgaria, 283
Bunin, Ivan, 255
Bureaucracy, 14–15; and Khrushchev's reforms, 16–17, 21–22, 35–36, 52, 57, 58, 59–62, 74–76, 79, 86–87; under Stalin, 21–22, 35–36, 52, 72–73, 79, 86–87,

Bureaucracy (*cont.*)
115–17, 118–19; and political participation, 50–67; under Brezhnev, 76–89
Burma, 329

Cambodia, 328
Campbell, Robert W., 116, 122
Ceausescu, Nicolae, 320
Censorship, 3, 17, 19, 253–54
Central Asia, 155, 159–60, 161–62, 163, 173, 229
Central Treaty Organization (CENTO), 329
Chapman, Janet, 116
China, 283, 314, 316, 317, 320
Chubar, Vlas, 37
Churchill, Sir Winston, 282
Civil libertarians, 97, 104
Coal, 159–60
Cohn, Stanley H., 113
Collective farms, 137–39, 140, 148–49, 233–35, 240
Command planning, 114–17, 118–19, 122–23, 129
Communist International, Seventh Congress (1935), 282, 295
Communist Party (CPSU), 12, 14–15, 181; under Stalin, 1, 15–16, 71–72; Central Committee of, 3, 33, 35, 39–40, 44, 46–48, 60, 63, 95–96, 212, 214, 215; Twentieth Party Congress, 5, 32–35, 38–40, 44, 45, 46, 53; Twenty-second Party Congress, 5, 40–44, 45, 46, 54, 58–59, 64, 202, 214; restoration of, 15–16, 21, 74–75; and the Stalin question, 32–49; Nineteenth Party Congress, 33, 307; Twenty-third Party Congress 45–46; Twenty-fourth Party Congress, 48, 64, 76, 80; Twenty-fifth Party Congress, 48, 82; under Khrushchev, 54–59, 64, 74–76, 78, 79; and political education, 56, 59, 64; Twenty-first Party Congress, 56–57, 58; under Brezhnev and Kosygin, 63–65, 77–85, 88, 97, 100, 118; in "developed socialism," 80–85, 88; in regional development, 164–65; and Eastern Europe, 313, 314, 315–16, 317, 320, 321
Connally, Senator Tom, 298
Conservatism, 14, 17–19, 22–25, 63, 106–7, 119, 280; and reformism, 12–15, 18, 26; and the Stalinist past, 16–17, 18, 20–21
Constitution, Soviet, 93–94; of 1936 ("Stalin"), 93, 94–95, 98–100, 101, 102,

103–4; of 1977 ("fourth Soviet"), 93–107, 203, 240
Council for Mutual Economic Assistance (CMEA), 173, 315, 316, 317–20
Council of Ministers, 40, 99–100
Council of Nationalities, 204
Cuba, 296, 324, 327, 328
"Cult of personality," 2, 4, 33, 34–38, 39, 41–42, 43–45, 46, 51, 87–88, 117
Czechoslovakia, 6, 293n, 317, 320

Dallin, Alexander, 285–86
Daniel, Yuli, 45, 46
"Deheroization," of the past, 15
Demichev, P. N., 42
Derevenshchina, 258–60
De-Stalinization, 4–7, 21–22, 24, 117; and the legal system, 93–107; in foreign policy, 279, 281, 316, 321
Detente, 4, 6, 32, 288, 298, 308–9, 330–31
"Developed socialism," 80–85, 88
D'iakov, Boris, 45
Diet, enrichment of, 135–36, 141, 186
Diplomatic Dictionary, 289
Dissidents, 6, 7, 25, 96, 104–5, 180, 187, 218–19
Divorce, 227, 229, 230, 231–36, 239–40, 242, 243, 246, 247
Doctors Plot, 3
Dubcek, Alexander, 6
Dudintsev, Vladimir, 255
Dulles, John Foster, 298
Dunham, Vera, 195
Dvor, 233–34
Dzhugashvili, Iosif, 206. See also Stalin

Eastern Europe, 25, 191–94; and Soviet foreign policy, 2, 4, 282, 283, 293, 296, 306, 309, 312–21
Economic assistance, in the Third World, 326–28
Economic performance, 114, 116–17, 123–29, 130–31, 180, 185–96. See also Agriculture
Economic policy: under Stalin, 1, 2, 19–20, 71, 73, 113–19, 120, 122–23, 129–30, 163, 306, 307; after Stalin, 5–6, 17, 18, 52–55, 57–60, 74, 77, 78, 117–23, 129–30, 149–50, 210–11; and regional development, 155–74; and Eastern Europe, 312–13, 315, 316, 317–20. See also Agriculture; New Economic Policy
Education, 71, 102, 142, 146–47, 181; by the party, 56, 59, 64; in the Georgian SSR, 211, 213–14

Egypt, 326, 327, 328, 329
Ehrenburg, Ilya, 255, 263
Engels, Friedrich, 140
Energy policy, 158–61
Environmental protection, 97, 163
Erofeev, Venedikt, 264
Ethiopia, 327, 328, 329
Ethnicity, 83, 162, 203–4, 206; in the Georgian SSR, 208–9, 212–14, 217, 219–20, 221–22
Eurocommunism, rise of, 314, 320

Fainsod, Merle, 72
Family, 71, 227–44
Fedoseev, P. N., 83
Finland, 4, 308
Finley, David D., 290
Florinsky, Michael T., 298
Food: prices, 147–48, 150–51; shortages of, 183–84
Foreign policy, 2, 3–4, 6, 32–33; in Eastern Europe, 2, 4, 282, 283, 293, 296, 306, 309, 312–21; and the Third World, 280, 295, 324–31; influences on, 284–99; and the United States, 293–94, 298–99, 305–6, 308–11, 326, 329–31; moderation in, 307–11. See also Brezhnev; Khrushchev; Stalin
Furtseva, Ekaterina, 42

Gamsakhurdia, Zviad, 218–19
Gati, Charles, 305, 307–10, 324
Gelbakhiani, rector of the Tbilisi Medical Institute, 216
Georgian Communist Party, 210–11, 212, 214, 215
Georgian SSR, 201–2, 206–22
German Democratic Republic, 313, 320–21
Gerschenkron, Alexander, 113, 116
Ghana, 327, 328, 329
Ginzburg, Evgeniia, 44
Gisser, Mischa, 117
Gladilin, Anatoli, 272
GOELRO plan, 157
Gomulka, Stanislaw, 128–29
Gomulka, Wladyslaw, 48, 314
Gorbatov, General A. V., 44
Gosgrazhdanstroy, 168
Gosplan, 157, 164, 167, 168
Gosstroy, 168, 171
Grain imports, 136, 139, 141, 149–50, 151
Granin, Daniil, 256, 262–63, 265, 268–71
Great Purges (1936–39), 1, 20, 33n, 71–72

Grekova, I., 265
Grossman, Gregory, 122–23
Gross national product (GNP), 124–26, 141, 296
Guinea, 327

Harriman, Averell, 3
Harvard Russian Research Center, 181–82
Helsinki accords (August 1975), 218
History, controversy concerning, 15, 18–19, 217
Holloway, David, 85–86
Hough, Jerry, 80
Housing, 97, 102, 182
Hungary, 40, 48, 283, 293n, 313, 315, 317, 320

Ilichev, L. F., 42
India, 326, 327, 328, 329
Indonesia, 328, 329
Industrialization, 3, 6, 32, 124–29, 130, 195; under Stalin, 71, 73, 114–17, 157–58; and regional development, 158–59, 163; in Siberia, 158, 161, 165–66, 171–72; in Georgia, 205–6; in Eastern Europe, 313, 316
Inkeles, Alex, 182
Inozemtsev, Nikolai, 160–61
Institute of Marxism-Leninism, 45, 47, 48
Institute of World Economy, 160, 289
Institute on the USA and Canada, 289
Intellectuals, 180, 183, 184–85, 187
Intelligentsia, the, 46, 53–54, 61, 85, 180, 219
Intermarriage, among Georgians, 208
Internal security forces. See Secret police
Iran, 327, 329
Iraq, 328, 329
Iskander, Fazil, 265

Japaridze, Revaz, 219
Jasny, Naum, 116–17, 135
Jen Min Jihn Pao (journal), 38
Jews, 283; emigration of, 6, 184, 219–20, 257
Johnson, D. Gale, 143
Jonas, Paul, 117
Jones, Christopher, 319
Juvenile delinquency, 83, 230–31

Kadar, Janos, 48
Kaganovich, Lazar M., 35, 36, 40, 41, 42

Kamenev, Lev, 37
Kapitonov, I. V., 220
Kataev, Valentin, 264
Kazakov, Yuri, 265–66
Kennan, George F., 283–84, 298
Khandzhian, A. I., 40
Khozraschet, 121
Khrushchev, Nikita S., 94, 99, 189, 195; agricultural policies of, 3, 74, 136, 137, 138, 139, 162, 163, 234; foreign policies of, 4, 6, 33, 74, 281, 296, 306, 308, 313–16, 325; reforms of, 4, 5, 16, 17, 19, 20, 21–22, 25, 45; denounces Stalin, 4–5, 21, 33–38, 39, 40, 41–42, 53, 183, 314; overthrow of, 5, 16, 17, 41, 44, 63, 76; and political participation, 6–7, 50–67, 74–76, 106, 117–18; and cult of personality, 51, 87–88; economic policies of, 52–55, 57–60, 74, 117, 119, 120, 210–11; and leadership, 55–57, 59, 61–62, 65–66, 74–76, 78, 79, 86–87; and the Communist Party, 56–59, 64, 74–76, 78, 79
Kirov, Sergei, 20, 34, 39–40
Kissinger, Henry A., 297, 298
Kochetov, Vsevolod, 47
Kolkhoz, 149, 233–35
Kommunist (periodical), 40, 47
Komsomolskaia Pravda (newspaper), 182–83
Kosinski, Jerzy, 183
Kosior, Stanislav, 33, 37
Kosygin, Alexei, 5–6, 7, 62–66, 77–78, 311; economic reforms of, 5–6, 87, 99, 120–22. *See also* Brezhnev
Krestinsky, Nikolai, 39
Kupradze, Viktor, 212
Kuznetsova, Larisa, 237–38

Labor, 99, 128, 229; in agriculture, 145, 146–47, 150; and regional development, 158–59, 161–62, 170, 171–73
Labor camps, 2, 3, 16, 33, 38
Lakoba, N., 40
Lane, David, 85
Language, use of national, 202, 206, 208, 211, 219
Law, 71, 93, 98–100; and individual rights, 7, 100–106; family law, 229–33, 236, 240, 242. *See also* Constitution, Soviet
Leadership, 55–57, 59, 61–62, 65–66, 71–89, 94, 100–1; and public opinion, 194–96; and foreign policy, 284–91, 294, 296–97, 330–31

Lenin, Vladimir, 19, 81, 137, 140, 236, 263–64; nationality policy of, 203, 214; foreign policy of, 280, 292, 295. *See also* Marxism-Leninism
Leningrad purge (1949–50), 20, 33
Leningrad Union of Writers, 268
Liberalism, in economic planning, 119–20, 121, 122
Liberation (film), 47
Liberman, Evsei G., 99, 119, 121, 122
Libya, 329
Linden, Carl, 74
Lippmann, Walter, 308
Literature, 3, 44, 45, 252–75
Litvinov, Maxim, 282
Livestock, 136, 139, 143, 146, 149–50, 151
Locational planning, 157–58, 164–72
Lowenthal, Richard, 325
Lysenko, T. D., 45, 162

Machine Tractor Stations (MTS), 137–38, 139, 140
Magnitizdat, 257
Maisky, Ivan, 45
Makarova, 265
Malenkov, Georgi, 3, 35, 36, 37, 40, 41, 42, 117, 288–89, 296, 307
Mamleev, Yuri, 264
Mandelstam, Osip, 255
Maoism, 62, 65
Maramzin, Vladimir, 264
Marriage, 208, 229, 230, 231, 232–36, 242, 246
Marxism-Leninism, 24–25, 34, 118, 140, 201, 222, 228, 282–83, 284, 307, 314
Mazurov, K. T., 42
Mensheviks, in Georgia, 205, 207, 209
Metropol (anthology), 264–65
Meyer, Alfred, 73
Mezhevich, M., 171
Middle class, 179–96
Mikoyan, Anastas I., 33, 36
Milenkovitch, Deborah, 122
Military, 4, 34, 39, 130–31, 205, 296, 331; in Eastern Europe, 6, 314, 315, 316, 317, 319, 321
Military assistance, 327, 328–29
Molodaia proza, 272
Molotov, Vyacheslav M., 13, 35, 36, 40, 41, 42, 296
Montias, J. M., 113
Mzhavanadze, V. P., 210, 212, 215, 216–17, 218

Nagibin, Yuri, 256, 265

Nationalism, 17, 19, 203; in the Georgian SSR, 206–9, 213–22
Nationality policy, 201, 202–4, 214, 220–22
Nekrich, Alexander, 45
Neo-Stalinism, 7, 12, 13, 20, 45–49
New Economic Policy (NEP), 1, 19, 37, 71, 98, 137, 140
"New Soviet Man," 59, 182
Nomenklatura, 23, 35–36
North Atlantic Treaty Organization (NATO), 2, 282
Nove, Alec, 122
Novyi mir (journal), 31n57, 44, 47, 48

Obshchestvenniki, 57
Oktiabr' (journal), 47
Olesha, Yuri, 255
Opinion surveys, 179, 181–84
Ordzhonikidze, Sergo, 39–40
Osetins, in Georgia, 217, 219
Oshchepkov, P., 45

Pakistan, 327, 329
Panferov, Fedor, 238
Pasternak, Boris, 256
Pavlenko, V. F., 167
"Peaceful coexistence," 4, 6, 33, 283, 289, 296, 297, 298, 306, 308
Peasants, 1, 53, 59, 61, 137
Pechilintsev, O. S., 171
Pervukhin, Mikhail, 40
Petroleum, 158–61, 173
Pipes, Richard, 206
Platonov, Andrei, 255
Poland, 40, 48, 313, 314, 315, 318, 320
Political participation, 6–7, 50–67, 74–76, 94–97, 105–6, 117–18, 119, 289–91
Political police. *See* Secret police
Political prisoners, 3, 16, 33, 38–40
Politicheskii dnevnik (journal), 46n
Polyansky, Dmitri, 42
Population, 135, 143, 161–62, 205–6, 207–8. *See also* Birth rates
Pospelov, Petr, 45
Prague Spring (1968), 317
Pravda (newspaper), 38, 47–48, 289
Privlechenie, 51, 56
Procuracy, 1955 reform of, 99
Public opinion, 179–96

Rakowska-Harmstone, Teresa, 216
Raskolnikov, Fedor, 39
Rasshirenie prav, 56
Red Army, 34, 39, 205

Reformism, 12–17, 18, 19–22, 23–25, 26
Refugees, surveys of, 181–82
Regional development, 155–74
Renationalization, of Georgia, 206–9, 218, 220
Revolution, 22, 24
"Revolutionary diplomacy," 295
Romania, 314, 315, 316, 317, 320
Romm, Mikhail, 11
Rustavi metallurgical complex, 211

Saburov, Maxim, 40
Samizdat, 25, 31n57, 44n, 45, 257, 264
Savchenko, V., 147
Schwartz, Morton, 286
Science, 45, 53–54, 97
"Scientific and technological revolution" (STR), era of, 81, 82–85, 88–89
Secret police, 3, 16, 33, 35, 52, 313, 314
Serdyuk, Z. T., 42
Seton-Watson, Hugh, 312
Shalamov, Varlam, 44
Shelepin, Alexander, 42
Shepilov, Dmitri, 40, 41
Shevardnadze, E. A., 215, 216–18, 219
Shevtsov, V. S., 81
Sholokhov, Mikhail, 42
Shukshin, Vasili, 258
Shulman, Marshall D., 290, 306
Shvernik, Nikolai M., 42
Siberia, 155–56, 158, 159–61, 163, 164–66, 169, 171–73
Singur, N., 168
Sinyavsky, Andrei, 45, 46, 264
Slavophilism, 13, 18–19
Solomentsev, M. S., 231
Solzhenitsyn, Alexander, 5, 44, 256, 257, 259–60, 263–64, 267
Somalia, 327, 328, 329
Southeast Asia Treaty Organization (SEATO), 329
Soviets, local, 100, 105
Sovkhoz, 149, 234
Sovnarkhozy, 119, 120
Stalin, Josef V.: death of, 1, 2–3, 15, 21, 200; economic policies of, 1, 2, 19–20, 71, 73, 113–19, 120, 122–23, 129–30, 163, 306, 307; agricultural policies of, 1, 53, 71, 137–39, 140, 146, 162; and the Communist Party, 1, 15–16, 71–72; political dictatorship of, 1–2, 16, 24, 34, 35–36, 42, 52, 71–73, 79, 86; and Stalinism, 1–2, 20–21, 24, 38, 86; and the "cult of personality," 2, 4, 34–38, 39, 41–42, 43–45, 46, 87–88; and World

Stalin, Josef V. (*cont.*)
War II, 2, 24, 34, 72–73, 158, 281; foreign policy of, 2, 73, 279–83, 284, 285–86, 287–89, 292, 295–96, 297, 305–8, 312–13, 316, 321, 325; repudiation of, 4–5, 34–38, 39, 41–44, 53; and reform, 19–21; rehabilitation of, 24, 45–49; and Soviet constitutionalism, 93, 94–95, 98–100, 101, 102, 103–4, 106; family policies of, 228, 229–30, 233. *See also* De-Stalinization
Standard of living, perception of, 182–83, 185, 188–89, 195
State farms, 138–39, 148–49, 234
Students, 183–85, 187–88, 189–90, 232
Subbotniki, 65
Syomin, Vitali, 266–68
Syria, 327, 328, 329

Tamizdat, 257
Tbilisi City Committee, 215
Tbilisi demonstrations, 211–13
Terebilov, V. I., 95
Territorial-production complexes, 166–72
Third World, the, 280, 295, 324–31
Thomson, David, 11
Tito, Josip, 2, 65, 281, 282, 296, 313, 316
Tourism, 191–92, 257
Trade: with the West, 128, 131, 173, 318; with Eastern Europe, 313, 318–19
Trade unions, 56, 59
Transcaucasian Bureau, 214
Trapeznikov, Sergei, 45
Trifonov, Yuri, 45, 256, 261–62, 263
Triska, Jan F., 290
Trotsky, Leon, 37, 280, 295
Trud (newspaper), 59
Truman Doctrine, 282
Tsarist Russia, 23, 24, 25
Tsvetaeva, Marina, 255
Tucker, Robert C., 73
Tukhachevsky, Mikhail, 39
Turkey, 327, 329
Tvardovsky, Alexander, 44, 47, 48

Ulam, Adam, 283
Unen (newspaper), 48
Union of Writers, 253, 254, 264–65
United Nations, 326–27
United States, and Soviet foreign policy, 305–6, 308–10, 326, 329–31
Urals-Kuznetsk Combine, 157, 158, 164
Urbanization, 170–71, 172, 205, 228, 233

Varga, Eugen, 73, 293, 294, 306
Vietnam, 310–11
"Virgin Lands," campaign, 138–39, 144, 162
Von Thunen, 157
Voprosy istorii (journal), 38
Voroshilov, Klimenti E., 35, 36, 40, 42
Voznesensky, Andrei, 256, 265
Voznesensky, Nikolai, 20

Wage differentials, 148–49
Warsaw Treaty Organization, 309, 319
Water resources, 163–64
Weber, Alfred, 157, 169
Weitzman, Martin, 127–29
Werth, Alexander, 182
Wiles, Peter, 135
Women, 96; in the labor force, 146, 236–37, 238–39, 242–43
Women's liberation, 227–28, 236–44
Working class, discontent among, 195

Yakir, Petr, 39
Yepishev, General A. A., 45
Yevtushenko, Yevgeny, 42–43
Youth, and the constitution of 1977, 96
Yugoslavia, 2, 4, 123, 282, 296, 313, 315, 316

Zaleski, Eugene, 121
Zhenotdel, the, 230, 236
Zhukov, Georgi K., 37
Zimmerman, William, 289, 292–93, 297–99
Zinoviev, Alexander, 264
Zinoviev, Grigori, 37
Zoshchenko, Mikhail, 255

turnover: broker commissions from, 215–16; earnings as basis of, 206–7; of low P/E ratio stocks, 145–50, 182–86, 197, 203–7; performance relationship to, 55, 56
Tversky, Amos, 118
Twark, Richard D., 157, 158

underwriters: of new issues, 88–91; New York Stock Exchange Study of, 77
unemployment: in Great Britain, 5, 280; in Phillips curve, 277–81
unions, 285–87
University Computing, 45, 83, 165
upgrading, 215–16
Upjohn, 49
uranium, 284, 285
Uranium Institute, 284
U.S. Government bonds, 6, 130
U.S. savings bonds, 316
U.S. Treasury notes, 310

Value Line, 147n, 202, 217
variable annuities, 252–53
variable interest bonds, 248–49

Vartan, Vartanig G., 22, 238, 319–20
Victims of Groupthink (Janis), 262–63
volatility, Beta as measure of, 54n
Volcker, Paul, 276, 277, 280

Wall Street Journal, 5, 25, 104n, 129, 156–57, 186, 203, 210, 211, 217, 228
Warner-Lambert, 88
Washington Power, 253
wash sales, defined, 239
Watson, Thomas J., 48
Welling, Kathryn, 227–28
Western Oil Shale Corporation, 89
whisky, investing in, 291–92
whole life (ordinary life) insurance, 255–56, 312–13
Williams, John Burr, 40–41
Williamson, J. Peter, 42–43

Xerox, 48, 49, 74, 79, 164, 165

yield: imputed, on zero-coupon bonds, 247–48; on money market funds, 242–43. *See also* interest rates

zero-coupon bonds, 247–48